THE STONE CRUSHER

The Kleinmann family in April 1938. *From left*: Herta, Gustav, Kurt, Fritz, Tini, Edith.

THE STONE CRUSHER

The True Story of a Father and Son's Fight for Survival in Auschwitz

JEREMY DRONFIELD

CHICAGO
REVIEW
PRESS

First edition
Published by Chicago Review Press Incorporated
814 North Franklin Street
Chicago, Illinois 60610
ISBN 978-1-61373-963-1

Library of Congress Cataloging-in-Publication Data

Names: Dronfield, Jeremy, author.
Title: The stone crusher : the true story of a father and son's fight for
    survival in Auschwitz / Jeremy Dronfield.
Description: First edition. | Chicago, Illinois : Chicago Review Press
    Incorporated, [2018] | Includes bibliographical references.
Identifiers: LCCN 2018005240 (print) | LCCN 2018005978 (ebook) | ISBN
    9781613739648 (Adobe PDF) | ISBN 9781613739655 (Epub) | ISBN 9781613739662
    (Kindle) | ISBN 9781613739631 (hardback)
Subjects: LCSH: Kleinmann, Gustav, 1891-1976. | Kleinmann, Fritz, 1923- |
    Jews--Austria--Vienna--History--1933-1945--Biography. | Holocaust, Jewish
    (1939-1945)--Austria--Vienna--Personal narratives. | Buchenwald
    (Concentration camp)--Biography. | BISAC: HISTORY / Holocaust. | HISTORY /
    Jewish. | HISTORY / Military / World War II. | BIOGRAPHY & AUTOBIOGRAPHY /
    Historical.
Classification: LCC DS135.A93 (ebook) | LCC DS135.A93 K574 2018 (print) | DDC
    940.53/18092243613aB--dc23
LC record available at https://lccn.loc.gov/2018005240

Typesetting: Nord Compo

Printed in the United States of America
5 4 3 2 1

Contents

Part IV: Survival

To Kurt

and
in memory of

Gustav
Tini
Edith
Herta
Fritz

Preface

THIS IS A TRUE STORY. Every person in it, every event, twist, and incredible coincidence is taken from historical sources. One wishes that parts of it were not true, that they had never occurred, so terrible and painful are they. But it all happened, within the memory of the still living, the survivors.

There are many Holocaust stories, but not like this one. The tale of Gustav and Fritz Kleinmann, father and son, contains elements of all the others but is quite unlike any of them. Very few Jews experienced the Nazi concentration camps from the first mass arrests in the late 1930s through to the Final Solution and eventual liberation. None, to my knowledge, went through the whole inferno together, father and son, from beginning to end, from living under Nazi occupation, to Buchenwald, to Auschwitz and the prisoner resistance against the SS, to the death marches, and then on to Mauthausen, Mittelbau-Dora, Bergen-Belsen. Fewer still went through all that and made it home again alive. Luck and courage played a part, but what ultimately kept Gustav and Fritz living was their love and devotion to each other. "The boy is my greatest joy," Gustav wrote in his secret diary. "We strengthen each other. We are one, inseparable."

This book tells not only their story, but also that of their family: Gustav's wife, Tini; their daughters, Herta and Edith; and younger son, Kurt. Two escaped to freedom overseas; two met their end in a Nazi death camp. Between them, the Kleinmann family's experiences track all those who lived through the Shoah or perished in it. This single family's story is a history of a people's suffering in microcosm, from invasion to liberation, by way of Auschwitz, English internment, American immigration, and the death camps of the Reichskommissariat Ostland.

Remembering the Kleinmanns' experiences is timely now more than ever. Like hundreds of thousands of other Jews, they did all they could to escape the Nazi regime but were frustrated by other nations' hostile immigration policies—Britain and America shunned all but a handful, while the press and public condemned and disparaged the foreign refugees.

I have brought the story to life with all my heart. It reads like a novel. I am a storyteller as much as historian. And yet I haven't needed to invent or embellish anything; even the fragments of dialogue are authentic, quoted or reconstructed from primary sources. The bedrock is the concentration camp diary written by Gustav Kleinmann between October 1939 and July 1945, supplemented by a memoir by Fritz and a lengthy interview he recorded in 1997. None of these sources makes easy reading, either emotionally or literally—the diary, written under extreme circumstances, is sketchy, often making cryptic allusions to things beyond the knowledge of the general reader (even Holocaust historians would have to consult their reference works to interpret some passages). Gustav's motive in writing his diary was not to inform the public but to help preserve his own sanity; its references were comprehensible to him at the time. Once unlocked, it provides a rich and harrowing insight into living the Holocaust week by week, month by month, and year after year. Most strikingly, it reveals Gustav's unbeatable strength and spirit of optimism: "... every day I say a prayer to myself," he wrote in the sixth year of his incarceration. "*Do not despair. Grit your teeth—the SS murderers must not beat you.*"

Interviews with surviving members of the family have provided additional personal detail. The whole—from Vienna life in the 1930s to the functioning of the camps and the personalities involved—has been backed up by documentary research, including survivor testimony, camp records, and other official documents, which have verified the story at every step of the way, even the most extraordinary and incredible.

The witness has forced himself to testify. For the youth of today, for the children who will be born tomorrow. He does not want his past to become their future.

—Elie Wiesel, *Night*

Prologue

Austria, January 1945

Fritz Kleinmann shifted with the motion of the train, shuddering convulsively in the subzero gale roaring over the sidewalls of the open freight car. Huddled beside him, his father watched, face drawn, exhausted. Around them sat dim figures, moonlight picking out the pale stripes of their uniforms and the bones in their faces. It would soon be time for Fritz to make his escape; if he left it any longer, it would be too late.

Eight days had passed since they'd left Auschwitz on this journey. They had walked the first sixty kilometers, the SS driving the thousands of surviving prisoners westward through the snow, away from the advancing Red Army. Fritz and his father had heard intermittent gunshots from the rear of the column as those who couldn't keep up were murdered. Nobody looked back.

At Gleiwitz they'd been put on trains for other camps deeper inside the Reich. Fritz and his father managed to stay together, as they had always done. Their transport was for Mauthausen concentration camp in Austria, where the SS would carry on the task interrupted by the Russian advance, draining the last dregs of labor from the prisoners before finally exterminating them. One hundred and forty men were crammed into each open-topped freight car. At first they'd had to stand, but as the days passed and the cold killed them off one by one, it gradually became possible to sit down. The corpses were stacked at one end of the car and their clothing taken to warm the living.

They might have been on the brink of death, but these prisoners were the lucky ones, the useful workers—most of their brothers and sisters, wives, mothers, and children had been murdered or were being force-marched westward, dying in droves.

Fritz had been a boy when the nightmare began, seven years ago; now he was twenty-one, grown to manhood in the Nazi camps, learning, maturing,

1

resisting the pressure to give up hope. He had foreseen this day and prepared for it. Beneath their camp uniforms he and his papa wore civilian clothing, which Fritz had obtained through his network of friends in the Auschwitz resistance. (Unfortunately, in the hurry of the evacuation he'd had to leave behind the guns he'd acquired.) Besides the clothing they had full heads of hair, having avoided the regular head-shaving for two months. They were back in their homeland now, and once they were free they could pass for local workmen.

The train had paused at Vienna, the city that had once been their home, then turned west through St. Pölten, then Amstetten, and now they were only fifteen kilometers from their destination. It was now or never. Fritz had been delaying the decision, worried about his father.

Gustav was fifty-three years old, exhausted—it was a miracle he had survived this far. In the last day or two Gustav had begun to realize that he couldn't make the escape attempt. The strength wasn't in him anymore. Yet he couldn't deny his son the chance to live. It would be a wrenching pain to part after so many years of helping one another to survive, but he urged Fritz to go alone. Fritz resisted, begged him to come, but it was no good: "God protect you," his father said. "I can't go, I'm too weak."

If Fritz didn't make the attempt soon, it would be too late. He stood up and took off the hated uniform; then he embraced his papa, kissed him, and with his help climbed the slippery sidewall of the car.

The full blast of the wind at twenty-two degrees below zero hit him painfully hard. He peered anxiously toward the brake houses on the adjacent cars, occupied by armed SS guards. Fritz had tested their alertness by heaving some corpses over the side, and they hadn't noticed. But the moon was brighter now—two days from the full, rising high and laying a ghostly glow across the snowy landscape, against which any moving shape would be starkly visible.[1] The train was thundering along at its maximum speed. Screwing up his courage and hoping for the best, Fritz launched himself into the night and the freezing air.

Part I

Vienna

1 | "When Jewish Blood Drips from the Knife . . ."

אבא

Vienna, March 1938

Gustav Kleinmann's lean fingers pushed the fabric under the foot of the sewing machine; the needle chattered, machine-gunning the thread into the material in a long, immaculate curve. Next to his worktable stood the armchair it was intended for, a skeleton of plain beechwood with taut webbing sinews and innards of horsehair. When the panel was stitched, Gustav fitted it over the arm, stretching the fabric taut; his little hammer drove in the nails—plain tacks for the interior, studs with round brass heads for the outer edge, tightly spaced like an orderly row of soldiers' helmets; in they went with a *tap-tapatap*.

It was good to work. There wasn't always enough to go around, and life could be precarious for a middle-aged man with a wife and four children. Gustav was a gifted craftsman but not an astute businessman, and once or twice he'd gotten into severe financial trouble, but always muddled through.[1] Born in a tiny village by a lake in the historic kingdom of Galicia,* a province of the Austro-Hungarian Empire, he'd come to Vienna aged fifteen to train as an upholster, and then settled here.[2] Called to military service in the spring of his twenty-first year, he'd served in the Great War, been wounded twice and decorated for bravery, and at war's end he'd returned

---

* Now part of southern Poland and western Ukraine

5

to Vienna to resume his humble job as a journeyman upholsterer, working his way up to master craftsman. He had married his girl, Tini, during the war, and together they raised four fine, happy children. And there was Gustav's life: modest, hardworking, and if not entirely content, at least inclined to be cheerful.

The droning of airplanes interrupted Gustav's thoughts, and he paused with a tack between his fingers and his hammer raised; it grew and receded as if planes were circling over the city. Curiosity overcoming him, Gustav laid down his tools and stepped out into the street.

Im Werd was a busy thoroughfare, noisy with the clop and clatter of horse-drawn wagons and the grumbling of motor trucks, the air thick with the smells of humanity, fumes, and horse dung.[3] For a confusing instant it appeared to Gustav to be snowing—in March!—but it was a blizzard of paper, fluttering from the sky, settling on the cobbles and the market stalls of the Karmelitermarkt. Gustav picked one up.

PEOPLE OF AUSTRIA!
For the first time in the history of our Fatherland,
the leadership of the state requires an open commitment
to our Homeland . . .[4]

Propaganda for this Sunday's vote. The whole country was talking about it, and the whole world was watching. For every man, woman, and child in Austria it was a big deal, but for Gustav, as a Jew, it was of the utmost importance—a national vote to settle whether Austria should remain free from tyranny.

For five years, Nazi Germany had been looking hungrily across the border at its Austrian neighbor. Adolf Hitler, an Austrian by birth, was obsessed with the idea of bringing his homeland into the German Reich as the first step toward building his "Greater Germany." Although Austria had its own homegrown Nazis eager for unification, most Austrians were opposed. For two years Hitler had been putting pressure on Austria's chancellor, Kurt Schuschnigg, to give members of the Nazi Party—which was banned in Austria—positions in his government, threatening dire consequences if they continued to be excluded. Now it looked as if the Führer would get his way; unless decisive action were taken, before long Schuschnigg would be forced out of office and replaced with a Nazi puppet; unification would follow, and Austria would be swallowed by Germany. The country's 183,000 Jews regarded this prospect with dread.[5]

The world watched keenly for the outcome—on the far side of the Atlantic, *TIME* magazine was preparing a cover picture of Chancellor Schuschnigg, a dapper fellow in round spectacles with a Ronald Colman mustache, with his nationalist slogan, "We are good Germans, but always good Austrians."[6] In a desperate last throw of the dice, he had announced a plebiscite—a referendum—in which the people of Austria would decide for themselves whether they wanted to keep their independence. Schuschnigg was confident of victory, while Hitler fumed. It was a courageous move; four years earlier, Schuschnigg's predecessor had been assassinated during a failed Nazi coup—and right now Hitler was ready to do just about anything to prevent the vote going ahead. The date had been set for Sunday, March 13, 1938, now only two days away.

Nationalist slogans ("Yes for Independence!") were pasted and painted on every wall and sidewalk. Government planes were carpeting Vienna with Schuschnigg's propaganda. Gustav looked again at the leaflet.

> . . . For a free and Germanic, independent and social, Christian and united Austria! For peace and work and equal rights for all who profess allegiance to the people and the Fatherland.
>
> . . . The world shall see our will to live; therefore, people of Austria, stand up as one man and vote YES![7]

These stirring words held mixed meanings for the Jews. They had their own ideas of Germanism—Gustav, immensely proud of his service to his country in the Great War, considered himself an Austrian first and a Jew second.[8] Yet he was excluded from Schuschnigg's Germanic Christian ideal. He also had mixed feelings about what Austria had become under Schuschnigg's Austrofascist government. As a younger man, Gustav had been an active socialist, an organizer for the Social Democratic Party of Austria.[9] With the rise of the Austrofascists in 1934, the party had been violently suppressed and outlawed (as had the Nazis). As a Jew and a socialist, Gustav was doubly excluded.

But for the Jews of Austria at this moment, implicit disdain was preferable to open persecution of the kind going on in Germany. The Jewish newspaper *Die Stimme* had a banner in today's edition: "We support Austria! Everyone to the ballot boxes!"[10] The Orthodox paper *Jüdische Presse* made the same call: "No special request is needed for the Jews of Austria to come out and vote in full strength. They know what this means. Everyone must fulfil his duty!"[11]

Through secret channels, Hitler had threatened Schuschnigg that if he didn't call off the plebiscite, Germany would take action to prevent it. At this very moment, while Gustav stood in the busy street reading the leaflet, German troops were already massing at the border.

אמא

With a glance in the mirror, Tini Kleinmann patted down her coat, gathered her shopping bag and purse, left the apartment, and woke the echoes in the stairwell with her neat little heels click-clacking briskly down the flights. She found Gustav standing in the street outside his workshop, which was on the ground floor of the apartment building. He had a leaflet in his hand; the road was littered with them—in the trees, on the rooftops, everywhere. She glanced at it and shivered; Tini had a feeling of foreboding about it all that Gustav the optimist didn't quite share. Gustav had little religious faith but he always thought things would work out for the best; it was both his weakness and his strength.

Tini walked briskly across the cobbles to the market. A lot of the stall-holders were peasant farmers who came each morning to sell their produce alongside the Viennese traders. Many of the latter were Jews; indeed, more than half the city's businesses were Jewish-owned, especially in this area. Local Nazis made a big issue of this prosperity, stirring up anti-Semitism among the workers suffering in the economic depression—as if the Jews were not suffering from it too. Leopoldstadt, Vienna's Second District, had once been its official Jewish quarter, and it still retained much of that character. Gustav and Tini held only lightly to their heritage; they weren't particularly religious, going to synagogue perhaps a couple of times a year for anniversaries and memorials, and like most other Viennese Jews, their children bore Germanic rather than Hebraic names, yet they followed the Yiddish customs like everyone else.

From Herr Zeisel the butcher Tini bought veal, thinly sliced for Wiener schnitzel; there would be leftover chicken for the Shabbat* evening soup, and from the farm stalls she bought fresh potatoes and salad; then bread, flour, eggs, butter . . . Tini progressed through the bustling Karmelitermarkt, her bag growing heavier. Where the marketplace met Leopoldsgasse, the main street, she noticed the unemployed cleaning women touting for work; they stood outside the Klabouch boarding house and the coffee shop, some equipped with pails of soapy water. The lucky ones would be picked up by well-off ladies from the surrounding streets who needed their kitchens cleaned. Those who brought their own water got the full wage of one schilling.† Tini and Gustav sometimes struggled to pay their bills, but at least she hadn't been reduced to *that*.

The government's pro-independence slogans were everywhere, painted on the sidewalks in big, bold letters like road markings: the rallying cry for the plebiscite—"We say yes!"—and everywhere the symbol of the Austrian *Kruckenkreuz*.‡ From the open windows of houses and businesses came the sound of radios turned up high, playing cheerful patriotic music. As Tini watched, there was a burst of cheering and a roar of engines as a convoy of trucks came down the street, filled with uniformed teenagers of the Austrian Youth displaying the red-and-white national colors, waving patriotic banners, and flinging out more leaflets.[12] The people crowding on the sidewalks greeted them with fluttering handkerchiefs, doffed hats, and cries of "Austria! Austria!"

It looked as if independence was winning . . . so long as you took no notice of the sullen faces among the crowds. The Nazi sympathizers. They were exceptionally quiet today—and exceptionally few in number, which was strange.

Suddenly the cheerful music was interrupted and the radios crackled with an urgent announcement—all unmarried army reservists were to report immediately for duty. The purpose, said the announcer, was to ensure order for Sunday's plebiscite, but his tone was ominous. Why would they need extra troops for that?

Tini turned away and walked back through the crowded market, heading for home. No matter what occurred in the world, no matter how near danger might be, life went on, and what could one do but live it?

---

* Sabbath; from just before sundown on Friday to darkness on Saturday evening
† 1 schilling = 19 cents in 1938, equivalent to about three or four dollars in 2018
‡ "Crutch cross," a cross with T-bars at the ends of the arms; symbol of the governing Fatherland Front

בן

Across the city the leaflets lay on the waters of the Danube Canal, in the parks and streets. At the end of the afternoon, when Fritz Kleinmann left the trade school on Hütteldorfer Strasse on the western edge of Vienna, they were lying in the road and hanging in the trees that lined it. But the propaganda trucks of the Austrian Youth, which had dominated the streets that morning, were long gone; instead, roaring down the street came column after column of trucks filled with soldiers. Hütteldorfer Strasse was one of the main routes west; the troops were heading for the German border, two hundred kilometers away. The boys coming out of school watched excitedly, as boys will, as rows of helmeted heads sped past, weapons ready.

Fritz headed for home. At fourteen years old, he already resembled his father—the same handsome cheekbones, the same nose, the same mouth with its full lips curving like gull's wings. But whereas Gustav's countenance was gentle, the gaze from Fritz's large, dark eyes was penetrating, like his mother's. He'd left high school and for the past six months had been training to enter his father's trade as an upholsterer.

As Fritz and his friends made their way homeward through the city center, they saw a new mood taking hold of the streets. At precisely three o'clock that afternoon the government's campaigning for the plebiscite had stopped due to the developing crisis; now the spirit of optimism was fading away. There was no official news, and rumors had begun to spread—rumors of fighting on the Austrian-German border, of Nazi uprisings in the provincial towns, and most worrying of all, a rumor that the Viennese police would side with local Nazis if it came to a confrontation. Bands of enthusiastic men roamed the streets— some yelling "Heil Hitler!" and others replying defiantly "Heil Schuschnigg!" The Nazis were louder, growing bolder, and most of them were youths, empty of life experience and pumped full of ideology.[13]

This sort of thing had been going on sporadically for days, and there had been occasional violent incidents against Jews.[14] But this was different; when Fritz reached Stephansplatz, right in the very heart of the city, where Vienna's Nazis had their secret stronghold, the space in front of the cathedral was teeming with yelling, baying people. Here it was all "Heil Hitler" and no counter-chant.[15] Policemen stood nearby, watching, talking among themselves but doing nothing.

It looked as if this rumor was true, that the police sympathized with the Nazis. Also watching from the sidelines, not yet revealing themselves but content to see the fervor rising, were the secret members of the Austrian Sturmabteilung—the SA, the Nazi Party's storm troopers. They had discipline, and they had their orders; their time was coming but hadn't yet arrived.

Avoiding the knots of demonstrators, Fritz crossed the Danube Canal into Leopoldstadt and was soon back in Im Werd, his boots clattering up the stairs to apartment 16—home, warmth, and family.

משפחה

Little Kurt stood on a stool in the kitchen-dining room, watching as his mother prepared the noodle batter for the chicken soup, the traditional Shabbat Friday meal. It was about the only Shabbat practice they maintained; Tini lit no candles, said no blessing. Kurt was proving to be the exception to the family's lack of interest in religion—only eight years old, he sang in the Stadttempel choir and had made friends with an Orthodox family who lived across the hallway (he'd made it his role to switch on the lights for them on Shabbat evenings), and was becoming quite devout. Kurt was the baby and the beloved; the Kleinmanns were a close family, but Kurt was Tini's particular darling. He loved to help her cook.

While the soup simmered, Kurt watched, lips parted, as she whipped the egg batter to a froth and fried it into thin pancakes. This was one of his favorite cooking duties. The very best was Wiener schnitzel, for which his mother would gently pound the veal slices with a tenderizer until they were as soft and thin as velvet; she taught him to coat them in the dish of flour, the batter of beaten egg and milk, and finally the breadcrumbs; then she would lay them two by two in the pan of bubbling buttery oil, the rich aroma filling the little apartment as the cutlets puffed and crinkled and turned golden. Tonight, though, it was the smell of fried noodles and chicken.

From the next room—which doubled as bedroom and living room—came the sound of a piano; Kurt's sister Edith, eighteen years old, played well, and had taught Kurt a pleasant little tune called "Cuckoo," which would remain in his memory forever. His other sister, Herta, aged fifteen, he simply adored; she was closer to him in age than Edith, who was a grown woman. Herta's place in Kurt's heart would always be as an image of beauty and love.

Tini smiled at his earnest concentration as he helped her roll up the cooked egg, slicing it into noodles that she stirred into the soup.

The family sat down to their meal in the warm glow of the Shabbat—Gustav and Tini; Edith and Herta; Fritz and little Kurt. Their home was small, just this room and the one bedroom they all shared—Gustav and Fritz in together, Kurt with their mother, Edith in her own bed, and Herta on the couch. Yet home it was, and they were happy here.

Outside, beyond these walls, a shadow was gathering over their world. That afternoon, a written ultimatum had come from Germany, insisting that the plebiscite be canceled; that Chancellor Schuschnigg resign; that the figurehead President Wilhelm Miklas replace him with the right-wing politician Arthur Seyss-Inquart (a member of the illegal Austrian Nazi Party) with a sympathetic cabinet under him. The justification given by Hitler was that Schuschnigg's government was repressing the ordinary Germans of Austria ("German" being synonymous with "Nazi" in Hitler's mind). Finally, the Austrian Legion, a force numbering thirty thousand Nazis living in exile, must be brought back to Vienna to keep order on the streets. President Miklas had been given until 7:30 PM to comply.[16] Though the public had no knowledge of this ultimatum, many could sense that something was wrong.

After dinner, Kurt had to hurry off to the Shabbat evening service at the Stadttempel. He was paid a schilling a time for singing in the choir, so it was an economic as well as a religious duty, and a personal delight. As usual, Fritz escorted him; he was an ideal elder brother—friend, playmate, and protector. The streets were busy this evening, but the unruly noise had subsided, leaving behind a sense of a lurking malevolence. Usually Fritz would accompany Kurt as far as the billiard hall on the other side of the Danube Canal—"You know your way from here, don't you?"—and head off to shoot billiards with his friends. But this evening was different.

Back in the apartment, the radio was playing. The program was interrupted by an announcement. The plebiscite had been postponed. It was like an ominous tap on the shoulder. Then, a little after half past seven, the music broadcast was halted and a voice declared: "Attention! In a few moments you will hear an extremely important announcement." There came a pause, empty, hissing; it went on and on for three full minutes, and then Chancellor Schuschnigg came on. His voice wavered with emotion: "Austrian men and Austrian women; this day has placed us in a tragic and decisive situation." Every person in Austria who was near a radio at that moment listened intently, many with fear, some with excitement, as the chancellor described the German ultimatum. Austria must take its orders from Germany or be destroyed. "We have yielded to force," he said, "since we are not prepared even in this terrible situation to shed Germanic blood. We decided to order the troops to offer no serious . . ."—he hesitated—". . . to offer no resistance." His voice cracking, he gathered himself for the final words. "So I take my leave of the Austrian people, with a German word of farewell, uttered from the depths of my heart: God protect Austria."[17]

The Kleinmanns, like families across Austria, sat stunned as the national anthem began to play. In the studio, unseen and unheard by the people, Kurt Schuschnigg broke down and sobbed.

בן

The sweet, exalting phrases of the "Hallelujah," led by the cantor's tenor and fleshed by the voices of the choir, filled the great oval space of the Stadttempel, embracing the marble pillars and the gilded ornamentation of the tiered balconies in harmonious sound. From his place in the choir on the very top tier behind the ark,* Kurt could look right down on the bimah† and the congregation. It was far more crowded than usual, packed to bursting—the less devout Jews of Vienna seeking comfort in their religion. The religious scholar Dr. Emil Lehmann, unaware of the latest news, had spoken movingly about Schuschnigg, exalting the plebiscite and closing with Schuschnigg's rallying cry: "We say yes!"[18]

After the service, Kurt filed down from the balcony, collected his schilling, and found Fritz waiting. Outside, the narrow cobbled lane was thronged with the departing congregation. From the outside there was little to show the synagogue's presence; it appeared to be part of a row of apartment houses. The main body was behind the façade, squeezed between this street and the rear of the Fleischmarkt. While Leopoldstadt was properly the Jewish quarter of Vienna, this little enclave in the old city center, where Jews had lived since the Middle Ages, was the cultural heart of Jewish life in Vienna. Their legacy was in the buildings and the street names—Judengasse, Judenplatz—and their

---

* Ornate cabinet in which the scrolls of the Torah are kept
† Reading table used by a rabbi, facing the ark

blood was in the cobblestones and in the crevices of history, in the persecutions and the medieval pogrom that had driven them to live in Leopoldstadt.

By day the narrow Seitenstettengasse was insulated from much of the noise of the city, but this night was different. In the Shabbat evening darkness, Vienna was bursting to life. A short distance away, on the Kärtnerstrasse, a long thoroughfare on the other side of the Nazi enclave in Stephansplatz, a mob was gathering. The brown-shirted storm troopers of the SA, free now to bring out their concealed weapons and put on their swastika armbands, were on the march. The police marched with them. Trucks rolled along filled with storm troopers; men and women danced and yelled by the light of flaming torches. A British journalist who witnessed it called the procession "an indescribable witches' sabbath."[19]

Across the city came the full-throated roar—"Heil Hitler! Sieg heil! Down with the Jews! Down with the Catholics! One people, one reich, one Führer, one victory! Down with the Jews!" Raw, fanatical voices rose in song—"Deutschland über alles"—chanted, "Today we have all Germany—tomorrow we have the world!"[20] The playwright Carl Zuckmayer described what he saw that night: "The netherworld had opened its portals and spewed out its basest, most horrid, and filthiest spirits … What was being unleashed here was the revolt of envy; malevolence; bitterness; blind, vicious vengefulness."[21]

The echoes reached the Seitenstettengasse, where the Jews outside the Stadttempel were dispersing. Fritz shepherded Kurt down the Judengasse to the canalfront and across the bridge. Within minutes they were back in Leopoldstadt.

The Nazis were coming, along with hordes of newfound weathercock friends, flooding in thousands, tens of thousands, northeast across the city center, heading for the Jewish district. The tide poured across the bridges into Leopoldstadt, washing into Taborstrasse, Leopoldsgasse, the Karmelitermarkt, and Im Werd. A hundred thousand chanting, roaring men and women, filled with triumph and hate. "Sieg heil! Death to the Jews!" The Kleinmanns, like every Jewish family in Vienna, sat in their home, listening to the tumult outside, waiting for it to burst in through the doors.

But it didn't come. For hours the mobs ruled the streets, all noise and fury, but doing little physical harm. Some unlucky Jews were caught in the streets and abused, people who "looked Jewish" were beaten up, known Schuschnigg loyalists were attacked, a number of homes and businesses were invaded and plundered—but the storm of destruction did not break over Vienna that night.

Amazed, some people wondered whether the legendarily civilized nature of the Viennese people might temper the behavior even of its Nazis.

It was a vain hope. The reason for the restraint was simple: the storm troopers were in charge. They were disciplined, and they intended to strip and destroy their prey methodically, not by riot. Already that night the police were wearing swastika armbands and the SA, on Seyss-Inquart's orders, had taken over public buildings. They were in total control. The time of the Nazis had arrived. But this was just a prelude. Germany itself was coming.

By next morning, the first columns of German troops had crossed the border. During the night, prominent members of Schuschnigg's party and cabinet were seized or fled. Schuschnigg himself was under arrest. The European powers—Britain, France, Czechoslovakia—objected to Germany's invasion of sovereign territory, but Mussolini, supposedly Austria's ally, refused to consider any military action; he wouldn't even condemn Berlin. International resistance to Germany fell apart before it had even formed. The world left Austria to the dogs.

And Austria welcomed them.

אבא

Gustav woke to the sound of engines. A low drone that entered his skull with the stealth of an odor and grew in volume. Airplanes. For a moment it was as if he were in the street outside his workshop; it was still yesterday, the nightmare had not happened. He came awake. It was scarcely breakfast time. The rest of the family, apart from Tini, who was clattering quietly in the kitchen, were still in their beds, just stirring from their dreams.

As Gustav rose and dressed, the drone of airplanes grew louder. There was nothing to be seen from the windows—just rooftops and a strip of sky—so he put on his shoes and went downstairs.

In the street and across the Karmelitermarkt there was little sign of the night's terrors or the previous day's hopes, just a few stray "Vote Yes!" leaflets, trampled and swept into corners. The traders were setting out their stalls and opening their stores—fewer than usual, but life must go on. Everyone looked to the sky as the rumbling engines grew louder and louder, rattling windows, drowning out the sounds of the streets. This wasn't like yesterday at all. This was an oncoming thunderstorm. The planes came into view over the rooftops. They were bombers, dozens of them in tight formation, with fighters darting loose above them. They flew so low that even from the ground their German markings could be picked out and their bomb-bay doors could be seen opening.[22] A ripple of terror swept across the marketplace.

What came out, though, was not bombs but another blizzard of paper fluttering down over the roofs and streets. Here was a political climate that produced actual weather. Gustav picked up one of the leaflets. It was briefer and simpler than yesterday's message, but infinitely more chilling. At the head was the Nazi eagle, and a declaration:

> National Socialist Germany greets her National Socialist
> Austria and the new National Socialist government.
> Joined in a faithful, unbreakable bond!
> Heil Hitler![23]

The storm of engines was deafening. Not only the bombers but over a hundred transport planes flew over; while the bombers banked and circled, the others headed southeast. Nobody knew it yet, but these were troop-carrying aircraft, heading for Aspern aerodrome just outside the city—the first German spearhead into the Austrian capital. Gustav dropped the slip of paper as if it were toxic and went back indoors.

Breakfast was bleak that morning. From this day forward a specter would haunt every move, word, and thought of every Jewish family. Catholics and Communists too, all those who had reason to fear what was coming, experienced the same sensation, but none with the certainty of the Jews. They were all aware of what had happened in Germany in the past five years. What they didn't yet know was that in Austria there would be no gradual onset; they would experience five years' worth of terror in one frantic torrent.

The Wehrmacht was coming, the SS and Gestapo were coming, and there were rumors that the Führer himself had reached Linz and would soon be in Vienna. The city's Nazis were mad with excitement and triumph. The majority of the populace, wanting only stability and safety, began to sway with the times. Jewish stores in Leopoldstadt were systematically plundered by squads of SA storm troopers, while the homes of wealthier Jews began to be raided and robbed. Envy and hatred against the success of Jews in business, in skilled trades, and in the legal and medical professions had built to a head during the economic depression, and the boil was about to be violently lanced.

There was a myth that it wasn't in the nature of civilized Viennese to conduct politics through street-fighting and rioting. "The real Viennese," they said in dismay as the Nazis filled the streets with noise and fury, "discusses his differences over a café table and goes like a civilized being to the polls."[24] But in due course "the real Viennese" would go like a civilized being to his doom. The savages were calling the tune in this country now.

Yet Gustav Kleinmann, a hopeful man by nature, believed that his family might be safe. They were, after all, Austrians more than Jews. The Nazis would surely only persecute the devout, the openly Hebraic, the Orthodox . . . wouldn't they?

בת

Edith Kleinmann kept her head high and her gaze steady as she walked. She felt she had no reason to be fearful, although there were were signs everywhere that she should be. Like her father she thought herself an Austrian more than a Jew. The boys she went out with were rarely Jewish. This made Gustav uneasy; being Austrian was a fine thing, but he felt that one should still cleave to one's people. If there was a contradiction there, Gustav didn't recognize it. Edith thought little of such things—she was eighteen years old. By day she was learning the craft of millinery and had ambitions to be a hat designer; in her free hours she had a good time, went out with boys, and loved music and dancing. She was, above all else, a young woman, with the drives and desires of youth.

A couple days had passed since the arrival of the Germans. They had marched in on the Sunday, when the abandoned plebiscite had been scheduled to take place. Most Jews had stayed indoors, but Edith's brother Fritz, typically daring, had ventured out to watch. At first, he reported, a few brave Viennese threw stones at the German troops, but they were quickly overwhelmed by the cheering, Heil-Hitlering multitude. The next day came the grand parade, when the full German force made its triumphal entrance into the capital, led by Adolf Hitler himself. The columns seemed endless: fleets of gleaming staff cars, motorcycles, armored cars, thousands of helmets, rifles, crisply peaked caps, field-gray uniforms, and tramping jackboots. The scarlet, white, and black flags were everywhere—held aloft by the soldiers, hanging from the buildings, fluttering from the cars. Behind the scenes, Reichsführer-SS Heinrich Himmler had flown in the day before and begun the process of taking over the police, filling its upper ranks with SS men.[25] The plundering of wealthy Jews went on, and suicides were reported daily.

Edith walked briskly. There was some kind of disturbance going on in the little *platz* at the corner of the Schiffamtsgasse and Leopoldsgasse. A large crowd had gathered along the street near the police station;[26] Edith could hear laughter and cheering. Some kind of celebration. She went to cross the road to skirt around it, but slowed her step. She had seen a familiar face in the press—a young man named Vickerl Ecker, an old schoolfriend. His bright, eager eyes met hers.

"There! She's one!"[27]

Faces turned toward her, she heard the word *Jüdin*—Jewess—and suddenly hands were gripping her arms and propelling her toward the crowd. She saw Vickerl's brown shirt, the swastika armband. Then she was through the press of bodies and in the midst of a ring of leering, jeering faces. About half a dozen men and women were on their hands and knees with brushes and buckets, scrubbing the sidewalk. They were all Jews, all well-dressed. One bewildered woman clutched her hat and gloves in one hand and a scrubbing brush in the other, her immaculate coat trailing on the wet stones.

"On your knees." A brush was put in Edith's hand and she was pushed to the ground. Vickerl pointed at the Austrian crosses and SAY YES! slogans. "Get rid of your filthy propaganda, Jewess." The spectators crowed as she began to scrub with the others. There were faces she recognized—neighbors, acquaintances—smartly dressed businessmen, prim wives, rough working men and women, all part of the fabric of Edith's world, all melded into a gloating mob. She scrubbed, but the paint wouldn't come off. "Work suitable for Jews, eh?" somebody called out, and there was laughter. One of the storm troopers picked up a man's bucket and emptied it over him, soaking his camel hair coat, to a storm of guffaws from the crowd.

After an hour or so, the victims were given "receipts" for their "work" and permitted to go. Edith walked home, struggling to contain herself, brimming over with shame and degradation.

In the coming weeks these *Reibpartien*—"scrubbing games"—became an everyday part of life in the Jewish neighborhoods. The patriotic markings proved impossible to shift, and often the SA added acid to the water so that it burned and blistered the victims' hands.[28] Fortunately for Edith she wasn't taken again, but her fifteen-year-old sister Herta was among a group forced to scrub the Austrian crosses from the clock pillar in the marketplace. Other Jews were forced to paint anti-Semitic slogans on Jewish-owned shops and businesses in livid red and yellow.

The suddenness with which the genteel Viennese civilization had turned was breathtaking, like tearing the soft, comfortable fabric of a familiar couch to reveal unimagined ugliness inside. Gustav was wrong; the Kleinmanns were not safe. Nobody was safe.

משפחה

They all dressed in their best outfits before leaving the apartment together. Gustav wore his finest suit; Fritz too, in schoolboy's knickerbocker pants; Edith, Herta, and Tini in their smartest dresses; little Kurt in a sailor suit. In Hans Gemperle's photography studio they gazed into the camera's lens as if looking to their own futures. Edith seemed uneasy, and rested a hand on her mother's shoulder. Kurt looked contented—at eight he understood little of what the changes in his world might mean—and Fritz displayed the nonchalant ease of a cocky teenager. Herta, just turning sixteen and a young woman already, was radiant. As Herr Gemperle (who was not a Jew and would thrive in the coming years) clicked his shutter, he caught Gustav's apprehensiveness and the stoicism of Tini's dark eyes. They knew something of the world, and perhaps they saw more clearly now where it was going, even the sanguine Gustav. It had been Tini's will that had brought them to the studio. She had a foreboding that the family might not be together for much longer. She wanted to capture and preserve them like this, while there was still happiness.

The poison was already on the streets, fomented by the SA; now it began to flow from the offices of government and justice.

Under the Nuremberg Laws of 1935, Austrian Jews were stripped of their citizenship. On April 4 Fritz and all his Jewish schoolfellows were expelled from the trade school; he also lost his work placement. Edith and Herta were fired from their jobs, and Gustav was no longer able to practice his trade. Along with many other Jewish businesses, his workshop was seized and locked up. People were warned not to buy from Jews; those who were caught doing so were made to stand with a sign: "I am an Aryan, but a swine—I bought in this Jewish shop."[29]

One Saturday four weeks after the Anschluss,* Adolf Hitler returned to Vienna. He gave a speech at the huge Nordwest train station—which stood on the far side of the great Augarten public park, just a few hundred meters away from Im Werd—to a crowd of twenty thousand members of the SA, SS, and Hitler Youth. "I have shown through my life," he thundered, "that I can do more than those dwarfs who ruled this country into ruin. In a hundred years' time my name will stand as that of the great son of this country."[30] Providence, he declared, had made him leader of the Reich, and he called on all Germans to hold it in their fists. The crowd exploded into a storm of "Sieg heil!" repeated over and over, ear-splitting, echoing over Leopoldstadt.

Officially this was a day of thanksgiving for Greater Germany, and Hitler's speech was broadcast across the whole Reich. Vienna was decked with swastikas, every newspaper filled with pictures glorifying the Führer. The next day Austria would at last have its long-awaited vote, and once again citizens were being exhorted to vote Yes—not for independence but to affirm the Anschluss and Hitler's rule. Jews, of course, were barred from voting. The ballot was firmly controlled and closely monitored by the SS, and to nobody's surprise the result was 99.7 percent in favor. Hitler remarked that the result "surpassed all my expectations."[31] The bells of Protestant churches across the city rang for fifteen long minutes, and the head of the Evangelical Church ordered services of thanksgiving. The Catholics remained silent, not yet certain if the Führer meant to deal them Jews' wages.[32]

Encouraged by the result, the Nazis tightened their hold. Foreign newspapers were banned. Swastika lapel pins began to appear everywhere, and suspicion fell on any man or woman not wearing one; it became known as the "safety pin."[33] In all schools, the heil Hitler salute became part of daily routine after morning prayers. Jews were expelled from universities and most elementary schools, Jewish businesses were seized and transferred to Aryan ownership, there were ritual book-burnings, and the SS took over the Israelitische Kultusgemeinde, the Jewish cultural and religious affairs center near the Stadttempel, humiliating and baiting the rabbis and other officials who staffed it.[34] From now on the IKG would become the govern-

* Lit. joining; the forcible unification of Austria with Germany

ment organ through which the "Jewish problem" was handled, and it would have to pay "compensation" to the state for permission to occupy its own premises.[35] The regime seized Jewish property worth a total of two and a quarter billion Reichsmarks (not including houses and apartments, which would be taken in time).[36]

Gustav and Tini struggled to hold their family together. Gustav had a few good Aryan friends in the upholstery trade who gave him employment in their workshops, but it was infrequent. During the summer, Fritz and his mother managed to get work from the owner of the Lower Austrian Dairy, delivering milk in the neighboring district—it was only possible because the delivery round was early in the morning and the customers wouldn't know that their milk was being brought by Jews. They earned two pfennigs for each liter they delivered, making up to one mark a day—starvation wages. The family subsisted on meals from the Jewish soup kitchen along the street.

Nazism spread itself everywhere; there was no escaping its touch. Groups of brown-shirted storm troopers and Hitler Youth marched in the streets singing:

> *Wenn das Judenblut vom Messer spritzt,*
> *Dann singen wir und lachen.*

"When Jewish blood drips from the knife, then we sing and laugh." Their songs extolled the hanging of Jews and putting Catholic priests against the wall. Some of the singers were old friends of Fritz's. The local SS unit, the 89th Standarte, also had familiar faces in its ranks. They were everywhere, demanding identification from passing citizens, proud and pleased in their crisp uniforms and unalloyed power. It infected everything. The word *Saujud*—Jew-pig—was heard everywhere. Signs saying "Aryans only" appeared on park benches. Fritz and his remaining friends were barred from playing on sports grounds or using swimming pools—which struck Fritz hard, because he loved to swim.

As summer progressed, the violence against Jews subsided but official sanctions went on, and beneath the surface a pressure was building. A name began to be heard, a name replete with fear. "Keep your head down and your mouth shut," said Jews to one another, "or you will go to Dachau." People began to disappear: prominent figures first, politicians and businessmen, then they began to take able-bodied men. Sometimes they were delivered back to their families in ashes. Then another name began to be whispered: Buchenwald.

The *Konzentrationslagern*—concentration camps—which had been a feature of Nazi Germany since the beginning, were multiplying.[37]

The persecution of the Jews was becoming thoroughly systematized, bureaucratized. Their identities were a matter of special attention. In August it was decreed that if they didn't already have recognized Hebraic first names, they had to take new middle names: "Israel" for men, "Sara" for women.[38] And each person's identity card had to be stamped with a J—the *Juden-Kennkarte*, or *J-Karte* as they called it. In Leopoldstadt, a special procedure was employed. The cardholder, having had their card stamped, was taken into a room with a photographer and several male and female assistants. After being photographed, head and shoulders, from all sides, they were made to strip naked. "Despite their utmost reluctance," one witness recorded, "people had to undress completely before all these men and women in order to be taken again from all sides." They were fingerprinted and measured, "during which the men obviously measured the women, hair strength was measured, blood samples taken and everything written down and enumerated."[39] Every Jew was required to go through this degradation, without exception. Some bolted as soon as they got their cards stamped, so the SS began doing the photography *before* stamping the cards.

By September the situation in Vienna was quiet, and a semblance of normal life began to resume, even for Jews within their communities.[40]

But the Nazis were far from content with what they had done against the Jews; what was needed was a spur to push the people to the next level of Jew-hatred. In October an incident occurred in Belgium that foreshadowed what was to come. The port city of Antwerp had a large and prosperous Jewish quarter, with a particularly thriving diamond trade. On October 26, 1938, two journalists from the Nazi propaganda paper *Der Angriff* came ashore from a passenger steamer and began taking photographs of the Jewish diamond exchange. They behaved in an intrusive and offensive manner, and several Jews reacted angrily; they tried to eject the journalists, and there was a scuffle. One of the Germans was hurt and their camera taken. The police dispersed the crowd and two Jews were arrested.[41] In the German press the incident was magnified to a Jewish outrage against innocent and helpless German citizens. According to Vienna's *Neues Wiener Tagblatt*, a small party of German tourists had, without provocation, been set upon by a gang of fifty Jewish thugs, beaten bloody, and had their property stolen from them as they lay unconscious. "A large part of the Belgian press is silent," the paper fumed. "This attitude is indicative of the inadequacy of these papers, which are not afraid to make a fuss when a single Jew is held accountable for his crimes."[42] The Nazi paper *Völkischer Beobachter* issued a dire warning that any further acts of Jewish violence against Germans "could easily have consequences beyond their sphere of influence, which might be extremely undesirable and unpleasant for both individual Jews and Jewry as a whole."[43]

The threat was clear and tensions high.

As November began, anti-Semitic feelings in Vienna and all across the Nazi Reich were looking for an outlet. The trigger was pulled far away in Paris, when a Polish Jew named Herschel Grynszpan, in a blaze of rage over the expulsion of Polish Jews from Germany—including his own family—took a new-bought revolver into the German Embassy. Looking to kill the ambassador, instead he fired five bullets into Ernst vom Rath, an official chosen at random.

In Vienna the newspapers called the assassination an "outrageous provocation of the German people."[44] The Jews must be taught a lesson.

Vom Rath lingered for two days in the hospital before dying on Wednesday, November 9. That night, the Nazis came out in force on the streets of Berlin, Munich, Hamburg, Dresden, Salzburg, Vienna, and every other town and city. Local party officials and the Gestapo were the masters of ceremonies, and under their lead came the SA and the SS, armed with sledgehammers, axes, and combustibles. The targets were homes and businesses still in Jewish hands. Jews were beaten and murdered out of hand if they got in the way. The storm troopers tore down and burned wherever they could, but it was the shattering of glass that onlookers remembered most vividly; the sound of it was the dominant theme of the night. The Germans called it Kristallnacht, night of crystal glass, for the glittering shards that carpeted the sidewalks.[45] The Jews would remember it as the November pogrom.

The general order was that there was to be no looting, only destruction.[46] The orders were strict, but in the chaos that ensued they were broken many times over, with Jewish homes and businesses robbed under cover of searching for weapons and "illegal literature."[47] Homes were invaded, possessions broken, furnishings and clothes slashed and torn by brown-shirted men; mothers shielded their terrified children close and couples clung to each other in petrified despair as their homes were violated around them.

In Leopoldstadt, Jews caught out of doors were driven into the Karmelitermarkt and beaten. After midnight the city's synagogues were set ablaze, and the rooftops within sight of the Kleinmanns' apartment glowed orange, illuminated by the flames of the Polnische Schul, the synagogue in Leopoldsgasse. The fire brigade turned out, but the storm troopers barred them from fighting the fire until the magnificent building had been completely consumed. In the city center, the Stadttempel, which couldn't be burned because it adjoined other buildings, was gutted instead; its gorgeous carvings, fittings, and beautiful gold and white paintwork were smashed and violated, the ark and the bimah thrown down and broken.

Then, before dawn, the arrests began. Jews in their thousands, mostly able-bodied men, were seized on the streets or dragged from their homes by the storm troopers.

Among the first taken were Gustav and Fritz Kleinmann.

2 | Traitors to the People

אבא

THEY WERE TAKEN TO the district police headquarters in Ausstellungsstrasse, an imposing building of red brick and ashlar near the Prater public park.[1] The Kleinmann family had spent many a holiday afternoon in the Prater, in the acres of green parkland, in the beer garden, the children delighting in the slide, the bathing pools, the rides and sideshows of the funfair. Now, in the gloomy winter morning, the gates were still and the steel spiderweb of the Riesenrad ferris wheel loomed over the rooftops like a threat. Gustav and Fritz passed by the park entrance without seeing it, in a truck packed with other Jewish men from Leopoldstadt.

Father and son had been given up to the storm troopers by their own neighbors: by men who had been Gustav's close friends, *Du-Freunden**, men he had chatted to, smiled at, known and trusted, who knew his children and his life story. Yet without coercion or provocation they had pushed him over the cliff.

The police station had some disused stables, and the prisoners were herded into one of the larger buildings.[2] There were hundreds of men and women in there already. The arrests had swept the city like a flash flood. Most were taken from their homes like Gustav and Fritz; hundreds more were seized the next morning while lining up outside the embassies and consulates of foreign nations, seeking escape; others had been snatched randomly off the streets.[3]

---

* Friends close enough to call one another *du*, the intimate form of "you," rather than the formal *Sie*

The barked question: *"Jude oder Nichtjude?"** And if the answer was *"Jude,"* or if the victim's appearance even hinted at it—into the back of the truck. Some were marched through the streets, abused and assaulted by crowds. The Nazis called it the *Volksstimme*—the voice of the people. It howled through the streets with a sound of sirens, and in the light of dawn it went on and on, a nightmare from which there would now be no waking.

Six and a half thousand Jews—mostly men—had been taken to police stations across the city, and none was fuller than the one by the Prater.[4] The cells had overflowed with the first arrivals, and now people were crammed so tightly in the stable building they had to stand with hands raised; some were made to kneel so that newcomers could crawl over them.

Gustav and Fritz stuck together in the press. The hours wore by as they stood or knelt, hungry, thirsty, joints aching, surrounded by muttering and groans and prayers. From out in the yard, leaking through the walls and around the rafters, came the jeering and the sounds of beatings. Every few minutes, two or three people would be called from the room for interrogation. None came back.

Fritz and his father didn't know how many hours they had been there when at last the finger pointed at them and they struggled through the mass of bodies to the door. They were seized and marched to another building, into the presence of a panel of officials. The interrogation, like every contact with the SA and SS, was held together by a glue of insults—*Saujud, Volksverräter, jüdische Verbrecher* . . . Jew-pig, traitor to the people, Jewish criminal. Each prisoner was forced to identify with these calumnies, to own them and accept them. And the questions were the same for every man: *How much money have you in savings? Are you a homosexual? Are you in a relationship with an Aryan woman? Have you ever helped to perform an abortion? What associations and parties are you a member of?*

Following interrogation and review, the prisoners were assigned to categories. Those labeled *Zurück* (return) were put back into confinement to await further processing. The ones marked as *Entlassung* (dismissal) were released, mostly foreigners arrested by mistake, women, the elderly, and adolescents. The category every man dreaded to hear was *Tauglich* (able-bodied), because

---

* "Jew or non-Jew?"

they guessed that this meant Dachau. Or Buchenwald, or the new name that was being whispered: Mauthausen, a camp they were building in Austria itself.[5]

While they waited for their verdicts, the interrogated were put in a mezzanine room overlooking the yard. Here Gustav and Fritz could see the source of the noises they had heard. The men outside had been forced into packed ranks with their hands raised, lambasted and abused by SA and SS storm troopers armed with sticks and whips. They were made to lie down, stand up, roll around, whipped, kicked, laughed at, their coats and smart suits smeared with dirt, their hats trampled on the ground. Some were singled out for severe beatings. Those not taking part in the "gymnastics" were made to chant "We are Jewish criminals! We are Jew-pigs!"

Throughout this, the Schutzpolizei, the regular police, men of long service who knew the Jewish folk of Leopoldstadt, many of them as friends, stood by, assisting as required, as they had ever since the persecutions began. Although most behaved with restraint and few participated in the abuse, neither did any resist it. At least one senior policeman joined in with the beatings in the courtyard, although his men did not.[6]

After a long wait, Fritz's and Gustav's verdicts came through. Fritz, only fifteen years old, had been tagged *Entlassung*. He was free to go. Gustav was marked *Zurück*: back to the cells. Fritz could do nothing but watch in sick dismay as his papa was force-marched away.

בּ

It was evening when Fritz finally left the police station. He walked home alone, passing the familiar entrance of the Prater. He had walked this route many times before—after swimming with his friends in the Danube, after days out in the park, in a bliss of sweet cakes or abuzz with adrenaline. Now there was just emptiness.

The streets were sullen and bloodshot, hungover after the previous night's debauch. Leopoldstadt was devastated, the sidewalks in the shopping streets and the Karmelitermarkt carpeted with glass shards and splintered wood.

Fritz came home to the apartment in Im Werd, to the arms of his mother and sisters. Where was his papa? He couldn't tell them. Again the terrible names pushed to the front of their minds: Dachau, Buchenwald. They waited through that night, but no word came; they inquired tentatively, but could learn nothing.

Around the world, the news of the pogrom was met with revulsion. The United States recalled its ambassador from Berlin in protest,[7] the president declaring that the news "has profoundly affected the American people ... I had difficulty believing that such things could occur in the 20th century."[8] Former president Hoover compared the Nazis to Torquemada and said they were bringing on themselves "the condemnation of the public opinion of the world ... for centuries to come."[9] In London, the *Spectator* magazine said that "this week's outbreak of barbarism in Germany is on so vast a scale, is marked by an inhumanity so diabolical and bears marks of official inspiration so unmistakable that its consequences internal and external are yet beyond prediction."[10]

But the Nazis shrugged off these condemnations, dismissing the atrocity claims as false reporting designed to distract from the real outrage—the terroristic Jewish murder of a German diplomat. They congratulated themselves on having dealt the Jews a deserved punishment, an "expression of a righteous disgust amongst the broadest strata of the German people" toward the malign influence of Judaism.[11] Condemnations from abroad were dismissed as "dirt and filth fabricated in the known centres of immigration of Paris, London and New York, and guided by the Jewish-influenced world press."[12] The Nazis declared that the destruction of the synagogues meant that Jews "can now no longer hatch plots against the State under cover of religious services."[13]

Fritz, Tini, Herta, Edith, and Kurt waited through that Friday, and could discover nothing about Gustav. Dusk fell and Shabbat began, and with it at last he came home; exhausted, famished, dehydrated, gaunter than ever, walking in through the door like a resurrection from the grave, to an outburst of joyful relief. He told his story. The officials at the police station had taken note of his service in the Great War, and friends among the police had eventually vouched for his multiple combat wounds and Silver Medal for Bravery First Class. Even the Nazis wouldn't go so far yet as to condemn a war hero to a concentration camp. The standing order from the top of the SS was that veterans were excluded from the round-up, along with the sick, the elderly, and juveniles.[14] Gustav Kleinmann was free to go.

Most were not. Over the next few days, the transports began. Fleets of *Grüne Heinrich** police trucks drove in relays from police stations all over the city,

---

* Green Henry: equivalent to Black Maria

packed with Jewish men tagged as able-bodied—some of them war veterans too, but lacking Gustav's decorations or acquaintances in the police. Many drove through Leopoldstadt and the city center, past the men's homes, all headed toward the same destination: the loading ramp of the Westbahnhof train station. There the prisoners were herded into freight cars. Some went to Dachau, some to Buchenwald. Many would never be seen again. The camps were sprouting like toxic weeds, and the transports would grow fuller and more frequent.

בת

To the sound of hammering, Gustav absently twisted a strip of fabric round his fingers. An off-cut, a scrap of waste, a remnant of his livelihood. Across the street a workman's hammer drove nails into the planks covering the broken panes that had once looked in on a Jewish-owned shop. It was Jewish no longer.

His own business had gone months ago, and now, looking along Im Werd, the market, Leopoldsgasse, he picked out the businesses that had once belonged to Jewish friends and were now either empty or in the hands of non-Jews. Like the neighbors who had turned him and Fritz over to the SA, many of the new owners were friends of his, and of the people whose shops they had taken. There was Ochshorn's perfumery on the far corner of the market square, now owned by Willi Pöschl, a neighbor from Gustav's building. The butchers, poulterers, and fruit sellers had lost their market stands. Another friend of Gustav's, Mitzi Steindl, had eagerly taken part in pushing out the Jews and seizing their businesses; she'd been poor before all this, and Gustav had often given her work as a seamstress just to help her out.

With a whole class of people labeled as dangerous enemies of the people, and the chance of an instant profit, friend had turned on friend without hesitation or qualm. These men and women who had taken Jews' livelihoods; the old school friend who had forced Edith to scrub the sidewalk; the many old schoolmates of Fritz who were now in the Hitler Youth; they reveled in the baiting, the intimidation, plundering, beating, and deportation of Jews. In the eyes of all but a few, Jews could no longer be friends, for how can a dangerous, predatory animal be a friend to a human being, much less an equal? It was inconceivable.

מִשְׁפָּחָה

Shortly after Kristallnacht, an English journalist observed: "It is true that Jews in Germany have not been formally condemned to death; it has only been made impossible for them to live."[15] In the face of this impossibility, some took their own lives; dozens each day accepted what they saw as the inevitable, and chose to take themselves out of this hopeless nothing of a life. Many more decided to leave and find life elsewhere. Ever since the Anschluss, Austrian Jews had been trying to leave the country, and now their numbers and their desperation increased.

For the Kleinmann family there was no easy way out. No way at all, it seemed. Leaving the Reich for a better place was impossibly difficult for a poor family. In the five and a half years since the Nazis had taken power in Germany, tens of thousands of Jews had emigrated. The Zionists and the desperate went to Palestine; others went wherever they had relatives or prospects. Failing that, they fled to any country that would let them in: France, Holland, Britain, the Americas North and South. But every nation on Earth resisted the influx of immigrants and refugees. Even Palestine, which was under British control, could take only strictly limited numbers.

In Austria, Jewish life and emigration came under the overall control of SS-Lieutenant Adolf Eichmann. Formerly a clerk with the SD, the intelligence and security arm of the SS, the Austrian-born Eichmann had made himself the organization's foremost expert on Jewish culture and affairs.[16] Accordingly, despite his low rank and his youth (he was only thirty-two), he had been put in charge of managing the Jewish problem in Austria. The solution to the problem was, first and foremost, to encourage Jews to leave. To this end, Eichmann ran the Central Office for Jewish Emigration. He reactivated the Israelitische Kultusgemeinde, Vienna's Jewish cultural and welfare organization, and coerced its leaders into becoming part of the apparatus of emigration. Eichmann also roped in the Palestine Office and the Zionist Association. The IKG's role was to maintain information on Jews and to coordinate the bureaucracy—including contacts with Jewish organizations in other countries—required for their departure.

But the Nazis, despite wanting the Jews gone, couldn't resist making it as hard for them as possible. They intended to strip them of their wealth as they passed through the system, imposing a variety of extortionate taxes and fines on them—including an "escaping the Reich" tax of 30 percent of their assets and an "atonement" tax of 20 percent (a punishment for Jewry's "abominable crimes," in the words of Reinhard Heydrich, who came up with the idea), plus other impositions including hefty bribes and an exchange rate for foreign currency that was positively ruinous.[17] Moreover, the applicant's tax clearance, once granted, was only valid for a few months, and securing a visa often took longer than that. Impoverished would-be emigrants would then be flung right back to the start. As a result, the Nazi government had to *lend* the IKG money in order to help pay for impoverished Jews to obtain their travel tickets and foreign currency.[18] In this way, the Nazis' own hatred gummed up the workings of the very machine they had created to carry it out.

Finding a place to immigrate to was the hardest part. Little help came from abroad. Around the world, people—especially Jews—condemned the regime and criticized their own governments for doing too little to take in refugees. But little was done. The campaigners were outnumbered by those who did not want immigrants in their midst, taking their livelihoods and diluting their communities.

In July 1938, President Roosevelt, who wished to help the Jews but had neither the power nor the will to force the issue under the United States' tight, discriminatory immigration law, had called an emergency international conference. It had been held with a great fanfare of press attention at Évian in France. But the prevailing anti-immigration mood had hobbled it before it even began, the conference invitation stating that "no country will be expected to receive a greater number of emigrants than is permitted by its existing legislation."[19] So that was that. The German press jeered at the hypocrisy of a world that made so much indignant noise about the supposedly pitiful plight of the Jews but did little or nothing to help.

While the right-wing Western press advocated standing firm against immigration, many journalists spoke out. In London, the *Spectator* declared, "It is an outrage, to the Christian conscience especially, that the modern world with all its immense wealth and resources cannot give these exiles a home, and food and drink, and a secure status."[20] Immigrants and refugees could be cared for without harming the settled population, and "civilised governments must accept the duty and responsibility of undertaking such a task. Anti-Semitism, the root of the refugee problem as it is now and as it is likely to develop . . . demands world co-operation to overcome its evils."[21]

The same magazine had a correspondent in Vienna, who reported that "the city of gaiety, as everyone knows, has become a city of persecution, a city of sadism . . . no amount of examples of cruelty and bestiality, can convey to the reader who hasn't felt it the atmosphere of Vienna, the air which the Austrian Jews must breathe. For it is not so much individual acts of persecution as the atmosphere these produce, the terror at every ring of the-front-door bell, the smell of cruelty in the air, which drive elderly Jews to stay behind locked doors all day and mothers to keep their children indoors . . . Feel that atmosphere and you can understand why it is that families and friends split up to emigrate to the corners of the earth."[22]

And then had come Kristallnacht. This unprecedented atrocity galvanized the liberal press and politicians, and some of the public. It should have changed everything, but it didn't. Governments, the conservative press, and the prevailing democratic will continued to stand firm against letting in more than a trickle of Jewish migrants. When people in the West looked to Europe, they saw not only the few hundred thousand Jews in Germany and Austria, but looming behind them the hundreds of thousands in other Eastern European countries, and the three million in Poland; all these nations had recently enacted anti-Semitic laws.

Again the Nazi press jeered: "The fundamental hypocrisy of this whole staged campaign is best shown by the attitude of numerous countries on the issue of Jewish emigration. Nobody wants to take Jewish immigrants."[23] "It is a shameful spectacle," said Adolf Hitler, "to see how the whole democratic world is oozing sympathy for the poor tormented Jewish people but remains hardhearted and obdurate when it comes to helping them."[24]

Hitler sneered at Roosevelt's "so-called conscience" and while the *Chicago Tribune* headlined that the United States had taken in over twenty-seven thousand Jews that year, on the same page it reported that a proposal to open up Alaska to Jewish immigrants had met determined resistance from the local populace.[25] Congressional leaders argued that Roosevelt's proposed relaxation of immigration laws to help Jewish refugees "might cause an upset of this nation's settled immigration policies" and "aggravate unemployment and relief problems."[26] In the British Parliament, members from all sides spoke earnestly about the need to help the Jews, but the home secretary warned of anti-Semitism in the country—"an underlying current of suspicion and anxiety about an alien influx"—and that the government must "be careful to avoid mass immigration." On the other hand, the politicians said, there should be a concerted move to help Jewish children, to save "the younger generation of a great people" who "had never failed to make their contribution to the destinies of the nations which had befriended them."[27]

Many fine words were spoken and calls to action were made. And little changed.

Meanwhile, the hundreds of thousands of Jews remaining in the Reich could only live out their days, queue at the consulates of Western nations, and wait and hope that their applications would be successful. Thousands were in concentration camps; for them an emigration visa was their only hope. Hundreds in Vienna were homeless, and many were reluctant to apply to emigrate for fear of being arrested.[28]

The Kleinmanns, who still had their apartment, were luckier than some, but no more free. Gustav had no money and no property, so it was difficult to raise the funds to buy his way through the bloodsucking bureaucracy. He also felt little confidence in his ability to begin a new life in a strange country. Tini couldn't bear the thought of leaving; she was rooted in Vienna, born and bred. At her age, where could she possibly go without feeling torn from her natural place?

Her children were another matter. She feared for them, especially fifteen-year-old Fritz; the Nazis had taken him once and might do it again at any time. It wouldn't be long before he lost the flimsy protection of his age.

Foreign countries were more receptive to child refugees than to adults. In December 1938, two parties totaling over a thousand Jewish children left Vienna for England—just part of a projected five thousand accepted by the United Kingdom government, living up to its fine words for once.[29] Eventually over ten thousand would find safety in Britain through the *Kindertransport*. Yet even this was just a fraction of the children needing refuge. The UK government proposed opening up Palestine to ten thousand Jewish children, in addition to the numbers already migrating there from Germany. Tini heard about this proposal and had hopes of placing Fritz on one of the transports when they began;[30] he was old enough to cope with being sent away and to support himself through work, which eight-year-old Kurt could not. Talks began in Palestine and dragged on for months with no agreement between

the British authorities, the Jewish Agency, and the Palestinian Arab delega-
tion. The Arabs feared that they would be swamped in their own land, losing
the majority rights they currently enjoyed and sacrificing all their hopes of a
future independent Palestinian state. The talks were doomed, and eventually
broke down.[31]

While the rest of her family fretted and wavered, Edith Kleinmann was
absolutely determined to leave. She could never forget the abuse she had suffered. A lively, outgoing spirit, she couldn't bear this confinement, which
amounted to a kind of captivity. Edith had her eyes on America. The application process was slow and complicated, and for most people hopeless. But she
had acquired the two affidavits she needed from relatives in the United States
who were willing to provide her with shelter and support. Thus prepared, at
the end of August 1938 she had registered at the American consulate to begin
the process of applying for one of the limited number of US visas granted each
year.[32] Weeks turned into months, and there was no visa, no hope of escape.
The system was flooded with applicants and was deliberately squeezed tight at
both ends, by the State Department and the Nazi regime. With the end of the
year looming, Edith faced the prospect of being stuck in Vienna forever. After
Kristallnacht, the need took hold in earnest. She had to get out, and England
looked like the best bet.

Since the early summer, large numbers of Austrian Jews—mostly women,
who passed more easily through the bureaucratic vetting process—had fixed on
England as the place to try for. Hopeful advertisements had begun to appear in
the classified section of the London *Times* ("the recognized medium for successful results").[33] The advertisers ranged from maids, cooks, chauffeurs, and
nannies, to jewel-setters, goldsmiths, doctors of law, piano teachers, mechanics,
skiing instructors, language tutors, gardeners, housekeepers, and bookkeep-
ers. Many offered themselves for more lowly work than they were qualified
for. The same self-recommendations recurred: "good teacher," "perfect cook,"
"good handyman," "experienced," "perfect in household," "excellent character." After Kristallnacht, the advertisements became palpably desperate: "any
work," "urgently seeks," "with boy aged 10 (in children's home if necessary),"
"immediately" . . . the clamoring of people with prison walls rising around
them and doors slamming shut.

Domestic servants received preferential treatment in applying for visas. If a
potential refugee could obtain certification as a domestic servant via the IKG,

the British government would issue a visa.[34] A near neighbor of the Kleinmanns, Elka Jungmann, who lived in apartment 19, placed an ad typical of the hundreds of others:

> Cook, with long-service testimonials (Jewess), also housekeeper, knows all housework, seeks post. — Elka Jungmann, Vienna 2, Im Werd 11/19.[35]

This might be Edith's way out. But as an apprentice milliner she had no domestic skills to offer, and to secure a contract she would need proof of experience. Edith, who dressed well, lived well, and saw herself as a lady—perhaps even a prima donna—wasn't keen on the idea. Clean the house? It wasn't in her nature. But Tini took her in hand, teaching her what she could. Then she obtained her a placement as a maid with a middle-class Jewish family in Vienna. Edith worked there for one month, and they generously gave her a testimonial certifying that she had worked for six. Applying through a neighbor's friend, with amazing good fortune Edith managed to obtain a work contract.[36] All she needed now was a visa and clearance from the Nazi authorities.

This was the hard part. Despite its fair words in public, the British government was still resistant to taking adult migrants, and only a handful of visas were given out each day.[37] The family all took turns standing in line at the British consulate in Wallnerstrasse, in the government district. Twenty-four hours a day, turn by turn, for a week they held Edith's place in line. By now the year was reaching its end and the cold was bitter, but they kept the place as it inched forward day by day. It was dangerous—not only the cold but exposure to the SA. The consulate queues clogged the sidewalks, and were periodically dispersed by the police; sometimes SA men would come by and beat the Jews with rope-ends. This practice was curtailed after the US consul-general asked the police to intervene.[38]

Gradually Edith's place reached the grand doorway of the Palais Caprara-Geymüller, which housed the consulate.[39] She was admitted and lodged her application. Then she waited. At last, in early January 1939, she was granted her visa.

Edith's parting was painful for everyone. None of them could imagine how or when or even if they would ever meet again. She boarded a train and vanished from their lives, into a new existence, leaving behind a void in the family. Another young Viennese girl tried to imagine what it must be like to set out on such a journey: "Away from here! . . . You lean back in the compartment, close your eyes and then you look out of the window. The train sings and your hair wafts. Abroad, a foreign land. Then being Jewish no longer means being tortured and martyred. I can hardly believe it any more. It must be wonderful, marvellous!"[40]

Within days Edith was aboard a ferry crossing the English Channel, leaving behind the terror and the abuse and the danger, but also everything she knew and everyone she loved. In later years, when she grew old and talked to her children about this time, she would fall silent at this point, as if the pain still remained too sharp, long after all else had lost its bite—this memory of parting more potent than anything that had gone before.

מִשְׁפָּחָה

In Vienna life went on. The Jewish population diminished; fortunate émigrés left in ones and twos, or hundreds at a time, while the unfortunate went in small batches to Dachau and Buchenwald.

The besieged, intimidated Jewish community was a ghost of its former self. A visitor who came in the early summer of 1939 believed it was worse than anything in Germany; he was unsettled to find whole streets of shops and houses in Leopoldstadt empty where Jews had been evicted and their properties left unoccupied. "Streets that had been blocked with traffic were now quite empty, and it looked to us just like a dead city."[41]

Less than half of Vienna's Jews still lived there, and they went out as little as they could. The Zionist Youth Aliyah, whose official purpose was to prepare young Jews for kibbutz life in Palestine, did heroic work among the children who remained, providing community, teaching, training in crafts and medicine, and succor. Over two thirds of Vienna's Jews, deprived of their means of support, now depended on charity, most of which was organized within their own communities. Soup kitchens sprang up—including one in a disused girls' school which served sixteen hundred meals a day to needy children. Only one meal could be provided per child per day, so constrained were the resources.[42] In most districts it was dangerous for Jews to be out after dark, especially on evenings when Nazi Party meetings took place; there would always be some brutality after the SS and SA had wound themselves up with speeches. Some districts were too dangerous for Jews at any time of day or night.

In their apartment, the Kleinmann family held together, closing in around the empty space left by Edith. Kurt attended one of the improvised schools, while his brother and sister did what they could to help their parents. Fritz was required to have a new identity card issued in summer 1939, having turned sixteen in June.[43] Of all the family's *J-Karte* photos, Fritz's—in which the adolescent verging on manhood, dressed only in his undershirt, glared with detestation into the camera—was the only one that would ultimately survive.

Occasional letters from Edith found their way to Vienna. They were short, communicating little more than that she had settled in her work as a maid and was doing well. She lived in the suburbs of Leeds, a large industrial city in the north of England, and worked for a Russian Jewish lady called Mrs. Brostoff.

Edith's letters continued to arrive during that summer; then in September they abruptly stopped. On September 1, 1939, Germany invaded Poland. Everything changed on that day—for Germany, for Europe, for the whole world, and almost immediately for the Kleinmann family. Britain and France declared war on Germany, and an impenetrable barrier fell between Edith and her family.

Nine days later an even worse blow hit them. On Sunday, September 10, Fritz was seized by the SS.

אבא

A new wave of arrests had swept through the Reich. Now that Germany was at war with Poland, all Jews of Polish origin were classed as enemy aliens. Thousands were rounded up for internment.[44] As an Austrian, Gustav should have been safe, but those who knew him were aware that he'd been born in the old kingdom of Galicia. At that time, Galicia had been part of the Austro-Hungarian Empire, but since 1918 it had been part of southern Poland.

The men who reported this fact to the Nazis were the same friends and neighbors who had betrayed Gustav and Fritz during Kristallnacht. One was now the building's official Nazi political leader.

It was a Sunday. Tini was alone in the apartment with the children. There was a hammering at the door, making them all flinch. Any loud, confident knock on the door these days was a prelude to insult, theft, and potential danger. Tini opened it warily and peeked out. There were four men looming over her. She recognized every face; every line under the eyes and every bristle on their cheeks was a familiar sight. They were neighbors in the same building, working men like her husband, friends with wives she knew, whose children once played with hers. The ones she knew best were Friedrich Novacek, an engineering worker, and foremost among them Ludwig Helmhacker, a coalman.[45] This wasn't the first time Ludwig and his little gang had called.

"What do you want from us now, Wickerl?" Tini said in exasperation as they pushed past her into the little apartment. (Even after all he had done, she couldn't help calling Ludwig by the friendly diminutive.) "You know we've got nothing—we don't even have food."[46]

"We want your husband," he said. There was no mistaking his tone, or the purposeful demeanor of all four men. Gustav wasn't there, as they could see perfectly well for themselves. Wickerl cut short her protest. "We have orders; if Gustl* isn't here, we're to take the lad." He nodded at Fritz.

It was as if she'd been physically kicked. There nothing she could say to change what was happening. They took hold of her son and marched him out the door. Wickerl paused before leaving. "So, we'll take Fritzl to the police, and when Gustl reports, the boy can come home again."

Later that day, Gustav came home to find his family in a state of panic and grief. When he heard what had happened, he didn't hesitate. He turned right around and headed out, intending to go straight to the police. Tini barred his way. "Don't," she said. "You have to get away, go somewhere and hide."

There was no shaking him. Gustav went out and walked quickly to the police station in Leopoldsgasse. Taking his courage in both hands, he walked right in and up to the desk. The police officer on duty looked up at him. "I'm Gustav Kleinmann," he said. "I'm here to turn myself in. You have my son. Take me and let him go."

The policeman glanced around. "Get out," he muttered. "Get the hell out of here."

Bewildered, Gustav left the building. He went home to find Tini both relieved to see him again and distraught that Fritz was still gone. "I'll try again tomorrow," he said.

---

* Affectionate diminutive used in eastern Austria; e.g., Fritzl, Gustl

Again Tini pleaded with him not to, begged him to run and hide. She realized, as Gustav apparently did not, that the Nazis would come back for him, and that their word could never be trusted. The policeman's dismissal had been a reprieve. "Get out now, or I'll turn on the gas—I'll kill myself."

Eventually she got through to him, and he went. All that day and evening they waited on eggshells, listening out for the knock on the door. Late that night, Gustav returned. He had nowhere else to go, and he couldn't leave Tini and the children alone all night long. There was no knowing who might be taken next.

At two o'clock in the morning it came. The thundering on the door, the tide of men surging into the apartment, the snapped orders, the hands seizing Gustav by his arms, the weeping, pleas, the last desperate words between husband and wife. He was allowed to pack a little bundle of clothes—a sweater, a scarf, a spare pair of socks.[47] And then it was all over. The door slammed, and Gustav was gone.

Part II

Buchenwald

3 | Blood and Stone: *Konzentrationslager* Buchenwald

אבא

MAKING SURE HE WAS ALONE, Gustav took out a little pocket notebook and pencil. He opened the book and wrote in his clear, angular hand: "Arrived in Buchenwald on the 2nd October 1939 after a two-day train journey."

He'd managed to keep the notebook concealed, knowing that it would be the death of him if he were found with it. But he felt a need that he couldn't ignore, to record what had occurred and what would yet happen. There was no way of telling how long he could keep going, or whether he would ever get out of this place. Whatever happened, this diary would be his witness.

Over a week had passed since that dreadful arrival, and there was a lot to record. Even the most concise account would eat up the notebook's precious leaves. He smoothed down the page and wrote on:

"From Weimar train station we ran to the camp . . ."

בן

The boxcar door groaned and clanged open, flooding the inside with light; instantly a hell's chorus of shrieked orders and snarling guard dogs erupted. Fritz blinked and looked around, stunned by this barrage on his senses.[1]

Over three weeks had passed since Wickerl Helmhacker and his pals had torn Fritz away from his family. The only thing he had to console him was that, since he had not been released, that must mean his papa had got away safely. Fritz's arrest had been utterly terrifying. The local police had brought him across the Danube Canal to the Hotel Metropole, headquarters of the Vienna Gestapo. He was just one among thousands of Jews who had been arrested in recent days. As in the November pogrom, the Viennese authorities struggled to accommodate them; they were transferred to the Praterstadion, the huge international football stadium on the far side of the Prater. They were kept there under guard for nearly three weeks. Eventually, on September 30, they were taken by relays of police cars and trucks to the Westbahnhof, where they were loaded into cattle cars.

For two days Fritz had been confined in the press of bodies inside the car, hardly able to move, rocked by the jolting of the train and oppressed by the proximity of strangers, a sixteen-year-old boy among a crowd of anxious, sweating, muttering men. They gradually resolved into individuals as the journey went on, Fritz growing used to the darkness and each man's unique presence: the middle-class father, the businessman, the spectacled intellectual, the bristle-cheeked workman, the ugly, the handsome, the portly, the terrified, the man who took it all calmly, the man simmering with indignation, the man scared to his bowels. The frightened far outnumbered the angry; some were silent, some muttered or prayed, some chattered incessantly. Each man an individual with a mother, a wife, children or cousins, a job, a place in the life of Vienna. But to the men in uniforms outside the boxcar—just livestock.

"Out! Out, Jew-pigs—now! Out-out-out!"

Out they came, into the dazzling light. One thousand and thirty-five Jews—bewildered, seething, confused, scared, dazed—pouring down from the boxcars onto the loading ramp of Weimar train station, into a hailstorm of abuse and blows and snarling dogs.[2] A crowd of local people had turned out to watch the transport come in; they stood beyond the SS guards, jeering, smirking, calling out insults.

The prisoners, some of them carrying bags and suitcases, were pushed, beaten, and yelled into ranks. From the loading ramp they were herded into a tunnel, then out into the air again. They were driven along at a run. The crowd followed for a while along the northbound city street and out onto the open road. "Run, Jew-pigs, run!" Fritz ran with the rest. If a man paused or dropped back, turned aside, even looked like he was slackening his pace, or if he spoke to another, the hammer-blow of a rifle-butt would fall on his shoulders, his back, his head.

These camp SS were worse than any Fritz had seen before. Christened by Himmler Totenkopfverbände—Death's Head Units—their caps bore skull-and-crossbones badges and their cruel brutality was beyond all human reason. Drunkards, sadists, stunted or twisted minds, deformed souls—inadequate human beings vested with a sense of destiny and almost limitless power, trained to believe that they were soldiers in a war against the enemy within.

Fritz ran and ran into a seemingly endless hell. Block after block of city street went by, then turned to country road. The prisoners were mocked and spat on. Men stumbled, weakened by age or fatigue or the burden of their luggage, and were shot. A man might stoop to tie a shoelace, or fall over, plead for water, and he would be gunned down without hesitation. The road, climbing a long slope, led into a thick forest, then forked. The prisoners were driven up the left branch, onto a new concrete road called by veterans the Blutstrasse, Blood Road. Built by hundreds of prisoners—many of whom had died in its making—it was still under construction. Their blood was joined by that of new arrivals driven along it.

They had gone about four kilometers when Fritz thought he recognized a familiar figure running ahead of him. He increased his pace and drew level. He had been right—here, in spite of all reason, all justice, was Papa, laboring along, dripping with sweat, with his little package of spare clothing under his arm. To Gustav, it was as if Fritz had miraculously materialized out of nowhere. This was no occasion for emotional reunions. Sticking close together, they edged deeper into the pack to avoid the random blows, shutting their minds to the sporadic gunshots, and ran on with the herd, up the hill, deeper and deeper into the forest.

This was the Ettersberg, a broad-backed hill covered in dense beech woodland. For centuries it had been a hunting ground of the dukes of Saxony-Weimar, and more recently a popular spot for picnics. It was known best as a retreat for the artists and intellectuals of the ducal court of Weimar and famously associated with writers like Schiller and Goethe, whose plays had been performed in an amateur theater in the parkland.[3] The city of Weimar was the very epicenter of German classical cultural heritage, and for that reason it had been chosen after the First World War as the seat of the new democratic republic. The Weimar Republic was now long dead, and with the founding of a concentration camp on the Ettersberg, the Nazi regime was placing its own imprint upon Weimar's heritage. Buchenwald—named for the picturesque beech forest that made the mountain so pleasant—was more than just a prison camp; it was a model SS settlement whose scale would eventually rival that of the city itself.[4] What happened here among the beeches would one day cast all of Weimar's Germanic heritage in shadow. Many of the people imprisoned here called it not Buchenwald but Totenwald: Forest of the Dead.[5]

At last, after eight uphill kilometers—more than an hour's worth of grueling running—the Blood Road bent northward and emerged into a vast open space cleared in the forest. Scattered across it were buildings of all shapes and sizes, some complete, some still under construction, many hardly begun.[6] They had reached Buchenwald.

Ahead the road was straddled by a wide, low gatehouse in a massive fence studded with guard towers. This was the entrance to the prison camp itself; the small town being built outside its fences comprised the barracks and facilities of the SS, the infrastructure of the machine in which the prisoners were both fuel and grist. On the gateway were two slogans declaring the ideology that made the machine. Above, on the gate lintel, was inscribed:

RECHT ODER UNRECHT—MEIN VATERLAND

My country, right or wrong: the very essence of nationalism and fascism. And wrought into the ironwork of the gate itself:

JEDEM DAS SEINE

To each his own. It could also be interpreted as *Each person gets what he deserves*.

Exhausted, sweating, bleeding, the new arrivals were herded through the gate. There were now one thousand and ten of them; twenty-five of those who had set out from Vienna were now corpses along the Blood Road.[7]

They found themselves within an impenetrable cordon: the huge camp was surrounded by a barbed wire fence with twenty-two watchtowers at intervals, decked with floodlights and guns; the fence itself was three meters high and electrified, with a lethal 380 volts running through it. The outside of the fence was patrolled by sentries, and within was a sandy strip called the "neutral zone"; any prisoner stepping on it would be shot.[8]

Immediately inside the gate was a large parade ground—the *Appellplatz*, or roll-call square. Ahead and along one side were long, low barrack huts that marched in orderly, radiating ranks down the hill slope, with bigger two-story blocks beyond, and a grid of streets between the blocks. The newcomers were ordered into ranks in the roll-call square, and stood there at gunpoint, awkward and disheveled in their assortment of soiled and ruined business suits and work clothes, sweaters and shirts, raincoats, fedoras and office shoes, caps and hobnail boots, bearded, bald, slicked hair, tousled mops: a thousand men and boys with a thousand identities. While they stood, the bodies of the men who had died along the road were carried in and dumped among them.

A group of finely uniformed SS officers appeared. One, a middle-aged, pouchy-faced man with a slouching posture, stood out. This, they would learn later, was Camp Commandant Karl Otto Koch. "So," he said, "you Jew-pigs are here now. You cannot get out of this camp once you are in it. Remember that—you will not get out alive."

The men were entered one by one in the camp register and each assigned a prisoner number: Fritz Kleinmann: 7290; Gustav Kleinmann: 7291.[9] Orders came at them in a confusing barrage that Fritz and many of the Viennese found hard to understand, unaccustomed to the German dialects. They were made to strip naked and march to the bath block, where they showered in almost unbearably hot water (some were too weak to stand it and collapsed), followed by immersion in a vat of searing disinfectant.[10] They sat in a yard to have their heads sheared, and under yet another rain of blows from rifle-butts and cudgels, were made to run naked back to the roll-call square. There they were issued with ill-fitting camp uniforms: long drawers, socks, shoes, shirt, and the distinctive blue-striped pants and jacket. If desired, for twelve marks a prisoner could buy a sweater and gloves, but few had so much as a pfennig, and would never know warmth again.[11] All their own clothes and belongings—including the little package of warm clothing Gustav had carried from home—were taken away.

With their hair gone, in uniform, the new arrivals were no longer individuals but a homogeneous mass, the only distinguishing features a rare fat belly or a head standing higher than the rest. The violence of their arrival had impressed on them that they were the property of the SS, to do with as it saw fit; they had no identities beyond their numbers. Each man had been issued a strip of cloth with his prisoner number on it, which he was required to sew onto the breast of his uniform, along with a symbol: in this assembly all were Jews. They were given a Star of David made up of a yellow and a red triangle superimposed; the red denoted that, having been arrested on the pretext that they were Jewish-Polish enemy aliens, they were under *Schutzhaft*, so-called protective custody, a rubric under which political opponents were imprisoned as "protection" for the state.[12]

Looking at the new prisoners, Deputy Commandant Hans Hüttig, a dedicated sadist with a flat face like the back of a shovel, shook his head and said, "It's unbelievable that such people have been allowed to walk around free until now."[13]

These annulled humans were marched to the "little camp," an enclosure on the western edge of the muster square surrounded by a double cordon of barbed wire fences: the quarantine area. Inside, rather than barrack huts, were four huge tents lined with wooden bunks four tiers high.[14] There wasn't nearly enough room for all. In recent weeks, over eight thousand new prisoners had arrived at Buchenwald, more than twenty times the usual rate of intake, and the largest since the Kristallnacht pogrom nearly a year earlier.[15] The tents were full to bursting. Gustav and Fritz found themselves sharing a bunk space only two meters wide with three other men. There were no mattresses, just bare wooden planks, but they had a blanket each, so they were at least warm. Squeezed in like sardines and their bellies empty, they were so dead tired they fell asleep right away.

The next day, the new prisoners were registered with the political department—the camp Gestapo. They were photographed, fingerprinted, and briefly interrogated, a process that took all morning. In the afternoon they received their first warm food: a half-liter of soupy stew containing unpeeled potatoes and turnips, with a little fat and meat floating in it. The evening meal consisted of a quarter-loaf of bread and a little 50-gram* piece of sausage. This proved to be the standard camp ration. The bread was provided in whole loaves, and as there were no knives, sharing it out was a haphazard business which usually led to disputes and jealous quarrels.

For eight days they were left in quarantine, then on October 10 they were put to work. Most were set to hard labor in the nearby stone quarry, but Gustav and Fritz were put to work on maintaining the canteen drains. All day long the workers were hazed and slave-driven. Gustav wrote in his diary: "I have

---

* 1¾ ounce

seen how prisoners get beaten by the SS, so I look out for my boy. It's done by eye-contact; I understand the situation and I know how to conduct myself. Fritzl gets it too."

So ended his first entry. He looked back over what he had written so far, just two and a half pages to bring them this far, through this much distress and danger. Eight days gone. How many more to come?[16]

אבא

As Gustav had observed, to stay safe it was vital to remain unnoticed, invisible. But within two months of arriving in Buchenwald, both Gustav and Fritz had drawn attention to themselves—Gustav unwillingly, Fritz deliberately.[17]

On their second day at work they were both switched to the quarry detail. Each morning, an hour and a half before dawn, shrill whistles yanked them from the exquisite forgetfulness of sleep in their comfortless bunk. Then came the *kapos* and the block senior, yelling at them to hurry. The kapos and block seniors were a shock to new arrivals; they were fellow prisoners—mostly "green men," criminals who wore the green triangle on their striped uniforms—appointed by the SS to act as straw bosses and barrack overseers. The kapos drove the workforce, did the dirty work of slave-driving, and enabled the SS guards to keep a distance from the mass of prisoners. A kapo was expected to be harsh, if not downright sadistic, and was motivated by the knowledge that if the SS removed his status, he would be placed back among the prisoners, who would exact their revenge.[18]

As the whistles shrilled, Fritz and Gustav put on their shoes and scrambled down, sinking to their ankles in cold mud on the bare floor. Outside, the camp was ablaze with electric light along the fence lines, atop the guard towers, and in the walkways and open areas. They were herded to the square for roll call, and dished out a cup of acorn coffee each. It was sweet but caffeine-free, with no power to stimulate, and always cold by the time they got it. Doling it out was a long process, and they all had to stand there in silence, motionless and shivering in their thin clothes for two hours. When it was time to go to work, dawn was lightening the sky.

The mass of men in the quarry detail were marched out through the main gate, turning right to follow the road leading between the main camp and the

SS barrack complex, a set of uniform two-story brick buildings, some still under construction, arranged in a great arc like the blades of a fan. The Nazis adored their grand designs, even in their concentration camps—*especially* in their concentration camps—creating an illusive appearance of elegance, order, and meaning to screen the chaotic nightmare played out within.

A little way down the hill, the prisoners passed through the inner sentry line. Out here there were no fences, and the work areas were surrounded by a well-manned cordon of SS sentries about a dozen meters apart. Every second sentry was armed with a rifle or sub-machine gun, and every other with a cudgel. Once inside it, any prisoner who crossed the sentry line was shot without hesitation or challenge. For the desperate, those who had been driven to the limit of what they could endure, running into the sentry line was a common means of suicide. For certain SS guards, forcing prisoners to run over the line to their deaths was one of their favorite means of entertainment. An "escape register" was maintained, recording the names of the SS marksmen and awarding credit for kills, which added up to rewards of vacation time.

The quarry was large—a pale, raw limestone scar on the green wooded hillside. From it, if one raised one's head, and the mist and rain permitted, a broad, rolling countryside stretched to the hazy western horizon. But one didn't raise one's head, not for more than a moment. The work was hard, grueling, dangerous; the men in stripes dug stone, broke stone, carried stone, and were beaten if they slacked, beaten if they carried too little.

There was a narrow railroad in and out, on which huge steel dump wagons ran, each the size of a farm cart, carrying the stone from the quarry to the construction sites around Buchenwald. Gustav and Fritz were assigned as wagon haulers—which meant they and fourteen other men had to heave and push a laden wagon weighing around four and a half tonnes up the hill, a distance of half a kilometer, intermittently lashed and yelled at by kapos.[19] The rails were laid on beds of crushed stone, which slipped and grated under the men's flimsy shoes or painful wooden clogs. Speed was imperative, and as soon as the wagon was emptied, it had to get back to the quarry with all haste, running down the return track propelled by its own weight, with the sixteen men holding on to prevent it speeding out of control. Falls were frequent, with fractured limbs and broken heads. Often a wagon would jump the rails, sometimes directly in the path of the next wagon, leaving a trail of men crushed, broken, and dismembered. The badly injured would be carried off to the infirmary if they weren't Jews, or to the death block—a holding barrack for the terminally sick—if they were.[20] Men with crippling injuries would be given a lethal injection by an SS doctor.[21] With no hospital treatment, even slight wounds could be life-threatening in the insanitary conditions in which the prisoners lived and worked. For a man with poor eyesight, losing his spectacles could effectively be a death sentence.

Gustav and Fritz toiled on, managing to avoid both punishment and injury. "We are proving ourselves," Gustav wrote in his diary.

So it went on for two weeks. Then, on October 25, dysentery and fever broke out in the little quarantine camp. With over three and a half thousand weakened men crammed into its bunks (about one third of them Jews, the rest Poles), and sanitation consisting of nothing but a latrine pit, it was a fertile ground for disease. Each day the population was eroded by twenty-five to fifty deaths. And the grinding life of the camp went on. Each day, impoverished rations; each day, standing for hours at roll call in the cold and rain; each day, beatings and injuries. The SS waged a special vendetta against a chief rabbi called Merkl, who was singled out every day and beaten bloody until eventually he was forced to run through the sentry line. And all the while the dysentery went on unchecked and the death toll rose.

Some Poles, driven by hunger, cut their way out of the little camp and broke into the main camp kitchens. They managed to bring back twelve kilos of syrup, a delight that brightened the prisoners' diets a little. It was a short-lived pleasure. The theft was discovered, and the whole of the little camp was punished with two days' withdrawal of rations. A few days later, on November 5, a crate of jellied meat was stolen from the store. Again the prisoners were starved for two days, this time with an additional punishment: they were forced to stand at attention on the roll-call square from morning until evening. While the punishment parade was still going on, there was a break-in at the piggery in the farm site at the north end of the camp, and a pig was taken. Camp Commandant Koch—who lived in a pleasant house in the Buchenwald complex with his wife and went for Sunday walks in Buchenwald's own zoo just outside the main camp—personally ordered starvation for everyone until the thieves were caught. Every prisoner's clothing was inspected for signs of blood or sawdust from the pigpen; there were interrogations for three days. It was finally discovered that the culprits were some SS men.[22]

Weakened by starvation, subjected to soul-breaking labor, with dysentery running unchecked in the camp, the prisoners died in dozens each day. The living walked silent and hunched like specters of the already dead.

Then, suddenly, things got even worse.

בן

On Wednesday, November 8, 1939, Adolf Hitler flew to Munich. He was there to lead the Nazi Party's annual commemoration of the failed 1923 Beer Hall Putsch, when he and his followers made their first attempt to seize power in Bavaria. The following day the Nazi leaders who were veterans of the putsch were scheduled to reenact their legendary march through the city.[23] Tonight, according to tradition, Hitler would open the occasion with an address before an audience in the grandiose Bürgerbräukeller beer hall.

With the war only just begun and his planned invasion of France facing postponement due to bad weather, the Führer's participation in the commemorations were hurried and brief; tonight he would be rushing back to Berlin, and therefore he gave his beer hall address an hour earlier than scheduled. Afterward, at two minutes past nine, he left the Bürgerbräukeller for his train. Eighteen minutes later—when he should have been in the midst of his speech— a bomb concealed in a pillar next to Hitler's podium exploded with colossal force, bringing down a gallery above, blowing out doors and windows, obliterating the handful of people standing nearby, and injuring dozens of others.[24] The perpetrator was apprehended the same evening. Georg Elser, a German communist paramilitary, had spent a year planning the operation and weeks carefully building and concealing the time bomb, hiding in the beer hall after hours and working through the night. His plan had been perfect—only thwarted by a last-minute change of plan.

Germany was appalled, and the reaction predictably furious. Although Elser was a Protestant with no Jewish connections, in Nazi eyes the Jews were responsible for every ill deed.[25] In the concentration camps next day—which happened to be the anniversary of Kristallnacht—they took brutal revenge. In Sachsenhausen the SS subjected the inmates to intimidation and torture, while at Ravensbrück the Jewish women were locked in their barracks for nearly a month.[26] But these cruelties paled beside what occurred that day at Buchenwald.

Early in the morning, all the Jewish prisoners, including Gustav and Fritz, were taken from the quarry and marched back to the confines of the main camp, along with all the Jews from the construction, farm, and other work details. They were ordered back to their barrack blocks, and when all were confirmed present and correct, SS-Sergeant Johann Blank went to work. Blank was a born sadist, addicted to all forms of cruelty. A former forestry apprentice and poacher from Bavaria, he was a particularly enthusiastic participant in the game of forcing prisoners to cross the sentry line and be shot, carrying out many of the murders personally.[27] Blank, accompanied by other SS men, still hungover from the previous night's Putsch celebrations, went from block to block, picking out twenty-one Jews (including a seventeen-year-old boy who had the bad luck to be outdoors on an errand). They were marched to the main gate, where they had to stand while the SS men performed a little parade to coincide with the commemorative march taking place in Munich. When it was over, the gate was opened, and the selected Jews were herded out and down the hill toward the quarry.

Inside their tent, Gustav and Fritz knew nothing of what was going on, other than the sounds that carried their way. For a long while, there was silence broken only by the shouts of the SS and the faint sounds of the remaining work details. Then, suddenly, there came a crackle of gunfire; then another and another, followed by sporadic shots. Then silence again.[28]

It didn't take long for the story of what had happened to circulate around the camp. The twenty-one had been marched to the quarry entrance, where they had all been shot. A few had managed to run, only to be hunted down and murdered among the trees.

The day wasn't over yet. SS-Sergeant Blank, accompanied by Sergeant Eduard Hinkelmann, who between them were the principal tyrants of the little camp, now turned their attention to their own domain. They carried out an inspection, finding fault with everything and working themselves into a fury. They ordered a ritual punishment. When the prisoners were mustered outside, the kapos went among them, counting, grabbing every twentieth man and shoving them forward. They came along Gustav and Fritz's line: *one, two, three . . .*

the counting finger danced along, pulsing the beats . . . *seventeen, eighteen, nineteen*: the finger went past Gustav . . . *twenty*: the finger jabbed at Fritz.

He was seized and pushed toward the other victims.[29]

A heavy wooden table was being dragged onto the roll-call square. Any prisoner who had been here more than a week or two recognized it as the *Bock*—the whipping bench, a table with a sloping top, straps, and ankle loops. The Bock had been introduced by Deputy Commandant Hüttig both as a means of punishment for the prisoners and of entertainment for his men.[30] Every prisoner had witnessed its use and was terrified by the sight of it. Blank and Hinkelmann very much enjoyed putting the Bock to work.

Fritz was gripped by the arms and, with his insides dissolving, was rushed to the Bock. His jacket and shirt were removed and his pants pulled down. Hands shoved him facedown on the sloping top, forced his ankles through the loops, and tightened the leather strap over his back.

Gustav watched in helpless horror as Blank and Hinkelmann prepared; they relished the moment, stroking their bullwhips—ferocious weapons of leather with a steel core. Camp rules allowed for a minimum of five lashes, and a maximum of twenty-five. Today the rage of the SS could be sated by nothing less than the maximum.

The first lash landed like a razor cut across Fritz's buttocks.

"Count!" they yelled at him. Fritz had seen this ritual before; he knew what was expected. "One," he said. The bullwhip cut across his flesh again. "Two," he gasped.

The SS men were methodical; the lashes were paced to prolong the punishment and heighten the pain and terror of each blow. Fritz knew that he must concentrate, that if he lost count the lashes would start over again. Three . . . four . . . an eternity, an inferno of pain . . . ten . . . eleven . . . fighting to concentrate, to count correctly, not to give in to despair or unconsciousness . . . twenty-four . . . twenty-five.

At last the strap was loosed and he was forced to his feet. Before his father's eyes he was helped away, bleeding, on fire, his mind stunned, as the next unfortunate was dragged to the Bock.

The obscene ritual dragged on for hours; dozens of men, hundreds of blows. Many succumbed to the distress of the moment, miscounted their strokes and had to begin again. None walked away unbroken.

אבא

Gustav and Fritz stood side by side at roll call—Fritz with some difficulty. Only two days had passed since the dreadful day of the shootings and the Bock, and Fritz had hardly begun to heal. But to succumb to pain or sickness here was to give in to death. Besides, he was worried about his papa. The starvation punishment had been renewed, and there had been no food for days; dysentery and fever still plagued the camp, and now Gustav, weakened by labor and hunger, had caught the disease. He was pale, feverish, and afflicted by diarrhea. Fritz watched him anxiously as they stood there and the minutes ticked slowly by. He couldn't possibly work; he could scarcely stand through roll call. Gustav swayed, shivering, his senses withdrawing. Sounds grew faint and muffled, a black haze closed in around his vision, his extremities growing suddenly numb, and he felt himself falling, falling, into a black pit. He was unconscious before he hit the ground.

When Gustav woke, he was on his back somewhere indoors. Not the tent. Above him floated the faces of Fritz and another man. They had carried him here—Fritz struggling with his still-unhealed injuries. He appeared to be in one of the barrack buildings in the main camp. It couldn't be the infirmary, which was closed to Jews. In his hazy, febrile state, Gustav was dimly aware that this must be the block set aside for Jews and hopeless cases, the one from which people rarely emerged alive. The air was thick, stifling, filled with a susurrus of groans and an atmosphere of hopeless, helpless death. But it was the closest thing there was to medical care for Jews.

There were two doctors. One, a German named Haas, was callous and stole from the sick, leaving them to starve. The other was a prisoner, Dr. Paul Heller, a young Jewish physician from Prague, who dedicated himself to doing the best he could for his patients with the meager resources the SS provided.[31] Gustav lay helpless, running a temperature of 38.8°C,* sometimes lucid, sometimes in a fever dream, for days.

Meanwhile, in the little camp the prisoners were starving. The announcement on the loudspeakers had been heard so many times it was like a mantra: "Food deprivation will be imposed as a disciplinary measure." In November alone the little camp had endured eleven days of total starvation. Some of the

---

* 102°F

younger prisoners suggested begging the SS for food. Fritz, who had scarcely begun recovering from his whipping, was among them. But the older, wiser prisoners, many of them veterans of the First World War, warned them against it. Taking action meant exposure, and exposure usually meant punishment or death.

Fritz talked it over with a Viennese friend, Jakob Ihr—nicknamed "Itschkerl"—a boy from the Prater. Itschkerl was determined to do something: "I don't care if we have to die—I'm going to speak to Dr. Blies when he comes."

SS-Lieutenant Dr. Ludwig Blies was the camp doctor and made regular inspection visits to the little camp. He was hardly a kind man, but he was more humane—or at least less brutally callous—than some other SS doctors. He had on rare occasions intervened to halt excessive punishments.[32]

Fritz agreed but didn't trust Itschkerl to do it alone. "All right," he said. "But I'm coming with you. And I'll do the talking; you just back me up."

When Dr. Blies entered the little camp for his next inspection, Fritz and Itschkerl caught his attention. Blies was, at first sight, an approachable figure: in his late forties, some found him disarmingly comical in appearance.[33] Fritz, being careful not to seem demanding, made his voice quaver with weepy desperation. "We have no strength to work," he pleaded. "Please give us something to eat."[34]

Blies stared at them. Fritz had hardly needed to adapt his voice; his thinness and gait said it all. It was sensible to appeal to the SS view of prisoners as a labor resource—but it was also extremely dangerous to draw attention to one's current uselessness in that regard. This apparently went through Blies's mind, competing with his humane streak, as he surveyed the two boys. Abruptly he said, "Come with me."

Fritz and Itschkerl followed the doctor across the roll-call square to the camp kitchens. Commanding them to wait, Blies went into the food store and came out a few minutes later with a large 1½-kilo loaf of ration-issue rye bread and a two-liter bowl of soup. "Now," he said, handing over this astonishing bounty, "back to your camp. Go!"

They shared the food—equivalent to half a dozen men's rations—with their closest bunkmates. The following day the whole camp was put back on full rations, apparently on Blies's orders. The boys' appeal to the doctor was the talk of the camp, and from that day forward Itschkerl became one of Fritz's best friends.

While this was going on, Gustav still lay sick in the death block. So far, the dysentery had failed to kill him. Fritz visited when he could, but although the worst was past, it was obvious to Gustav that he would never recover in this unhealthy environment. After two weeks in the pestilential block, Gustav begged to be discharged, but Dr. Heller refused to let him go. Gustav was determined; disobeying the doctor's orders, he asked Fritz to help him get out. Father and son slipped away and made their way back to the little camp, Fritz guiding his papa's faltering steps. The moment he was out in the fresh air Gustav began to feel better, and even in the tent the atmosphere felt fresher than in the death block.

The following day he was given light work as a latrine cleaner and furnace stoker;[35] he ate well, and regained his health a little. Fritz too was recovering from his injuries. But there was always a limit to one's health in Buchenwald. They were both thin; Gustav, who had always been lean, had declined to 45 kilos* during his illness, although he was regaining some weight now. On the whole, he felt that things were looking up, since they could hardly get any worse. Fritz's new reputation for cleverness had made him popular not only with the regular prisoners but even with the camp seniors—the very highest of the prisoner functionaries, who had authority over the block seniors and ordinary kapos; they all thought highly of him.

But still the reality remained: the perks were menial and the consolations little more than a stay of death. "I work to forget where I find myself," Gustav wrote.

The only thing that held a man together was comradeship. Fritz would often wonder, now and in later years, how he survived all this: "It was not good luck; neither was it God's blessing." Rather, it was the kindness of others, especially the older prisoners, many of whom were long-term veterans of Gestapo dungeons and concentration camps; they knew nothing about Fritz, yet sometimes they would risk their lives to help him. He was just a boy, and short for his age. "All they saw was the Jewish star on my prison uniform, and that I was a child."[36] He and Itschkerl often got extra tidbits of food, sometimes medications when they needed them. Later, when systematic exterminations and transportations began, the older prisoners would help the boys evade the selections.

With winter beginning to bite, Fritz and Gustav were grateful to receive a parcel of fresh underwear from home. They were allowed to receive such

---

* 99 pounds

things but could send out no communications; the SS was extremely sensitive about what went on in the camps, even though the atrocities were known throughout the world by now.

Little news accompanied the parcel. Tini was still trying to arrange for the children to leave the Reich and getting nowhere. Of Edith there was no news at all. With Germany and Britain at war, the family was entirely cut off from their eldest daughter. Where she was and what she might be doing were a blank.

4 | The Stone Crusher

בת

THE WINTER NIGHT SKY over the north of England was deepest black, speckled with stars and banded by the mist of the Milky Way, with a bright slice of a first-quarter moon floating in it. The city, the whole nation, was in blackout, and the heavens had all illumination to themselves.

Edith Kleinmann looked up at the same stars that tracked the skies over Vienna, where her family, God willing, were all keeping safe. She had no news at all, only fears. If only this barrier didn't exist, if only she could know how her mother and father, sister and brothers, friends and relatives were. And she had news of her own that she was bursting to share. She had met a man; not just any man this time, but *the* man.

Her first few months in England had been uneventful enough. Her work placement, arranged through the Jewish Refugees Committee, was as a live-in maid with a Mrs. Rebecca Brostoff, a Jewish lady in her sixties who had a prominent wart on her nose and a home in the quiet suburbs on the outskirts of Leeds. Her husband, Morris, was a bristle merchant, and they were modestly well off. Both had been born in Russia in the days of the pogroms and had been refugees themselves in their youth. Their children had flown the nest, and Mrs. Brostoff took the opportunity to give something back to the world by helping this generation of Jewish refugees.[1]

The house, semidetached from its neighbors with yards front and back, wasn't a mansion, but it was opulent compared with the Kleinmanns' apartment in Vienna. Leeds was a sprawling industrial city, all soot-blackened brick and English Victorian architecture, long streets of small, begrimed factory-workers' houses, grand public buildings, and gray, smoky skies. Even the public parks seemed rustic and unsophisticated compared with the palatial gardens of Edith's home city. The countryside north of the city was wild, wind-blown moorland, the landscape of the Brontë novels. Street Lane, six kilometers out from the city center and blandly suburban, was neither country nor metropolis.

Not many would choose Leeds for its charms. But there were no Nazis here. No conflict, no danger, and although anti-Semitism existed (was there any nation on Earth where that toxin hadn't spread?) there was no Jew-baiting, no exclusion, no scrubbing games, no Dachau.

Britain was mired in a war that was going nowhere; after months of buildup—soldiers marching, politicians talking up a storm, the people prepped with air raid drills, gas masks, sandbags, and blackouts—there had been no bombs, no gas, no Nazi parachutists shooting it out with the Home Guard in the local high street. It was all rather a letdown; wound to a high state of anxious expectation, here they were, still living their normal lives but with a whole new panoply of restrictive regulations. They called it the Phony War, or the Bore War.

And there were the Jewish refugees. Many British people welcomed them, but some did not, and the government was caught between the two poles. The press spoke out for and against them, arguing for the contribution they made to the economy and pleading the plight they faced in their home country while on the other hand British workers worried about their jobs, and their fears were played upon by a right-wing press. There were claims about the criminal tendencies and shiftlessness of Jews and the threat they posed to British life. But still, there were no actual Nazis, no SA or SS, and no repression. With the outbreak of war, the government had begun screening and interning enemy aliens; Edith, as an Austrian, was examined and placed in Category C—refugees from Nazism, exempt from internment.[2] And that was that.

Mrs. Brostoff treated Edith—who wasn't the world's most natural domestic servant—kindly, and Edith was content on a good weekly wage of three pounds. For eight months she wrote brisk, brief letters home—and then it came to an end. Germany invaded Poland; Britain and France demanded withdrawal and set a deadline.

In a chilling echo of Chancellor Schuschnigg's ominous announcement of capitulation, Austrian refugees heard Prime Minister Neville Chamberlain's address on the radio, the stiff, leaden voice precisely and mechanically intoning, "I have to tell you now that no such undertaking has been received, and that consequently this country is at war with Germany . . . Now may God bless you all. May He defend the right. It is the evil things that we shall be fighting against—brute force, bad faith, injustice, oppression and persecution—and against them I am certain that the right will prevail." The nation was by no means so sure. But when autumn turned to winter and the Germans didn't invade England and no bombs fell, the British began to grow complacent.

For Edith Kleinmann, that first winter in England was marked not by war but by romance. She had known Richard Paltenhoffer in Vienna but only as an acquaintance. He was the same age as she and had lived with his mother in an apartment in Novaragasse, a long street between the Augarten and the Prater, and had moved in the same circles as Edith and her friends. In England they met again, and fell in love.

Richard had been through hell since Edith had last seen him. In June 1938, only three months after the Anschluss, by sheer bad luck he'd been picked up by the Vienna SS. The Nazi regime in Berlin had instituted what they called *Aktion Arbeitsscheu Reich*—Action Work-Shy Reich. It was intended to sweep the "asocial" element in German society off the streets and into the concentration camps, the "useless mouths" and "community aliens": the unemployed and work-shy, beggars, drunks, drug addicts, pimps, and petty crooks. Around nine and a half thousand people were caught up this way and despatched to Dachau, Sachsenhausen, and Buchenwald. The "asocial" category was loosely defined, and local police, especially in Vienna, swept up many Jews and Roma who had the bad luck to be in the wrong place at the wrong time.[3] On June 24, 1938, Richard Paltenhoffer, nineteen years old and ejected by the Nazis from his job as an apprentice bookbinder, was one of the unlucky victims of Action Work-Shy Reich.

Arrested by the security police—the Sipo—Richard was sent to Dachau, where he remained for three months; then he was transferred to Buchenwald.[4] At that time Buchenwald was an even worse place than when Fritz and Gustav Kleinmann arrived there a year later. Its facilities were even more rudimentary, with no proper water supply, and with the arrival of the thousands of Jews arrested in Vienna after Kristallnacht, conditions became truly diabolical. It was then that the ramshackle tents of the little camp were put up (although Richard, accommodated in one of the regular blocks, never experienced those). The food supply was not only meager but sporadic, and the shortage of water led to dehydration and disease, especially among the "November Jews," who were so numerous that work and uniforms couldn't be found for them and they had to live in their increasingly soiled civilian clothes.[5]

Richard, although spared the ordeal of the November Jews, endured the nightmare of a Buchenwald winter, with its regime of terror, violence, and grueling labor. On one of the regular punishment parades that usually followed evening roll call, a man standing in front of him was bayoneted by an SS guard. The blade passed right through the man, who fell back against Richard, and impaled Richard's leg. The wound gave him trouble for months afterward, but luckily he didn't succumb to infection.

In April 1939, Richard's life was saved by an extraordinary stroke of luck. The SS had been relieving pressure inside the camps by releasing Jews who had emigration papers. There was no chance of that for Richard, who didn't have the means. However, to mark Adolf Hitler's fiftieth birthday on April 20, Himmler agreed to a celebratory mass amnesty of nearly nine thousand concentration camp prisoners.[6] Among them was Richard Paltenhoffer, who gained his freedom on April 27.

He had more sense than to return to Vienna, where he would likely be picked up again before long. Instead he crossed the border into Switzerland. Through his involvement with the Österreichischer Pfadfinderbund—the Austrian Boy Scouts—he obtained the necessary travel permit to go to England. By the end of May he was in London and on his way to Leeds, where friends of his had already found refuge. Lodgings had been arranged for him by the JRC, as well as a job as an apprentice baker in a factory making kosher crackers. The same committee promised to arrange for his bayonet wound to be treated at a Jewish hospital. He was eager to get to Leeds and start raising the money from friends to pay for the treatment.[7]

Richard's lodgings proved to be a room in a house close to the city center, in a cobbled street of tall townhouses that had once been genteel but were now run-down, with cracked window panes and soot-blackened bricks.

There was a large and thriving Jewish community in the city, which had its own active branch of the JRC run by David Makovski, who ran a tailoring business. He was known for a sometimes irascible temperament and a belief that each person should know his or her place in society and stick to it. With a tiny budget of £250 a year, Makovski and his small staff of volunteers helped hundreds of Jews find homes and work in Leeds.[8]

It was through a social club for young Jews that Edith and Richard were reunited. Although they'd only been acquaintances before, they quickly became much more than that. Soon they were dating, and by Christmas 1939 they were deeply involved. In Edith's eyes, Richard Paltenhoffer was a reminder of home and the life she had lost—the lively society, and a career in fashion rather than in sweeping carpets. Richard was a genial, attractive figure. He had a beaming smile and liked to laugh, and he dressed sharp—nicely cut chalk-stripe suits and a fedora to match, always with a handkerchief tucked just so in the breast pocket. Among the regular Yorkshire working men in their serge, woollen scarves, and flat caps, Richard stood out like an exotic bloom in a potato field. A war, even a phony war, was a time of possibility for the young, and with two high spirits far from home it was almost inevitable that they would enjoy themselves to the fullest. They met at a dance and swept each other off their feet. Christmas came, and the New Year celebrations, and January was scarcely through when Edith discovered that she was expecting a baby.

Hectic romances and whirlwind marriages were a fixture of wartime life, and in February Edith and Richard started making arrangements for a wedding. It wasn't a simple business—they were refugees, and any change of status had to be registered with the government. At 9:30 sharp on Monday, February 19, they presented themselves at the office of Rabbi Arthur Super at the Leeds New Synagogue, and from there they all went to the police station to fill out the required forms. Then, with help from the United Hebrew Congregation in Leeds, David Makovski's Control Committee, and a Rabbi Fisher, late of the Stadttempel in Vienna, now based in Leeds, the prospective marriage was arranged with the Registrar General.[9]

With bureaucracy satisfied, on Sunday, March 17, 1940, Edith Kleinmann married Richard Paltenhoffer at the New Synagogue in Chapeltown Road, a remarkable modern building of green copper domes and brick arches in the heart of Leeds' own equivalent of Leopoldstadt.

Two months later, on May 10, Adolf Hitler launched his long-anticipated invasion of Belgium, the Netherlands, and France. The British Expeditionary Force and its French ally were driven back and divided by a German spearhead. In the last week of May and the first week of June, the remainder of the British force, with its back to the sea, was evacuated from the beach at Dunkirk by a fleet of hundreds of warships, merchant vessels, fishing smacks, and private boats.

The Phony War was over. The Germans were on their way, and seemingly unstoppable. The English Channel was an obstacle, but one way or another, Hitler was coming.

אבא

"*Left*–two–three! *Left*–two–three!"

The rasping voice of the kapo barked out the time as the team pulled the quarry wagon up the rails. It was relentless: "*Left*–two–three! *Left*–two–three!" Their shoes slithered on the ice and loose stones, their hands and shoulders raw on the ropes or numbed on the bare metal of the wagon. Winter had come savagely to the Ettersberg, but the kapos could always be relied on to outdo it. "Pull her, dogs! *Left*–two–three! Onward, pigs! Isn't this fun?" A man who flagged was kicked and beaten. The wheels squealed and scraped, the men's feet thumped and ground on the stones, their hot breath clouded in the bitter air. "At the double! Faster or you'll be in the shit!"[10] A dozen backbreaking wagonloads to be drawn up this slope to the construction sites every day, an hour's round trip. "Forward, pigs! *Left*–two–three!"

"The men-beasts hang in the reins," Gustav wrote in his diary, turning his daily hell into a series of stark poetic images. "Panting, groaning, sweating . . . Slaves, cursed to labor, like in the days of the Pharaohs."

There had been a brief respite in the new year; in the middle of January, Dr. Blies, concerned about the extreme death rate from disease in the little camp, and with the SS worrying that it might spread to them, ordered that the survivors be moved to blocks in the main camp.[11] They were showered and deloused, then put into quarantine in block 8, a wooden barrack close to the roll-call square. So began a remarkable and most welcome eight days of rest and recuperation. The barrack seemed almost luxurious after the tents, with waxed wooden floors, solid walls, toilets, a washroom with cold running water, and tables to eat off. Everything was kept immaculately clean; the prisoners even had to remove their shoes in an anteroom before entering the barrack. Severe punishments were inflicted for dirt and disorder. During that one blessed week they got regular food, and every day was relaxed. Gustav had regained his strength, while Fritz was put to light work doing odd jobs. "He's doing well," Gustav had recorded in his diary.

Of course it couldn't last. On January 24 the quarantine period ended. Gustav was transferred to a block near the camp stores and kitchens while Fritz was placed in block 3, the "youth block," with the other young boys.[12]

The newer inmates got to know the main camp better—the ordered ranks of barrack blocks radiating down the hill with streets between them, and the centerpiece: the Goethe Oak. This venerated tree stood next to block 29, near the kitchens and bath block, and was reputed to have been a landmark in Goethe's walks from Weimar up the Ettersberg. So potent were its cultural associations that the SS had been obliged to preserve it and build the camp around it.[13] They put it to use for punishments. One of their favorite techniques, used throughout the concentration camp system, was to tie a man's hands behind his back and hang him by his wrists from a beam. The Goethe Oak made a spectacular venue for this abominable ritual. The hanged men would be left for hours—enough to cripple them for days or weeks—and often beaten bloody while they hung. Two of Gustav's workmates were among those suspended from the Goethe Oak for not working hard enough.

Fritz and his father, having absorbed the whispers about the camps that had spread in Vienna, were surprised on emerging from quarantine to learn that Jews made up only a fraction of Buchenwald's prisoner population; Fritz estimated a tenth, although it was actually closer to a fifth.[14] There were criminals, Roma, Poles, Catholic and Lutheran priests, and homosexuals, but political prisoners—mostly communists and socialists—made up the largest group. Many had been transferred here from other camps, having been prisoners for years, in some cases since the beginning of the Nazi regime in 1933. However, it was for the Jews and the Roma that the SS reserved its harshest treatment.

"*Left*–two–three! *Left*–two–three!" A dozen loads a day, up the hill, a dozen dangerous high-speed rolls back to the quarry. Fingers burning with cold on the metal, scorched by ropes, minds numbed, shoes and wooden clogs skittering on the ice and stones, abuse and battery from the kapos.

After a few months, Gustav and Fritz were taken off wagon duty and put to work within the quarry, carrying stones. Although it appeared initially to be less dangerous work, it was, if possible, even worse. Carriers had to pick up stones and boulders from where they were hewn out of the rock face and carry them in their bare hands to the waiting wagons. Palms and fingers were chafed and quickly blistered and bled. The shift lasted ten hours, with a short break at midday. That was just the baseline of laboring in the quarry—on top came the abuse for which the place was infamous.

"Every day another death," Gustav wrote. "One cannot believe what a man can endure." He could find no ordinary words to describe the living hell of the quarry. Turning to the back pages of his notebook, he began composing a poem, titled "Quarry Kaleidoscope," translating the chaotic nightmare into precise, measured, orderly stanzas.

> Click-clack, hammer blow,
> Click-clack, day of woe.
> Slave souls, wretched bones,
> At the double, break the stones.[15]

In these lines he managed to find a midpoint between the experiences he lived each day and how it was perceived through the eyes of the kapos and the SS.

> Click-clack, hammer blow,
> Click-clack, day of woe.
> Hear how all these wretches moan,
> Whimpering while they tap on stone.[16]

The slave-driving, each endless day, and the murderous abuses, all transmuted into poetic imagery. "Shovel! Load it up! Think you can take a breather? You think you're some kind of celebrity?" Hands slipping, grazing on the boulders, staining the pale limestone with rust-red blood; struggling, laden, to the wagons. "On, you shirkers—wagon number two! If you don't have it full soon, I'll beat you to a pulp!" The stones clattering and banging into the hollow iron belly of the wagon. "Finished? You think you're free now? D'you see me laughing? Wagon three, at the double! Faster, or you'll be in the shit. On, pigs!" Driven along with kicks and curses; the filled wagon wheeling slowly away up the steep rails: "Left–two–three! Left–two–three!"

The kapos and guards entertained themselves with the prisoners. One of Gustav's fellow carriers was made to take a huge rock and run with it in circles, uphill and down. "But be funny, understand?" the kapo ordered him. "Or I'll beat you crooked." The victim tried to run in a frolicsome manner, and the kapo laughed and applauded. Around and around he ran, chest heaving, straining for breath, bruised and bloodied. At last, overcome by sheer fatigue, the droll performance faltered; yet he kept moving, struggling around the circle twice more. But the kapo was bored now; he pushed his victim to the ground and delivered a savage, fatal kick to the head.

A favorite game was to snatch the cap off a passing prisoner and hurl it away—up a tree, in a puddle, always just beyond the sentry line. "Hey, your cap! Go get it, there by sentry four. Go on, mate, go get her!" This would often be a new prisoner, who didn't know the game. "And the dumbass runs," Gustav wrote. Past the sentries—*bang!*—and he was dead. Another entry in the guards' escape register, another credit toward an SS man's bonus vacation time: three days for each escapee shot. An SS sentry named Zepp was in cahoots with several kapos, including Johann Herzog, a green-triangle prisoner whom Gustav described as "a murderer of the worst sort." A former Foreign Legionnaire, Herzog had been arrested on his return to Germany; he was a killer and a brutal sexual sadist.[17] Zepp would reward Herzog and his fellows with tobacco each time they sent a man into the line of his rifle.

Some men despaired and ran of their own volition across the line to death. But most of the prisoners would not give up, couldn't be tricked. And some seemed unbeatable, no matter what abuses the guards and kapos inflicted on them. A blow with a rifle butt:

> Smack!—down on all fours he lies,
> But still the dog just will not die.[18]

In the middle of the quarry, dominating everything, stood a machine. A massive roaring engine drove a series of wheels and belts connected to a great hopper, into which stones were shoveled. Inside, heavy steel plates worked up and down and side to side, a colossal iron jaw chewing the stones, crushing them down to gravel. On the machine's footplate, a kapo worked the throttle and gears. When the quarry laborers were not filling the wagons, they were feeding this monstrous machine.

For Gustav, the stone crusher seemed emblematic not just of the quarry but of the camp and the entire system in which Buchenwald was just a component—the great engine in which he and his fellows were both the fuel driving it and the grist that it ground.

> It rattles, the crusher, day out and day in,
> It rattles and rattles and breaks up the stone,
> Chews it to gravel and hour by hour
> Eats shovel by shovel in its guzzling maw.
> And those who feed it with toil and with care,
> They know it just eats, but will never be through.
> It first eats the stone and then eats them too.[19]

Some men tried to resist being consumed. One prisoner on the crusher-filling detail, a comrade of the man who had been made to run in circles, kept his head down and shoveled the stones, anxious to avoid the attention of the kapos. He was a tall, powerfully built man, and he shoveled well. The kapo on the footplate of the stone crusher saw the opportunity for a game; he edged the throttle up until the machine was running at double speed, rattling and banging diabolically. The prisoner shoveled faster. Man and machine labored: the man panting, muscles straining; the crusher grinding and clattering fit to explode. Slaves working nearby left off their labors to watch, and the kapos, also enthralled, let them. On and on the contest went, shovel by shovel, clattering plates, roaring gears, the man dripping with sweat, the crusher thundering and defecating a cascade of gravel. The man seemed to have tapped within himself a threefold seam of strength and will. But the crusher's strength and stamina were limitless, and little by little the man weakened and slowed. Summoning his will, he rallied for one more titanic effort, stretching his muscles to shovel as if for his life; the machine would win, it always won, but still he tried.

Suddenly there was a bang and a long, grinding groan from inside the machine. The stone crusher shuddered, coughed, and stood still. The kapo on the footplate, dismayed, delved into the machine's innards and found that a stone had got into the gears.

There was a silence pregnant with dread. The prisoner, having heroically crippled the stone crusher, was liable to be murdered. The senior kapo, stunned for a moment, burst out laughing. "Come here, tall guy!" he called. "What are you, a farmhand? A miner, I'll bet?"

"No," said the prisoner. "I'm a journalist."

The kapo laughed. "A newspaperman? Too bad. I've got no use for one of those. Wait, though, I do need someone who can write. Go and wait in the hut there. I have other work for you."

Man against machine; on this occasion, man had won a small victory. The machine, it seemed, could be beaten by a person with the necessary strength and will. Whether this was also true of the greater machine remained to be discovered.

The mechanic cleared the stone from the gears and restarted the engine. Rattling, clattering, the stone crusher went back to work, consuming the rocks fed into its insatiable gullet by the laboring prisoners, eating their strength, their sweat and blood, grinding them down as it ground down the stone.

5 | The Road to Life

אמא

ON MAY 4, 1940, a curfew was introduced for Jews in Vienna, lasting from 9:00 PM to 5:00 AM.[1] One might think, after 1938, that there were no ways left in which the Nazis could further blight the lives of Jews, but one would be wrong. There was always another stick with which to beat them.

In October the previous year, two transports of Jews had left Vienna bound for Nisko in German-occupied Poland; they were to be resettled there in some kind of agricultural community.[2] The program—organized with the cooperation of Josef Löwenherz, head of the IKG—sputtered out, but it served as a practice run for mass deportations and added to the sense of insecurity among the Jews remaining in Vienna. When the survivors returned home in April, they brought back a story of abuse and murder.[3]

For Tini Kleinmann, the mission to get her children out of Austria became more urgent. Her chief priority was to have Fritz released from the camp while he was still a minor and eligible for higher priority emigration. In the spring, Tini received her first letter from him and Gustav. Until now there had been no communication, but suddenly they were allowed. The letters weren't much: the camp provided a form in which the prisoner had to fill in his name, prisoner number, and block number. Most of the space was taken up by a list of restrictions (whether money and packages could be received, whether that prisoner could write or receive letters, a warning that inquiries to the commandant's office would be futile, and so on). There was a tiny space in which the prisoner could write a short message, subject to SS approval. Tini gleaned little other than that her husband and son had been separated, as they gave different block numbers. She replied with news of home and scraped together money to send them, earned from occasional illegal work. She wrote that she missed them, and pretended that all was well.[4]

Meanwhile, she lodged applications for emigration with the IKG and the United States consulate for Fritz, Herta, and Kurt. Each application needed two affidavits from friends or relatives living in America pledging to provide shelter and support to the applicant. The affidavits were no problem, as Tini had several connections. There was a cousin, Bettina Prifer, who had emigrated to New York in January with her two teenage children.[5] Bettina's husband, Ignatz, was from Lemberg.* Like Gustav Kleinmann he had been categorized as a Polish Jew and had been deported on the Nisko transport in October.[6] Another of Tini's American cousins was Bettina's brother, Alfred Bienenwald, an itinerant merchant seaman who had made his home in America before the First World War and now lived in Atlantic Highlands, New Jersey.[7] Finally, Tini had an old and dear friend, Alma Maurer, who had emigrated many years ago and lived in Massachusetts.[8] Support and connections were plentiful—it was the bureaucracy of the Nazi regime and United States consulate that presented a problem.

America's resistance to taking in refugees had not abated in the past two years. If anything, it had grown stronger. President Roosevelt—who wanted to increase the numbers—could do nothing against Congress and the press. The United States had a theoretical quota of sixty thousand refugees per year, but chose not to use it. Instead, Washington employed every bureaucratic trick it could dream up to obstruct and delay applications. In June 1940, an internal State Department memo advised on policy for its consuls in Europe: "We can delay and effectively stop for a temporary period of indefinite length the number of immigrants into the United States. We could do this by simply advising our consuls to put every obstacle in the way and to require additional evidence and to resort to various administrative devices which would postpone the granting of the visas."[9]

Tini Kleinmann trekked from office to office, stood in line, wrote letter after letter, filled out forms, suffered the abuse of Gestapo officials, lodged inquiries, and waited, and waited, and waited, and feared every new message in case it was a summons for deportation, her every turn blocked by the State Department's obstacles and devices—obstacles specifically designed to pander

---

* Lemberg, Austro-Hungarian Empire, later became Lwów, Poland, now Lviv, Ukraine

to congressmen and newspaper editors, businessmen, workers, small town wives, and storekeepers, in Wisconsin and Pennsylvania, Chicago and New York, Florida, California, and Washington, who mistrusted Jews and objected stridently to a suffocating new wave of immigrants.

בן

For ten-year-old Kurt, this world was a bewildering place; as a child, it affected him erratically and left sporadic, vivid impressions on his memory.

It was a perpetual struggle for his mother to keep him and Herta warm and fed on the little money she could scrape together. In the summer, they were allowed to go to a farm owned by the IKG to pick peas. They got lunch there, which helped. There were still a few wealthy Jewish families in Vienna who managed to eke out their remaining fortunes and charitably helped support those who were destitute. One such family invited Kurt to dinner. His mother coached him strictly—"Sit up straight, behave yourself, do as you're told."

She fretted all the time about Kurt's behavior—he was a good boy, but he had a lot of energy and like most boys his age he could be volatile. In the precarious situation they were in, the countless little instances of naughtiness bred a fear in Tini's mind that he would do something to jeopardize himself, and she never let up drumming into him how vital it was that he behave himself. Kurt went to dinner and enjoyed a magnificent meal. Except for the Brussels sprouts. He'd never had them before and took against them right away, but after his mother's fearsome coaching he felt obliged to eat them. He threw up right afterward.

Kurt coped with being a child in the new Vienna as best he could. He existed in a kind of limbo. Many of the boys and girls who had been his friends were now inexplicably his enemies. He was separated from them, and his social world shrunk down to his relatives. His mother had a large extended family. There was an uncle called Sigmund, of whom the family saw relatively little. Tini's eldest sister, Charlotte Popper, was married to an upholsterer who had helped Gustav get established in the trade. They had a son who had emigrated to Chile, and the family was hoping to join him there. Another of Kurt's aunts, Bertha, lived nearby in Haidgasse. She had married young, several years before the First World War, and her husband, Richard Teperberg, had died in it; he went missing in action in May 1915, and two months later was declared dead. Bertha, left alone with her children, had never remarried.[10] Jeanette Rottenstein, two years older than Tini, had never married at all.[11] Jenni was a seamstress, and until 1935 she'd shared an apartment with their elderly mother, Eva, in the old Jewish quarter, not far from the Stadttempel. After Eva's death, Jenni had moved to Leopoldstadt. She lived alone with her cat and told the children it spoke to her—Jenni would ask it a question, and it would say *mm-jaa*. Kurt was charmed by this performance, although it was never clear whether Jenni was joking. She had a childlike sense of humor and loved animals. She and Kurt had a scheme wherein she would give him money to buy caps for his cap pistol, and Kurt would stalk the city pigeon-catcher; when he was about to net some birds, Kurt would fire his pistol, sending them up in a flapping gray cloud and leaving the catcher with an empty net. Jenni was Kurt's favorite aunt.

He had several others, a few of whom had married out to non-Jews and now lived in a state of uncertainty, their children classed as *Mischlinge*—mongrels—under Nazi law. One such child was his cousin Richard Wilczek, son of a gentile housepainter named Viktor who was married to Hilda, the daughter of Bertha Teperberg. The same age as Kurt, Richard Wilczek was not only a cousin but his best friend. He wasn't around anymore; his father had sent him and his mother to the Netherlands for safety after the Anschluss. What had become of Richard now that the Nazis were there too, Kurt didn't know. Another playmate lost.

They had been a happy band, the children from the streets around the Karmelitermarkt, before the Nazis came. On a Saturday morning Tini would make Kurt sandwiches, pack them in his little rucksack, and he would meet up with his best friends in the street. "So whose turn is it today?" They took turns to decide their destination, and off they would go, hiking across the city like a band of pioneers to some distant park or landmark or, if the weather was hot, to the Danube to swim. It was a perfect little society of friends, with no notion that some of them were marked with any stigma.

Kurt's awareness that grown-ups had decreed that some children were not like others had come on him violently. He'd been conscious of Nazi regulations since 1938, but they had made little impact on his eight-year-old mind. Then, one day in winter, a boy in the uniform of the Hitler Youth had called him a Jew and pushed him down. Kurt began to realize he was marked, that although he didn't know this boy, he'd hated Kurt enough to knock him down and shove his face hard into the snow.

When the hate came from an actual friend, that was when the injustice of it stuck in Kurt's brain. He'd been with a little group of friends in the market, playing as they had always done. The boy who was the dominant personality in the group suddenly decided that he needed to pick on somebody—as such boys will—and he singled out Kurt, calling him by the slurs he'd heard adults use against Jews. He began pulling off Kurt's coat buttons and taunting him. Kurt wasn't easily bullied; he hit the boy. Shocked, the boy pulled a metal bar off his little scooter and laid into Kurt with it, battering him on the head so badly that Kurt had to go to the hospital. He remembered his mother looking down at him anxiously as his cuts and bruises were treated. She understood the consequences that would follow. A complaint had been made to the police by the boy's parents; Kurt, a Jew, had dared to strike an Aryan. That was a matter for the law.

Probably because of his age, Kurt was let off with a caution. The incident left a scar on his mind. He understood now the malevolence and injustice of the Nazis.

There was another *Mischling* cousin Kurt's own age with whom he liked to play: Viktor Kapelari, who lived with his parents in Vienna-Döbling, the suburban Nineteenth District. Viktor's mother, Helene, was another of Tini's sisters; she had converted to Christianity when she married. They were wealthy; Viktor's grandfather owned a factory.

Viktor and his mother had always been fond of Kurt and often took him fishing. Mingled with the pleasant memories of these trips, Kurt would always retain a haunting image of Viktor's father in the sinister field-gray uniform of a Nazi.

After one of their fishing trips, Kurt came home with a bone-handled hunting knife belonging to Viktor, which he had pocketed. One day, one of the periodic orders came out from the Gestapo or the Sipo for all the Jews in the district to report to the local police station for some inspection or registration or selection. Putting on his coat, Kurt slipped the knife into his pocket. He knew now what the Nazis could do. They had taken his father and Fritz away, they had tormented his sisters, they had pushed him down in the snow, beaten him and made it into *his* crime. There was nothing they would not be allowed to do. Kurt was determined to defend his mother and Herta against them. Walking along, fingering the knife blade in his pocket, he could sense his mother's anxiety. He understood, in a vague way, that when Jews were ordered to report, something bad could happen. To soothe her fears, he showed her the knife.

She was horrified. "Get rid of it! Throw it away!" There was no convincing her of the necessity for it. Reluctantly, he tossed the knife away. They walked on, Kurt almost heartbroken. How in the world was he to defend the people he loved now? What would become of them?

בן

Another dawn, another roll call, another day of woe. The prisoners in their stripes stood in ranks in the cool summer air, motionless except to take the sustenance doled out, soundless except to answer to their numbers. Any breach of roll-call discipline meant punishment, as did any infraction of the immaculate neatness and cleanliness of one's locker, one's bunk, and one's barrack block: a veneer of precise order glued over a morass of bestial barbarism.

At last the slow ritual began drawing to a close and the prospect of the day's labors settled on each man. For Fritz, that meant working in the vegetable gardens attached to the farm complex—hard labor still but infinitely better and safer than the killing ground of the quarry.[12] For Gustav, it was back to the murderous task of stone-carrying. He'd had a reprieve during the second half of the winter when Gustav Herzog, one of the younger Jewish block seniors, employed him as an orderly in his block's bunk room. He'd discovered that Gustav was an upholsterer and had skill with mattresses, as well as a knack for keeping things in order. It was completely illegal, and would have led to punishment for both of them, but it helped the block pass inspections by the SS and kept Gustav in safe, easy work for two months. Eventually, though, the assignment had to end, and in mid-May Gustav had been sent back to the hell of the quarry.

Now that they were neither living in the same block nor working in the same place, he and Fritz saw little of each other, but they met when they could. Receiving a little money from home enabled them to buy occasional comforts from the prisoner canteen, which helped brighten their days.

As the morning parade was dismissed and the men were just beginning to move, the camp senior bellowed out:

"Prisoner 7290 to the main gate, at the double!"

In their separate sections of the assembly, both Gustav's and Fritz's hearts froze. Each man's number was as familiar to him as his name; officially within the camp it *was* his name, and the instant he heard those digits, Fritz felt as if he'd been physically seized. There were normally only two reasons for a prisoner to be summoned to the gate at roll call: punishment, or assignment to the stone quarry expressly for the purpose of being murdered.

"Prisoner 7290 to the main gate, at the double!" the camp senior repeated.

Fritz pushed through the mass of prisoners as they milled about, forming into their various work details, and ran to the main gate. Gustav watched him go with his heart in his mouth.

In an extremity of fear, Fritz reported to the adjutant, SS-Lieutenant Hermann Hackmann. Known as "Jonny," Hackmann was a clever, slender young man with a boyish grin that concealed a brutal, cynical nature; he carried a hefty bamboo cudgel and presided over roll call each morning.[13] He looked Fritz up and down, glanced at his number, and said, "Wait there. Face the wall."

Fritz stood by the gatehouse, staring at the whitewashed bricks while behind him the work details marched out through the gate. When everyone had gone, SS-Sergeant Schramm, Fritz's Blockführer,* came to fetch him. "Come with me."

Outside the gate, Schramm led him to the administrative complex that straddled the Caracho Way, as the home stretch of the Blood Road was known.† On the left was the camp Gestapo building. Fritz was led in and left standing for a long time before being called into a room. "Cap off. Take off your jacket." The habit of obeying strange orders without question was ingrained by now, and Fritz did as he was told. "Put these on." He was handed a civilian shirt, tie, and jacket.

They were rather large for him, especially in his half-starved condition, but he put them on, knotting the tie neatly into the rumpled collar. They sat him before a camera and took mugshots from all sides. Wary of the Gestapo's intentions, Fritz stared with deep, hostile suspicion into the lens. When it

---

* SS guard in command of a barrack block
† *Caracho*: an exclamation of surprise (Spanish)

was over he was ordered to put his prison uniform back on and run back to the camp. He obeyed, puzzled but also relieved to still be in one piece. His surprise increased when he was informed that he didn't have to work for the rest of that day.

Fritz sat in the empty barrack wondering what this could possibly be about. Clearly the jacket and tie had been intended to give the impression that he was living as an ordinary civilian, not as a prisoner, but beyond that he couldn't imagine.

That evening, when the work details marched back to their blocks, weary and gaunt, Gustav, who had been in a state of sick anxiety all day, slipped away and went across to Fritz's block. When he looked in through the door and saw him there, alive and well, the relief was immense. Fritz described what had happened, but neither they nor any of their friends could tell what it meant. Anything that involved being singled out for attention by the Gestapo surely couldn't be healthy.

A few days later, the same thing happened again; Fritz was summoned from roll call and taken to the Gestapo office. A copy of his photograph was put in front of him, and he was ordered to sign it: *Fritz Israel Kleinmann*, in his strong, confident hand. The image of himself was unsettling: his eyes glowering into the camera, and the mockery of the oversize jacket and the brutally cropped hair. If this was meant to give the impression that he lived a normal life, it was miserably unsuccessful; nobody living normally in the world could look like that.

At last he was told the purpose of it all, and it was wonderful. His mother had obtained the affidavit she needed from America and had applied for Fritz to be released so that he could emigrate.

בן

Hope glimmered in the back of Fritz's mind while he went on enduring the sick fever dream that passed for life in Buchenwald. It was troubling that the hope did not include his papa, who was being slowly worn down in the quarry.

Fritz's life and his father's were diverging; first through his being transferred to the youth block, and then through his move from the quarry detail to the gardens. Fritz was discovering a wider world through the older prisoners who helped and befriended him.

Foremost among them was Leopold Moses, who had helped Fritz survive in the early months and had remained a friend. Fritz had first encountered him in the quarry. During the early days, there had been almost no water supply, and none at all in the little camp. Workers in the quarry would drink from puddles, which had caused the epidemic of dysentery and typhus. Leopold Moses had offered Fritz some little black pills: "Swallow them," he said, "they'll prevent the shits." Fritz showed the pills to his father, who recognized them from his time in the trenches in World War One; they were veterinary charcoal, and they did help.

Leo Moses took Fritz under his wing when he was transferred to the youth block, and Fritz learned his story. Aged thirty-nine, he'd been in the concentration camps since the very beginning. A laborer from Dresden, Leo had been a member of the German Communist Party and had taken part in the so-called March Action, an attempted communist revolution in 1921. As a known communist, Leo Moses been arrested as soon as the Nazis came to power—long before his Jewishness became an arrestable crime. At first he'd been held in the notorious Columbia Haus, the Gestapo prison in Berlin, and then he spent years in Oranienburg and Lichtenburg concentration camps. When the latter became a women's camp in 1937, Leo had been transferred to the newly opened Buchenwald.[14] As a well-behaved camp veteran, he'd been made a kapo on the haulage column—one of the first kapos in Buchenwald with a Jewish star. But he hadn't been able to live with being a slave-driver, and the SS soon demoted him and subjected him to twenty-five lashes on the Bock.

Through Leo Moses, his first friend and protector, Fritz got to know some of the other veteran Jewish prisoners, all of whom befriended this slight, frail-seeming boy, took care of him, and did what they could to keep him and his fellow youngsters in block 3 safe. Despite being known as the youth block, it was mostly occupied by adults, with just forty or so boys. Many came from the ghetto at Tomaszow, Poland, and spoke Yiddish or Polish; Fritz and the other Viennese boys could scarcely communicate with them, but they ate together and stuck by one another.

Among their patriarchs was Gustav Herzog, the block senior, the man who had employed Fritz's father as a room orderly and given him his brief reprieve from the quarry. At thirty-one, Gustl was young for a block senior.[15]

He was the son of a wealthy Viennese family, owners of the Herzog international news agency, and Gustl himself had been a journalist and a keen hockey player. He'd been arrested in the Kristallnacht pogrom and had failed to secure emigration papers.

The appointment of Gustl Herzog and a number of other Jews as block seniors had helped to break down the dominance of the brutal green triangle men.[16] His deputy was Stefan Heymann, who made a strong impact on Fritz's young mind. A decade older than Herzog, Stefan had the face of an intellectual: high-browed, bespectacled, with a narrow jaw and sensitive mouth.[17] He had been an officer in the Germany army in the last war and been wounded several times. As an active communist and a Jew, he'd been among the first arrested in 1933, and after years in Dachau he had ended up in Buchenwald.

Stefan and Gustl obtained extra soup for the boys, and on evenings when there was no night work, Stefan would tell stories to take their minds off their plight. One evening he read to them from a treasured book, a forbidden work of communist origin: *Road to Life* by the Russian author Anton Makarenko. It told the story of Makarenko's work at two Soviet rehabilitation colonies for juvenile offenders. In the pages of the book, as Stefan conjured it, his voice low in the barrack gloom, the boys' camps were brought to life as magical idylls, a universe away from the daily reality of Buchenwald:

> We transferred to the new colony on a fine, warm day. The leaves on the trees not yet begun to turn, the grass was still green, as if at the height of its second youth, freshened by the first days of autumn. The new colony itself was at that time like a beauty of thirty years—lovely for itself as well as for others, happy and calm in its assured charm . . . The whispering canopy of the luxuriant treetops of our park spread generously over the Kolomak. There was many a shady mysterious nook here, in which one could bathe, cultivate the society of pixies, go fishing, or, at the lowest, exchange confidences with a congenial spirit. Our principal buildings were ranged along the top of the steep bank, and the ingenious and shameless younger boys could jump right out of the windows into the river, leaving their scanty garments on the window sills.[18]

The boys listened, enraptured. Most were alone, their fathers having been killed already, and many had grown increasingly apathetic and listless; but hearing this story of another, better world brought them back to life, enthused and cheered.

Other cultural delights were to be had under the tutelage of their seniors. One evening Stefan and Gustl came into the barrack with an air of conspiratorial mystery. Urging the boys to be quiet, they led them across the camp to the clothing store, a long building adjacent to the shower block and kitchens. It was quiet and still, the hanging racks and shelves stuffed with uniforms, boots, and underwear, and the clothing confiscated from new prisoners, deadening the echo of the boys' footsteps. Within, some older prisoners had gathered; they gave each boy a piece of bread and some acorn coffee, and then four prisoners appeared with violins and woodwinds. There, in the midst of this musty, cloth-lined room, they played chamber music. For the first time Fritz heard the jaunty, impudent melody of "Eine kleine Nachtmusik." Like him, it was a Viennese composition; the cheerful skipping of the bows on the strings brought the room to life and smiles to the lips of the men and boys gathered round. So the evening passed in music and joy, a memory Fritz would treasure forever: "For a very short time we were able to laugh again."[19]

Outside these walls, outside these few borrowed hours, there was no laughter. Working in the vegetable gardens, whose produce was sold in Weimar market and to prisoners in the canteen, was an improvement on the quarry but tougher than the boys had expected.

Fritz and his friends had anticipated being able to pilfer a few of the carrots, tomatoes, and peppers they planted. But it hadn't turned out that way; they never had the chance to get close to the ripened crops. The gardens were under the overall authority of an Austrian officer, SS-Lieutenant Dumböck, who had spent time in exile in Germany with the Austrian Legion during the period when the Nazi Party was outlawed and now took a special pleasure in persecuting Austrian Jews. "You pigs ought to be annihilated," he yelled repeatedly at them, and he did his best to make it come true; Dumböck was later reported to have murdered forty prisoners with his own hands.[20]

While some garden workers did general labor as backbreaking and injurious as in the quarry, others were put on the loathsome task of *Scheissetragen*—shit carrying.[21] Fritz was among them. They had to collect the slop of feces from the prisoner latrines and sewage plant in the main camp and carry it in buckets to the vegetable beds. Every trip, there and back, had to be done at top speed, running as fast as one could bear with the noisome, glooping pails of filth. The only job worse than shit carrying was that of the so-called 4711 detail, named after a popular German eau de cologne; their job was to scoop out the feces from the latrines—often with their bare hands—to fill the shit-carriers' buckets. The SS typically allotted this task to Jewish intellectuals and artists.[22]

Fritz and the other boys had some of the pressure taken off them by their kapo, Willi Kurz. A former amateur heavyweight boxing champion, Willi was a disillusioned soul; having once been on the board of an Aryans-only sports club in Vienna, he had been deeply hurt when the authorities branded him a Jew. But it was his position as an officer in the militia wing of Schuschnigg's Fatherland Front that had condemned him; within weeks of the Anschluss he'd been arrested and sent to the camps. Willi was kind to the boys on his detail; he let them ease off the pace and take a rest if no SS were around. Whenever a guard appeared, Willi would make a show of driving the boys along at full pace, yelling savagely at them and brandishing his cudgel, but he never beat them. His performance was so convincing that the guards never bothered inflicting beatings themselves if Willi was in charge.

אבא

"*Left*–two–three! *Left*–two–three!"

Gustav, with his shoulder to the ropes, heaved. There was no release, no pause, no reprieve from the daily ordeal—just heave, step, heave, step, into eternity. On either side the other cattle heaved and stepped, sweated in the burning sun, dappled by shade from the trees. Twenty-six men with Jewish stars on their uniforms, twenty-six half-starved bodies hauling the wagon with its load of logs from the forest, up the slope, along the dirt road, wagon wheels groaning under the load, men sweating at the ropes.

For Gustav, transfer to the haulage column had been a lifesaver, and he owed it to Leo Moses. The quarry had become intolerable, worse than ever. Sergeants Blank and Hinkelmann, along with a notorious kapo named Vogel, had taken to chasing prisoners over the sentry line every day. Hinkelmann had invented a new torture; if a man collapsed from exhaustion, Hinkelmann would pour water into his mouth until he choked. Blank, meanwhile, entertained himself by standing on the high ground at the top of the quarry and throwing rocks down on the prisoners as they left at noon break or at the end of the day; men who failed to get out of the way quickly enough were hit and killed. The SS men also took up extortion against those Jewish quarry workers who received money from home; every few days, each had to pay up five marks and six cigarettes or risk being beaten and tormented. With two hundred prisoners, the guards made a good little income from their "paydays," although the sum declined week by week as the prisoners died or were murdered.

Leo Moses had stepped in and saved Gustav's life. On Leo's advocacy, in July Gustav was transferred out of the killing ground of the quarry to the haulage column, in which Leo had once been a kapo. Gustav and twenty-five other Jews were hitched to a wagon and hauled building materials around the camp complex all day long—logs from the forest, stone from the quarry, cement from the stores. The kapos forced them to sing as they worked, and the other prisoners referred to them as the *singende Pferde*—singing horses.[23]

"*Left*–two–three! *Left*–two–three! *Left*–two–three! Sing, pigs!"

Whenever they passed an SS guard, he would lash out at them. "Why don't you run, you dogs? Faster!"

But still it was better than the quarry. "It is hard work," Gustav wrote, "but one has more peace and is not hunted . . . Man is a creature of habit, and can get used to everything. So it goes, day after day."

The wheels turned, the man-horses sang and heaved, the kapos yelled time, and the days passed.

בן

SS-Sergeant Schmidt screamed at the group of men as they ran in circles around the roll-call square. "Run! Faster! Run you pigs, run! Faster, you shits!" While all the other prisoners walked back to their barracks, Fritz and the other block 3 inmates had been made to stay. Schmidt, their Blockführer, had found fault in his inspection again—a bed not properly made, a floor insufficiently pristine, belongings not stowed away—and it was punishment time once more—*Straf-sport*, it was called. Thickset and flabby, like so many of his fellows, Schmidt was a notorious sadist and killer, as well as a noted goldbrick; he held a post in the prisoners' canteen and skimmed off tobacco and cigarettes in large quantities. Fritz and the other boys called him "Shit Schmidt" for his favorite word, which decorated virtually every sentence.[24]

"Faster, you Jew-shits!" Fritz and the other boys, who were at the front, stepped up their pace to avoid the blows Schmidt aimed at any man going too slowly. Some of the runners struggled with painful stomachs or testicles where Schmidt had kicked them for answering too slowly at roll call.

"Run! March! Lie down ... get up ... lie down again. Shit! Now run!" *Thwack* went his bullwhip on the buttocks of some poor man who couldn't keep up. "Run!"

For two hours the ordeal went on, as the hot sun went down and the square cooled, the men sweating and laboring for breath. At last Schmidt dismissed them with a curse and they limped back to their barrack.

Starving, they sat down to the only warm meal of the day: turnip soup. If they were lucky there might be a little scrap of meat. When they had finished and were about to get up, Gustl Herzog, the block senior, told the boys to stay where they were. "I have to talk to you," he said. Once the older men had gone, he said, "You boys mustn't run so fast during the *Strafsport*. When you run fast, your fathers can't keep up and they get beaten by Schmidt for lagging behind."

The boys were ashamed, but what could they do? *Someone* would get beaten for going too slow. Gustl and Stefan Heymann showed them the solution. "Run like this—lift your knees higher, take smaller steps." That way, they would give the illusion of running flat-out, but still go slowly enough for the others to keep up. It would be enough to fool Shit Schmidt.

As time went on, the old hands taught the boys all the veterans' little tricks—absurd things, some of them, but they could mean the difference between safety and pain, or between life and death.

And all the while, as Fritz labored in the gardens and Gustav hauled with the *singende Pferde*, the war went on in the world outside, the months dragged by, and all hope of release slowly waned.

His mother's application to have him released, which had sustained Fritz's hopes for a while, came to nothing. She went on applying for all her family—especially the children—but with each month passing by, the prospect receded.

6 | A Favorable Decision

בת

AFTER MONTHS OF LIMBO, at the start of June 1940 Britain was launched into an all-out shooting war. The quiet home front began to transform into a place of bombs and blood and death.

Before a seaborne German invasion could take place, Goering and Hitler had to break the Royal Air Force. The Bore War gave way to the Battle of Britain. Every day, Luftwaffe bombers flew in swarms from their bases in France and Belgium to attack Britain's airfields and factories, and every day the Spitfire and Hurricane fighters scrambled to oppose them. The RAF had become a coalition force, its British and Commonwealth pilots joined by exiles from Poland, France, Belgium, Czechoslovakia, and even some volunteers from the United States defying their country's Neutrality Act.

During that hot early summer, the Luftwaffe's targets were military, and the cities were mostly left alone. The press fixated on two things: the progress of the battle, and growing fears about a German fifth column infiltrating Britain—spies and saboteurs paving the way for the main invasion. The rumors had begun in April, before the Battle of France had even begun. The press—with the right-wing *Daily Mail* at the forefront—had played a major role in whipping up paranoia about fifth columnists, and although the *Mail* claimed to speak for "the people," in fact the majority of Britons had had no notion of what a "fifth column" even was until the *Mail* began its campaign.[1] In fact, there were spies and saboteurs at work in Britain, and dozens were eventually caught and convicted, but most were natural-born British citizens, not immigrants.

Nevertheless, the paranoia had quickly evolved into hysteria, and suspicious eyes were turned toward the German refugees who had settled in the country. At the very start of the war, thousands of German and Austrian nationals had been interned as enemy aliens. But the fifty-five thousand Jewish men, women, and children living in Britain were hardly likely to be spying for Hitler. Most were placed in Category C—exempt from internment—although 6,700 had been categorized B (subject to some restrictions), and 569 were judged a threat and interned.[2] The overwhelming majority were allowed to get on with their lives.

But with the country under threat of imminent invasion, the *Daily Mail* and some politicians were strident in their demands that the government do something about the fifth column threat. All male German and Austrian nationals, regardless of status, ought to be interned for the sake of national security. When Winston Churchill took over as prime minister on May 9, he took the matter firmly in hand. Measures began for moving interned nationals to Canada and extending the categories subject to internment. Churchill's cabinet considered them all: aside from Germans and Austrians, there were members of the British Union of Fascists and the Communist Party, and Irish and Welsh nationalists. When Italy declared war on June 10 and Italians were added to the list, Churchill lost patience and issued the order: "Collar the lot!"[3]

On June 21, the government instituted a new internment policy and issued instructions to local police forces. To avoid putting too much pressure on infrastructure, it would proceed in stages. Initially, Germans and Austrians—Jews, non-Jews, and anti-Nazis alike—who did not have refugee status or who were unemployed were to be arrested and interned. The second stage would sweep up all remaining Germans and Austrians living outside London, and the third would take those in London. The first-stage arrests began on June 24.[4]

Churchill told Parliament, "I know there are a great many people affected by the orders . . . who are the passionate enemies of Nazi Germany. I am very sorry for them, but we cannot . . . draw all the distinctions which we should like to do."[5]

The Anglo-Jewish community was equivocal on the whole affair; they shared the fifth column paranoia and worried deeply about the rise in anti-Semitism that had been triggered by the influx of refugees. People in the north of England were circulating the kind of slurs that always arose against Jews in times of stress: they were black-marketeers, profiteers, evaded military service, enjoyed special privileges, had more money, better food, better clothes.[6] Desperate to curtail the growth of anti-Semitism, the *Jewish Chronicle* breathtakingly recommended taking "the most rigorous steps" against refugees and supported the extension of internment.[7]

In Leeds, Edith Paltenhoffer's fears had been growing for months. After marrying Richard, they had set up home together in an apartment in a large and rather run-down Victorian house in the Chapeltown Road district, close to the synagogue.[8] Edith had left her live-in position with Mrs. Brostoff and switched to a daily job as a cleaner with a Mrs. Green, who lived nearby. This was no light undertaking, as changes of employment by refugees had to be registered and approved by the Home Office.[9] Richard, for the time being, continued with his journeyman cracker baking, although it was hardly his ideal metier.

They should have been happy, but Edith was deeply unsettled. When the fifth column paranoia began in the press, life became uncomfortable for anyone with a German accent. Synagogues in England stopped allowing sermons in German, and the Board of Deputies of British Jews—also keen to avoiding provoking anti-Semitism—worked to suppress gatherings of German Jewish refugees.[10]

When France fell and a German invasion looked certain, Edith and Richard were consumed by fear. They had seen how quickly Austria had fallen to the Nazis, and it was only too easy to imagine storm troopers in Chapeltown Road and Eichmann or some other SS ghoul issuing orders from Leeds Town Hall.

Edith went through her belongings and dug out the affidavits from her relatives in America. It was time to try again to get out of Europe altogether. At the beginning of June, she inquired of the Refugee Committee whether her affidavits would still be valid now that she was married. It took nearly two weeks for the reply to find its way back from London: no, they were not. Edith would need to write to her sponsors and ask them to either issue new affidavits or swear a statement transferring the old ones to her married name. Because US immigration law did not give automatic entitlement to her husband, the sponsors would need to extend the affidavits to include him.[11] And of course, there would remain the formalities of applying for an emigration visa at the US Embassy in London.

With the Battle of Britain escalating in the skies over their heads and the calls for internment growing louder in the press, Edith and Richard were looking at an excruciatingly long process. Edith had been through it before in Vienna, and it would be no better here. They would never discover just how long it would take; at the beginning of July, events overtook them. The second stage of the government's program came into force, and the Leeds police arrested Richard.

It was only by luck that they didn't take Edith too. Women with children were not exempt, but pregnant women were. This, the politicians reasoned, was where the public might draw a line; if they saw pregnant women being subjected to barrack-room life in camps, they might turn against the whole idea of internment. The same applied to mothers with very sick children.[12]

Edith wasn't standing for this outrage. Her poor husband, only twenty-one years old, with the scars of a Nazi concentration camp on his body, had fled to this country seeking sanctuary. And now, to be torn from his wife and unborn child and sent to some awful internment camp by the very people who should be shielding him from the Nazis . . . It was beyond belief.

Applications for release could be submitted to the Home Office; it was no easy process, as the internees had to prove that they were not only no threat to security but that they could make a positive contribution to the war effort.[13] Edith immediately lodged an application and submitted a medical report. Meanwhile, both the Leeds and London branches of the Jewish Refugee Committee lobbied the Home Office on behalf of the thousands now incarcerated. Many weren't even in real camps with proper facilities—the numbers had been too great for existing camps to hold, and improvised centers had been set up in derelict cotton mills, disused factories, racecourses, anywhere that could be found. Many went to the main internment center on the Isle of Man, a small island between the coasts of northern England and Ireland, a popular vacation spot before the war.[14]

The weeks of July and August went by, Edith's pregnancy advanced, and no word came. She wrote again to the JRC in late August. The secretary in London replied, advising her against pressing the matter: "We . . . feel that you have done everything possible at the present time and think it would be most unwise for our Committee to intervene. We have been advised by the

Home Office that additional appeals and letters of enquiry . . . can result in delaying any decision."[15]

A few days later, the decision was reached—and it went against Richard. He would stay in the camp.

For a concentration camp veteran, life in an internment camp could be relatively mild. There was no forced labor, no real punishments, no sadistic guards; internees—many of whom were scholars, scientists, and artists—played sports, set up newspapers, concerts, and educational circles. But they were prisoners nonetheless. And although there was no SS, Jews sometimes found themselves confined in the same camps—or even the same rooms—as Nazi sympathizers. Richard had the additional torment of knowing that Edith was having to cope with her pregnancy alone and without his wages.

In early September, now well into her third trimester, Edith submitted a second application for Richard's release. The JRC assured her, "We sincerely trust that the application will receive a favourable decision."[16] The waiting began again. After two weeks, a brief note came from the Aliens Department of the Home Office, telling her that Richard's case would come before committee "as soon as possible."[17]

Two days later Edith's contractions started. In no fit state to give birth at home, she was taken to the Maternity Hospital in Hyde Terrace in the center of Leeds. On Wednesday, September 18, 1940, she gave birth to a healthy boy, and named him Peter John. A real Yorkshire-born English baby son. Peter was five days old when the news came through from the JRC—his father had been released.[18]

The public mood had turned against interning harmless refugees. The catalyst had come in July, when a ship bound for Canada carrying several thousand internees—including some Jews—was sunk by a U-boat. The loss of life made Britain look at itself and realize what it was doing to innocent people. The policy was gradually reversed, and by the end of the year most interned refugees had been released. In Parliament, politicians expressed regret for what they had done in a fit of panic; one Conservative member said, "We have, unwittingly I know, added to the sum total of misery caused by this war, and by doing so we have not in any way added to the efficiency of our war effort."[19] A Labour member added: "We remember the horror that sprang up in this country when Hitler put Jews, Socialists and Communists into concentration camps. We were horrified at that, but somehow or other we almost took it for granted when we did the same thing to the same people."[20]

אבא

Gustav opened his notebook and leafed through the pages. So few of them— just three sides covered in his strong script summed up the eons of the year 1940. "Thus the time passes," he wrote, "up early in the morning, home late in the evening, eating, and then straight to sleep. So a year goes by, with work and punishment."

A new punishment had been devised for the Jews by the deputy commandant in charge of the main camp, SS-Major Arthur Rödl, a bumptious crook whose low intelligence had not hindered his rise to senior rank. Each evening, when they returned from the quarry and the gardens and the construction sites, exhausted and hungry, while all the other prisoners went to their barracks, the Jews—thousands of them—were made to stand on the roll-call square under the glare of the floodlights and sing.

The "choirmaster" stood on top of a gravel heap at the edge of the square and conducted. "Another number!" Rödl would call out over the loudspeakers, and the weary prisoners would draw breath and struggle though another song. If the singing wasn't good enough, the loudspeakers would bark out: "Open your mouths! Don't you pigs want to? Lie down, the whole rabble, and give us a song!"

And down they had to lie, whatever the weather, in the dust, the dirt, muddy puddles or snow, and sing. The Blockführers would walk between the rows, kicking any man who didn't sing loudly enough. The ordeal often went on for hours. Sometimes Rödl would grow bored and announce that he was going for dinner, but the prisoners would have to stay and practice: "If you can't get it right," he said, "you can stay and sing all night." The SS guards, who resented having to stand by and supervise, would take out their wrath on the prisoners, administering kickings and beatings.

The most common tune was the "Buchenwald Song." Composed by two Austrian prisoners, it was a stirring march tune, with words extolling courage in the midst of wretchedness. The song had been commissioned by Rödl himself, though he had nothing to do with its substance; "All other camps have a song," he had declared in 1938. "We must get a Buchenwald song."[21] He offered a prize of ten marks to the successful composer (which was never paid) and was delighted by the result. The prisoners sang it when they marched out to work in the mornings:

> When the day awakens, ere the sun smiles,
> The gangs march out to the day's toils
> Out into the breaking dawn.
> And the forest is black and the heavens red,
> In our packs we carry a scrap of bread
> And in our hearts, in our hearts, just sorrow.
>
> Oh Buchenwald, I cannot forget you,
> For you are my fate.
> He who has left you, he alone can measure
> How wonderful freedom is!
> Oh Buchenwald, we do not whine and moan,
> And whatever our fate may be,
> We will say yes to life,
> For the day will come when we are free!

The song had been composed by the Viennese songwriter Hermann Leopoldi with words by celebrated lyricist Fritz Löhner-Beda, both of whom were prisoners. The SS, including Major Rödl himself, abjectly failed to recognize the spirit of defiance. "In his weakness of intellect he absolutely did not see how revolutionary the song actually was," recalled Leopoldi.[22] Rödl had also commissioned a special "Jewish Song" with defamatory lyrics about the crimes and pestilence of the Jews, but it had been "too stupid" even for him, and he banned it. Some other officers later resurrected it and forced the prisoners to sing it late into the night.[23] But still it was the rousing "Buchenwald Song" more often than not. The Jews sang it times without count on the roll-call square under the lights; "Rödl enjoyed dancing to the melody," said Leopoldi, "as on one side the camp orchestra played, and on the other side the people were whipped."[24] They sang it marching to work in the red dawn, investing it with all their loathing and hatred of the SS. Many died singing it. "They cannot grind us down like this," Gustav wrote in his diary. "The war goes on."

בן

Buchenwald continued to expand, month by month. The forest was eaten away and logged, and among the littered waste the buildings rose like pale fungus on the blighted back of the Ettersberg. The SS barracks were gradually completing their arc—a semicircular fan of sixteen two-story blocks, with the administrative building at one end and an officers' casino in the center, all encompassing a large spruce grove.[25] There were handsomely designed villas with gardens for the officers, a small zoo, riding and stable facilities, garage complexes and a gas station for SS vehicles, and even a falconry. This strange addition, which stood among the trees on the slope between the commandant's villa and the quarry, comprised an aviary, a gazebo, and a Teutonic hunting hall of carved oak timbers and great fireplaces, stuffed with trophies and heavy furniture. It was intended for the personal use of Hermann Goering, in his capacity as Reich Hunt Master, but he was destined never to even visit the place, let alone use it. The SS was so proud of it that for a fee of 1 mark local Germans could come in and look around.[26]

All of this—houses, barracks, garages, offices, entertainment facilities—was built from the bones and timbers of the hill on which it stood, and fashioned with the blood of the prisoners whose hands transported and laid the stones and bricks and lumber.

Along the roads between the construction sites, Gustav Kleinmann and his fellow slaves hauled their wagons of materials, and his son was now one of those whose hands put up the buildings. Fritz's nightmare period in the gardens had ended. His tireless benefactor, Leopold Moses, had used his influence again to have Fritz transferred to the construction detail building the SS garages, a sprawling complex laid out around a huge open area.[27] The kapo of Construction Detachment I, which was undertaking the project, was Robert Siewert, a friend of Leo Moses.

Siewert, a German of Polish extraction, wore the red triangle of a political prisoner. He'd been a bricklayer in his youth, and he had served in the German army in the last war. A dedicated communist, he'd been a member of Saxony's parliament in the 1920s. In 1935 the Nazis had imprisoned him for treason, transferring him to Buchenwald in 1938. Siewert was in his fifties but had an air of resilient strength and energy: thickset, with a broad face and narrow eyes under dark, heavy brows. On Leo's request, he arranged Fritz's transfer to his detachment.

At first the labor was as arduous as any Fritz had known. Again it was all about carrying—bring this here, bear this burden, and *run*! A sack of cement weighed fifty kilograms,* whereas Fritz himself weighed little over forty. Other laborers in the yard would lift the sack onto his shoulders, and he would carry it, staggering, trying to run, to wherever it was needed. But even this was better than the gardens or the quarry, for there was no abuse, no beatings—only grueling, crippling work. The SS valued the construction detachment highly, and therefore Siewert was able to prevent them abusing the prisoners under him.

For all his stern appearance, Robert Siewert had a kind heart. He took a liking to Fritz and couldn't stand to see such a young, slightly built boy being worked into the ground. He took Fritz off carrying and reassigned him to mixing mortar. He also taught Fritz how to gain favor with the SS. "You have to work with your eyes," he told him. "If you see an SS man coming, work fast. But if no SS are about, then you take your time, you spare yourself." Fritz became so adept at watching for the guards and making a show of intense productive labor that he acquired a reputation for industriousness. Siewert would point him out to the construction leader, SS-Sergeant Becker, and say, "Look how diligently this Jewish lad works."

One day Becker arrived at the building site with his superior, SS-Lieutenant Max Schobert, deputy commandant in charge of protective custody prisoners. Siewert called Fritz away from his work and presented him to the officer, extolling his performance. "We could train Jewish prisoners as bricklayers," he suggested. Schobert, a brutal-faced individual with a perpetual sneer, looked down his large nose at Fritz. He didn't like this suggestion at all; all that expense to train Jews! Nonetheless, a seed had been planted which had the potential to grow into a lifeline.

During that summer a large unit of SS troops arrived at Buchenwald to bump the garrison up to full strength. Their barrack buildings weren't complete, and work had to be accelerated—a task beyond the capacity of the construction detail. Robert Siewert took the opportunity to press his case again, complaining to the camp administration that he didn't have enough bricklayers. The only solution would be to train young Jews for the job. Commandant Koch's reac-

---

* 110 pounds

tion was the same as Schobert's. But Siewert insisted that he simply couldn't provide the labor force in any other way. Eventually Koch relented.

Fritz Kleinmann was the first apprentice. Siewert began by having him taught to lay bricks to build a simple wall under the supervision of Aryan workmen. With a string laid out as a guide, he pasted on the mortar and laid down brick after brick, neatly and correctly. Fritz had inherited his father's aptitude for manual craft, and he learned quickly. Having mastered the basics, he was taught how to do corners, pillars, and buttresses, then lintels, fireplaces, and chimneys. In wet weather he learned plastering. Every day Siewert would come to talk to him and check on his progress. In double-quick time Fritz became a fully trained mason and builder—the first Jew in Buchenwald to do so.

His progress was so impressive, and the need so urgent, that the SS allowed Siewert to start up a training program for Jewish, Polish, and Roma boys. They would spend half of each day working on-site, and half in their block in the camp being taught construction theory and science.

In Fritz's young mind, Robert Siewert became a hero, representing the spirit of resistance to the Nazis and the ethos of humane kindness. The young were his greatest concern, and he had set himself the goal of doing whatever he could to equip them with skills and knowledge that could save their lives. "He spoke to us like a father," Fritz would recall, "with patience and kindness, to which we had grown unaccustomed."[28] Fritz wondered where Siewert got the strength, at his age and after so many years of Nazi imprisonment.

Robert Siewert's Jewish apprentices wore green bands on their sleeves with the inscription "Bricklayers' School" and enjoyed certain privileges. A particular delight was the heavy laborers' special food allowance; twice a week, they shared an extra ration of 2½ kilos of bread and half a kilo of blood pudding or meat pâté, which was brought to the construction site for them. This was on top of their standard daily ration of 2½ kilos of bread, 250 grams of margarine, a spoonful of curd or beet jam, acorn coffee, and three quarters of a liter of cabbage or turnip soup with little bits of meat in it.

When winter began to set in, Siewert got permission to set up oil drums as braziers on the construction site, on the pretext that the plaster and mortar was liable to crack in freezing conditions. His real purpose was the welfare of his workers, who labored all day in the bitter cold with only their thin prison uniforms to protect them. A humane and courageous man from heart to backbone, Robert Siewert was absolutely devoted to the well-being of his fellow men, and never failed in that duty, knowingly putting himself at unthinkable risk by interceding with the SS on behalf of Jews, Roma, Poles, and other oppressed people.

But Siewert's influence did not extend far beyond the limits of the construction site and the bricklaying school. As soon as the day's work ended and the prisoners returned to the main camp, they returned to the direct jurisdiction of the camp guards and the regime of enforced singing parades long into the night, random beatings, food deprivation, and capricious murders. Fritz would look at his fellow prisoners and silently give thanks that at least he ate better than they did and was not beaten at work or at risk of being driven over the sentry line or kicked to death. He ached for his papa, who slaved each day on the haulage column. Fritz saved what he could from his additional rations to give to him when they met in the evenings.

Extra morsels of food came to Fritz from an unexpected source. While working on the construction of a heating plant for the SS barracks, he was befriended by an Austrian prisoner who worked as a welder in one of the SS technical facilities.[29] All Fritz knew of him was that he spoke in the dialect of Styria in southern Austria. He would meet Fritz every few days behind the heating plant and give him a piece of bread. Fritz never knew his name, only that he pitied the young Jewish boys in the camp and helped others besides Fritz, stealing from the SS food store to provide for them. Fritz asked Robert Siewert about the Styrian; he reluctantly gave his approval, warning, "Boy, be careful you don't get caught." To be apprehended by the SS would mean punishment for both of them—and death for the Styrian. Fritz's heart was warmed by these gifts of food, and by the sense of solidarity.[30]

Gustav's mind was eased by his son's new status and the safety it brought. "The boy is popular with all the foremen and kapo Robert Siewert," he wrote. "From Leo Moses we get our greatest support, which gives us further confidence." To Gustav's indomitably optimistic mind, it was beginning to seem that they might survive this ordeal. Meanwhile, for the poor men in the quarry their hell had no end, and they died in dreadful numbers every day. The fear of being sent back there was constant.

During his time on the construction detachment, Fritz was moved out of the youth block and transferred to block 17, which was on the same north-south street as his father's block. It was painful to part from his friends. But the move proved formative; block 17 was where the Austrian VIP and celebrity prisoners—the *Prominenten*—were housed. Most had been incarcerated for their political activities but were of a higher status than most of the red-triangle men in the camp.[31] Some of their names were familiar to Fritz, his father having known them—or at least known *of* them—during his time as an activist in the Social Democratic Party.

Fritz was welcomed into this new community by one of the room seniors, Josef Jellinek, who was in his forties and a veteran of left-wing politics. Along with his sister Adele, Josef, or Seppl as he was known,* had been a writer and editor with the Viennese social-democratic newspapers *Das Kleine Blatt* and *Der Arbeiter-Sonntag*. It was Seppl Jellinek who introduced the starstruck Fritz to the society of block 17.

They included Robert Danneberg, a Jewish socialist who had been president of the Vienna provincial council, a member of the National Assembly, and one of the leading figures in "Red Vienna"—the socialist heyday that had lasted from the end of the First World War until the right-wing takeover in 1934.

Contrasting with Dannenberg's sober presence was the droll, round-faced Fritz Grünbaum, star of the Berlin and Vienna cabaret scenes, *conférencier*,† scriptwriter, and movie actor. He had also written librettos for the operetta composer Franz Léhar (who was one of Hitler's favorite composers despite having a Jewish wife). As a prominent Jew and a political satirist, Grünbaum had been taken by the Nazis soon after the Anschluss. Aging and slightly built, with his bald, shaved pate and bottle-bottom spectacles he resembled Mahatma Gandhi. He had survived periods in the quarry and latrine details. His health and spirit had been broken by it, and he had attempted suicide. Even so, he managed to keep up a semblance of his old persona and would, on occasion, perform cabaret for the other prisoners. His comment on his plight as a Jew was simple and to the point: "What does my intellect benefit me when my name damages me? A poet called Grünbaum is done for." He was right; he would be dead within months.[32]

Fritz got to know other artists in block 17, including another prominent librettist, the bespectacled, somber-looking Fritz Löhner-Beda. Like Grünbaum he had written librettos for Léhar's operettas and operas. Also like Grünbaum, as a famous Jew living in Vienna, Löhner-Beda had been arrested

---

* Seppl: Austrian diminutive of Josef
† Cabaret emcee

in April 1938 and sent to the camps. He always hoped that Léhar, who had influence with both Hitler and Goebbels, would be able to have him freed, but he hoped in vain. To add to his torment, songs from Léhar's operettas *Giuditta* and *The Land of Smiles* were often played over the camp's loudspeakers, the SS apparently unaware that Löhner-Beda had authored the librettos for those very works. Even more hurtfully they played the popular song "I Lost My Heart in Heidelberg," for which he had written the lyrics. Another of his works was sung every single day in the camp, for it was Fritz Löhner-Beda who had written the poignant, defiant lyrics of the "Buchenwald Song" to music by his friend and fellow prisoner, the composer and cabaret star Hermann Leopoldi. Leopoldi at least had managed to escape this miserable place; he'd been released in early 1939 and was now living with his wife in America.

One of the brightest of the block 17 *Prominenten* was Ernst Federn, a young Viennese Jew from a family of intellectuals and academics; his father, Paul Federn, was a well-known psychoanalyst who had studied under Freud, and Ernst himself had followed his father into the profession. He was also a Trotskyist, and wore the red-on-yellow star of a Jewish political prisoner. Ernst was a little forbidding to look at, with heavy features set in an almost thuggish-looking expression beneath his cropped scalp. But he was a soul of kindness. He had become known as the prisoners' psychoanalyst, and anyone could come to him to talk about themselves or their problems. His irrepressible optimism gave marvelous encouragement to the other prisoners, some of whom regarded him as a little crazy for it.[33]

There were other men too who had been active social-democrats, Christian-socialists, Trotskyists, communists. In their free time in the evenings, young Fritz would sit and listen to their conversations about politics, philosophy, the war . . . Their talk was intellectual, sophisticated, and Fritz, keen to learn, strained to comprehend what they said. One thing that came through clearly was the strength of their belief in the idea of Austria. Despite their own hopeless situation, their country's obliteration as an independent state, and its relegation as the mere "Ostmark" of the German Reich, they shared a vision of a future Austria, free from Nazi rule, renewed and beautiful. These men believed firmly that the Nazis must lose the war in the end, even though the trickles of news that found their way into the camp indicated that right now they were winning it on all fronts.

Fritz felt his faith and his courage grow in the light of these men's vision of a better future. What he did not know, but could easily guess, was that few of them would live to see it. "The camaraderie I learned in block 17 changed my life fundamentally," he would recall. "I became acquainted with a form of solidarity unimaginable in life outside the concentration camps."[34] Fritz would always recall Fritz Grünbaum's birthday celebration, it being the same day as Fritz's sister Herta's. The other blockmates saved portions of their rations to give old Grünbaum a decent dinner, and a little extra was stolen from the kitchens. After their meal, Löhner-Beda gave a speech and Grünbaum himself sang a few verses. As the youngest inmate present, Fritz was permitted to congratulate the humbled star.

Dozens of men—politicians, intellectuals, entertainers, from Vienna, Silesia, Bohemia, Brno, Prague, and one young apprentice upholsterer from Leopoldstadt, a playmate of the Karmelitermarkt—what could they possibly have in common? That they were Austrians by birth or by choice, and that they were Jews. In here, they had the whole world in common; they were a tiny nation of survivors surrounded by a poison sea.

And the deaths went on.

One of the first from block 17 was Hans Kunke, a young Jewish political radical and writer. Square set and good-looking, Hans was a musician by nature and a revolutionary by calling. In the days of Red Vienna he had been active in the Socialist Workers' Youth organization, and even after socialist parties were suppressed after 1934, he and his wife, Stefanie (who was now in Ravensbrück concentration camp), had remained members of the central committee of the illegal Revolutionary Socialist Youth. Hans, who ate at the next table to Fritz, had a fine baritone voice and was said to be an accomplished pianist. He was only thirty-four years old, but his experiences in Buchenwald had damaged him severely, and he had been assigned to the sock-darning detail, a labor allotted to invalids. The SS would not let him be. One morning at roll call, a week after Fritz Grünbaum's birthday celebration, Hans Kunke was called out and transferred to the quarry. He endured six months there as a stone carrier under the torment of kapos Vogel and Johann Herzog and the SS overseers Blank and Hinkelmann. On the last day of October 1940, Hans Kunke, utterly broken and driven by despair, ran across the sentry line and was shot.[35]

Another fatality was Rudi Arndt, a young Jewish communist from Berlin, who was block senior in block 22 (originally designated the "Jewish block" and still known by that name even though the Jewish prisoner population had long since overflowed it). Rudi organized secret musical performances and Jewish cultural celebrations. The SS called him the *Judenkaiser* because he had no fear of remonstrating with them on behalf of the other Jews when their rations were cut or they were barred from the prisoners' infirmary. He conspired to steal medicines from the stores to treat sick Jews, smuggled them into the infirmary and hid them from the SS doctors, and set up an improvised hospital in block 22. To Stefan Heymann, who was his friend and assistant, and to Fritz and to every other Jew in Buchenwald, Rudi was a hero. But he was betrayed to the SS by a group of green-triangle prisoners and sent to the quarry, where he met the usual fate on the sentry line.[36]

The killings in the quarry were growing more frequent, and many of the dead were friends of Fritz's or Gustav's, some from the old days in Vienna. That year—the first full year of the war—across all the Nazi concentration camps prisoner deaths through murder and suicide increased tenfold, from around thirteen hundred to fourteen thousand.[37] The atmosphere of war was the cause of it. While their fellows in the Waffen-SS and the Wehrmacht fought and conquered Germany's enemies in Poland, France, Belgium, Denmark, the Netherlands, Norway, and Great Britain, the Totenkopf SS in the concentration camps felt their blood stirring and their tempers fired up, and they ramped up their war against the enemy within. News of military victories triggered spurts of triumphal aggression, and setbacks—such as the failure to subdue Britain, the only enemy still fighting—inspired retribution.

With the numbers of corpses needing to be disposed of rising beyond its ability to cope, in 1940 the SS began to equip all its concentration camps with their own crematoria.[38] Buchenwald's was constructed in a corner of the main camp, immediately beyond the now-defunct little camp. It was a small, unremarkable square building with a yard surrounded by a high wall. From the roll-call ground the square spike of its chimney could be seen rising, brick upon brick, until it was complete; then it began pouring out its first acrid smoke. From that day on, the smoke would scarcely stop. Sometimes it blew away across the treetops, often it drifted over the camp. But always there was the smell of it; the smell of death.

A change was coming to the concentration camps. Its first tremors had been felt during 1940; during the coming year of 1941 they would grow louder.

אמא

In the New Year, after endless months of frustration, a result came at last from the United States consulate in Vienna.

For more than a year Tini had struggled through every obstacle the authorities could throw in her way. Since March 1940, there had been a standing summons for an interview for emigration, but Tini had been advised that she needed to wait until Gustav and Fritz had been freed if she wanted the family to be able to go together.[39] But since the SS would not release concentration camp prisoners unless they had all the necessary papers to emigrate, this was a hopeless dead end. Accordingly, Tini had registered her children separately from herself and Gustav, so as to give them the best chance.

All the affidavits were in place from the various relatives—affidavits for Tini herself, separate ones for Gustav, and for the children. The problem was getting American visas and valid tickets for travel (which had to be paid for) *and* having everything coordinated. Several opportunities for travel had been missed; when France remained free, it had provided a route out of Europe to America. But the German invasion in May 1940 had closed the French ports. In the fall, Lisbon in Portugal had become available to German Jewish emigrants, but the United States consulate in Vienna had simultaneously put a near-total freeze on issuing visas. Only three or four per month were given out. Tini was close to despair.

There was friction between refugee charities and the US government. Margaret Jones, a charity worker with the American Friends Service Committee in Vienna—an institution set up by the Quakers—inquired at the consulate why the flow of visas had all but dried up. A State Department official told her that tensions between President Roosevelt, Congress, and the press and public over refugees had hit a sticking point. Roosevelt's stance in favor of giving a haven to refugees had withered in the face of America's growing anti-Semitism and purported evidence that Jewish refugees were involved in fifth column activities. Capitulating to public opinion, the president had instructed the State Department to reduce the number of visas to near zero: "No more aliens."

What particularly appalled Margaret Jones was the lack of any public announcement on policy, and no outward change in procedure. The consulate staff still called applicants for the standard succession of interviews, which was tortuous in itself, requiring expenditure of money they didn't have for notarized documents, police certificates, steamship tickets, local anti-Jewish taxes, shuttling them back and forth from consulate to IKG to police and back again. And then, at the final interview, when the anxious applicant had miraculously got every document in order, hoping against hope that their visa would be granted and they could go to safety at last, they were told that they had failed to show they could make a contribution to the United States, and that they were therefore likely to "become a public charge."[40] *Visa refused.*

As of October 1940, virtually all applicants—people who were living in constant terror and had beggared themselves in their efforts to get everything they needed—received this verdict and went away heartbroken. The consular staff found it unpleasant, but had no choice but to obey orders.[41]

"We have everything," Tini wrote to the German Jewish Aid Committee in New York, "but none of us has emigrated . . . Our local consulate is not giving us adequate answers."[42] She couldn't understand the endless frustration; her husband was a hard worker with good skills—and a decorated war veteran—and they had affidavits in plenty.

Her only hope was for the children. At the beginning of 1941, Tini made her breakthrough. Her old friend, Alma Maurer, who had been at her wedding and now lived in Massachusetts, had obtained an affidavit for Kurt from a prominent Jewish gentleman in the town where she lived—a judge no less. And then a miracle—rare as a hen's teeth or a pot of gold at the end of the rainbow, a *visa for immigration.* The United States was willing to make an allowance—albeit a small and tightly guarded one—for Jewish children. In conjunction with the German Jewish Children's Aid organization in New York, a limited number of unaccompanied minors would be received and placed with appropriate Jewish families in the United States. Kurt had been accepted.

It would hurt both Tini and Herta to let him go, but it was the only way to get him to safety. And there was more good news—the kind gentleman in Massachusetts would be willing to sponsor Herta as well. She wasn't a child, but perhaps this extra step up would help Herta climb over America's wall.

7 | The New World

אבא

BENEATH A CLOUD-PACKED GRAY SKY the Ettersberg was a white tumor in a white landscape striated with the black streaks of hedge lines, buildings, and scraped roads. On the hill, the thick covering of snow softened but did not hide the radiating outlines of the barrack blocks and the tower-spiked fences.

Gustav leaned on his shovel. The kapo's back was turned, and Gustav snatched the moment to catch his breath. His frozen fingers were purple, and when he breathed on them there was no feeling of warmth: no sensation at all. He knew that when he returned to the barrack in the evening and the bone-cold numbness leached out of him, they would gripe and ache abominably. He could sense his bones complaining now as they gripped the haft of the shovel, but they did so silently with teeth clenched.

A new year, but nothing had changed in this world except the passing of seasons and the daily passing of lives. Smoke from the crematorium drifted foully in the freezing air over the camp and into the nostrils of the prisoners, the scent of their own futures.

Gustav, his senses trained by more than a year in this place, felt the kapo turning toward him and was already plying his shovel before the man's eyes reached him. The work of the haulage column had been interrupted by the snow; each day the prisoners shoveled the camp streets clear, hauled the snow away, and each night nature buried them deep once more.

The light was fading. Sensing that no eyes were upon him, Gustav rested again. He looked up at the southeastern sky, marbled gray and scintillating with falling flakes, smeared with smoke from the chimney. Somewhere over there, far beyond these fences and woods, was his home, his wife, Herta, little Kurt. What were they doing right now? Were they safe? Warm or as cold as him? Frightened or hopeful? Despairing? He and Fritz still received regular letters and a little money from Tini, but it was no substitute for being there. He knew only that Tini's world right now revolved around trying to get the children out of the country, and that her hopes were pinned most on Kurt.

With a last glance at the sky, Gustav bent his back and drove his shovel into the snow.

כן

The sky above Kurt's head was warm and blue as only skies in childhood memories can be, shimmering with the sunlight-dappled leaves of horse chestnuts and studded with snowy heaps of blossom. He put one foot before the other, gazing upward, dizzying himself with pleasure.

Looking ahead, he realized that he had lagged behind the rest of the family. There were Mama and Papa walking arm in arm, and Fritz, sauntering with his hands in the pockets of his smart knickerbocker pants, Herta strolling prettily, Edith upright and elegant.

They had spent the morning in the Prater, and Kurt was replete with delight. He'd lost count of the number of times he'd shot down the great slide—if you helped out by carrying bundles of mats back up to the top, the man in charge gave you a free ride, and Kurt and Fritz and the other less well-off kids always took a few turns. Now, strolling along the Hauptallee, the broad avenue that ran arrow-straight for over a kilometer through the Prater woods, Kurt was amusing himself by walking with one foot on the path and one on the raised grass bank between it and the road. His senses full, Kurt didn't notice that the rest of the family was getting farther and farther ahead. One foot up, one foot down, he hummed to himself, enjoying the sensation of boosting himself up on each high step. All awareness of time slipped away, and when at last he looked up again, he was alone.

An instant's shiver of terror flickered through his chest. Before him, the rows of trees receding into the distance, the woods on either side, the families, the couples, bicycles and carriages and cars swishing by on the road; through the trees the colors of the amusement park and more people—but nowhere could he pick out the familiar shapes of his parents or his sisters or Fritz. They had simply vanished. Were they hiding from him? Had they forgotten him? It was as if they had been snatched away in an instant.

The momentary terror passed, and Kurt reasoned with himself. There was no need to panic. He knew his way around the Prater like he knew the face of a friend; it was little more than a kilometer from home, about a dozen blocks. He could find his own way. And when he got home his mama and papa would remember that they had another son. He kept going along the Hauptallee, past the amusement park, close by the foot of the Riesenrad ferris wheel, and to the Prater entrance. But as he emerged from the park, he met an obstacle. The Hauptallee opened out onto the Praterstern, a huge star-shaped interchange where six other great boulevards and avenues met, in the center of which stood the tall column of the Tegethoff monument. After the peace of the woods, it was a maelstrom of noise and movement. Trucks, motor cars, and trams streamed roaring from left to right across his vision, pouring in and out of the nearest boulevards onto the interchange; the sidewalks teemed with people hurrying, idling, standing about.

Kurt stood there, stunned by the realization that he had no idea what to do now. He had come through this place times without count, but always with a grown-up or older sibling. He'd never needed to pay attention to how you got through this torrent.

After a while he became aware of a presence and a woman's voice. He glanced up and found a lady peering down at him with concern. "Are you lost?" she asked. Well of course he wasn't lost; he knew exactly where he was, but he didn't know how to get from this *where* to the *where* he wanted to be. He knew the direction but couldn't figure out how to physically accomplish it. But he also didn't know quite how to explain this complex concept. The lady frowned anxiously at him.

From out of nowhere a policeman appeared and quickly took control. He took Kurt by the hand and led him back toward the Prater, bearing left along Ausstellungsstrasse. Eventually they came to the police station, a large and extremely important-looking building of red brick and stone. Kurt was led into a world of dark uniforms, anxious-looking citizens, and quietly efficient bustle filled with strange smells and sounds. The policeman spoke with another officer, and Kurt was given a seat in an office. A policeman working there smiled at him, chatted, played with him. Kurt had a roll of caps, and to his delight the policeman, using the buckle of his dress belt, set them off one at a time, the banging echoing round the office like rifle fire.

Distracted and enjoying the policeman's company, Kurt scarcely noticed the time passing. Then, "Kurtl!" said a familiar voice. "There you are!" He turned and saw his mama in the doorway, and his papa behind her. His heart lit up within him; he jumped up and ran toward his mother's open arms.

בן

Kurt woke, staring and shaking, with his heart pounding in his chest. For a moment he had no idea where he was. A rush of sound, thudding, clattering in his ears; beneath him a hard wooden bench; around him strange people; a sensation of rocking rhythmically. A train—he was on a train. Then he noticed the flat packet hanging against his chest, and remembered.[1]

This was the train to his new life. The old life, the familiar life, the beloved, was behind him, inexplicably, inexorably receding into a different dimension. Or perhaps it was the other way round—Vienna, Im Werd, his home, all were real and of the present, and it was he who had been pushed into this unreal existence.

The slatted wooden bench had numbed his backside, but he'd been so tired, sleep had taken hold of him, and he'd slumped against the passenger beside him. He sat up and touched the packet. He recalled his mother hanging it around his neck.

That image was vivid in his memory: They were in the kitchen in the apartment. She sat him on the table—the same worn surface where he had once helped her coat the velvety veal cutlets for Wiener schnitzel and roll up the noodles for chicken soup. He could see her face, hollowed by hunger, etched by worry, close before him, telling him how vital it was to look after this wallet. It contained his papers, and in this world now, that was as much as to say that it held his very soul, his permission to exist. He must preserve and guard it, for his life depended on it. On the front was written his name and date of birth. She smiled and kissed him. "You behave now, Kurtl," she said. "Be a good child when you get there—no tricks, be obedient so they will let you stay." She produced a gift for him, a new-bought harmonica, all gleaming and sweet, and he clutched it to him.

... And then she was gone. Blinking out in his memory like a light switched off.

Kurt looked around at the people on the train, glanced out the window at the unfamiliar countryside flowing by under its February frost, and wondered. He knew in that part of his mind where he kept facts that this was the train from Berlin, where he had collected his final papers from the German Jewish Children's Aid and the travel money he was required to have—fifty crisp green American dollars tucked safe in his luggage—and he knew likewise that he had got to Berlin from Vienna on another train, and that that train must have left from the Westbahnhof or Hütteldorf . . . but in the other part of his mind the memory of it was fading. In time, to his lifelong regret, he would be utterly unable to remember saying good-bye to his mother, or to Herta.

Most of the other people on the train were refugees, and to Kurt most seemed elderly. There were families too, with young children. German, Austrian, Hungarian Jews, a few Poles, all crammed into their seats. Mothers murmured to their little ones while their husbands read or talked or dozed, old men with hats low on their brows stooped in their sleep, snoring and sighing into their gray beards, and children stared at them wide-eyed. Every few stops the refugees had to change trains, gathering themselves and their luggage. German soldiers or police herded them onto whatever trains were available, and sometimes when they boarded they found themselves in luxurious first-class compartments, sometimes second, but more often the aching wooden slats of third. Kurt preferred third class, because at least he got to sit properly; the seats in first had armrests, and the children had to perch on them, squeezed and elbowed between the adults. On a few occasions Kurt got so desperate for comfort that he clambered up onto the luggage rack and stretched out on the valises.

There were only two other unaccompanied children on the train, a boy and a girl, and Kurt gradually got to know them. Both were sponsored by the German Jewish Children's Aid. One was a fellow Viennese named Karl Kohn, who was fourteen and came from the same part of Leopoldstadt as Kurt. He wore glasses and seemed kind of sickly and a little small for a teenager. The girl could not have been more different; Irmgard Salomon was from a middle-class family in Stuttgart, Germany; despite being only eleven, she was taller than either of them by a clear two inches.[2] Drawn together by their isolation in this train of families and old people, the three formed a bond as the train carried them farther and farther from their homes and mothers—hundreds, then thousands of kilometers slipping by.

אמא

Apartment 16 had become a hollow shell. Where there had been family, now there were just two women: one aging, one just blooming. Tini was forty-seven years old—an age when she should have been looking forward to a future filled with grandchildren. And Herta, two months away from her nineteenth birthday, should have been settled in her occupation and considering which of her admirers she might marry, and where in Vienna they might choose to live. They should not have been sitting here alone with each other, trapped in this desolate apartment, with their few possessions robbed from them and their dear ones—husband, father, sons, brothers, sister, daughter—stolen or fled.

Vienna was a place of forbidden zones with all the opportunities of life withdrawn, and the apartment, which they were fortunate to have kept at all, was a prison.

Saying good-bye to Kurt had been a pain beyond pain. He was so small, so slight, such a sliver of humanity to be sent out into the world through the press of people crowding the station. Tini and Herta had not been able to accompany him to the train—only people with travel permits were allowed on the platforms—and they had had to say their farewells outside and watch from a distance as the crowd of refugees swept him away.[3]

Flesh of her flesh, blood of her blood, soul of her soul, gone from her. Her children were all leaving her. Kurt was her hope; not yet formed, he would have a new beginning in an altogether new world. Perhaps he would return one day, and she would see a new person in his place, shaped by a life that was wholly strange to her.

בן

Kurt lay on his back and gazed up at the stars. He had never in his life seen them like this—a skyscape deeper, blacker, more brilliant than any other on Earth; a vault unadulterated by street lights and houselights. The ship, rolling steadily beneath him, was in blackout, and there were no other visible presences anywhere on the vast disc of starlit black ocean surrounding it.

He felt like the last survivor of a great exodus. After the train arrived in Lisbon, he and Karl and Irmgard—all of whom had acquired their travel papers and tickets with plenty of time to spare before the voyage—had been kept waiting for weeks. There were supposed to be thirty-eight other Jewish children joining them for the voyage to America, and they were all intended to sail in one group. Kurt and his two friends were put in the care of a young woman. Although her name did not remain in Kurt's memory, the impression of her did; an image of prettiness. He developed a crush on her, and people teased him about it—how could an eleven-year-old boy take a fancy to a grown woman? He retorted that in Vienna you grew up fast, and any eleven-year-old Viennese would know how to respond to a pretty lady.

When the time had come to sail, it was apparent that the thirty-eight other children weren't going to make it. Somehow they'd been trapped in the bureaucratic tangle of emigration. So at three in the afternoon of Monday, March 17, Kurt, Karl, and Irmgard were taken to the dock with just one another for company. There was their ship, tall as an office block, fixed to the dockside with great ropes and gangways.

SS *Siboney* wasn't the largest passenger liner afloat, but she had a certain elegance: two slender funnels and upper decks lined with covered promenades like arcades. Along the hull, partly hidden by the dock and the gangways, were identification markings to protect her from German U-boats: AMERI-CAN - EXPORT - LINES in giant white letters, flanked by Stars and Stripes the size of buses.

Kurt handed his papers to the officer at the foot of the gangway and went aboard. There were many familiar faces from the train journey among the passengers; by far the majority of people aboard appeared to be refugees, with a few returning tourists and commercial travelers among them. Kurt and Karl went in search of their cabin, following directions along a maze of corridors and down flight after flight of steps. Eventually they found it, right down in the depths of the ship, where it was unpleasantly stuffy and the engines could be heard throbbing loudly. There was a bunk bed; Kurt claimed the top bunk while Karl had the bottom. Having staked out their turf and disposed of their luggage, the two boys left the cabin and rarely went back to it.

Along with most of the other passengers, they watched from the rail as *Siboney* pulled away from the dock and, with engines thundering, turned her bow westward. The port rotated around them, then receded, Lisbon shrank to a smear, then Portugal to a sliver, then all of Europe dwindled and sank beneath the horizon.

Kurt remained on deck for three hours after sailing, looking out across the expanse of the ocean. Out of sight, beyond the northern horizon, convoy after convoy of merchant ships dragged slowly eastward toward Britain with Royal Navy escorts circling like nervous herdsmen; in the east, German U-boats slid out from their pens and cruised the vast ocean with torpedoes couched in their tubes. All *Siboney* had for protection was the set of painted markings on the sides. Kurt descended to his cabin that night tired and replete with new sensations.

That first night was unpleasant in the noisy, overheated cabin, and the next day was marred by seasickness (all Kurt could keep down was fruit). Reluctant to spend another night in the cabin, after dark Kurt and Karl took their blankets and sneaked up on deck. There was nobody to stop them; Nurse Sneble, a compact middle-aged woman from New York, was supposed to look after the children, but she was so busy with the elderly passengers she scarcely had time to cast a glance at them.

It was chilly in the night air, but wrapped up and reclining in deck chairs, the two boys were warm enough. They luxuriated in the quiet and the fresh air. Kurt watched the stars overhead and wondered at this new situation and the place he was going to. He knew a tiny smattering of English from school; under Nazi rule, English had been on the school curriculum, even in the Jewish charity schools. But Kurt hadn't picked up much; he could say *hello, yes* and *no*, and *OK*, but that was about all. His class had learned the rhyme "Pat-a-cake, pat-a-cake, baker's man" by rote, but in Kurt's mind the words had little meaning. To his ears, the *Siboney*'s American crew and passengers just spoke gibberish.

Somewhere back there, beyond the horizon where the eastern starfield met the black line of the ocean, were his home and family. He no longer had the harmonica his mother had given him. The train had stopped somewhere in France, and while he and the other kids were waiting to change trains, some German soldiers had stopped and spoken with them, and played with them a little. Kurt had shown them the harmonica. They took it and wouldn't give it back. When he boarded the train again, he left behind his last link with his mother and home.

בן

A cloud lay over Europe, roiling black and flickering with lightning. Somewhere in mid-Atlantic, *Siboney* steamed out from under it and into a bright American dawn.

Kurt and Karl, asleep on their deck chairs, were woken by a dash of cold spray. Jumping up, they realized that it wasn't sea spray but a splash from the mop of a sailor swabbing the deck. Gathering their blankets, they retreated indoors.

Somehow Nurse Sneble found out about their night al fresco, and her gaze finally fell on the two boys. They were reprimanded and ordered to sleep in their cabin from now on. Cowed, they obeyed, but together with Irmgard they continued to have the run of the ship all day long, exploring, playing games, making friends with the sailors. This rich environment of new experiences helped to distract them from thoughts about what they had left behind and the uncertainty of where they were going.

Day by day the weather grew warmer as *Siboney* steered a southwesterly course. The days passed with island-spotting, lifeboat drills, watching sharks cruise by the ship. It was an idyll that seemed set to last forever. On the eighth day they reached Bermuda, where some of the passengers disembarked. It was announced over the ship's loudspeakers that in two days they would reach New York. *Siboney* turned her bow northwest and left the warm tropics behind. Kurt sensed a changed atmosphere aboard; the cruise was done, and people were preparing for the most momentous arrival of their lives.

Around noon on Thursday, March 27, 1941, with every man, woman, and child lining the rails, *Siboney* passed between Staten Island and Long Island and steamed into the Upper Bay. Kurt pressed between the others to watch the gray waters and distant shores slip by. Then he saw it, off the port bow, the glittering outline of the Statue of Liberty growing and growing from a little spike until she towered above the ship, pale green and magnificent. *Siboney* steered into the Hudson, past the skyscraper skyline of Manhattan. Around Kurt, children and adults exclaimed and pointed as they picked out the sights, talking excitedly, wreathed in smiles. Many children had been given little American flags, and they held them up, fluttering in the wind, tiny, fragile offerings of hope.

בן

Seventh Avenue was a cascade of noise and color. Canary-yellow taxicabs with flared black wings stuttered at the curbs and barked their way angrily into the streaming, halting, screaming traffic of automobiles and buses, disputing the Forty-Second Street intersection with bell-ringing trams. Broadway and Times Square were like the innards of a racing engine with the throttle wide open. Kurt's senses were drowning. He clutched the hand of the lady from the aid society like a lifebelt as they waded through the dense sidewalk traffic of skirts and overcoats, swinging umbrellas and canes, bobbing hats, flapping newspapers and flying cigarette ash, all flashing past his face too rapidly to register.

He had been in New York for one day, and it wasn't enough to even begin getting used to it. Kurt was a city boy to his bones, but this was nothing like Vienna. The old place had its feet in the twentieth century but its heart had never caught up. New York was a city of modernity from foundations to sky, a town built out of automobiles and gasoline and glass and concrete and people and people and people and still more people who themselves seemed more of the modern world than any in Europe. Kurt and his friends were aliens in every way.

When *Siboney* had docked at the pier, Kurt, Karl, and Irmgard had been released from its charge with their papers stamped. There was a medical inspection, during which they were prodded and scrutinized and tested. Kurt had been fine, the doctor noting only that his eyes were mismatched: one brown, one hazel. But Karl gave cause for concern; the doctor frowned and wrote on the form that he suspected pituitary disease, as well as defective vision.[4] After going through customs, they had been met by a lady from the Hebrew Immigrant Aid Society, which partnered with the German Jewish Children's Aid in helping refugees. She took them to a hotel.

There was a lot to arrange for all of them. They were immigrating to the United States, not merely for the duration, and they needed to be settled. Of the three, only Kurt had definite arrangements in place. Karl and Irmgard had no friends or relatives in America; their only point of contact was the Children's Aid, which had arranged places for Irmgard here in New York and for Karl in distant Chicago. After a night in the hotel the time came for them to part. Kurt would never see either of his friends again.[5]

The bell rang and "Sixth and West Thirty-Fourth Street!" yelled the conductor as the bus jolted to a halt. The aid society lady took Kurt's hand, and they joined the knot of people spilling from the bus onto the sidewalk and into another maelstrom of traffic and indifferent, noisy humanity. Kurt looked upward. And there it was—the mythic epicenter of New York's ultramodernity, climbing up and up, impossibly, inhumanly high: the Empire State Building. Kurt, humanly tiny and insignificant, gazed up at it in wonder. Of all the sights he saw in New York, the visit to the Empire State Building left the clearest impression. Then there was another bus, heading for Pennsylvania Station and an unmissable appointment with the eastbound train.

דוד

The strange place names ticked by, stop by stop, meaningless to Kurt's Austrian eyes but replete with the culture of a previous wave of religious immigrants who yearned for their home towns in England: Greenwich, Stamford, Old Lyme, New London, Warwick. The train had left New York behind, tracing the coast right through Connecticut and all the way to Providence, Rhode Island. There the main line ended.

When Kurt disembarked, accompanied by the lady from the aid society and the suitcase that had traveled with him all the way from Im Werd, they were met by a woman Kurt had never seen before. She was about his mother's age, but more expensively dressed. To his surprise, she greeted him familiarly in German. This was Mrs. Maurer, his mother's old friend from Vienna. Waiting with her on the platform was a middle-aged man accompanied by a woman, both regarding him with reserved benevolence. In respectful tones, Mrs. Maurer introduced the gentleman as Kurt's sponsor, Judge Samuel Barnet.

Judge Barnet was around fifty years old—almost exactly the same age, in fact, as Kurt's father, but in every other respect as different as New York from Vienna. Samuel Barnet was rather short and stocky, with gray, receding hair, a large, fleshy nose, and thick, bushy eyebrows beneath which were set a pair of deceptively sleepy-looking eyes.[6] At first sight, he had a rather grave demeanor, even a little frosty. The lady with him, who wasn't much taller than Kurt himself, was the judge's sister, Kate; she was small, neat, and stolidly built like her brother.

Mrs. Maurer, who had taken responsibility for housing Kurt, explained that he wouldn't be staying with her. She and her husband, George, who was a cotton mill inspector, weren't very well off and rented a small apartment in a town house;[7] instead, she had arranged accommodation with Judge Barnet himself. It didn't seem to make much sense that he be housed with a stranger rather than with the only person in this new world of Kurt's who actually knew Vienna, was friends with his mother, and spoke German. But much of this passed right over Kurt's uncomprehending head.

Leaving the aid society lady to head back to New York, they climbed into the Barnets' automobile. From Providence they drove into Massachusetts, crossing a seemingly endless succession of rivers, bays, and inlets. Eventually they reached their destination: New Bedford, a large town on the bank of the Acushnet River estuary. This southeast corner of the state was a dense little patch of immigrant England whose traces were visible on almost every road sign for miles around, from here to Boston by way of Rochester, Taunton, Norfolk, and Braintree.

It was all meaningless to Kurt, and New Bedford was even less like Vienna than New York had been—a town of river ferries and broad streets, small, genteel public buildings, cotton mills, and long, straight avenues of suburban homes of gray shingle and white clapboard, where automobiles hummed, children played, and sober citizens went about their business with decorum.

Judge Barnet's house was on Rotch Street, one of a grid of quiet, leafy suburban avenues between Buttonwood Park Zoo and the center of town. As a Special Justice of the District Court of New Bedford and a pillar and keystone in the town—especially its Jewish community—Samuel Barnet might well be expected to be of titanic proportions, intimidating and mighty, living in an imposing mansion on the edge of town; instead, the car turned in at the driveway of a regular clapboard home standing shoulder-to-shoulder with others almost but not quite identical to it.

Kurt's reception into Judge Barnet's home was warm but, in keeping with the man's demeanor, reserved. Communication was near-impossible. *Yes* and *no* weren't really sufficient, and "Pat-a-cake, baker's man" would be of no use at all in this situation. Once Mrs. Maurer had left, an invisible barrier settled between them—a barrier which the judge was determined to break down without delay. Fortunately, he wasn't alone in this endeavor.

Samuel Barnet had been a widower for more than two decades, his wife, Mollie, having died in the 1919 influenza epidemic when she was only nineteen years old. They'd been married in 1915 when she was sixteen and he was a young and ambitious attorney.[8] They had no children, and Samuel had never remarried. But his house was neither a widower's mausoleum nor a bachelor's den; with him lived his three sisters, aged between thirty-eight and forty-three, and like their brother all resolutely unmarried.

The sisters were Kate, Esther, and Sarah, and they had already appointed themselves aunts to the new arrival. Sarah, the youngest, had trained as a dental hygienist but hadn't had work for several years. Esther, bespectacled and lean and a little flustered-looking, taught chemistry at the City High School. And Kate, the eldest, who had come to the station at Providence, had a matronly air; she kept house and worked for Samuel as a clerk in his office downtown.[9] There was a fourth sister, Goldie, who was married and lived in Brockton.

They welcomed the bewildered Kurt and showed him where he would sleep. His arrival had been long-expected, and a bedroom had been prepared for him on the first floor. Exhausted, he slept his second night on American soil in his own bed in—for the first time in his life—his very own room.

The next morning he woke to find a strange presence in his room. A tiny boy aged about three, dressed in a little camelhair coat, was standing at his bedside, gazing at him in wonder. He opened his mouth and spoke—and out poured a stream of the same incomprehensible English gibberish that Kurt had been hearing since boarding ship at Lisbon. The tiny boy seemed to want or expect something, but Kurt had no idea what it was. The boy's face fell in disappointment, and he burst into tears.

He turned to an adult standing behind him, and wailed, "Kurt won't talk to me!"

The little boy, Kurt learned, was a member of the family. His name was David, the son of Judge Barnet's younger brother, Philip, who lived right next door with his much younger wife, Roberta, and their two children. Together they made up one large, extended household.

As they grew accustomed to one another, Kurt was assimilated into the household and the family—much more rapidly than could ever have been expected. Judge Barnet—or Uncle Sam as Kurt quickly learned to call him—belied his somber appearance and proved as warmly welcoming as any guest could wish, and Kurt would never be allowed to feel out of place.

The family were Conservative Jews,* a concept unfamiliar to Kurt. All he had known were his family's lightweight religious observances—in which synagogue and Torah played little role—and the strictly Orthodox who were common around Leopoldstadt. Conservatives—who were not necessarily politically conservative—were somewhere in between; they believed in preserving ancient Jewish traditions, rituals, and laws, but departed from the Orthodox in recognizing that human hands had played a part in creating the Torah and that Judaic law had evolved to meet human needs. So they were both conservative and progressive. Also unlike the Orthodox, they didn't follow any traditional dress code. As Kurt got to know New Bedford, he would discover that the Barnets were leading lights in a large and active Jewish community, within which he was welcomed as readily as he had been in the Barnet household.

Spring came to New Bedford along with Kurt, and the trees lining Rotch Street turned green. If you squinted along it, you could almost imagine that you were in the Hauptallee in the Prater, and that none of this had happened—the Nazis coming, the family split and sundered. As strange as this place was, Kurt could already sense that, but for the lack of his mother and father, and of Fritz and Herta and Edith, and the thousands upon thousands of kilometers that lay behind him, he had found something that felt like a home.

---

* Conservative Judaism is known outside America as Masorti Judaism

8 | Unworthy of Life

אה

NOBODY EVER REALLY KNEW the reason for Philipp Hamber's death, but everyone heard about the circumstances in which it was done. The camp SS required no reasons for their brutalities; a bad mood, drunkenness, a hangover, a perceived slight, a prisoner looking askance at a guard, or just a sadistic impulse— these were enough. When SS-Sergeant Abraham knocked Philipp Hamber to the ground and killed him, nobody took note of the cause because there was none; but they remembered the atrocity itself vividly, and its terrible repercussions.[1]

Like Gustav Kleinmann, Philipp Hamber was a Viennese Jew and worked in the haulage column, but he was in a different team under a kapo called Schwarz. They had made a delivery to the site where the camp's economic affairs building was under construction.[2] SS-Sergeant Abraham happened to be on-site. He was one of the cruelest, most feared Blockführers in Buchenwald. Something—some misdirected glance from Philipp, a mistake, perhaps a dropped sack of cement, or just something about the way he looked or moved—drew Abraham's attention. He singled Philipp out, shoved him, knocked him to the ground, and kicked him. In a sadistic fury, he dragged the helpless prisoner through the churned mud of the building site and heaved him into a foundation trench full of rainwater. As Philipp floundered and choked, Sergeant Abraham planted a boot on the back of his head and held him beneath the surface. Philipp's struggling gradually subsided, and his body went limp.

News of the drowning of Philipp Hamber spread through Buchenwald. The prisoners were used to murder as a constant presence in their everyday lives, but whereas they had learned to live in spite of it and to avoid it as best they could, now they were becoming resentful.

"Again there is unrest in the camp," Gustav wrote. He hardly ever took his diary from its hiding place these days. During the past nine months he had scarcely filled two of the notebook's little pages. His last entry had been in January 1941, when they were moving snow. Now it was spring. In the intervening months the prisoners' submission to SS oppression had been tested more severely than ever.

At the end of February, a transport of several hundred Dutch Jews had arrived. Since falling to German invasion the previous year, the Netherlands had been ruled by Arthur Seyss-Inquart—the Austrian Nazi who had helped facilitate the Anschluss in 1938. The large Jewish population had been confined to their own districts and expelled from certain professions but were otherwise not persecuted by the German occupiers to the same degree as in Germany, Austria, and Poland. The homegrown Dutch Nazis were not content with this situation; they persistently harassed the Jews, who sometimes responded violently. In February 1941 violent clashes took place in Amsterdam in which the Nazis suffered a severe beating at the hands of young Jewish men. A German police officer was killed. The SS rounded up four hundred Jewish men as hostages, a move which triggered a wave of strikes by communist trade unions, paralyzing the docks and transport system. Open warfare erupted between the strikers and the SS, and at the end of the month, 389 of the Jewish hostages were transported to Buchenwald.[3]

They were all fit, spirited men, many of them dock workers, and had already proven themselves unwilling to submit to abuse. A few were housed in block 17, where Fritz lived with the Austrian *Prominenten*, but most were put in block 16, where Gustl Herzog was now block senior (and where Richard Paltenhoffer had once been confined). Fritz spent a lot of time with the Dutchmen, many of whom spoke German. They were astonished to find so many Austrians in the camp; they had come to associate the Austrian accent with the Nazi forces occupying their country, and strangely it hadn't occurred to them that there were Austrian Jews.

Fritz and the others taught the Dutchmen the ways of the camp, but it did them little good. They weren't easily cowed, and the SS treated them with an unprecedented level of brutality. All were put to work as stone-carriers in the quarry, and in the first couple months around fifty were murdered. Many fell sick or suffered injuries and were barred from medical treatment. Gustl Herzog did what he could to help; when the SS doctors had left the building, he and a couple other functionaries smuggled sick and injured Dutchmen into the prisoner infirmary. Pneumonia and diarrhea were rife, and some of them had festering wounds, but the SS, determined to grind them down to dust, still forced them to work.

Gustl Herzog wasn't the only prisoner who helped them; the political prisoners did everything they could for their fellow socialists. By spring, the SS had decided that under these circumstances the Dutch could not be broken quickly enough, and so in May all the survivors were transferred to Mauthausen concentration camp in Austria. None ever returned.

Gustav had recorded none of this in his diary, but the murder of Philipp Hamber—which occurred in the atmosphere of resistance generated by the treatment of the Dutch—prompted him to bring it out of hiding to set down how Philipp had been "drowned like a cat" and that the prisoners were not taking it quietly. There was unease and resentment, and much of it came from one man: Philipp's brother, Eduard, who also worked in the haulage column and had witnessed the murder.[4] They were unusually close. Both had been movie producers in Vienna before the Anschluss, and Eduard was politically active in the Social Democratic party, hence they had been arrested soon after the Nazi takeover. Eduard wanted justice for his brother.

Unfortunately for the SS, the murder—having occurred on a large construction site outside the main camp fences—had been witnessed by a civilian visitor, and Commandant Koch had no option but to enter the death in the camp log and hold an inquiry. At the same time, Eduard Hamber lodged an official complaint with Koch's deputy. He knew the danger he was putting himself in. "I know that I must die for my testimony," he told a fellow prisoner, "but maybe these criminals will restrain themselves a little in the future if they have to fear an accusation. Then I will not have died in vain."[5]

At the next roll call, all the members of kapo Schwarz's haulage detail were called to the gatehouse. Their names were taken, and they were asked what they had seen. They all denied having seen anything. Only Eduard persisted in his accusation. They were all sent back to their blocks. Eduard was interrogated again by several officers, including Commandant Koch and the camp doctor. Koch assured him, "We want to know the whole truth. I give you my word of honor that nothing will happen to you."[6] Eduard repeated his account of how Abraham had beaten his brother and deliberately, brutally drowned him.

They let him go back to his block, but late that night he was called out again and was placed in a cell in the Bunker—the cell block that occupied one wing of the gatehouse. The Bunker had an evil reputation; tortures and murders were known to be perpetrated in there, and no Jew who entered it ever came out alive. Its principal jailer was SS-Sergeant Martin Sommer, whose boyish looks belied years of experience in concentration camps and a hideous cruelty. All the prisoners knew Sommer well from his regular performances wielding the whip when victims were taken to the Bock, besides his reputation as the Bunker's chief torturer. After four days, Eduard Hamber's corpse was brought out for disposal. Sommer claimed that he had committed suicide, but everyone knew that Sommer had beaten him to death.[7]

This wasn't enough to satisfy the SS. At intervals over the following weeks, three or four of the witnesses from the Schwarz detail would be named at roll call and brought to the Bunker. There they were interrogated by Deputy Commandant Rödl (the music lover) and the new camp physician, SS-Doctor Hanns Eisele. A virulent anti-Semite, Eisele was known to the prisoners as the *Spritzendoktor* (Injection Doctor) because of his willingness to dish out lethal injections to sick or troublesome Jews. He was also known by the nickname *Weisser Tod*—White Death.[8] He used randomly selected prisoners for vivisection for his own personal edification, administering experimental injections and unnecessary surgery—including amputations—and then murdering the victims.[9] He would be remembered as perhaps the most evil doctor ever to practice at Buchenwald. As with Eduard Hamber, the prisoners were told by Koch and Eisele that they had nothing to fear if they told the truth; again they denied that they had seen anything. Their silence didn't save them; they were murdered to the last man.

"Three or four of the thirty men are brought daily to the Bunker," Gustav wrote in his diary, "and taken care of by Sergeant Sommer: even Lulu, a foreman* from Berlin, and (so kapo Schwarz believes) Kluger and Trommelschläger from Vienna are among the victims. Thus our rebellion shrivels up."[10]

---

* A semi-unofficial designation beneath kapo in rank

Eduard Hamber's heroic sacrifice had been fruitless, based on the idea that the SS could be brought to account for their crimes, or at least be made to fear that they might. They were immune and their power was limitless.

אבא

Summer returned to the Ettersberg, and more besides. "Fritzl and I are now receiving money regularly from home," Gustav wrote. Somehow or other, Tini was managing to scrape together whatever she could from charity or work, knowing that it would make their lives in the camp a tiny bit more comfortable. She also sent occasional packages of clothing—shirts, underpants, a sweater— which were invaluable. Whenever something arrived for them, Gustav or Fritz would be called to the office to collect and sign for the items; usually the package would be opened and the contents itemized on their record cards.[11]

Gustav's love for his son had grown to fill his whole heart during their time in Buchenwald, as had his pride in the man he was becoming—this June he would turn eighteen. "The boy is my greatest joy," he wrote. "We strengthen each other. We are one, inseparable."[12]

On Sunday, June 22, the camp loudspeakers announced momentous news. That morning, the Führer had launched an invasion of the Soviet Union. With three million troops, Operation Barbarossa was the biggest military action in history, with a front spanning the whole of Russia, north to south, intended to engulf it in one huge wave. The war had entered a new phase. Before the summer was out, Buchenwald would come to feel the change.

אמא

Tini sat at the table where her family had once eaten together.

"My beloved Kurtl," she wrote. "I am extremely happy that you are doing fine and you are well. I am really curious to hear about your summer vacation. Actually, I almost envy you; one cannot go anywhere anymore here . . . For that reason, I would be so glad if I could be with you now. Here, we cannot enjoy ourselves anymore . . ."[13]

It was true. Existing restrictions on Jews had been tightened in May 1941 with the issue of a declaration reinforcing long-standing laws: Jews were forbidden to visit all theaters, concerts, museums, libraries, pleasure parks, sports grounds, and restaurants; they were barred from entering shops or buying goods outside certain specified times. Some rules were expanded: whereas previously Jews had been barred from sitting on designated public benches, now they were forbidden to enter public parks at all. The declaration also introduced some new and deeply sinister rules: Jews were not allowed to leave Vienna without special permission, were barred from making inquiries to high government offices, and the spreading of rumors about resettlement and emigration was strictly forbidden.[14]

Everything was conspiring to keep the Jews in Europe. Not long after Kurt's departure, Portugal had implemented a temporary ban on transmigrants, due to a bottleneck at Lisbon, and in June President Roosevelt, pandering again to the xenophobes, banned the transfer of funds from the United States to European countries, hamstringing the refugee aid agencies.[15] Liberal organizations lobbied for the rights of Jewish refugees and *New Republic* magazine accused the State Department of caving in to bigotry, calling the refugee effort "a football for anti-Semitism." Roosevelt and the State Department were victims of a "clever German strategy" to spread Nazi propaganda in democratic nations "where the seeds of anti-Semitism and anti-liberalism are already sprouting."[16] They had been germinating since the early 1930s through what Elmer Holland, Democratic congressman from Pennsylvania, called the "Vermin Press"—papers like the *New York Herald Tribune*, which called for "a fascist party to be born in the United States." There were accusations of undue Jewish influence in Washington from the *Chicago Tribune*, the *Washington Times-Herald*, and the *New York Daily News*, along with apologetics on behalf of Hitler.[17] And—as in Britain—there was a rising panic over a mythic immigrant fifth column. Suspected fifth columnists were threatened and even murdered; the finger was pointed at the Jehovah's Witnesses for refusing to salute the flag; vigilante groups formed; and even Jewish child refugees were labeled by some as potential spies. Even before the nation joined in the war, the FBI was receiving up to twenty-eight hundred reports from the public every single day about alleged spies.[18]

Accordingly, the inflow of refugees was squeezed tight until it became barely a trickle. By June 1941, there were 44,000 Jews still in Vienna, only 429 having been able to emigrate to the United States so far that year.[19] In July, US immigration regulations were altered, making existing affidavits invalid.[20] Escape became all but impossible, especially with the meager sums of money

Tini could scrape together. She'd had a brief stint working in a grocery store but had been fired because as a Jew she was not a citizen.

But still Tini went on trying. It wore her down; some days the depression weighed so heavily on her soul that she couldn't drag herself out of bed. During the past two months, news had come to the neighboring Orthodox families of Friedmann, Heller, and Hermann that their menfolk had died in Buchenwald. They had been persecuted by Blank and Hinkelmann to the point that they committed suicide by running through the sentry line. All the time Tini expected to hear similar news about Gustav or Fritz, knowing the kind of grueling labor her husband was being made to do. "He is not a young man anymore," she wrote. "How can he bear that?"[21] Every time a letter from them was delayed, it sent her into a panic. So she persevered and fought on, refusing to give up hope of at least getting Herta to safety.

"Life is getting sadder by the day," she wrote to Kurt. "But you are our sunshine and our child of fortune, so please do write often and in detail . . . Please give my regards to your aunts and Uncle Barnet. Millions of kisses from your sister Herta, who is always thinking of you."[22]

בֶּן דּוֹד

That first summer was all about absorbing the new world.

Judge Barnet and his sisters hadn't wasted any time in putting Kurt to school, despite his speaking no English. Rather than waiting for September, the judge used his influence to have him enrolled right away in the local grammar school. Although he was eleven, they put him in second grade; after two weeks he was bumped up to third grade, then the fourth. Kurt picked up English quickly, thanks in large part to Ruthie, the Barnets' niece, who came to live with them that summer.

Having his own room hadn't lasted long; soon after Kurt's arrival, Ruthie moved in. She was from Brockton, near Boston, where her father had a hardware store; she'd graduated college and taken a job as a teacher at Fairhaven, across the estuary from New Bedford. Sam Barnet gave her Kurt's room, and Kurt moved in with Uncle Sam. This was more like back in the old apartment, when the whole family had shared a room. Each day Kurt would come home from school and Ruthie tutored him in English. She was a good teacher, kind and good-natured, and Kurt grew to adore her; in time she would become a surrogate sister to him. Cousin David next door would become a little brother, their relationship echoing Kurt's bond with Fritz.

In those first months, the presence of a Viennese refugee boy in the Barnet household caused a stir in New Bedford society. Kurt was photographed for the newspaper sitting on Sarah Barnet's knee, with David and his baby sister, Rebecca, alongside; he was interviewed for the radio, and when he graduated fourth grade in June, the teacher placed him front and center in the class photograph. It seemed like Kurt could hardly move without having his picture in the paper.

The Jewish community of southeast Massachusetts was a warm, welcoming place for him, insulated from the colder, darker places into which some of his fellow refugees were sent. In later years, Kurt would be surprised and dismayed to learn of other children placed with uncaring, neglectful families or in neighborhoods where their German accents or Jewishness brought hostility. Judge Barnet and his huge extended family seemed to know everyone and everything, and they were all eager to make Kurt feel right at home. He spent weekends with Ruthie's parents, Abe and Goldie, in Brockton and at their summer home on the coast. Abe's hardware store was a wonderland, and Abe an amiable soul. Later on, after the United States joined the war, Uncle Sam played an active role in the war effort, recruiting Kurt as a mascot to help sell war bonds.

That first summer of 1941, when he was still finding his feet, Kurt went away to camp. Avoda was a camp for Jewish boys, founded in 1927 by Sam and Phil Barnet through the Young Men's Hebrew Association. It ran on an ethos of taking boys from deprived urban environments and giving them a grounding in traditional Jewish family and social values. But in every other respect Camp Avoda was a typical boys' summer camp, set among the trees on the shore of Tispaquin Pond, near Middleborough, halfway between New Bedford and Boston. It was a simple environment: a group of utilitarian dorm huts surrounding a baseball field. Kurt had the time of his life, playing sports and swimming in the warm, shallow waters of the lake. In Vienna he had floundered in the Danube Canal with a rope tied around his waist and a friend on the bank holding the other end; here he learned to swim properly. Had Fritz been able to see this place, he might have been reminded of the paradise of the camp in Makarenko's *Road to Life*.

Normally Kurt didn't like to write letters, but now he wrote profusely to his mother, telling her all about this wonderful new world he had found.

Tini was heartened to hear that at least two of her children were now safe. But she couldn't shed her anxiety that something would go wrong, that somehow Kurt's idyll would be destroyed. "Please be obedient," she wrote back, "be a joy for your uncle, so that the counselors have good things to say about you . . . Darling, please be well-behaved." A photograph he sent her with the other Barnet children filled her with pleasure: "You look so nice . . . so handsome and radiant. I almost didn't recognize you."[23]

Kurt was losing his old life in the brightness of the new. Looking back on this later, he might have hardly recognized himself.

אבא

"Every day the roar of the radio," Gustav wrote despairingly. The camp loudspeakers, which had always been an intermittent source of unwelcome noise—regularly blaring out Nazi propaganda, German martial music, terrifying commands, and morale-grinding announcements—were now set to an almost constant stream of Berlin radio, crowing with triumphal news from the Eastern Front. The glorious crushing of Bolshevik defenses by the might of German arms, the encirclement of this division or that corps, the seizing of city after city, the crossing of rivers, the triumph of some Waffen-SS division, the glory of a victorious Wehrmacht general, the surrender of hundreds of thousands of Soviet soldiers. Germany was devouring the lethargic Russian bear like a wolf disemboweling a sheep.

For the Jews under Nazi rule—especially those in the Polish ghettos—the news had been received as a glimmer of hope; Russia might win, after all, and liberate them from this miserable existence. But to the political prisoners in the concentration camps, most of whom were communists, the news was depressing and stirred up resentment. "The Politicals hang their heads," Gustav noted. The unrest that had been felt in the camp throughout the year—with the Dutch arrivals and over the Hamber murder—was stirring again, and there were disturbances in the labor details, incidents of disobedience, minor acts of resistance. The SS dealt with it in their usual way. "Each day the shot and slain are brought into the camp," wrote Gustav. Each day, more grist for the crematorium, more smoke from the chimney.

In July 1941, a new horror came to Buchenwald. It was supposed to be veiled in secrecy, but the veil was thin and full of holes. The previous September, the American journalist William L. Shirer, based in Germany, had reported a "weird story" told to him by an anonymous source who "says the Gestapo is now systematically bumping off the mentally deficient people of the Reich. The Nazis call them 'mercy deaths.'"[24] The program, codenamed T4, involved a number of specialized asylum facilities equipped with gas chambers, together with mobile gas vans that traveled from hospital to hospital, collecting and exterminating mentally handicapped and physically disabled patients—those deemed by the regime as "unworthy of life." The scheme had drawn some negative public attention, particularly from the church, and this, together with the demands of the war in the Soviet Union, had led to the T4 program being suspended. However, the Nazis did not terminate it altogether; instead, they began to experiment with using the techniques on concentration camp inmates, specifically those judged mentally or physically deficient. This new program, given the codename Action 14f13, was to focus particularly on disabled Jewish prisoners.[25]

Sometime in April or May 1941, Commandant Koch summoned his camp doctors and senior SS officers to a meeting, and informed them that a secret order had been received from Himmler: all "imbecile and crippled" inmates, especially Jews, were to be exterminated.[26]

The first the inmates of Buchenwald knew of Action 14f13 was in June, when a small team of doctors arrived in the camp to inspect the prisoners. "We got orders to present ourselves at the infirmary," Gustav Kleinmann wrote. "I smell a rat; I'm fit for work."[27] The doctors selected 187 prisoners, variously classed as mentally handicapped, blind, deaf-mute, and disabled, including some who had been injured by accidents or abuse in the camp. They were told that they would be going to a special recuperation camp, where they would be properly looked after, and in due course they would be allotted easy work in textile factories. The prisoners were suspicious, but many—especially those most in need of care—chose to believe the hopeful lies. A month later, on July 13 and 14, transports came to the camp and took away the 187 men. They were taken to an asylum at Sonnenstein and murdered. "One morning, their effects came back," wrote Gustav. The grim delivery included clothing, prosthetic limbs, and eyeglasses. "Now we know what game is being played: all of them gassed." They were the first of six transports of predominantly Jewish prisoners murdered under Action 14f13.

At the same time, Commandant Koch began an ancillary program: the elimination of prisoners carrying tuberculosis. SS-Doctor Hanns Eisele was in charge. It was for his part in this program that Eisele earned his sobriquets as the Injection Doctor and the White Death. In July, a few days before the first transports left for Sonnenstein, two transports arrived from Dachau carrying 2,008 transferred prisoners. Those identified as having tuberculosis—around five hundred, diagnosed on the basis of general appearance rather than a proper medical examination—were sent to the infirmary. There they were immediately killed by Dr. Eisele with lethal injections of the sedative hexobarbital.[28]

Within a handful of months, the character of Buchenwald had altered irrevocably, and with it what it meant to live as a prisoner. From now on, sickness or injury or anything that incapacitated a man was as good as a death sentence. Such things had always carried a severe risk of death here, but now it became a stone certainty that being rated unfit for work or "unworthy of life" was enough to put a man's name on a list to be exterminated.

And then the first Soviet prisoners of war arrived, and a door opened into a new department of hell.

In the Nazi mind, Jews and Bolsheviks were one and the same—Jews, they claimed, had created Bolshevism, had spread it and now ran it (along with the global capitalist conspiracy they were also, contradictorily, alleged to be running). It was true that many of the leading Bolshevik revolutionaries of 1917 had been Jews, and it was also true that the Soviet regime had liberated Russian Jews from the repression they had suffered under the tsars. But the hopeful dawn of the early revolution had turned to gloom under Lenin and Stalin, and the alleged connection between Jewishness and communism was just a fantasy in the minds of Nazi ideologues, a banal modern equivalent of the blood libel. But it was a mythology potent enough to inspire the invasion of the USSR and breed a campaign of murder across the conquered Soviet territories, with death squads following behind the army and slaughtering Jews in tens of thousands. Captured Red Army soldiers, meanwhile, hundreds of thousands of whom had been rounded up in the first weeks of the invasion, were regarded as subhuman—if not Jews, then the thralls of Jews: degenerate, dangerous Bolsheviks and Slavs who were not fit to live. At the same time, their own leader, Josef Stalin, was labeling them cowards and traitors; beset from all sides, Soviet prisoners of war were among the most wretched men on Earth.

Within this mass of the despised, some were more hated and feared by the Nazis than others—political commissars, fanatical communists, intellectuals, and Jews. These were singled out for immediate disposal. The task couldn't be accomplished in the POW camps because of the risk of spreading panic among the bulk of the prisoners; thus the SS decided to use the concentration camps. The program was codenamed Action 14f14.[29]

The first small group of fifteen Soviet POWs arrived in Buchenwald in September 1941 and were dispatched immediately.[30] During roll call, the Russians were marched off by SS-Sergeant Abraham and four other guards toward the eastern sector of the main camp. On the roll-call square, the other prisoners were ordered to give a loud, spirited rendition of the "Buchenwald Song." Their thousands of voices filled the camp. As they sang, from the corners of their eyes they glanced in the direction the Russians had been taken. That area was occupied by a small factory—the Deutsche Ausrüstungswerke (DAW), whose prisoner workforce manufactured military equipment for the Germany army. Behind the factory was an SS shooting range. Under cover of the singing, the Russians were lined up there and shot.

A couple of days later, another thirty-six Russians were brought to the camp, and again the prisoners at roll call had to sing to drown out the gunshots as the Russians were dispatched in the same way.

"They say they were commissars," Gustav wrote, "but we know everything . . . How we feel is not to be described—now shock is piled upon shock."

This method of execution was an improvisation; in the long term it would be far too inefficient. Therefore, while these small groups of Russians were being murdered on the shooting range, a new facility was being prepared. In the woods a little way off the road to the quarry, the SS had a riding hall. Its stable building was no longer required, and a team of carpenters from the construction detail was hard at work inside building interior walls, dividing the building into rooms. The facility was officially code-named Commando 99, a reference to the telephone number of the stables.[31]

The work was completed in mid-October, and a few days later a contingent of around two thousand Soviet POWs arrived from Stalag X-D, near Hamburg. Barrack blocks 1, 7, and 13, in the southwest corner of the main camp, were fenced off with barbed wire, forming a special camp for them. They had been brought in primarily as laborers; with around three million Russians now in captivity, they were both plentiful and, in the Nazis' eyes, eminently expendable.[32] But they also served to test the new facility.

Each day, the Russians selected for liquidation were taken in groups to Commando 99, where they were told they would undergo a medical inspection. They were greeted by blaring music from loudspeakers outside the building. Inside, they were shepherded into a reception room under SS guard. Men in white coats took them, one at a time, along a corridor to the far end of the building. There the prisoner passed through a series of small rooms filled with medical paraphernalia and staffed by more men in white coats. His teeth were examined, his heart and lungs listened to with a stethoscope, his eyesight tested. Finally, he was led into a room with a measuring scale marked on the wall. He was ordered to stand with his back against it to have his height measured. What was not apparent, unless the prisoner was exceptionally perceptive, was that the men in white coats were not doctors but disguised SS guards; also that there was a narrow slit in the wall at neck-height, obscured by the measuring scale. Behind it was a tiny cubicle in which stood an SS man armed with a pistol. While the prisoner was being measured, the white-coated attendant tapped on the partition, and the concealed guard shot the prisoner in the back of the neck.[33] The body was removed through the back door into a truck. Outside and in the waiting room, the loud music drowned out the sounds of the shots. While the next victim was being brought through, the previous man's blood was hosed off the floor of the measuring room.

Some of the Soviet victims were taken from the Russian enclosure within the main camp, but the majority were driven in from POW camps for the sole purpose of extermination. Despite the cloak of secrecy, the prisoners of Buchenwald knew perfectly well what was going on. The carpenters who converted the stable were prisoners, and the others saw the truckloads of Russians arriving daily. And even without this clear evidence, most were astute enough to guess the nature of the "adjustments" (as the SS officially called the executions) being carried out in the former stable.[34]

Before long, the SS ceased even attempting to be discreet about Action 14f14, especially when the camp crematorium became unable to cope with the number of corpses coming out of Commando 99—sometimes several hundred in a day. Mobile ovens had to be brought up from Weimar to cope with the overload. They were parked outside the crematorium, on the very edge of the roll-call square, incinerating the bodies right in front of the other prisoners.[35]

"In the meantime the shootings continue," Gustav recorded. The closed truck that carried the bodies from Commando 99 dribbled trails of blood along the road, all the way up the hill to the gate and across the square to the crematorium. After a while, the truck was fitted with a metal-lined container to prevent leakage and keep the camp tidy.

אחים

Surely one must finally lose one's ability to be appalled? It must get worn down like a stone with the passage of use, blunted like a tool, numbed like a limb. One's moral sense must scar and harden under an unending series of lacerations and concussions.

For some, perhaps that was so; for others, the opposite was true. Even some of the butchers of the SS could only withstand so much. The effect of murdering thousands of Soviet prisoners of war produced varied effects on the camp guards, who all had to take turns handling the victims in the execution room and wielding the pistol behind the killing slot. Continuous, orchestrated shootings, every single day—this was not the same as the sporadic, random murders they were accustomed to. Many of them reveled in it; they saw themselves as fighting soldiers, and these killings were their contribution to the war against Bolshevik Jewry. Others were shaken and even broken by it and tried to avoid duty in Commando 99; some fainted when faced with the carnage or suffered mental breakdowns after prolonged exposure; a few worried that if word got out, as it inevitably would, it could lead to retaliatory murders of captured German troops by the NKVD, the Soviet Gestapo.[36]

For the other prisoners, all of whom were witnesses to the open secret of Action 14f14 and some of whom were forced participants in the cleaning-up, the effect was corrosive and traumatic. And it was far from being the end. The new demon introduced to Buchenwald at the end of 1941 was of a different kind, and was once again perpetrated by the camp's medical officers. There was no limit to the depths to which the Nazis would go in thinking up new monstrosities. That same year, prisoners began to be subjected to lethal medical experiments designed to develop vaccines for German troops.

Everyone knew that something was afoot when they fenced off block 46—one of the two-story stone-built barracks that stood down the hill near the vegetable gardens. The block's inmates were moved to other barracks, and the building surrounded by a double cordon of barbed wire. It was hardly the first time such a thing had happened, usually indicating the arrival of some new contingent of prisoners. But this time there was no such intake.

After roll call one winter's day, the adjutant produced a list and stood surveying the massed ranks of prisoners before beginning to call out numbers. The hearts of Fritz, Gustav, and every man there beat a little faster; whenever the SS compiled a list, or singled out any prisoner, it was almost never for anything good, and nearly always for something dreadful. The drone of numbers went on and on, dozens of them, and each selected man turned pale as his was called.

It was doubly unnerving that among the SS officers stood SS-Major Dr. Erwin Ding,* a trim, nervous-looking little man who had served with the Waffen-SS (and wore his hat in the crumpled style of a fighting soldier). Ding had been camp physician and was known for his incompetence, but although he was unfit to be a doctor, his skills were adequate for the task now assigned to him.[37] The same could be said for his deputy, SS-Captain Waldemar Hoven; a remarkably handsome fellow, Hoven had spent a few years in Hollywood working as a movie extra before returning to Germany to work in his family's sanatorium. He was even more medically incompetent than Ding; still unqualified, Hoven had pressed two prisoners into service to write his doctoral dissertation for him. But he was very handy with a needle, and he killed many hundreds of prisoners with lethal injections of phenol.[38]

The prisoners whose numbers were called—a mixture of Jews, Roma, and Aryan political prisoners and green-triangle men—were ordered to the gate, and from there they were marched to block 46 and disappeared inside.

What happened within block 46 only became known through rumor when the surviving prisoners were let back out. The whole truth was not revealed until much later. Dr. Ding and Hoven injected the prisoners with unknown substances; the subjects immediately fell ill, some of them gravely. They suffered bloating, headaches, bleeding rashes, hearing loss, nosebleeds, muscle pains, paralysis, abdominal pains, vomiting . . . the list went on and on. Many died, and the survivors were left in a pitiable state. The substances with which they

---

* Later known as Schuler or Ding-Schuler

were injected were typhus serums that were being developed in collaboration between the SS, the IG Farben chemical corporation, and the Wehrmacht, with the aim of producing a vaccine for German troops serving in Eastern Europe, where typhus was endemic.[39]

At periodic intervals, more batches of prisoners were sent to block 46 to be ruined and killed in the pursuit of incompetent medical research. Eventually, the Typhus Research Station was extended, with block 50 closed off and repurposed as a Serum Institute.[40] In this, prisoners were injected with typhus bacilli with the intention of extracting a serum from their blood. Several old friends of Gustav's from Vienna—Otto Herschmann, Oskar Kurz, Hans Kurzweil, Ludwig "Max" Matzner—were among the prisoners selected for this new torment, but they were saved when a conference of SS top brass deemed it improper for Jewish blood to be used in the development of a vaccine that was to be injected into the veins of German soldiers. The very idea was outrageous, and the Jewish subjects were released from block 50.[41]

אם ובת

Tini and Herta sat opposite each other at the table in the kitchen, plying their needles and thread. Mending had always been a part of Tini's life; with little income and four children, there had always been socks to darn, torn pants to stitch, jackets and sweaters with elbows worn through. Now, their sewing kits were in nearly perpetual use; they had scarcely enough money to keep from starving, and what little surplus Tini had she sent to Gustav and Fritz, guessing that their need was more urgent. It was little enough; she'd been able to send them each a package of spare bits and pieces of underclothing in May, and she might be able to send them something in the next few weeks—perhaps a pair of socks or a pullover.[42] Month by month her own and Herta's clothes got shabbier and more threadbare, and their needles worked overtime to keep them in one piece.

Their sewing today was not mending, however. On September 1, 1941, it had been announced by the Ministry of the Interior in Berlin that as of the nineteenth of the month, all Jews living in Germany and Austria must wear a yellow Star of David on their clothes—the *Judenstern*.

The yellow mark for Jews was a medieval practice. The Nazis had revived it for use in Poland and the other occupied territories, where the Jews were perceived as even more degenerate and untrustworthy than those in Germany. During the invasion of the Soviet Union, it was claimed that German soldiers had met "the Jew in his most disgusting, most gruesome form," and that this had made the state realize that *all* Jews, including those at home, must be deprived of their ability to be camouflaged within society.[43]

Along with everyone else, Tini and Herta had had to go along to one of the collection points set up by the IKG to get their stars. They were manufactured in factories, printed onto rolls of fabric, with the word *Jude* printed in black lettering styled to resemble Hebrew.[44] Each person was allotted up to four. The final bitter insult was that they had to pay for them: 10 pfennigs each. The price was set in Berlin; the IKG bought them in huge rolls from the government for 5 pfennigs a star and used the profit to cover administrative costs.[45]

Tini had fought to the very end to get Herta away from this nightmare. The closure of the US consulate in Vienna meant that all applications had to be routed via Berlin, which added to the already excruciating bureaucratic obstructions. There were girls Herta's age and even younger being sent to concentration camps now. In desperation, Tini had written to Judge Barnet in America, begging for him to act on her behalf. "Regarding Herta, I am devastated that she has to stay here. I was informed by an unofficial source that relatives in the US can petition Washington to obtain a visa. May I ask you to do something for Herta? I do not want to have to reproach myself like in Fritz's case."[46] Sam Barnet acted right away, filing the necessary papers and putting up 450 dollars to cover all Herta's expenses,[47] but it had done no good. The maze was too complex and the barriers impossible to surmount. Herta's visa had not been approved.

Their needles plied in and out, through the cheap yellow calico of the stars and the worn wool of their coats. Tini glanced across at Herta; she was fully a young woman now—nineteen, going on twenty, about the age Edith had been when she went away. Nineteen and pretty as a picture. Imagine how beautiful she could have been if there were nice clothes for her and there hadn't been this life of constant containment and deprivation. When Herta looked at her mother, she saw lines etched by worry and cheeks sinking below the bones from hunger.

The appearance of the Judenstern in Vienna over the following days and weeks produced varying reactions among non-Jews. They had grown so used to the idea that the Jews had largely disappeared from the country—vast numbers had emigrated, and the supposedly dangerous ones had been sent to the camps—that to the less perceptive Viennese it was as if thousands of Jews now suddenly materialized in their midst, clearly marked for all to see. Some people were ashamed of what the state had done; they believed that it was right and proper to send Jews away and bar them from public life, but to stigmatize them in this highly visible way was wrong somehow. Shopkeepers who had been willing to sell to Jews were faced with the embarrassment of having their other customers know that they did so. Some braved it out; others began to shut their doors to wearers of the yellow star. And for those Jews who had been willing—and sufficiently Aryan-looking—to ignore some of the restrictions about where one could go and what one could do, that was now out of the question. The Gestapo, conversely, was delighted by the measure, which enabled the thorough enforcement of racial laws. Some members of the public, shocked to find so many Jews still about, began to demand that harsh action be taken.[48] It seemed that life could not possibly get any worse.

But of course it could; the bottom of the pit had not yet been reached, not by any means. On October 23, 1941, the head of the Gestapo in Berlin relayed an order from Heinrich Himmler to all Reich security police: with immediate effect, all emigration of Jews from the Reich was banned.[49] From this moment on, removal of Reich Jews would be solely by resettlement to the eastern territories, where several large ghettos had been established in cities such as Warsaw, Łódź, and Minsk. Deportations from Vienna to the east had been going on sporadically since the beginning of the year; from now on, they would apply to all Jews. Tini's only hope, to which she had dedicated so much time, hard work, and motherly love—of sending Herta to join Kurt in America—was snuffed out in an instant with the stroke of a bureaucrat's pen.

In December America joined the war against Germany, and the final barrier fell.

9 | A Thousand Kisses

אבא

SPRING HAD COME TO Buchenwald again. The forest was alive with greenery, the singing of blackbirds in the warm mornings a counterpoint to the harsh *scrawk* of the crows. The breeze whispered in the leaves. Each morning, not long after the rising of the sun, would come the rasp of saws biting into tree trunks, the grunts of the slaves wielding them, and the snapped insults and orders of the kapos and guards. Occasionally there was a yell, a long, creaking tear, and a great beech or oak would come crashing down. The slaves set about its corpse, lopping branches, stripping twigs, reducing it to logs and a carpet of leaves.

Gustav and his team, already tired, their shoulders raw, stood by as sweltering laborers stacked up logs for them to transport to the construction sites. Gustav was doing well; he was a foreman now, in charge of his own twenty-six man team of Singing Horses. They'd had a terrible winter but had made it through. "My lads are true to me," he wrote in his diary; "we are a brotherhood, and stick tightly together." In February another transport of invalids had left Buchenwald—several of them Gustav's friends, "all strong fellows"—followed the next day by the usual returning crop of clothes, prosthetics, and eyeglasses. "Everyone thinks, *tomorrow morning it will be my turn*," he wrote. "Daily, hourly, death is before our eyes." More of Gustav's friends had died, including haulage column kapo Willi Gross and his brother, blamed for sabotage and sent to the punishment detail. Subjected to weeks of carrying earth in the gardens, they collapsed one by one and were killed off.

Around the same time, the SS had murdered another old acquaintance, Rabbi Arnold Frankfurter. Formerly the Austro-Hungarian army's Jewish chaplain in Vienna, Rabbi Frankfurter was the man who had married Gustav and Tini in 1917. Arrested in the summer of 1938, he'd been sent to Dachau then transferred here. The SS made his life hell, flogging him on the Bock and tormenting him until his aged body could take no more. In the wreck that remained of him, it was hard to recognize the portly, bearded rabbi of the Vienna barracks. Before he died, Rabbi Frankfurter spoke with an Orthodox friend, with whom he had shared long evenings debating the Talmud. The rabbi gave him a traditional Yiddish blessing, asking him to pass it on to his wife and daughters: *Zayt mir gezunt un shtark*—"Be healthy and strong for me."[1] Gustav remembered his wedding day clearly, in the pretty little synagogue in the Rossauer Kaserne, the grand army barracks in Vienna: Gustav in dress uniform, the Silver Medal for Bravery gleaming on his breast, Tini in a picture hat and dark coat, almost plump before decades of hardship and mothering sculpted her into handsome maturity.

Taking off his cap and running a hand over the bristles of his shaved scalp, Gustav looked up into the canopy of swaying leaves. With a feeling that was like a faint ghost of contentment, he replaced his cap and sighed. "In the forest it is wonderful," he had written in his diary. "If only we were free; but always we have the wire before our eyes."

During the first half of 1942, Buchenwald had completed its transformation. In January, Commandant Koch had been relieved of his position and replaced by SS-Major Hermann Pister, an aging administrator who'd served time in Himmler's motor pool. "From now on a new wind blows in Buchenwald," he had told the assembled prisoners at roll call upon his arrival, and he meant it.[2] In addition to Commando 99, the Typhus Research Station, and the invalid extermination transports, an exercise regime had been introduced, in which prisoners were roused half an hour earlier than usual for roll call and made to do exercises half-dressed.

For Jewish prisoners the situation had grown worse than ever. Hitler's hatred against Jews was swelling beyond all control or constraint. The invasion of the Soviet Union had failed to achieve the clean, decisive conquest envisaged by the Führer and had stalled badly during the winter. A food crisis had taken hold in the Reich, and German aggression against the USSR had inspired communist partisans in occupied territories from France to Belarus and Ukraine. In the dank workings of the Nazi mind, the Jews were behind communism—therefore they were behind the communist fifth column. Having caused the war in the first place, Jews were now hobbling German progress.[3] In January 1942 the Wannsee Conference had taken place in Berlin, at which the heads of the SS had agreed at last upon the Final Solution to the Jewish problem. For several years the final solution had been thought to be mass deportation and emigration. Now they decided it had to be something far more drastic and decisive. The exact nature of it was kept secret from the public, but it transformed the concentration camp system. In Buchenwald, Jews came under even closer, even more hostile attention than before. Euthanasia of invalids, starvation, abuse, and murder whittled down the Jewish population until by March there were only 836 left, out of a total of 8,117 prisoners.[4] The only thing keeping Buchenwald's remaining Jews alive was their usefulness as workers, and that might not hold out for long under the pressure from the top to bring about a "Jew-free Reich."

Commandant Pister had broken up the existing kapo appointments in the labor details and barrack blocks, replacing many of the Jewish and political kapos and block seniors with green-triangle men—career criminals—thereby sparking a conflict between the green men and the politicals known as the "inmates' war." Forty-eight politicals had been put into a punishment detachment, and four were put into the Bunker.[5] The atmosphere in the labor details had gone from brutal to fanatically harsh.

Gustav's momentary idyll, gazing up at the swaying trees, was ended by yells from the SS sergeants in charge of the logging detail. Under Gustav's direction, his team lifted and shouldered the logs. They had no wagon for this job; the timber had to be transported by hand up the steep wooded hillside. A few of Gustav's lads were worn out; they wouldn't survive another step with a tree trunk gouging their shoulders. He told them to just tag on with the others; so long as they were discreet and *looked* like they were carrying, they should pass. Gustav shouldered his own end of a log, and they set off.

Climbing the slope was arduous, and they had a long day of this ahead of them. It was best just to exist in the moment, to slog on, shut off the pain and weariness, not think at all. Reaching the destination was the worst part—under the eye of a construction kapo and SS supervisor, the last yards and the stacking of the logs had to be done at top speed. Men had been maimed and even killed by hastily stacked trunks slipping and rolling on them.[6]

"What do you think you're doing, Jew-pigs?" SS-Sergeant Greuel's face appeared in front of Gustav, apoplectic with fury, brandishing a hefty cane. "Some of these beasts aren't carrying anything!"[7]

Gustav began to explain that some of his lads weren't up to carrying, but he scarcely got a word out before Greuel's cane lashed him across the face, knocking him sideways. Gustav put up his hands to protect his head, and the cane whipped furiously back and forth, battering his fingers; he twisted, and the blows fell on his back. Then Greuel turned his rage on the other men, beating them until they bled. "You're a foreman, Jew," he seethed at Gustav. "So drive your Jew animals harder. I'll make a report about this lapse."

Greuel was a notorious sadist, and some said there was a sexual element in his cruelty; he occasionally held individuals back from work details and beat them alone in his room for his own pleasure.[8] Once he'd fixed on a victim, he wouldn't let up. The next day it happened again—Gustav and his men were beaten for not working hard enough. At roll call, Gustav was called to the gate and interrogated by the Rapportführer, the sergeant in charge of the SS Blockführers, who oversaw roll calls and handled camp discipline. Satisfied by Gustav's answers, he tore up Greuel's report.

On the third day, Gustav and his team were hauling stone from the quarry, supplementing the work of the teams on the rail wagons. Their wagon was loaded up with two and a half tonnes of rocks, and even with twenty-six men at the ropes it was a killing strain to haul it step by step up the road to the top of the hill. This time Gustav was reported for not driving his team fast enough, and this time the Rapportführer passed the report on for further action.

Gustav was given five Sundays on the punishment detail, without food. He was fifty-one years old, and tough as he was, his body couldn't take this treatment for much longer. Like Fritz before him, he was put on *Scheissetragen*—shit carrying. Each Sunday, while the prisoners not on punishment duty took it easy, he carried buckets of liquid feces from the latrines to the gardens, always at a running pace. Although his friends slipped him morsels of food, he lost 10 kilos* in the course of a month. He'd always been lean; now he was starting to become skeletal.

---

* 22 pounds

Eventually the punishment stint was over, and his weight loss halted. He was relieved of his position as a foreman on the haulage column, but his friends managed to get him less arduous work on the infirmary wagon, carrying food and supplies, although he still had to work evening shifts in the haulage column. He began to recover from his ordeal. That he had survived Greuel's persecution at all was little short of miraculous.

בן

Fritz Kleinmann had learned that even miracles couldn't last in a place like this. Every day the circle of probability was closing in on each man, his days shortening and the odds on his surviving the hardships and the lottery of selection growing longer.

In the spring Fritz lost one of his dearest friends, Leopold Moses, the man who had protected him, nurtured and tutored him in the art of survival, steered him toward safer work. A large transport of prisoners was being sent to a new camp the SS was building in Alsace, called Natzweiler. Leo was selected and sent off with them. Fritz never saw him again.[9]

One evening in June, Fritz was sitting in his regular spot at the table in block 17, having finished up his small ration of turnip soup and piece of bread, listening to the conversation of his elders. He would be nineteen in a couple weeks, still a boy in years and, by comparison with some of these men, a child in intellectual development and understanding of the world. He always listened, always keen to learn. His attention was taken by the appearance of his kapo and mentor Robert Siewert's distinctive figure in the doorway, beckoning.

Fritz went to him and found him looking grave, his heavy brows frowning. When they were outside, Siewert spoke softly and quickly: "There's a letter from your mother in the mail office. The censor won't let you have it." Through a contact in the mail room—which employed prisoners as staff—Siewert had managed to learn the letter's contents. It was like a stab to the heart. "She and your sister Herta have been notified for resettlement. They've been arrested and are waiting for deportation to the east."[10]

The words sank in. *Arrest . . . resettlement . . . deportation.* Fritz hurried down the street to block 29, with Siewert following behind. He asked one of the block inmates to tell his papa that he wanted to see him urgently. (Prisoners were forbidden from entering barracks other than their own.) After a few moments, Gustav came out, and Siewert repeated what he recalled of Tini's letter.

They could only speculate what it meant. They received news and rumor all the time and had acquired an acute sensitivity to the truth about Nazi actions, no matter how euphemistically they were named. It would be impossible to live three years in a concentration camp and not develop a fine nose for evil. But deportation? Resettlement? This was what the Nazis had wanted all along—to send the Jews away from the Reich. Perhaps they really had designed a way to do that. And yet Fritz, his father, and Robert Siewert all knew too well what was being done to the Soviet POWs and had heard whispers about the SS massacres in the Ostland, the conquered region east of Poland.[11] Only one thing could be known for certain—there would be no more packages, no more letters, no more link with their dear ones once they were gone from Vienna and sent to Russia or who-knew-where.

אם ובת

Tini stood by the gas cooker in the kitchen. That day when they took Fritz and she threatened to gas herself if Gustav didn't run away and hide was still a vivid memory. And now they had come for her.

She turned off the main gas tap, as she was required to do. The detailed list of instructions issued by the authorities lay on the kitchen table, along with the keyring with which she had been provided, with the apartment key attached to it.

Tini looked at Herta, who stood in her coat with her little suitcase by her side. That was all they were permitted—one or two cases per person, total not to exceed 50 kilos. There was little chance of that; all they possessed between them wouldn't come close. Everything was gone—taken from them or sold. They had clothes and bedding—as required in the resettlement instructions—along with plates, cups, spoons (knives and forks were forbidden), and food to last for three days' travel. Those who were able were required to bring equipment and tools suitable for establishing or maintaining a settlement. Tini would be permitted to keep her wedding ring, but all other valuables had to be surrendered. She'd never possessed many treasures, and they were all gone now, anyway; neither could she have conjured up more than a fraction of the 300 marks in cash the deportees were allowed to take to the Ostland.[12]

Tini picked up her small case and bulky pack of bedding, and, with a last look around the apartment, closed the door and locked it. Wickerl Helmhacker and his friends—the same men who'd been given authority over the building and its tenants and who had taken Fritz and Gustav—were waiting there on the landing. Tini handed Wickerl the key, and turned away. Their slow footsteps echoed mournfully in the stairwell as they descended.

Escorted by policemen, they crossed the Karmelitermarkt, passing between the stalls, conscious of eyes on them. Everyone—even those who didn't know them personally—knew where they were going, and why. Wearing the Jewish star, carrying luggage, accompanied by police—they were being sent away, like the thousands who had preceded them. "Evacuation" of Jews had begun the previous fall. After an interruption during the winter, they had resumed in May. The evacuees went once a week, hundreds of people at a time, and nobody knew quite where their destination was, other than that it lay somewhere in the vast, vague regions of the Ostland.[13] No news ever came back, and neither did any of the settlers; presumably they were too busy making new lives for themselves in the land that the Reich had established for them.

After passing through the market, Tini and Herta knew where to go: a few steps along Hollandstrasse, then left into Kleine Sperlgasse, where the Sperlschule—the local elementary school—stood. The cobblestones were as familiar as the soles of their own feet—especially for Herta. All the local children had attended the Sperlschule: Edith, Fritz, and Herta herself had spent a large part of their lives in its halls and classes. Kurt had been a student here when the Nazis came. He'd been barred for a while along with all the Jewish children but had returned later when the Sperlschule was redesignated as a *Judenschule*. It had no students at all now—the SS had closed it down in 1941 and turned it into a holding center for deportations.

Tini and Herta passed through the guarded gateway and walked along the alleyway between the tall buildings. The school consisted of a group of four-story buildings set back from the street, surrounding a large L-shaped schoolyard. Where children had once run and played ball on the cobblestones, SS guards now stood sentry. Trucks were parked, loaded with crates and bundles. Tini and Herta presented their identity cards and papers and were taken into a building.

The classrooms had been converted into makeshift dormitories filled with people. Everywhere they saw the faces of friends, acquaintances, neighbors, as well as strangers from more distant parts of the district. Most were women, children, and men over forty. There were very few young men; most had gone to the camps. There weren't many elderly people either; those over sixty-five were slated for separate deportation to the ghetto for elderly Jews at Theresienstadt.*

Tini and Herta were put in a room and left to join in with its little community. News was exchanged among them, little snippets of information and grapevine gossip, inquiries about relatives and mutual friends. The news was almost never good. Nobody knew for certain what their own fate was to be. Their resettlement in the Ostland had been presented to them not as a punishment or imprisonment but as an opportunity for a new life. Tini abhorred the very idea of being taken from her native city and was innately suspicious of the future. From the very beginning she had expected the worst from the Nazis, and they hadn't proven her wrong so far.

She had written to Fritz and Gustav but could tell them little other than the bare, devastating fact of their selection. Mistrusting the future, Tini had given some possessions to a non-Jewish relative, including her last photograph of Fritz—the one taken in Buchenwald—and had given a package of spare clothing for him to her sister Jenni, who lived around the corner in Blumauergasse. Two years older than Tini and unmarried, Jenni was in as precarious a position as Tini herself, but so far she'd been omitted from the deportations.[14] The same was true of their elder sister Bertha, who also lived nearby in Haidgasse. As a widow of the First World War who had never remarried, Bertha also lived alone.[15]

After a day or two, the detainees were alerted that they would be departing imminently.[16] Everyone was ordered out into the yard. Those who had brought equipment and materials were ordered to load it up onto waiting trucks. People crowded the corridors, spilling out through the doors, all carrying luggage and bundles. Some had come from Im Werd, many dozens of others from the streets around the Karmelitermarkt, and hundreds from all over Leopoldstadt. In all, they numbered just over a thousand. Their identity cards were inspected again, each one stamped *Evakuiert am 9. Juni 1942*,† and they climbed aboard the trucks.

The convoy passed down Taborstrasse and the broad avenue alongside the Danube Canal. Herta looked down at the water, drifting, gleaming under

---

* Now Terezín, Czech Republic
† Evacuated on June 9, 1942

the summer sun; come the weekend it would be teeming with pleasure boats and dotted with swimmers. She recalled the time she and her papa had challenged each other to a swimming race, as Fritz and his friends always did. Her beloved Papa, gentle and warm. Those had been good days. Sometimes her mother, who loved to row, would take the kids out in a boat, all of them together. It was like a dream now, vivid but remote. Jews weren't allowed to use the Danube Canal anymore, or to walk on the broad, verdant banks under the trees.

After crossing the canal, the convoy drove another three kilometers through the streets and pulled in at the Aspangbahnhof, the train station serving the southern half of the city.

There was a small crowd of spectators gathered around the entrance, held in order by dozens of police and SS troopers. Tini and Herta climbed down from their truck and joined the crush slowly filtering in through the doors into the gloom of the station interior.

Waiting at the platform was a train made up of sixteen passenger cars in the attractive cream and crimson livery of the Deutsche Reichsbahn. Well now, this didn't look so bad. Everyone knew of the awful cattle cars in which their menfolk had been taken away to the camps. This seemed much more promising.

The evacuees were ordered to load their luggage into a boxcar at the rear of the train; food supplies and medicines had already been stowed. It was a long, slow process, and the evacuees had been at the station several hours when there was a loud whistle and a voice boomed: "One hour to departure!"[17] The announcement was repeated all along the platform, and people began hurrying to their places. Each person had been assigned a car to go to. Tini, holding tightly on to Herta, pushed through the milling crowd to their assigned place, where a car supervisor equipped with a list and an air of flustered importance was marshaling his charges. He was an official appointed by the IKG, not a police officer or SS, and his presence was also reassuring.

The sixty or so people assigned to his car gathered about him. Tini recognized some of them: an elderly lady from Im Werd, all alone; a woman about Tini's own age from Leopoldsgasse, also unaccompanied; many of the women were on their own, their husbands and sons having gone to the camps. Their children—the fortunate ones—had been sent to England or America. Some remained, however. A woman Tini had never seen before, aged sixty or so, was traveling with four children, three boys and a girl, evidently her grandchildren. The youngest, a boy named Otto, was about Kurt's age, and the eldest was a girl of about sixteen.[18] Gray-bearded men in rumpled hats, fellows with pouchy cheeks and jowls, neat, careworn wives in headscarves, mingled with young women whose faces were prematurely lined, and the disorientated children, some as young as five, staring about in wonder and confusion. The car supervisor called their names from his list, checking them off against their transport numbers.

"One-two-five: Klein, Nathan Israel!" A man in his sixties held up his hand. "Here."

"One-two-six: Klein, Rosa Sara!" His wife answered.

"Six-four-two: Kleinmann, Herta Sara!"

Herta raised her hand.

"Six-four-one: Kleinmann, Tini Sara!"

"Here," said Tini.

The list went on: Klinger, Adolf Israel; Klinger, Amalie Sara . . . Along the length of the platform the fifteen other car supervisors were calling the rolls of their own sections of the list of 1,006 men, women, and children who were going on the journey.

At last they were told their destination: the city of Minsk, where they would either join the ghetto and work in the various local industries, or farm the land, depending on their skills.

When the car supervisors were satisfied that nobody was missing, the evacuees were finally allowed to board, with the stern instruction that they were to do so in silence and keep to their designated seats. The passenger cars were second class and divided into closed compartments—comfortable enough, if a little overcrowded. As Tini and Herta took their seats, it was almost like the old days, when they had been free to travel. For a long while now it had been illegal for Jews to venture outside their districts, let alone leave Vienna. It would be interesting to see a little of the outside world again.

Smoke and steam poured across the platform, and the axels squealed as the long train began to move, slowly snaking out of the station, heading north. It crossed the Danube Canal and rolled past the west end of the Prater on the bridge over the Hauptallee, past the Praterstern and the street where Tini had been born, and in a few moments reached the Nordbahnhof.[19] This would have been a more convenient station for the Jews of Leopoldstadt to depart from, but the Aspangbahnhof was more discreet and out of the way.[20] A few minutes later the broad River Danube passed beneath the compartment window, then the final suburbs and the rolling farmland northeast of Vienna.

The train went briskly, and although it stopped occasionally at stations, the evacuees were strictly forbidden to get off unless they had an extremely good reason. The hours of the long June day dragged by. People read, talked, slept in their seats. Children grew restless and fretful in their confinement, others catatonic with exhaustion, staring. At regular intervals the car supervisor came along and peered into each compartment to check that his charges were behaving themselves and had no problems. A doctor—also appointed by the IKG—was on hand if anybody felt unwell. It was a long time since any Jew had been looked after so solicitously by strangers.

They passed through what had once been Czechoslovakia and entered the land that had been Poland. It was all Germany now. To Tini and Herta the southern Polish landscape was of particular interest; this region had once been part of the kingdom of Galicia, in which Gustav had been born during the great days of the Austro-Hungarian Empire, when the Jews had enjoyed a golden age of emancipation. While Tini had experienced that era in Vienna, Gustav had spent his childhood here, in this beautiful landscape, in a little village called Zablocie bei Saybusch,* by a lake at the foot of the mountains. The train didn't go there, but it passed nearby, through countryside Gustav himself would have recognized if he were here, not just from his childhood but from his military service in the war, when he had fought for these same fields and towns against the army of the Russian tsar.

The train also passed near but did not visit another small town, about fifty kilometers north of Zablocie, named Oświęcim. The Germans called that town Auschwitz, and the SS had established a new concentration camp there. The Vienna train chugged in a wide arc to the west, then resumed its northeastward route.[21]

The sun sank behind them, dusk gathered, and the train steamed on, leaving the mountains of southern Poland and passing into rolling plain. The evacuees spent the night in comfortless dozing, with aching backs and dead limbs. The next morning they passed through the city of Warsaw, where there was a great Jewish ghetto, but they didn't halt there. Beyond Bialystok they crossed the border, leaving Greater Germany behind and entering the Reichskommissariat

---

* Now Zabłocie in Żywiec, Poland

Ostland, formerly part of the Soviet Union. About forty kilometers farther on, the train reached the small city of Volkovysk.*

Here it stopped.

For a while it seemed no different from any previous stop. Tini and Herta, like everyone else, glanced out the window, wondering where they were. The car supervisor looked in on the compartment, then moved off. Somehow there was a sense that something wasn't quite right. There was a sound of raised voices at the far end of the corridor, car doors opening, and heavy boots coming briskly along from both ends. Armed SS troopers appeared at the compartment door, and it was flung open.

"Out! Out! All out!" Although shocked and confused, the people had been conditioned by years of experience not to hesitate. They stood, grabbing for their belongings, mothers and grandmothers clutching their children. "Come on, Jew-pigs! Out now!" Tini and Herta found themselves in the corridor, crushed by people hastening to get to the doors. Any who were slow were kicked or shoved with rifle butts. They poured on to the platform, where there were more Waffen-SS troopers.

The SS men were like none that Tini had ever seen in Vienna: fiercer and with the Death's Head insignia of the concentration camp division on their collars.[22] They were accompanied by men in the uniforms of the dreaded Sipo-SD, the Nazi security police.[23] They yelled and cursed at the Jews, driving them along the platform—men and women, elderly and children; those who stumbled or fell, or who couldn't go fast enough, were kicked and beaten, some so badly that their unconscious bodies were left lying on the ground.[24]

They were herded to another train, this one made up of boxcars. Into these they were driven at gunpoint, crushed in with scarcely room to move. Then the doors slammed. Tini and Herta, clinging to each other, found themselves in a darkness filled with sobbing, the moans of the injured, and the crying of terrified children. Outside they could hear the guards yelling and car doors grinding shut all along the train.

After the last door had slammed, they were left in darkness for hours, not moving. A few people, broken by the sudden, violent shock, lost their reason during that awful night; they screamed and raved. The SS hauled out the mad

---

* Now Vawkavysk, Belarus

and the sick and put them all together in a separate car, where they suffered a special hell almost beyond imagining.

The next day, the train began to move. It went painfully slowly. The transport was no longer behind a speedy Reichsbahn locomotive but a plodder from the Haupteisenbahndirektion Mitte,* the network serving the German eastern territories. In the two days since leaving Vienna they had covered over a thousand kilometers; now it took a further two days to cover a quarter of that distance.[25]

Eventually the train came to a halt. The sounds coming from outside suggested that they were in some kind of station. The terrified people waited for the doors to open, but they didn't. Night came, and nothing happened, then another day. The train sat there, unattended except for periodic inspections by the Sipo-SD guards, for two whole days. It had arrived on a Saturday, and the German railroad workers in Minsk had recently been awarded the right not to work weekends.[26]

Cramped together in darkness, illuminated only by tiny cracks of daylight in the car walls, frightened, with little or nothing to eat or drink, and only a bucket in the corner as a toilet, the deportees endured the dragging nightmare hours in horrible uncertainty. Had the plan for them changed? Had they been tricked? What would become of them? On the morning of the fifth day since leaving the comfort of the passenger train, the imprisoned were jolted from their stupor; the train was moving again. Dear God, would this never end?

"Please dear child," Tini had written to Kurt, almost a year ago now, "pray that we are all reunited in good health." She had never quite let go of that hope. "Papa wrote . . . thank God he is healthy . . . the knowledge that you are well taken care of by your uncle is his only joy . . . Please, Kurtl, be a good boy . . . I hope they have good things to say about you, that you keep your things and your bed in order and that you are nice . . . You have a wonderful summer, soon the beautiful days will be over . . . All the kids here envy you. They don't even get to see a garden."[27]

With a shrieking of steel on steel and a thump and rattle of cars bumping, the train halted again. There was silence, and then the car door slammed wide open, flooding the imprisoned with blinding light.

---

* Main Railroad Administration, Central

✡

Precisely what befell Tini and Herta Kleinmann that day will never be known. What they witnessed, what they did or said or felt was never recorded. And the exact details of what happened to them were also lost to history. Not a single one of the one thousand and six Jewish women, children, and men brought to the freight yard at Minsk railroad station on the morning of Monday, June 15, 1942, was ever seen again or left any account.

But general records were kept, and there were other transports from Vienna to Minsk during that summer from which a handful of individuals brought back their stories.[28]

When the car doors opened, the people inside—bone-weary, aching, starving, dehydrated—were ordered out. They were yanked about and scrutinized by Sipo-SD men, and quizzed about their skills. An officer addressed them, reiterating what they had been told back in Vienna—that they would be put to work in industry or farming. Most of the people, unable to do without hope, were reassured by this speech. A few dozen of the healthier-looking adults and older children were selected and taken aside. The remaining multitude were herded to the station barrier, where their belongings were taken from them. The carloads of luggage, food, and supplies that had been brought from Vienna were also seized.[29] Trucks and closed vans were waiting in the road, into which the people were loaded.

The convoy drove out of the city, heading southeast into the Belarusian countryside—a vast, flat plain of field and forest, dusty under a huge sky.

When the German forces took this land from the Soviet Union the previous summer, they had rolled through it like a consuming wave. Immediately in their wake came a second wave: Einsatzgruppe (Task Force) B, one of seven such units deployed behind the front line armies. Commanded by SS-General Arthur Nebe, formerly head of the German criminal police, Einsatzgruppe B comprised a total of around a thousand men—mostly drawn from the Sipo-SD and other police branches—divided into smaller subunits, or Einsatzkommandos. The role of these units was to locate and exterminate Jews in captured towns and villages, a task in which they were often willingly assisted by units of the Waffen-SS and Wehrmacht, and in some areas such as Poland and the Baltic state of Latvia, by local police.[30]

Not all Jews were murdered immediately. That was impracticable, given the millions who inhabited these regions. Besides, the Nazis had learned in Poland how to make Jews contribute to the war economy. A ghetto was established in Minsk, and its industry made to serve the Reich and line the pockets of corrupt officials inside and outside the ghetto. It was to this ghetto that the first transports of German and Austrian Jews had been brought in late 1941, with local Jews massacred to make way for them. Then, in 1942, the implementation of the Final Solution had begun, and Minsk had been chosen as one of its principal centers.

The task of organization fell to the local commander of the Sipo-SD, veteran Einsatzgruppe officer SS-Lieutenant Colonel Eduard Strauch. He surveyed the area and chose a secluded spot in the countryside about a dozen kilometers southeast of Minsk. The little hamlet of Maly Trostinets had been a collective farm under the Soviets. Strauch took it over and ordered a concentration camp built there. Maly Trostinets camp was only small, never intended to hold more than about six hundred prisoners to work the farmland and provide a Sonderkommando* for its main purpose, which was mass murder. Another task was to sort the plundered belongings of the victims, which provided a cash source for the SS.[31]

Of the tens of thousands of people—mostly Jews—brought to Maly Trostinets, few ever saw the camp. When each trainload of deportees—usually around a thousand at a time—arrived at Minsk railroad station, the Sipo-SD selected a few dozen for the camp. The trucks carrying the remaining hundreds drove out in the direction of Maly Trostinets; accounts vary, but it seems that they would normally stop off at a meadow outside the city.[32] From there, at intervals of an hour or so, individual trucks would drive on while the rest waited.

The trucks drove to a half-grown pine plantation about three kilometers away from the camp. There, one of two possible fates awaited the captives. For the majority it was quick, for some slower. But the end was the same. There was a clearing among the trees where a huge pit had been excavated by a Sonderkommando, about fifty meters long and three meters deep. Waiting beside it was a platoon of Waffen-SS under SS-Lieutenant Arlt. Each of Arlt's men was armed with a pistol and twenty-five rounds of ammunition; more boxes of cartridges were stacked nearby.[33] About two hundred meters out

---

* Special labor detail: concentration camp prisoners forced to handle victims before and after executions

from the clearing, a ring of sentries from a Latvian police unit stood guard, to prevent any victims escaping or any potential witnesses venturing near.[34]

Disembarked from the truck, the women, men, and children were forced to strip to their underwear, leaving behind any possessions they had on them. At gunpoint, in groups of about twenty, they were marched to the edge of the pit, where they had to stand in a line, facing the edge. Behind each person stood an SS trooper. On the order, the victims were shot in the back of the neck at point-blank range, and fell into the pit. Then came the next batch. When they had all been shot, a machine-gun that had been set up at the end of the pit opened fire on any corpses that seemed to be still moving.[35] After a short interval, the next truck would arrive, and the process would be repeated.

What made those people submit? From the first who faced the empty pit to those who saw it already half-filled with the corpses of their neighbors and friends, and who heard the shots being fired—what enabled them to stand and be shot down? Were they paralyzed by terror? Had they resigned themselves to their fate, or suffered an existential self-negation? Or did they still retain, until the very last split second with the pistol at their neck, a hope that the shot would not fire, that somehow they would be reprieved? A few did try to run, although they didn't get far, but overwhelmingly the victims went quietly to their deaths.

At Maly Trostinets there was none of the undisciplined fury and euphoria that had often characterized Einsatzgruppe killings elsewhere, in which infants had their backs broken and were hurled into the pits, and the murderers laughed and raged as they killed. Here it was just cold, clockwork execution.

And yet it told on the killers' minds. Even these men had consciences of a sort—wizened, stunted consciences, just enough to be rubbed raw by the endless blood and guilt. It had happened among the murderers in Buchenwald's Commando 99. Arlt's men were provided with vodka to numb the feeling, but it didn't heal the damage.[36] For this reason the SS had experimented with alternative methods that would allow them to exterminate but avoid bloodying their hands.

At the beginning of June, mobile gas vans had been introduced at Maly Trostinets. They had three of them—two converted from Diamond cube vans, and one larger Staurer furniture removal van. The Germans called them S-Wagen, but the local Belarusian people called them *dukgubki*—soul suffocators.[37] While the majority of Jews were shot at the pit, some—probably two or three hundred from each transport—went to the gas vans. The lottery happened at the station in Minsk, where some were loaded into the regular trucks, and some into the S-Wagen parked among them, crammed in so tightly that they crushed and trampled one another.

Once the shootings had been completed, the gas vans started up and drove to the plantation, where they parked beside the corpse-filled pit. Each driver or his assistant connected a pipe from the exhaust to the van interior, which was lined with steel. Then the engine was started. The people trapped inside immediately began to panic; the vans shook and rocked with the violence of their struggle, and there were muffled sounds of screaming and hammering on the sides. Gradually, over the course of about fifteen minutes, the noise and shuddering lessened and the vans grew still.[38]

When all was quiet, each vehicle was opened. Some of the bodies, which had piled up against the door, fell out onto the ground. A Sonderkommando of Jewish prisoners climbed up and began hauling out the rest of the corpses, heaving them into the pit on top of the victims of the shootings. The van interior was a scene of indescribable horror; many of the bodies were streaked with blood, vomit, and feces; the floor was littered with broken eyeglasses, tufts of hair, and even teeth lying in the mess, where the victims had fought and clawed the people near them in their demented efforts to escape.

Before the vans could be used again, they were taken to a pond near the camp and the interiors thoroughly washed. The delay this caused, together with the small number of vans available and frequent mechanical failures, was the reason why firing squads were still used. The SS was still working to refine its methods of mass murder.

SS-Lieutenant Arlt wrote in his log for that day: "On 6/15 there arrived another transport of 1000 Jews from Vienna."[39] That was all. He had no interest in describing what was just another day's work, over which the SS felt it was better to draw a veil of discretion.

אמא

A summer sun lay hot and lazy on the slow-moving surface of the Danube Canal. The faint, delighted squeals of children drifted over the water from the grassy banks where families sat with picnics or strolled under the trees. Pleasure boats cruised along, and rowboats scudded across the expanse between them.

It was all far away from Tini's senses as she pulled on the oars—a pleasant, distant background music of laughter. Sunlight sparkled on the splashes with each lift of the oar blades from the water and illuminated the faces of her children. Edith, smiling serenely, Fritz and Herta still little kids, and Kurt, the last-born and beloved, a tiny speck scarcely out of diapers. Tini smiled at them, and heaved at the oars, sending the boat surging across the water.[40] She was good at rowing—had been since her girlhood. And she doted on her family; at the age of twelve she had been made a counselor to the younger children because she loved it so well; to nurture and to save was part of her makeup, and in motherhood it had its purest expression.

The sounds of the other boats and the revels on the far banks faded, as if a mist had descended, closing off the boat from the world. The oars dipped and splashed, and the boat glided on.

In a drawer in a chest in faraway Massachusetts, Tini's last letters to Kurt lay gathered. The German in which they were written was already leaking away from his comprehension as his child's mind adapted to his new world. He had absorbed her meaning, but was already slowly, insensibly beginning to forget how to read her words.

My beloved Kurtl . . . I am so happy that you are doing well . . . write often . . . Herta is always thinking of you . . . I am afraid every day . . . Herta sends hugs and kisses. A thousand kisses from your Mama. I love you.

✡

That night, after the Sonderkommando had backfilled the pit, dusk fell on the silent clearing among the young pines. Birds returned, night creatures foraged among the weeds and ran over the disturbed soil of the pit. Beneath lay the remains of Rosa Kerbel and her four grandchildren—Otto, Kurt, Helene, and Heinrich—and the elderly Adolf and Amalie Klinger, five-year-old Alice Baron, the spinster sisters Johanna and Flora Kaufmann, Adolf and Witie Aptowitzer from Im Werd, and Tini Kleinmann and her pretty twenty-year-old daughter Herta, along with the other nine hundred souls who had boarded the train in Vienna.

They had believed that they were going to eke out a new life in the Ostland, and that perhaps one day they would be reunited with their dear ones—husbands, sons, brothers, daughters—who had been scattered to the camps and far countries.[41] Beyond all reason, beyond all human feeling, the world—not only the Nazis but the politicians, people, and newspapermen of London, New York, Chicago, and Washington—had closed off that future and irrevocably sealed it.

10 | A Trip to Death

אבא

THE SUMMER SUN WAS LOWERING, glittering a blinding orange between the branches, sending long, coal-gray tree shadows across the forest floor. The rasp of saws on tree trunks and the urgent grunts of men filled Gustav's ears, along with the pumping of his own blood and the heave of his breath as he and his workmate, Friedmann, helped hoist a log up onto the wagon.

In a way it was pleasant to be working in the woods again, away from the grit and dust and mud. But it was exhausting. Gustav worked on the infirmary wagon during the day, but on the haulage column in the evening shifts that were routine during the longer daylight hours. The area being logged was at least accessible by track, so a wagon could be used rather than carrying by hand. But the two SS sergeants in charge—Chemnitz and Deuringer—rained abuse on them, and the kapo, a vindictive sadist called Jacob Ganzer, drove everyone harder than ever. The work had to be done at top speed, which made it not only exhausting but dangerous.

Gustav and his mates hefted their heavy log and launched it onto the stack already on the wagon. Not a second to spare to catch their breath or ensure that the stack was stable—already another was ready to be heaved up, and kapo Ganzer was barking at them to go faster. Gustav took one end of the massive trunk, Friedmann applied his shoulder to it, other hands took up the weight, and they strained it upward, over the sideboard of the wagon, up onto a space on the log pile. With Ganzer's hectoring voice in their ears, somebody let go before the trunk was quite settled—it shifted and rolled, an unstoppable mass weighing hundreds of kilos, bringing the others with it. It rolled over Gustav's hand, and his brain scarcely had time to feel the crushing, cracking pain in his fingers before the log slammed into his body, knocking him to the ground and landing on top of him.[1]

He lay there, pinned like a butterfly on a card, staring up at the swirling canopy of leaves flickering in the evening sun, his body a mass of pain, his ears filled with the screams and groans of other men. Then striped uniforms were in his vision, hands scrabbling at the trunk, lifting it off him. Looking around, he saw others picking themselves up, bloodied hands and faces, some sprawled and moaning with broken limbs. Friedmann lay a few feet away, motionless, whimpering hoarsely. He had taken most of the force of the falling trunk on his chest. Blood was leaking from his mouth.

Gustav was picked up and carried. Seven other injured men were either carried or managed to hobble up the road to the camp and were delivered to the infirmary.[2] Friedmann was brought in on a stretcher. He couldn't move; his ribcage was crushed and his spine broken. He lay helpless, shattered, and in agony. Gustav's injuries were less severe, but not by much; his chest had taken some of the impact, and his broken fingers were on fire with pain.

The lottery had finally run against him, as it did for nearly everyone. It could only run true so many times, and the longer one was forced to play it, the more certain it was that it would turn bad, until it became all but inevitable. Although there had been no invalid selections for several months, the prospects for any badly injured man were grim. The doctor's needle and a vein full of phenol or hexobarbital was the likely fate, and then—smoke from the crematorium chimney like the rest.

Friedmann died horribly but mercifully quickly from his injuries. The other men, most of whom were less badly injured, made it out of the infirmary in a short time. But Gustav remained, too sick to move. The days dragged by, and he was placed in a small ward adjoining Operating Room II. If he didn't know already what this meant, he would quickly learn; Operating Room II was where lethal injections were given, and each man in the ward would be taken in there at some point and never come back.[3]

It was probably the severity of Gustav's injuries that saved his life. Those who were badly but not mortally sick or hurt were usually selected for killing. But those like Gustav who were expected to die naturally from their illness or injuries were left to do so. Gustav was tended steadfastly by a friendly orderly called Helmut and managed to cling on to life. He was in the infirmary for six weeks, at the end of which he had recovered enough to be discharged.

He didn't have the strength to return to the haulage convoy or even the infirmary wagon, but his trade skills saved him. He was transferred to the Deutsche Ausrüstungswerke (DAW), the small factory within the main camp perimeter. It manufactured miscellaneous military supplies like cartridge cases, barrack-room lockers, aircraft parts, and so on, and handled conversion of trucks into mobile canteens, as well as various other tasks.[4] Gustav was given work as a saddler and upholsterer. For the first time since his arrival in the camp—almost the first time since the Anschluss four years earlier—he was able to practice his proper trade again.

Gustav was happy—or as happy as one could be—in his new position. The work was congenial, and he made good friends. His foreman was a German political prisoner named Peter Kersten, a former Communist Party city councilor—"a very brave man," Gustav thought; "I get along with him very well." He even managed to obtain a place for a Viennese Jewish friend, Fredl Lustig, who had been his foreman at one time on the haulage column. Together they made a contented band.

So it went on until the beginning of October. And then everything changed.

בן

Fritz and his workmate, Max, lifted a heavy concrete lintel from the scaffold bed and carefully eased it into the place prepared for it in the wall above the window space. Fritz positioned it, checking its level and fit.

Over the past two years, his skills as a builder had developed and grown under Robert Siewert's tutelage, as had those of all the other young men in the construction detachment. All kinds of brick and stone work, plastering, general construction—he had mastered it all. Since completing the heating plant, the Siewert detachment had been moved to the site of the new Gustloff-Werke, a huge factory that had been under construction since the spring on a site beside the Blood Road, opposite the SS garage complex. Once completed, it would turn out barrels for tank and antiaircraft guns, as well as rifle barrels and other armaments. When Fritz and his comrades arrived, most of the exterior walls were already up, and he had been put to work fitting window lintels. Fritz was expected to complete two large factory windows a day, constructing the fenestrations, setting the lintels, and fixing them in place, a job requiring a highly skilled bricklayer and a great deal of care.

His workmate, Max Umschweif, was a relative newcomer to Buchenwald, having arrived the previous summer. A slightly built Viennese with the intelligent face of an intellectual, he had fought with the International Brigade against the Fascists in the Spanish Civil War. After the defeat of the Republican forces, he and his comrades had been interned in France; returning to Vienna in 1940 he'd been picked up by the Gestapo as a known antifascist and sent to the camps. Fritz loved hearing his stories about the war in Spain but was utterly bewildered that he had voluntarily returned to Austria knowing that the Gestapo would be after him.

Using the butt of his trowel to knock the lintel into its final position, Fritz checked it with a spirit level, then quickly and skillfully mortared it in place. It was pleasant working up here on the scaffolding. While the SS overseers constantly harassed and beat the brick and mortar carriers, driving them to go faster, they never ventured up the ladders onto the scaffolding. Satisfied with the lintel, he turned and took a moment to stretch his muscles. There was a fine view over the forest from up here: beautiful in their October glory, the oaks and beeches were dappled with gold, pale oranges, and shades of red. Far away, the spread of Weimar could be seen, and the rolling farmlands around.

Fritz had been through some terrible experiences in recent months—the departure of Leo Moses, his father's accident and near death, close friends of his murdered by the SS, and the worrying news about his mother and Herta, which brought with it the agony of not knowing—but dreadfully fearing—what would become of them in the east.

His reverie was interrupted by a call from below. "Fritz Kleinmann, come down here!" He clambered down the ladder. "Kapo wants you," said one of the laborers.

Fritz found Robert Siewert. He had that grave look again, and took Fritz quietly to one side. He put his arm around Fritz's shoulders and pulled him close; he had never done such a thing before, and Fritz guessed that bad news was coming. "There is a list of Jews to be transferred to Auschwitz in the records office," he said simply. "Your father's name is on it."

The shock was beyond almost anything Fritz had experienced. Everyone knew the name of Auschwitz, one of the crop of newer camps the SS had been establishing in occupied territories. He also knew its reputation, and what a transfer there would mean. There had been talk in Buchenwald; rumor, gossip, and news from far away, as well as events in the camp itself, warned the prisoners that the drama of the Jews had entered its last act, that the Nazis meant to finally dispose of the remainder who had not emigrated or died already. And there had been disturbing whispers about the gas chambers being built in some camps, including Auschwitz.

Siewert explained what he had learned; the list was a long one, almost all the Jewish men in Buchenwald were on it, except for those like Fritz who were required for construction of the Gustloff factory. Fritz was dazed and appalled; he knew so many youngsters in the camp who had lost their fathers and always feared that he would become one of them. "You will have to be very brave," Siewert said.

"But Papa does useful work in the factory," Fritz objected.

Siewert interrupted him. "It is everyone," he said. "All the Jews except builders and bricklayers are going to Auschwitz." He looked Fritz in the eye. "If you want to go on living, you have to forget your father."

Fritz struggled to find words. "That's impossible," he said. With that, he turned on his heel, scrambled back up the ladder to the scaffold, and went back to work.

✡

There were just over four hundred names on the list drawn up by Buchenwald's command headquarters. A few days earlier they had received an order sent on behalf of Heinrich Himmler to all camp commandants: on the wishes of the Führer himself, the Reichsführer-SS required that all concentration camps located on German home soil be made Jew-free. All Jewish prisoners were to be transferred to camps in former Polish territory—namely Auschwitz and Majdanek.[5]

In Buchenwald's case there were only 639 Jews left: those who had survived the random murders, transfers, and euthanasia transports. Of that total, 234 were employed on construction of the Gustloff factory; they were to be retained for the time being, while the remaining 405 were slated for Auschwitz.[6]

In the evening of Thursday, October 15, a few days after Fritz's conversation with Robert Siewert, all Jewish prisoners were ordered to assemble in the roll-call square.[7] They all knew what to expect, and it was exactly as Siewert had foretold; the numbers of Fritz Kleinmann and the other skilled construction workers were called out. These men were ordered to return to their barrack blocks. The rest were informed that they were to be transferred to another camp. They were taken to block 11, which had been cleared to make way for them, and shut inside, barred from all contact with other prisoners. There they waited for the transfer to begin. They were kept in suspense for two days.

אב ובן

Fritz hadn't been able to rest since walking off the roll-call square and leaving his father behind. All night it tormented him. He knew that what Robert Siewert had said about learning to forget his father was sensible, wise advice, but Fritz could not imagine himself being able to follow it. The news about his mother and Herta had set a feeling of despair in him, and he couldn't imagine how he could possibly live if his papa were murdered. In the early hours a rumor passed through the block, claiming that three of the prisoners in block 11 had been taken to the infirmary during the night and killed by lethal injections. The rumor was false, but it helped push Fritz over the edge.

The next morning, before roll call, he sought out Robert Siewert and pleaded with him to pull whatever strings he could to get him placed on the Auschwitz transport.

Siewert was aghast. "You have to forget your father," he said again. "These men will all be gassed."

But Fritz was adamant. "I want to stay with my papa, no matter what happens. I couldn't go on living without him."

There was nothing Siewert could say to dissuade him. As roll call was ending, he went and spoke to SS-Lieutenant Max Schobert, the deputy commandant. While the prisoners began dispersing and setting off for morning work, the call went up: "Prisoner 7290 to the gate!" Fritz reported and explained himself to Schobert, requesting that he be transferred with the others. It was all the same to Schobert how many Jews were sent to be exterminated, and he granted the request.

Fritz was led to block 11 and pushed inside. He found himself looking into the surprised faces of old friends and mentors—the thin, intellectual Stefan Heymann was there, and Gustl Herzog. There was the courageous Austrian antifascist Erich Eisler and Bavarian Fritz Sondheim—their faces gathered in front of him, astonished and appalled when they realized why he was here. They protested and implored, just as Siewert had, but he pushed past them, looking for his papa. And there he was, among the crowd. They rushed to each other and embraced, both crying with joy.

Later that night, Robert Siewert came to take Fritz to sign a paper acknowledging that he was going on the transport of his own free will. Then he was taken back to block 11. His parting from Robert Siewert was painful; he owed him his position, his skills, his very survival during the past two years.

On the morning of Saturday, October 17, the 405 Jewish transferees—Poles, Czechs, Austrians, and Germans—were given a meager ration of food to take with them on their journey. Gustav's consisted of a single hunk of bread. They were ordered to take no possessions with them, and then they were led outside.

The mood in the camp was somber, even among the SS. Whereas previous transfers had been marched out under a hail of abuse and blows from the guards, the four hundred Jews marched to the gate in silence. Outside, a convoy of buses awaited them. Fritz and Gustav sat in almost civilized comfort as they drove down the Blood Road, up which they had run in terror almost exactly three years earlier. How much they had changed since then; how much they had seen. At Weimar station they were loaded into cattle cars—forty men in each.[8] Extra boards had been nailed on to close up any gaps and make the cars absolutely secure.

As it set off, the mood in Fritz and Gustav's car—which they shared with Stefan Heymann, Gustl Herzog, and many other good friends—was depressed. In the daylight leaking through cracks in the car walls, Gustav took out his diary, keeping it out of view of the others. Having been forewarned of the transfer, he'd ensured that he had it on him when they were moved to the isolation block. Whatever lay ahead, he felt better able to face it with Fritz by his side.

"Everyone is saying it is a trip to death,"[9] he wrote, "but Fritzl and I do not let our heads hang down. I tell myself that a man can only die once."

Part III

Auschwitz

11 | A Town Called Oświęcim

אחים

ANOTHER TRAIN, ANOTHER TIME . . .

Gustav woke from a doze with the sunlight rippling across his eyelids, and his nostrils filled with the odors of serge, sweaty male bodies, tobacco smoke, leather, and gun oil. His ears filled with the steady clatter of the train and the mutter of men's voices, suddenly raised in song. The boys were in good spirits, even though they might be on their way to their deaths. Gustav rubbed his neck, sore where he'd rested his head on his pack, and retrieved his rifle, which had slipped to the floor.

Standing up and peering out through the side slot, he felt the warm summer wind on his face and smelled the scents of the meadows, coming to him fleetingly through the shreds of smoke from the locomotive. The rolling wheat fields were at the green-gold stage, ripening toward the harvest. A village spire broke through a gap in the distant rise; beyond stood the green of the Beskid mountains, and beyond that the ghostly curtain of the Babia Góra, the Witches' Mountain. This was the land of his childhood. After six years in Vienna it looked strange, in that peculiar way of a vivid memory suddenly unearthed.

He'd been drafted into the Austrian Imperial and Royal Army in the spring of 1912, his twenty-first year.[1] As a born Galician he'd been placed in the 56th Infantry Regiment, which was based in the Cracow district.* For most young working-class men their three years' army service was a welcome interlude. Conditions for conscripts were good by military standards, and

---

* Now Kraków, Poland

it opened their horizons. Many were illiterate, most had never been farther than the next village, and all they knew was low-paid agricultural work or journeyman trades. In Galicia the majority didn't even speak German; many couldn't even tell the time.[2] Gustav had seen more of the world than most of his fellow recruits, having been a resident of Vienna for the past six years, and he spoke both Polish and German; but as an apprentice upholsterer he was poor, and the army provided some stability. It was a transition to manhood, and provided an exciting environment—the army was still in its imperial heyday of hussars and dragoons, colorful, dashing dress uniforms, and endless pomp with the flags and banners of the imperial Double Eagle fluttering over it all.

Austria was immensely proud of its imperial history and of its army, which contained in its ranks Slavs, Jews, Hungarians, and many other nationalities and ethnic groups besides Austrian Germans; it had once been the greatest empire in Europe, and although reduced considerably by its wars with Napoleon and various other nineteenth-century enemies, Austria-Hungary remained a great and extensive power, at least equal to its upstart neighbor, Germany. It was said that the cryptic Habsburg heraldic device *"AEIOU"* stood for either a German phrase meaning "All the Earth is subject to Austria" or a Latin one meaning "Austria will stand until the end of the world."[3] Either way, it was a nation of gigantic pride and hubris, and to be in its army was to be part of a martial history going back to the Holy Roman Empire.

For Gustav it had meant a return to his homeland, and he had spent most of the first two years in the garrison at Kenty,* a small town in the farmlands north of the Beskid mountains, about halfway between his home village of Zablocie and a town called Oświęcim, a pretty, prosperous, but otherwise unremarkable place on the Prussian border, remembered by soldiers of the neighboring 57th Infantry as the scene of a minor battle in the 1866 war against Prussia.[4]

And so it went on, barrack life week in, week out, parades, boot-blacking and brass-polishing, with occasional field exercises and maneuvers. And then, in 1914, just when the young men of the 1912 intake thought they would soon be done with the army and going back to their farms and workshops with their manhoods made, the war came. The ecstatic thrill of impending combat galvanized bored and glory-hungry young men all over Europe, none more so than those of Austria.

---

* Now Kęty, Poland

All of a sudden, the 56th Infantry Regiment was on alert, and along with the rest of the 12th Infantry Division, they marched to the train station to embark for the fortress town of Przemyśl on the right flank of First Army.[5] This would be the regiment's jumping-off point for the advance north into Russian territory.[6] Gustav and his comrades marched with a lively step under their heavy packs as the band blared out the vibrant tune of the regimental Daun march, immaculate in their gray field uniforms with steel-green facings, their mustaches waxed and backs straight, grinning to the waving girls and as pleased with themselves as only young men can be. They were with friends and comrades, and off to chase the Russians all the way to St. Petersburg.

They were marching with less spring in their step by the morning of August 22, five days later. The railheads were well short of the Russian border, and there had been a long, punishing forced march to the advance. After hours and many kilometers, under their twenty-kilo packs, with winter overcoats strapped on, carrying ammunition, spade, and rations for days, with their rifle straps chafing and feet sore, Lance Corporal Gustav Kleinmann and his platoon mates were more ready for bed and bottle than for battle. And they got neither that day. Their objective was the city of Lublin, where they were supposed to link up with a Prussian advance from the north. While I and V Corps on their left flank met heavy Russian resistance and took a lot of casualties, X Corps barely made contact, and just marched all day long, pushing into Russian territory.[7]

בן

Gustav eased his leg into a more comfortable position. Outside, a hard Galician frost bit at the edges of the window panes, and snow lay thick on the ground.

It had been a wretched winter, following on from a terrible fall. In that first glorious week of the war, they had achieved their objective, capturing Lublin and driving the Russian army back in disarray. But they'd been let down by poor leadership and tactics, and the Germans had failed to support them with an advance from the north. By the middle of September the Russians had rallied and begun recapturing ground.[8] Their counterattacks turned into a rout, with Austrian regiments breaking and falling back all along the line.

The civilian population, with their towns and villages under Russian bombardment or threatened with being swallowed up, panicked, and the train stations and roads were choked with refugees. The large Jewish population was especially terrified. They knew about Russia's anti-Semitic laws and had heard stories of dreadful pogroms; many, indeed, were the descendants of Jews who had fled Russia. In the territories captured by the tsar's army, Jewish property was expropriated, Jews were dismissed from public offices, and some were seized as hostages and taken away to Russia; throughout captured Galicia, Russian officials extorted money from the Jewish population with threats of violence.[9] A flood of refugees headed west and south toward the heartlands of Austria-Hungary. At first they sought sanctuary in Cracow, but by the autumn even that city was under threat, and the refugees began heading for Vienna; the authorities set up embarkation stations for them at towns behind the lines, including at Wadowitz* and Oświęcim.[10]

Eventually Austria's forces fought the Russians to a standstill, and the front line settled just short of Cracow, with Russia in possession of a swathe of eastern Galicia. All along the line, the armies dug trenches and began the dreadful attrition of bombardment, raids, and hopeless attacks.

In the New Year, Gustav and the 56th Regiment—what remained of them after the retreat—found themselves in the front line outside Gorlice, a town about a hundred kilometers southeast of Cracow. Their defenses were poor—the trench line was little more than a series of shallow ditches protected by a single strand of barbed wire—and they had little or no reserve line. What was more, to get from the rear to the trenches, units had to cross open ground that was subjected to Russian artillery fire.[11] The Russians held the town and dominated the ground in front of it from a stronghold in a large hilltop cemetery on the western outskirts.

And there they sat through the biting winter. For Gustav, it had been a kind of reprieve when he was wounded—a bullet through the left forearm and calf. He'd spent a short while in the auxiliary hospital at Bielitz-Biala,† a large town close by Zablocie; he knew the place well, having worked there as a baker's boy between the ages of twelve and fifteen. Then, in mid-January

---

* Now Wadowice, Poland
† Now Bielsko-Biała, Poland

he'd been moved here, to the reserve hospital in the next town—Oświęcim, or Auschwitz, as it was known in German.[12]

The town itself was pleasant in peacetime, with fine civic buildings and an ancient, picturesque Jewish quarter that attracted tourists.[13] Gustav knew it from childhood; it stood at the confluence of the Vistula and the Sola, the river that meandered down from the lake by the village where he'd been born. The military hospital at Oświęcim was a little way from the town, across the Sola in the outlying hamlet of Zasole. A complex of modern barracks had been constructed here, standing in neat rows near the riverbank. It wasn't an ideal spot; the ground was marshy and in summer plagued with insects. It had been intended as part of a transit camp for seasonal migrant workers flowing from Galicia into Prussia, but the outbreak of the war had curtailed it, and the lines of wooden workers' barracks stood empty.[14]

For Gustav, worse than the ache of the wounds—which were almost healed now—was the wrench of being away from his comrades when they were still in the line. Gustav was determined not to malinger; his wounds weren't debilitating, and despite his rather slight appearance, he was proving a tough young fellow with a surprising capacity for taking hardship and injury.

But for now there was peace here, and silence but for the brisk footsteps of the nurses and the low murmur of voices. The bandages and missing limbs were reminders of the howling, exploding hell from which he had come, and to which he would return soon enough.

אחים

Bullets smacked into sides of the tombs and the trees, flinging stone splinters in their faces. But Gustav and his men held on and returned fire, pressing ahead, meter by meter, into the cemetery.

Gustav was only a month out of the hospital and already back in the thick of it—back to Gorlice, back to the frozen trenches at the foot of the slope leading up into the town, back to the sporadic fall of shells and the steady attrition. Then came this day—February 24, 1915—when the regiment launched an assault on the heavily defended Russian positions in the cemetery.

To Corporal Gustav Kleinmann's eye it had looked like a suicide mission: an uphill frontal attack against a large force in a secure, easily defended position. The cemetery was a traditional Catholic one; rather than a field of headstones it was a city of little stone tombs—structures of limestone and marble packed close together with narrow alleys between. It was a veritable fortress, and Gustav's platoon was cut to pieces in the first approach. With their sergeant and platoon officer killed, Gustav and his right-hand man, Lance Corporal Johann Aleksiak, came up with a plan of their own to try to make a success of the attack without wasting any more lives.[15] Leading the remnants of the platoon—which now consisted of just themselves, two lance corporals, and ten privates—they skirted to the left flank of the enemy position, where they were sheltered from the Russian fire, and advanced from there.

They had infiltrated the fringes of the cemetery and were among the tombs before the Russians knew they were there. As soon as they were noticed, withering gunfire lashed at them. They returned fire as best they could and pressed on. The Russians began lobbing hand grenades, but still Gustav and his squad pushed forward, firing and driving back the Russians. The alleys between the tombs became too narrow for effective firing, so they paused and fixed bayonets. They were now about fifteen meters inside the enemy perimeter and might be encircled at any moment. With bayonets fixed and their blood hot and furious, Gustav and his men launched their final, savage assault.

It worked; the Russians were prized at bayonet-point out of their positions, and with the pressure taken off by Gustav's flank attack, the rest of 3 Company was able to advance into the cemetery. Between them they took around two hundred Russian prisoners that day, part of a total haul of 1,240 captured by the regiment.

In the face of the setbacks the Austrian army had suffered since the start of the war, the capture of the cemetery was a major achievement—significant enough to earn a passing mention in a report by Field Marshal von Höfer, Deputy Chief of the General Staff.[16] Not for the first time, nor the last, a knife-edge battle had turned on the initiative of two lowly noncommissioned officers.

בן

Rabbi Frankfurter chanted the last blessings of the Sheva Brachot, the seven blessings of marriage, his voice echoing hauntingly through the synagogue chapel. Beneath the wedding canopy held up by his soldier comrades, Gustav stood in his best dress uniform, the Silver Medal for Bravery 1st Class gleaming on his breast. Beside him was his bride, Tini Rottenstein, radiant, with bright splashes of her white lace collar and silk flowers against the dark fabric of her coat and broad-brimmed hat.

Two years had passed since that day on the cemetery hill in Gorlice. They hadn't been easy. Gustav and Johann Aleksiak had both received the Silver Medal 1st Class for their actions that day, one of Austria's highest awards. In his citation, their commanding officer had called it a "clever, unprecedentedly courageous approach" in which the two corporals had "excellently distinguished themselves."[17] The twelve men with them had received the 2nd Class medal. It had been a fierce battle, and over a hundred men of the 56th Infantry Regiment had received decorations.[18] It had all turned out to be for nothing, as the Russians later recaptured the cemetery. However, in May 1915 the Austrians launched the Gorlice-Tarnow offensive, which drove the tsar's army back across the Vistula and out of Galicia. Eventually they had retaken the fortress towns of Przemyśl and Lemberg,* as well as the Russian cities of Warsaw and Lublin. In August that year Gustav had been wounded again, this time a much more serious injury to the lung.[19] He recovered eventually and returned again to action.

And now had come the precious day—Tuesday, May 8, 1917—when he and his girl went with their friends and family to the pretty little synagogue chapel in Vienna's Rossauer barracks. Like Gustav's, Tini's ancestry was from the outer parts of the empire. Her father, Markus Rottenstein, and her mother, Eva, were from Neutra in Hungary,† and had moved to Vienna after their marriage.[20]

"May the barren one rejoice and be happy at the gathering in of her children in joy." Rabbi Frankfurter's chanting filled the room. "Blessed are You Lord, who created joy and happiness, groom and bride, gladness, jubilation, cheer and delight, love, friendship, harmony and fellowship . . . who gladdens the groom with the bride." Then he laid the traditional glass on the floor by Gustav, who brought his boot heel down and shattered it. "Mazel tov!" yelled the chorus of soldiers, family, and friends.

The rabbi spoke, reminding Tini of the solemnity of wedding a soldier, and touched on the goodness of the Austro-Hungarian empire to its Jewish people. He likened the new emperor, Karl, to the sun shining on the Jews; his forebears had brought down the walls of the old ghettos and "installed

---

* Later Lwów, Poland; now Lviv, Ukraine
† Now Nitra, Slovakia

Israel" in their realm.[21] Austria had always had its share of anti-Semitism, it was true, but since the emancipation of the Jews under the Habsburg emperors, they had lived well and achieved much. With this foundation, Gustav and Tini and their fellow Jews could make their way with their own hands and hearts.

Gustav and Tini Kleinmann walked out of the synagogue that day into a new era. Gustav wasn't done with fighting; he would see more action on the Italian front and earn more decorations, helping Austria and Germany fight their slow, inevitable, bloody defeat. But he survived in the end and came home to Vienna. In the summer of the first year of peace, Edith was born, the first child of many. The old empire had gone, broken up by the victorious Allies; Galicia had been ceded to Poland, Hungary was independent, and Austria was reduced to a rump. But Vienna was still Vienna, the civilized heart of Europe, and Gustav had more than earned his family's place in it.

Many didn't see it that way. In the last year of the war, trapped in a mire of impending defeat, people in Austria and Germany had begun telling themselves stories to relieve the shame of losing. It was the fault of the Jews, many said; they had thrived in the wartime black market, it was alleged. Fingers were pointed at the rivers of Jewish refugees fleeing the front, and how they had worsened the food crisis in the cities; stories were told about how Jews had shirked their duty to their country and avoided military service. The pernicious influence of Jews in government and commerce had been a knife in Germany's and Austria's back, people claimed. In the Vienna parliament there was anti-Jewish agitation from German nationalists and the conservative Christian Social Party; newspapers began to print dire threats of pogroms.[22]

Yet the promise lived on, the outburst of anti-Semitism settled down to a murmur, and the Jews of Vienna continued to thrive. Gustav struggled but never despaired, throwing himself into socialist politics in a bid to ensure a brighter future for all working people and to win prosperity for his growing family.

אבא

Another train, another time, another world . . . and yet the same.

Gustav sat in darkness, rocked by the motion of the train. Around him the air was thick with the familiar stench of unwashed bodies, stale uniforms, and the latrine pail, and alive with the dull murmur of voices. There were forty men in a space so small that they had barely half a square meter* per man, packed so close together they could scarcely move, and getting to the piss bucket in the corner was an ordeal. Two days had passed since boarding the train at Weimar; two days locked in darkness. Gustav's eyes had adapted to the slivers of light leaking through cracks around the door and gratings, just enough to write a few brief phrases in his diary. It must be around noon now; the light was at its brightest, and the faces of his comrades were discernible. Gustl Herzog was there, and the long, earnest features of Stefan Heymann, as well as Gustav's friend Felix "Jupp" Rausch, and Fritz sitting close to some of his young friends, including Paul Grünberg, a Viennese who was the same age as him and had been a trainee bricklayer. The mood was profoundly depressed, and without water or blankets they were thirsty and cold.

Although he could neither see it nor smell it, Gustav knew the landscape through which they must be passing by now; he knew those fields, those green distant hills and ghostly mountains, the quaint little villages and towns. He had been born here, grown up here, bled for his country here, and now the rail tracks were bringing him back one last time, to die. Behind him, the family he had begun with such hope lay broken and scattered. The promise of 1915, when they pinned the medal to his chest, and of 1917, when he'd stomped the glass beneath his heel and joined with Tini in marriage beneath the canopy in the blue and white synagogue, and the promise of 1919, when he'd held baby Edith for the first time, the promise that Israel had been built in Austria; that promise had now been crushed under the wheels of this vast, insane, malfunctioning machine in its unstoppable, senseless drive to jolt life into an Aryan German greatness that had never existed, and that never could exist because its blinkered puritanism was the very antithesis of all that makes a society great. Nazism could no more be great than a strutting actor in a gilt cardboard crown could be a king.

The train, huffing its way past fields of stubble where the wheat had been harvested and woods turning golden in the fall, began to lose speed. Slowing to a crawl, it turned south and heaved into the station in the small town of Oświęcim.[23]

---

* About five square feet

Shedding billows of steam, the locomotive shunted its train of cattle cars up to the loading ramp. And there it stayed. Inside the cars, the Jews of Buchenwald wondered if they had reached their destination yet. The hours of that October afternoon ticked by but nothing happened. The slivers of light faded, and Gustav and his companions were left in total darkness, aching, hungry, parched. And frightened. Would the door never open? Would they never move?

At least Gustav had the consolation of Fritz by his side; how Gustav would have coped if the boy hadn't come of his own free will did not bear thinking about. The spirit of that crushed promise of long ago lived on in Fritz, in the bond that held father and son together and had kept them alive so far. If they were indeed going to die here, at least it would not be alone.

Eventually they heard movement outside: car doors crashing open all along the line, accompanied by barked orders from the SS. Their door opened, and a blaze of flashlights and electric lanterns dazzled their eyes. "Everyone out!" They disembarked into a ring of light surrounded by the growling of guard dogs. They were ordered to form five ranks between the tracks. Well-trained by years of roll calls they quickly formed up, and expecting the usual rain of abuse and beatings, the Buchenwalders were astonished—and a little unsettled—to receive neither. The guards called out an order from time to time, but otherwise they were eerily silent, walking up and down the rows, observing the new prisoners closely. Time passed, and the men grew more and more nervous. Whenever no SS men were nearby, Gustav reached out and hugged Fritz close to him.

The last time Gustav had set foot in this station had been in 1915, when he was discharged from the reserve hospital and sent back to the front line. Nothing about it was familiar.

It was a little after 10:00 PM when a tramp of marching boots along the ramp heralded the arrival of the camp standby squad under the command of SS-Lieutenant Heinrich Josten of the detention department.[24] He was a hard-faced individual, middle-aged, with a grim slant to his mouth and steel-rimmed spectacles. Checking off the new arrivals on a list, he asked whether any man had any watches or other valuables, such as gold. "If so, you are to give them up. You will not need them now." Then he gave the nod to his men, and they began marching the prisoners in orderly fashion along the ramp.

They marched down a long, straight street between what looked in the gloom like a complex of light industrial buildings and rows of wooden huts or barracks. Now, this *did* look vaguely familiar to Gustav.

Turning left, they were marched along a short road to a gateway flooded with arc lights; the gates swung wide, the barrier before them lifted, and the 404 Buchenwalders marched in under the wrought iron arch with its slogan ARBEIT MACHT FREI—*work brings freedom.*[25] The barrier descended and the gates clanged shut behind them. They were marched along a camp street lined by large, well-built, two-story barrack blocks; they were similar to the SS barracks at Buchenwald, but to Gustav's eye there was a different kind of familiarity, more distant. He had been here before.

Arriving at a block in the far corner of the camp, they were ordered inside. It was constructed as a bathing block, with changing rooms. Their names were checked off against the transport list, and they were ordered through into a changing room staffed by prisoners. Here they were ordered to strip naked; they would be given a medical inspection, showered, and their uniforms deloused before going to their accommodation.[26]

Fritz glanced at his father and friends; the nervousness that had been growing among them increased still more. They knew this ritual from their first arrival at Buchenwald, but it felt different now; they had all heard the rumors of gassings at Auschwitz, and that the pretext for getting prisoners to enter the gas chamber was to tell them it was a shower room.[27] Nevertheless, the men did as they were told, stripping off their old, soiled uniforms and underwear. They filed through yet another room, where they were scrutinized by a doctor, and another, where their heads were freshly shaved—right down to the scalp, without leaving the furze of stubble they normally wore. Their bodies were also shaved, including their pubic hair. There followed a louse inspection. Fritz noticed a sign painted in sinister Teutonic letters on the white wall—"ONE LOUSE IS YOUR DEATH."[28]

Next came the shower room. Fritz and Gustav and the others watched anxiously as the first batch were herded through the door.

Minutes passed; a restlessness began to spread among the prisoners. Fritz could feel it growing and hear the low murmuring. When their turn came, would they obey and walk meekly to the lethal chamber? Suddenly, a face appeared in the doorway, gleaming wet, with water dripping from his chin, and grinning. "It's all right," he said, "it really is a shower!"

The next batches went through in much better spirits. Finally, certified louse-free, they were issued with their deloused and disinfected uniforms and fresh underwear.[29] To his relief, Gustav's diary, with its pages of priceless testimony, was still secreted inside his clothes.

When they were dressed, they were inspected by SS-Captain Hans Aumeier, deputy commandant and head of Department III—the "protective custody" section, which covered most Jews. Drunk and in a foul temper, Aumeier slapped the block senior who'd been sent to collect the new arrivals for turning up late. Aumeier was everything that caused the SS to be feared: a walking embodiment of malevolence, a glowering martinet with a tight little slit for a mouth and a reputation for torture and mass shootings. Once he was satisfied with the new prisoners, he ordered the block senior to take them to their accommodation.

They were placed in block 16A, in the middle of the camp. As soon as they were inside, the block senior—a German wearing a green triangle—demanded that they all hand over any contraband articles and told his room orderlies—all young Poles—to search them. The belongings taken ranged from paper and pencils to cigarette holders and pocket knives, as well as money and sweaters—all precious items in the camps. Some of the bolder spirits, including men like Gustl Herzog who had been block seniors in Buchenwald, argued and refused to hand over their possessions and were beaten with rubber hoses. Any man who spoke up got a beating. Somehow, Gustav managed to keep his little notebook concealed. Others lost objects they had treasured—keepsakes that had kept their spirits alive, or in the case of warm clothing, had kept body and soul together through the previous winter.

At last the room orderlies took the men to the bunk rooms and assigned them their places—two men to a bed, one blanket each. Gustav managed to get himself and Fritz assigned to the same bed. It was like their first night in the tent in Buchenwald, three years ago almost to the day. At least here there was a floor and a sound roof over their heads. But there was the same abuse, the same inhuman debasement, and the same prospect that life would be both cruel and brief.

אבא

On the third day they received their tattoos. This practice was unique to Auschwitz, introduced the previous fall. The new arrivals lined up at the registration office; each man rolled up his left sleeve and presented his forearm, and the tattoo was laid on the skin with a needle (the SS had experimented with a stamping device at one time, but it hadn't worked very well).[30]

The men were called in and registered in the order in which they had been placed on the original list in Buchenwald. Gustav laid out his forearm, where he still bore the scar from his bullet wound of January 1915, and the number 68523 was seared into his skin in blue ink. Like most of the others he was entered as *Schutz Jude*—a "protective custody" Jewish prisoner—and his place and date of birth were set down, and his trade.[31] Having volunteered, Fritz was near the end of the list, and he received the number 68629. His trade was listed as builder's mate.

All the while, the Buchenwalders wondered what would be done with them. Days passed, and they weren't assigned to any labor detail and were left more or less alone. As seasoned camp inmates, they kept their ears and eyes open and learned a lot about Auschwitz. The camp they were in was much smaller than Buchenwald, with only three rows of seven blocks. This, they learned, was the main camp, Auschwitz I.[32] A couple kilometers away, on the far side of the railroad, a second camp had been constructed at the village of Brzezinska, which the Germans called Birkenau—"the birch woods" (the SS did like their picturesque names for places of suffering).[33] Auschwitz II-Birkenau was vast, built to contain over a hundred thousand people and equipped to murder them on an industrial scale.

Auschwitz I had its own killing facility, which the new men learned about soon enough—the infamous block 11, the Death Block, in whose basement the first experiments with poison gas had been carried out, where interrogations were conducted, and in whose tiny *Stehzellen* ("standing cells") prisoners were tortured by being forced to stand upright for days at a time. Most notoriously, the enclosed yard outside block 11 was the location of the *Schwarze Wand*—the "Black Wall"—against which condemned prisoners were shot.[34] SS-Captain Aumeier had overseen many such executions. Whether the Buchenwalders would be sent to Birkenau or die here was yet to be discovered.

Day-to-day life during that first week was familiar yet strange. There was no square, and roll call took place in the street outside the block. Food was doled out by the Polish room orderlies and the block senior—the *Blockowi* as the Poles called him—and was wretched. The Poles hated and despised the Austrian and German Jews—both as Germans and as Jews—and made it plain to them that they stood no chance of surviving long in Auschwitz; they had been sent here only to be killed. They took out their loathing at meal times; the Jews were made to line up, and when a man's turn came, he was shoved forward by the Blockowi, who handed him a bowl and spoon and doled out a splat of stew from a bucket. A young Pole stood by with a spoon and quickly removed any pieces of meat he spotted in the bowl. Even the most laid-back and phlegmatic among the Buchenwalders were aggravated by this ritual, but any man who complained received a beating.

Gustav was a little better treated than others; he was regarded as Polish by birth and spoke the language. During those first few days he became acquainted with some of the older prisoners, and they told him about the ways of Auschwitz—about Birkenau, the gas chambers, and block 11, and confirmed what Gustav had heard about the terrible, fatal purpose of this place.

In daylight, the familiarity of the surroundings became clearer—the well-made brick buildings and the general air of the place. He *had* been here before. Auschwitz I had been created from the old military barracks built in the hamlet of Zasole by the Austrian army before World War I. The Polish army had taken it over after 1918, and now the SS had turned it into a concentration camp by constructing extra barrack blocks and surrounding it with an electrified fence. The familiar-looking huts and buildings Gustav had seen along the road from the station were the remnant of the barracks intended for migrant workers. This was where he had been in the hospital in 1915, in this very spot by the Sola, the river that flowed from the lake by the village where he'd been born. When he'd last seen it, it had been under snow and filled with soldiers, and he'd been a wounded hero. Now there was a prisoner tattoo beside the bullet wound for which he'd been treated here. It was as if this part of the world would not let him go; having birthed him, raised him, and nearly killed him once, it was determined to call him back.[35]

On October 28—the ninth day since the Buchenwalders' arrival—Auschwitz demonstrated its character. Two hundred and eighty Polish prisoners from block 3 were taken to the Death Block for execution. Realizing what was intended for them, some of them fought back in the vestibule of block 11. They were unarmed and weak, and the SS quickly butchered them and led the rest to the Black Wall. One of the doomed men passed a note for his family to a member of the Sonderkommando, but it was discovered by the SS and destroyed.[36] "Lots of scary things here," Gustav wrote. "It takes good nerves to withstand it." There were many whose nerves were beginning to fail them; one was Fritz.

בּ

Fritz had come to a decision. A sense of dread had been growing in him in the week since coming to Auschwitz. He'd become so accustomed to his daily work as a builder and to the fact that he owed his survival thus far to his position in the construction detail that to be without work in a place whose whole purpose was death was wearing away at his nerves. He felt that sooner rather than later, his turn would come; he would be selected as a useless eater and sent to the wall or the gas chambers. Misgiving turned to anxiety and dread, and then solidified into certainty. It preyed on his mind. He became convinced that the only way to save his life was to identify himself to the labor commander or someone else with authority and ask to be assigned work.

He confessed his thoughts to his father and some of his close friends. They argued strenuously against this rash idea. It was a fundamental principle of survival that you *never* drew attention to yourself in the slightest way. For Fritz to single himself out in such a blatant, obtrusive way was suicidal. But Fritz was young and headstrong, and he had convinced himself that he was doomed otherwise.

The first person he approached was the SS Blockführer. With the courage of desperation, Fritz identified himself and said he was a skilled builder and wished to be assigned work. The man stared at him, glanced at the yellow star on his uniform, and scoffed. "Who ever heard of a Jewish builder?" Nonetheless the Blockführer took him to the Rapportführer, SS-Sergeant Gerhard Palitzsch.

Palitzsch was a good-looking man—one of the few SS men who lived up to the Aryan ideal of athletic, chiseled handsomeness, pleasant and serene in his manner. In fact Gerhard Palitzsch had a reputation as a murderer second to none; not even his commander Hans Aumeier was more dedicated to killing. The number of prisoners Palitzsch had personally shot at the Black Wall was beyond counting. His preferred weapon was an infantry rifle, and he would shoot his victims in the back of the neck with an insouciance that impressed his fellow SS men. The commandant of Auschwitz, Rudolf Höss, often watched Palitzsch's executions "but never noticed the slightest stirring of an emotion in him. He performed his horrifying tasks nonchalantly, with an even temper and a straight face, and without any haste."[37] If any delay occurred, he would put down his rifle and whistle cheerfully to himself or chat casually to his comrades until the killing was resumed. He was proud of his work and felt not the slightest brush of conscience. The prisoners considered him "the biggest bastard in Auschwitz."[38]

And this was the man to whom Fritz Kleinmann had chosen to make himself conspicuous. Palitzsch's reaction was the same as the Blockführer's— he had never heard of a Jewish builder. "I will put it to the test," he said. "If you're trying to fool me, you'll be shot at once." He ordered the Blockführer to take the prisoner away and make him build something.

Fritz was escorted to a nearby construction site where the kapo provided materials and ordered him to try and make a pier—the upright section between two windows, an impossible task for anyone not properly trained. With death hanging over him, Fritz felt absolutely calm for the first time in two weeks. Taking his trowel and a brick, he began his task, scooping up the mortar and slapping it down deftly.

Within two hours he was back at the camp gate, escorted by a very surprised Blockführer. "He really can build," the man told Palitzsch. Palitzsch's impassive face registered displeasure; it went against his sense of what was proper. Nevertheless, he noted down Fritz's number and sent him back to his block.

Nothing changed immediately, but then, on October 30, the eleventh day since their arrival, the moment of reckoning came for the Buchenwalders. After morning roll call, all the Jewish prisoners recently transferred from other camps were paraded together for inspection by a group of SS officers. In addition to the 404 men from Buchenwald, there were 1,084 from Dachau, Natzweiler, Mauthausen, Flossenbürg, and Sachsenhausen, as well as 186 women who had just arrived from Ravensbrück—in all, 1,674.[39] They were ordered to strip naked and to walk slowly past the officers so that they could be evaluated. Those who appeared old or sick were directed to go to the left, the others to the right. The rate of selection appeared to be about half and half. Fritz approached; the officer looked him up and down and immediately indicated the right. Gustav's turn came. He was over fifty years old and had suffered badly that year. Several hundred other men who were Gustav's age—some even younger—had been sent to the left. They looked him up and down carefully, the hand went up—to the right. He walked over and stood beside Fritz.

By the end, more than six hundred people—including around a hundred Buchenwalders and virtually all the men from Dachau—had been condemned as unfit. Many were old friends and acquaintances of Gustav and Fritz. They were marched away to Birkenau and never seen again.[40]

"So this was the beginning in Auschwitz for us Buchenwalders," Fritz would recall later. "We knew now that we were doomed to death."[41]

But not yet. Following the selection, the remaining eight hundred men were also marched out. But instead of heading west toward the railroad and Birkenau, they were driven east. The SS had work for them; there was a camp to be built. They crossed the river, passing the town of Oświęcim, and marched on into countryside.

As they marched, driven in the familiar fashion with curses and blows from SS rifle butts and kapos' canes, the Buchenwalders felt a sense of relief not at all in keeping with their circumstances. They were alive, and that was everything. Whether Fritz's intervention had precipitated this move, nobody knew, but Gustav believed it was so. "Fritzl came with me willingly," he wrote in his diary. "He is a loyal companion, always at my side, taking care of everything; everyone admires the boy, and he is a true comrade to all of them." In at least some of their minds, Fritz's rash action had saved them all from the gas chamber.[42]

12 | Auschwitz-Monowitz

✡

IF AN AIRPLANE WERE to fly east over southern Poland on a day in November 1942—over the mountains and rolling hills smoothing to broad river plains and marshes—from it one would see little trace of the German occupation. Just small country towns and ancient mercantile cities straddling winding roads and bending rivers.

Flying high toward the gray scar of the city of Cracow, one would see a shape emerging from the woods and fields near the brown pen-stroke line of the railroad—a vast rectangle over a kilometer long and nearly a kilometer wide, filled with row after row after row of oblong barracks. Flying lower, one would make out the dots of the watchtowers in the perimeter fence, streets between the barracks, and on the near edge, among some trees, several buildings set apart, pouring out acrid smoke.

With the camp and crematoria of Birkenau passing out of sight, a dense cluster of buildings on the other side of the railroad would come into view. The Auschwitz camp, sitting beside the river Sola, would only be distinguished among the gray mass of workshops by the russet-colored roofs of its barrack blocks and its perimeter fence. To the right, the Sola winds away southward, a silver line fringed with the deep green of woods, meandering through the farmlands toward the old garrison town of Kenty and the green Beskid mountains. Beyond them, just out of sight, the lake and the village of Zablocie bei Saybusch, where Gustav Kleinmann was once a boy. To the left, the Sola bows north and east, cutting off the town of Oświęcim from the camp that has usurped its name and stained it forever. There the Sola flows into the Vistula and continues east toward Cracow and Warsaw.

Flying on, several kilometers beyond Oświęcim, another new scar emerges from the landscape: a massive, dark blight against the southern edge of the Vistula, edging out the once sleepy hamlet of Dwory: an area three kilometers long and over a kilometer wide, gridded with roads and tracks and filled from end to end with construction sites, vacant plots, dotted with offices, workshops, a few ridged roofs of factory buildings and the shells of many more, half-built, laced with cages of pipework, silos, and shining steel chimneys. This is the Buna Werke, belonging to chemical company IG Farben, under construction and already way behind schedule.

Tucked up beside it, at the far end where the little village of Monowitz stood until the SS emptied it, the beginnings of a new camp. A simple oblong marked out among the fields—minuscule beside the spread of the factory complex, with just a handful of barrack blocks, a few incomplete roads, and a grid of construction sites, speckled with the dots of prisoners hard at work.

בן

His hands moving with the quick deftness of experience and the urgency of fear, Fritz sliced mortar from the bucket and slapped it onto the first course of bricks, snaked the tip of the trowel through it, spreading the gray sludge, swiping the excess from the edges with quick strokes. He picked up a brick, buttered it, and laid it end-on to the last one, swiped off the mortar, then another. His mind focused on the task, as if that was all that existed, his whole world in that layering of mortar and brick.

"Tempo, tempo! Faster, faster!" The familiar voice of the Polish kapo, Petrek Boplinsky, cut into his thoughts. The man knew only a few words of German, and the only one they ever seemed to hear was *schneller!* as he strode around the site with his cane, urging on the brick and mortar carriers. The drive to build the camp was furious, and only the toughest and fittest could survive the pace. Few of the half-starved prisoners were up to it. "*Pięć na dupe!*"* Boplinsky yelled, followed by the thwack of the cane lashing some

---

* Polish: Five on the ass!

poor carrier five times across the buttocks. Without looking up, every other man put on a little extra speed.

A couple weeks had passed since Fritz and the others had arrived in the Monowitz camp.[1] It had been a living hell, as bad as the worst of Buchenwald, and many had not survived the initial onslaught. After the three-hour march from Auschwitz I, the new men had been herded into the barracks, where again they had to share bunks. Fritz and his father stuck together. The barracks were primitive and incomplete, with no lights, no washing facilities, and the only water supply a few faucets outside in the field. Jews weren't allowed in the barrack day rooms, which were reserved for Polish prisoners and Aryan kapos. The camp had no kitchens yet, so food was delivered each day from Auschwitz I.

Although work at Monowitz had begun in the summer, there was still almost no camp—just flat, open fields with a few wooden barracks, no fence, and only a sentry line to keep the prisoners in.[2] At first the new men were put to digging roads. It rained frequently, and the ground turned to mud that was hell to dig and bogged down the wheelbarrows. They would all return to the barracks each evening soaked to the skin and exhausted. There was no heating, but the SS Blockführers and Rapportführer still expected them to report each morning at roll call with clean, dry clothes and shoes. During those first days, Fritz had regarded his older and less fit comrades with concern—especially his papa. They wouldn't be able to stand this for long.

The camp was taking shape, with fences and the foundations for guard towers being laid, and more barracks. Fritz kept an eye on the progress; salvation lay in getting transferred to the construction detail.

One day as they were digging, SS-Sergeant Richard Stolten, Monowitz's labor manager, happened to pass near. It was doubly risky to attract the attention of the SS in Monowitz; there were no guard barracks yet, and they were trucked in from Auschwitz I each day in two shifts. The SS hated doing duty at Monowitz and could be particularly violent tempered. But Fritz reckoned it was worth the risk; he laid down his shovel and hurried after him. "Number 68629. I'm a bricklayer," he said, and indicated his workmates. "We're from Buchenwald; many of us are skilled construction workers."

Stolten stopped and looked him up and down, then called the kapo over. "Find out which of these Jews are builders," he said, "and take their numbers."

It had been as simple as that. The Auschwitz SS were under enormous pressure to complete the camp so that the labor force for the Buna Werke could be moved to full capacity. Fritz was transferred to construction along with several of his friends. As an upholsterer Gustav had some woodworking skills, and he passed himself off as a carpenter. While Fritz worked on laying foundations and floors, his father was put to work on the prefabricated wooden sections from which the barrack blocks were constructed.

The haste of the SS was such that they had to bring in paid outside workers from the German Plassmann construction company. For the first time since entering the concentration camps, Fritz and Gustav worked alongside civilians.

On the other side of the main Oświęcim–Monowitz road, the hulking shadow of the Buna Werke loomed. It represented the zenith of German industrial collaboration with the Nazi regime. The works belonged to the chemical giant IG Farben and was designed to produce synthetic fuel and rubber, as well as other chemical products, for the German war effort, and to do so at a healthy profit for the company.[3] Their deal with the SS allowed IG Farben to draw on an unlimited supply of slave labor from Auschwitz, for which they paid the SS three to four marks per day (which went straight into the SS coffers). This was less than the going wage for civilian workers and gave the company additional big savings on worker facilities, sickness benefits, recreation, and all the other usual costs of labor. Productivity was bound to be lower because of the poor physical condition of the maltreated, starved prisoners, but the company considered the savings worth it on their bottom line.[4] Any workers who were too sick or broken down to work could simply be sent to the gas chambers at Birkenau and replaced from the fresh intakes constantly arriving from all over Germany's conquered territories.

By the time the Buchenwalders arrived, there were around two thousand prisoners at Monowitz, mostly working on construction of the factory complex.[5] Previously, the construction workers for the Buna Werke had been brought in by train from Auschwitz I each day; with the labor requirement ballooning, having a satellite camp on-site had become imperative. The management of IG Farben, way behind schedule in getting their factory operational, were under pressure from Himmler and Goering to make progress. The war was proving far more intense and difficult than had been expected in early 1941, and the demand for fuel and rubber was frantic. The company wanted the number of prisoners more than doubled, and the Auschwitz SS were struggling to oblige.[6]

While some of the slaves were transferred from other concentration camps, a large proportion were Jews brought directly from the Netherlands, France, Belgium, and Poland. On arriving at Auschwitz, the vast majority went straight to the gas chambers, and a small number were selected as fit to work and sent to Monowitz. These people hadn't been through the winnowing process of the camps; they were less toughly made than the veteran prisoners and lacked their survival skills. Gustav, whose job was less skilled than Fritz's, worked alongside men from these transports. They were rapidly broken by the pace of the labor, the abuse, the starvation, and the lack of care for the sick. By Gustav's reckoning, between eighty and one hundred and fifty of these poor wretches disappeared from Monowitz each day, sent to the gas chambers. Nobody could survive this for long, and even the veterans were destroyed by it sooner or later.

Among the new arrivals Fritz met two old friends from Buchenwald: Jule Meixner and Joschi Szende, who had been transferred to Natzweiler a few months earlier and now transferred again to Auschwitz. From them he learned the heartrending news that Leo Moses had been murdered in Natzweiler. After surviving eight years in the camps, the SS had finally finished him off. The tragic injustice of it was agonizing. Fritz recalled that first encounter in the stone quarry, when Leo had offered him the little black pills to counter the endemic diarrhea; he remembered the influence Leo had used to have him moved to safer work details. Fritz owed his survival thus far to several people, but Leo Moses, the hard-bitten, gentle-hearted old communist, was the dearest, and Fritz would always grieve for him.

Fritz discovered that kindness could be found in unexpected places. The German civilian construction workers were too wary of the SS to talk openly with the prisoners, which was forbidden. But once some of the blocks had been built and the work detail moved indoors to install washbasins and fittings, they became a little more communicative. Fritz learned that they weren't dedicated Nazis, but neither were they hostile to the Nazi cause. When he tried to probe them about what they thought of the brutal slave-driving of the prisoners, they clammed up. And yet, some of them at least betrayed a little sympathy; their manner became a little warmer, and they began to leave pieces of bread lying around after eating their lunches, and the cigarette butts they discarded were longer than before, with a good deal of smoking left in them. The civilians' foreman, nicknamed Frankenstein because of his angular skull and constant ferocious expression, proved gentler than he looked; he never yelled or berated the prisoners, and his manner influenced kapo Boplinsky, who became more approachable and used his cane less on the carriers.

This slight relaxation of the labor regime did nothing to offset the hunger, and gifts of bread crusts did not take away the fact that every man was being ground down, some quicker, some slower, but all to the same terrible end. The older prisoners were usually the quickest. Fritz, seeing his father at work, could only marvel at his will to live.

אבא

Gustav had a short reprieve from outdoor labor once the first few barrack blocks had been completed. Trucks arrived loaded with bunks and bales of straw. Prisoners, including Gustav, were set to stuffing straw into jute sacks to make mattresses. Aside from working in the DAW factory at Buchenwald, this was the closest he had come to being back in his old trade, and he rather enjoyed himself, stuffing and stitching up the mattresses faster and more neatly than any of the others.

It didn't last, and before long he was back outdoors. Now that the erection of the barrack walls in their part of the camp was complete, he was faced with the prospect of being put to hard labor. Even worse was the possibility of being assigned to the Buna Werke sites. Some of his block-mates worked there and came back each evening exhausted, telling dreadful stories about the behavior of the SS guards and kapos. It was like the Buchenwald quarry all over again; there were constant beatings merely to alleviate the boredom and bad tempers of the SS. Often the prisoners came back to their blocks on stretchers. Any man whose productivity wasn't sufficient for the company was sent to Birkenau.

In Gustav's mind, it was imperative to avoid being transferred there. Each morning, when SS-Sergeant Stolten called out that day's skilled worker requirements, Gustav came forward. It didn't matter if Stolten wanted roofers or glaziers or carpenters, Gustav was there, swearing that he had that skill. And he managed to pull it off, day after day, bluffing his way on the roofs and windows or any other building work required. Fritz worried about the consequences if the SS found out that his father didn't really possess these skills. Gustav shrugged it off. He was smart, and good with his hands; he believed there was no craft he couldn't master sufficiently well to evade notice by the SS.

As more barracks were completed, they were filled with newly arrived transports of prisoners who were sent to work on the factory sites. Conditions in the camp were horrible beyond imagining, even for veterans: overcrowded, freezing cold, and dirty. The sanitary facilities still weren't completed, and dysentery began to spread. Prisoners died in frightening numbers every day.

And yet it was mild compared with what was occurring at Birkenau. Three or four rail transports came to Monowitz each day filled with Jews who had survived the selections at Birkenau. They told awful stories about the plundering of victims by the SS. "In Birkenau they are sleeping on dollar bills and pound notes," Gustav wrote angrily, "which the Dutch and others bring with them. The SS are millionaires, and every one of them abuses the Jewish girls. The attractive ones are allowed to live; the others go down the drain."

The Polish winter set in fiercely, freezing the ground. There was still no functioning heating in Monowitz, and the cooking facilities were ramshackle. At Christmas the cookers broke down, and the prisoners were without food for two days. They didn't even get the usual crusts from the civilian workers, who were on holiday. Eventually, food was delivered from the kitchens at Auschwitz I.

Fritz and Gustav were moved to separate blocks. They met in the evenings and talked about their situation. Fritz was losing hope. It was January 1943, and after only two and a half months in Auschwitz-Monowitz, most of their comrades from Buchenwald were already dead. The Austrian *Prominenten* had all been murdered: Fritz Löhner-Beda, lyricist of the "Buchenwald Song," beaten to death in December for not working hard enough; Robert Danneberg, the Social Democratic politician, the same fate; the lawyer and author Dr. Heinrich Steinitz . . . the list went on, all dead. Worst of all the deaths to Fritz was Willi Kurz, the boxer, who had been kapo in the Buchenwald garden detail and helped Fritz and his young friends survive their ordeal there.

Unable to see any hope in their situation, Fritz poured out all his fears to his papa when they met one evening. Gustav told him not to give up. "Hold your head up high," he said. "Lad, the Nazi murderers will not beat us!" Fritz wasn't reassured; his friends had all lived by the same philosophy, and most of them were dead.

In the privacy of his own thoughts, Gustav struggled to live by his own motto. "Every day the departures. Sometimes it is heartbreaking, but I tell myself, *Keep your head high; the day will come when you are free. You have good friends by your side. So don't worry—there are bound to be setbacks."* But how many setbacks could a man take? How long could he go on holding up his head and avoiding death?

Even the fittest had little chance, because the daily tide wrack of deaths was not due to chance or negligence or random outbreaks of malice, as had been the case in the early years at Buchenwald; the Final Solution was being enacted, and even the Jews who were useful laborers were being deliberately, methodically worked to death. If one died, well, that was one less Jew to trouble the world. There were a dozen more to do his work. If a person was to survive, it must be by skill, companionship, and an extraordinary portion of luck.

For Gustav, his skills came together with his luck that January. The SS finally recognized his trade and decided they had a use for it. He was appointed camp saddler, with responsibility for all saddlery and upholstery work in Monowitz—mostly repairs for the SS. It was indoor work, out of the savage weather, and once the heating system became operational, he was even warm. This felt almost like safety. Gustav was acutely conscious that others were not so fortunate, and that safety never lasted long.

13 | The End of Gustav Kleinmann, Jew

ב

BRICK BY BRICK, COURSE BY COURSE, the buildings rose in the Monowitz camp. The double electrified fence was up, the barrack blocks were all but complete, and the barracks for the SS were under way. Through the early weeks of 1943, Fritz helped build the headquarters garage and a command post for the SS Blockführers beside the main gate.

He worked beside a civilian bricklayer. Like many of the others, this man didn't speak to the prisoners, but whereas most avoided conversation, this man wouldn't even acknowledge Fritz's existence. The two of them laid bricks next to each other day in, day out, and he never said a word, never even noticed any gesture of Fritz's. Fritz grew accustomed to his eerily silent presence until one day, out of the blue, the man murmured, without looking up, "I was in the moors at Esterwegen." It was almost inaudible, but made Fritz jump. The man carried on working without missing a beat, as if he hadn't spoken.

That evening Fritz told his father and friends about this cryptic pronouncement. They understood immediately. Esterwegen had been one of the Nazis' earliest concentration camps, part of a group established in the sparsely populated moors of Emsland in northwest Germany in 1933. The Emsland camps had been set up by the local authorities to incarcerate political enemies—mostly members of the Socialist party. They were run by the SA and were so notoriously, chaotically brutal that when the SS took the camps over in 1934 their behavior seemed civilized by comparison—at least their viciousness was disciplined.[1] Many of those early political prisoners had later been released, and Fritz's silent workmate must have been one of them. No wonder he was so reluctant to associate with the inmates here—he must be in a state of constant fear of being singled out and incarcerated again.

In confiding to Fritz, the man had broken the spell. He maintained his Trappist silence, but each morning Fritz would find little gifts beside his mortar tub—a piece of bread and a few cigarettes. Little things, but truly heartwarming, and in this environment potentially lifesaving.

Working alongside free civilians, receiving acts of charity, finding his feet in this new camp, and enjoying the privileged existence of a skilled worker who didn't have to slave on the Buna sites, Fritz began to grow more relaxed about life. A great deal too relaxed, in fact; after more than three years in the camps he should have known better.

One day he was at work on the scaffolding around the shell of the half-finished Blockführers' building. He was musing on a remark his grandfather had once made; old Markus Rottenstein had been a bank clerk specializing in shorthand with Austria's prestigious Boden-Credit-Anstalt (bankers to the imperial family, no less),[2] and had firm views on the status of his people, believing that Jews shouldn't be in manual trades. Just then, a friend of Fritz's who worked on the haulage column arrived with a load of building materials and called up to him, "Hey Fritz, what's new?"

"Nothing," Fritz replied, and indicated his surroundings. "My grandfather always used to say, 'A Jew belongs in the coffee house, not on a builder's scaffolding.'"

The words were hardly out of his mouth when a furious voice called from below, "Jew! Down from that scaffolding!"

Heart racing, Fritz hurried down the ladder and found himself facing SS-Lieutenant Vinzenz Schöttl, director of the Monowitz camp, a terrifying nemesis with snake eyes in a face like dough. Schöttl was usually reserved, a father of four from Bavaria whose main interest was in acquiring booze and luxuries for himself through the black market; yet he had a capricious, volatile nature and was absolutely ruthless in ordering punishments.[3] On one occasion, when an inspection discovered some inmates in block 22 with lice, Schöttl had the whole block—including the seniors—sent to the gas chambers. He glared at Fritz. "*What* did you say?" he shouted.

Jumping to attention and whipping off his cap, Fritz repeated mechanically: "My grandfather said, 'A Jew belongs in the coffee house, not on a builder's scaffolding.'"

He stood, scarcely daring to breathe, while Schöttl stared at him. Suddenly the dough face split and let loose a guffaw. "Clear off, Jew-pig!" With that, Schöttl walked off laughing.

Sweating and palpitating, Fritz climbed back up the ladder. He had nearly paid the price for complacency. There was no safety.

With twenty-five blocks now complete, the influx of new Jewish prisoners to Monowitz was growing. Fritz and the other veterans were troubled by how naive some of them were. They had been through the selection at Birkenau, and their wives, mothers, children, and fathers had been sent one way, while they—the young men—had been sent the other. That was all they knew. They had no inkling of what would happen to their families, and hoped they would see them again. Although they appealed to the veteran prisoners for information, Fritz and the others couldn't bear to reveal the truth and shatter their hopes of being reunited. Eventually, inevitably, they found out that their wives and little ones, their mothers and sisters and fathers, had all been gassed. Some of these men fell into a depressed, helpless torpor. In their hearts, they died. They didn't look after themselves in body or soul; they moved about in a state of utter apathy, and gradually joined the ranks of the wasted and hopeless, starved, skin and bone, scabbed, with lifeless eyes and empty souls. In camp slang these walking dead were known cryptically as *Muselmänner*—Muslims. The origin of this term was lost in camp lore, but some said it was because when these poor souls could no longer stand, their collapsed posture resembled a Muslim at prayer.[4] They were doomed. Once a man became a Muselmann, the other prisoners would avoid him; their hearts closed, partly in disgust, partly in dread at the thought that they too might become like this.

Once the building work he'd been assigned to was complete, Fritz was among a group of six construction workers selected by SS labor manager Stolten for transfer to the camp bath block and its heating plant. He found himself cementing and mounting heating units for another civilian company whose foreman nearly drove Fritz mad. Jakob Preuss was all noise and bluster in front of the SS. If a guard or an officer came near, Preuss would throw out a salute and cry, "Heil Hitler!" He never ceased berating and yelling at the prisoners working under him. He grated on Fritz's nerves. After a while, Preuss called

Fritz into the foreman's office, and screamed at him: "What do you think you're doing, with your work rate?" Fritz was taken aback; he knew better than to slack, and his performance had never been criticized before. Preuss lowered his voice and said, "If you keeping working this fast, we'll be finished soon, and I'll be sent to the front!"

So that was the secret of his bad temper: fear. Fritz slowed his work rate, and Preuss became positively friendly, wangling extra food for his inmate workers. He was joined in this by another of the German civilian workers, a welder from Breslau called Erich Bukovsky. Both Preuss and Bukovsky, despite the former's ostentatious salutes, confessed that they hoped the Nazis would be defeated.

It was beginning to look as if they might. Until now it had seemed that Germany would go on winning and crushing and destroying without end, irresistible. And then, in February 1943, news came through the grapevine that the Germans had surrendered to the Russians at Stalingrad. The Nazis were not invincible. Fritz heard about this through a French worker, a man with an extravagant waxed mustache, whom Fritz only ever knew as Jean (the others just called him Mustache). Jean also told him about the Resistance in France. It was all heartening news, which Fritz shared eagerly with his father and friends when they met up in the evenings. And yet, Stalingrad, England, and Africa all the places where the Allies were beating the Germans—were a very long way from Auschwitz.

אבא

Gustav's fingers worked deftly at a leather panel, trimming, pushing the heavy needle through the tough, pliant material. He was content in his day-to-day existence, if not in his heart. There was no shortage of work, and he was, in effect, a kapo now, with the privileges of a kapo and a handful of semi-skilled workers under him. He had no cause to complain about them and plenty to occupy his hands. Being indoors had been a boon during the winter months, and even now, with May beginning and summer on its way, it was infinitely better than being on the haulage column or in the factories. He got on well with his block senior, Bernd Grath, a veteran Communist Party activist. Grath was a decent man; food was shared fairly in his block, and any inmate who came to him with a complaint or a request would always go away satisfied.

Taking each day as it came, Gustav doggedly reassured himself that he would survive—these Nazis might bend him but could not break him. Fritz didn't share his father's sanguine, dogmatic principle of determined optimism; he never ceased worrying about everything—his friends, his papa, the future. He wondered about Edith and Kurt; it was a year and a half now since America had joined the war and the last communication with Kurt had closed down.

Fritz also fretted about what had become of his mother and Herta. There was no way of finding out where they'd been sent or what had become of them—all he'd ever learned was that it was to the Ostland, a vast, vague region. Hearing the tales that came out of Birkenau—especially the terrible rumors leaked by the *Geheimnisträgern* (bearers of secrets) who served in the Sonderkommando in the crematoria—it was sickeningly easy to imagine what might have been waiting for them in the east. Fritz longed for information. Unlike in Buchenwald, where they'd been able to communicate with home, here they were cut off entirely, unable even to write to the relatives and friends who (they hoped) still lived in Vienna. An anger was growing in Fritz, born out of helplessness. His nature was not like his father's. Gustav tried not to dwell on things. He kept his head down, did his work, and lived from day to day. Fritz couldn't do that. It wouldn't be long before his hatred of the Nazis became too great to contain.

While Gustav stitched, a short distance away, across the road and rail tracks, a decision was brewing that could bring his comfortable existence to an abrupt end. Progress at the Buna Werke was still lagging far behind schedule, despite Himmler having been assured that the factories would be finished by now.[5] Anxious to find out what the problem was, a commission had been sent from the Reich Main Security Office (RSHA)* in Berlin, the umbrella organization for all SS security and policing. The RSHA was Himmler's enforcement and intelligence arm, and it wanted answers.

What the commission found didn't please them at all. The vast complex of factory buildings rising out of the construction sites was still only half-complete, and none of its units were ready to begin production. The methanol plant was almost set to go online—actually a few months ahead of schedule—but the far more important rubber and fuel factories were nowhere near finished, and wouldn't be for months, maybe another year. Accompanied by Monow-

---

* RSHA: *Reichssicherheitshauptamt*, Reich Main Security Office

itz director Schöttl, the SS top brass stalked around the site, scrutinizing and inspecting, under the guidance of managers and engineers from IG Farben.

They grew more displeased by the minute. They noticed that about a third of the construction workers were camp inmates, who were visibly weaker and less efficient than the paid civilians. Their effectiveness was hampered further by the necessity of constantly guarding them and keeping them together, which prohibited splitting them off and spreading them out more effectively. As if that weren't enough, they also noticed that many of the prisoner foremen were Jews. They quizzed Schöttl about this highly undesirable arrangement. He told them that there weren't enough Aryans in Monowitz; nearly all the prisoners he was sent were Jews, so he had little choice but to make some of them foremen. The visitors glowered and insisted that it would not do; Jews must not be put in positions of responsibility. They ordered Schöttl to do something about it.

A few days later, on May 10, the Monowitz prisoners were at evening roll call when Schöttl appeared in company with SS-Captain Hans Aumeier, the malignant murderer in overall charge of protective custody. They were armed with a list and looked grave, as if they had a very serious task to perform. From the list Schöttl read out the numbers of seventeen prisoners. As they stepped forward, they all turned out to be Jews who had foreman positions—mostly veteran Buchenwalders and Sachsenhauseners—and among them was prisoner 68523: Gustav Kleinmann. Everyone knew what this usually signified. Selections like this happened all the time, and typically meant one thing: the Birkenau gas chambers.

Aumeier inspected the selected men, looking with distaste at the Jewish stars on their uniforms. In most cases, they were of the two-color kind: a Star of David made up of a red triangle over a yellow triangle, a practice dating from the time when the Nazis still felt they had to have a pretext for sending Jews to the camps.

"Get rid of them," Aumeier ordered.

A kapo who was standing by unpicked Gustav's star from his jacket, separated the two triangles, and gave the red one back to him. The same was done to the other sixteen men, leaving them clutching their red triangles, utterly mystified.

"You are political prisoners," Aumeier announced. "There are no Jews in positions of authority here. From this moment you are all Aryans."

And that was that. As far as the regime was concerned, Gustav Kleinmann was officially no longer a Jew. Nobody cared that he was still the same man, with the same birth, the same character, thoughts, and history. By the mere alteration of a list and a badge, Gustav Kleinmann was no longer a threat and burden to the German people. And there, neatly played out in one simple, self-satirizing ritual, was the whole towering idiocy of Nazi racial ideology.

From that moment, life for the Jews in Monowitz was transformed. The seventeen who had been Aryanized were now on a higher plane, and although they weren't immune from punishment, they were safe from outright persecution and no longer disgusting in the eyes of the SS. From their positions as foremen and kapos, they were able to gain influence and help their fellow Jews acquire good positions. Gustl Herzog became a clerk in the prisoner records office, an enormously important position, and eventually rose to be its head functionary.[6] This office was where the master list of Monowitz prisoners used at roll call was maintained, updated, and organized according to block and labor assignments. Gustl oversaw a staff of several dozen prisoners, most of them women, who undertook this mammoth clerical task. Jupp Hirschberg, who'd been a block senior in Buchenwald, became kapo of the SS headquarters garage, where staff cars and other vehicles were maintained and washed; he became privy to all manner of gossip from the officers' chauffeurs, as well as intelligence about events in the wider camp and the world outside. Another Jew became a clerk assigned to labor detail organization, and another was made a block senior in the "re-educational" enclosure of the camp where Soviet prisoners of war were kept. Others acquired jobs ranging from carpenters' kapo to camp barber. Between them, they brought the conditions for other Jews to a new level of humaneness. They were able to speak out to prevent beatings, obtain decent rations, and resist the influence of the brutal green-triangle kapos.

For Gustav it meant his comfortable working life was given an additional security. There was no danger now of his being selected for the gas chambers, and so long as he continued to take reasonable care, he was safe from random acts of violence by the SS.

But his change of status brought with it an unexpected complication. He and Fritz were now living in different blocks and would meet in the evenings to talk. They had grown so used to this arrangement that they thought nothing of it. One evening they were deep in conversation—reminiscing about the old days, weighing up the future, discussing their inner thoughts, exchanging news about the camp—and failed to notice an SS Blockführer eyeing their intimate conversation with deep suspicion.

He interrupted, jabbing at Fritz. "Jew-pig, what do you think you're doing, talking to a kapo like that?"

They both jumped to attention, startled out of their wits. Fritz answered, more than a little puzzled, "He's my father."

The Blockführer's fist slammed into Fritz's face. "He has a red triangle; he can't be a Jew's father."

Fritz was stunned; in all his time in the camps he'd never been punched right in the face like that. "He *is* my father," he insisted.

"Liar!" Again the Blockführer punched him. Again—either from defiant courage or sheer incomprehension—Fritz repeated his answer, and received another savage punch. Gustav stood by in horror, helpless, knowing that if he intervened it would make things worse for both of them.

Fritz was battered to the ground by the enraged SS man. At last, the Blockführer ran out of steam. He ordered Fritz to get up and leave. Fritz picked himself up, bruised and bleeding, and walked away. "He really is my son," Gustav said.

The man stared at him in disbelief, as if he were a madman. It was impossible; an Aryan could not be the parent of a Jew; therefore prisoner 68629, Jew, could not be the son of 68523, Aryan, period. Gustav gave up; if he'd told the man he was in fact an Aryanized Jew, it would probably change nothing. Indeed, it was entirely possible that the Blockführer knew that Gustav had been Aryanized by Aumeier, but would still think the same way. The racism of Nazis was beyond fathoming.

אחים

Arriving at Auschwitz-Monowitz, turning off the main Auschwitz road that separated the camp from the huge Buna Werke, one entered through a simple gateway in the double electrified fence, passing the small Blockführers' building. Inside, a single street ran straight to the far end of the enclosure, a distance of just 490 meters,* with a turning circle at the end.[7] Barrack blocks lined the road, end-on; there were three rows to the left, two to the right. About halfway along, on the right, was the large open space of the roll-call square, with a

---

* 536 yards

smiths' workshop and the inmates' kitchen block to one side, and a neat grass border. The grass was carefully tended, as were the verges and flower beds in all concentration camps; the contrast between the care given to these patches of decoration compared with the abuse and murder of human beings was a paradox that drove some prisoners mad.[8]

A little farther along, on the left-hand side of the street, stood block 7. Outwardly it was no different from the others: a single-story wooden barrack, not particularly well made, measuring 17.5 by 8 meters.* But inside it was very special, for this block belonged to the *Prominenten*, the prisoner VIPs. Again, these were not like the *Prominenten* of Buchenwald; there were no celebrities or statesmen here. Monowitz's high-status prisoners were the kapos and foremen and men of special skills with special duties—the *Funktionshäftlinge*, functionary prisoners, the inmate aristocracy. Lesser men were not allowed here.[9] Gustav Kleinmann, camp saddler and newly minted Aryan, was now a *Prominente* and had a bunk in block 7. Having come here a despised Jew and ordinary laborer—the lowest of the low—he was now among the most privileged.

In his personal state of contentment, Gustav was becoming less conscious of the sufferings of others, or at least less disturbed by them now that they happened mostly out of his sight. On the rare occasions when he took out his notebook, it was to observe how peace had settled on the camp, and that fewer prisoners were being sent to the gas chambers—albeit because the selections at Birkenau were becoming more thorough in weeding out and murdering the weak. By Gustav's reckoning, about 10 to 15 percent survived from each transport—"The rest are gassed. The most gruesome scenes play out." But still, "Everything is more peaceful in Monowitz, a proper work camp." To Gustav's eye, trained by terrible experience, this camp's primary purpose was to exploit, not to break its inmates, and the horror of life within and without its fences was diminished compared with what he had seen.

Life would have been bearable in block 7 if it hadn't been for two things. One was separation from Fritz. The other was the man who fluttered above all the *Prominenten* like a malevolent, bloodsucking bat: Josef "Jupp" Windeck, the camp senior and chief of all the kapos and functionary prisoners. If the SS had designed their ideal prisoner enforcer, they could not have produced one more to their liking than Jupp Windeck.

---

* Approximately 57 by 26 feet

He wasn't much to look at—small and slight, with the look of a weakling. But his appearance was belied by the temperament of a tyrant.[10] His bland, characterless features expressed a disdain and scorn for all he saw; he loved to lord over his fellow men and trample them down to enhance his elevation. The son of a builder from northwestern Germany, Windeck had been a petty criminal since the age of sixteen, with twenty-two convictions to his name, and had been in and out of prisons and concentration camps since the early 1930s, including Esterwegen and Sachsenhausen. He'd been in Auschwitz since 1940 and wore the black triangle of an "asocial," a catch-all category that included addicts, alcoholics, the homeless, pimps, the unemployed, and the "immoral." He'd quickly become camp senior in Auschwitz I and was transferred to Monowitz at the same time as the Buchenwalders.

It had taken Windeck no time at all to establish a reign of corruption and terror. He enriched himself through thievery and extortion, and bribed certain SS sergeants. "Well, so much stuff came with the Jews," Windeck recalled later, "and we filched from it, of course we did . . . as kapos we always got ourselves the best."[11] His chief ally was SS-Sergeant Josef Remmele, the brutal Rapportführer, who shielded him from the SS and in return benefited from Windeck's moneymaking schemes. Windeck was permitted to dress as he liked, and favored riding boots with breeches and a dark jacket—probably in an attempt to mimic the look of an SS officer. He would stride about the camp, never without his dog whip, and in his strutting self-importance would have been a laughable figure if it hadn't been for the power vested in him. There were allegations that he sexually abused younger prisoners, and his temper was capricious and violent. He murdered several prisoners, beating or kicking them to death or drowning them in the washroom basins.[12] It was Jupp Windeck who had murdered the lyricist Fritz Löhner-Beda, lashing the weakened, broken old man with his dog whip.[13]

"A little man who always was a nobody and suddenly had power" was how Windeck's henchman Ephraim "Freddi" Diamant described him. "He particularly liked to beat up feeble, half-starved, and sick inmates . . . When these miserable fellows lay on the ground before him, he trampled on them, on their faces, their stomachs, all over, with the heel of his boots." He was particularly proud and vain of his riding boots: "God help the man who dirtied Windeck's boots, for he could be murdered for that."[14]

With their conversion to Aryan status, Gustav and the other Jewish kapos and functionaries were able to hold off Jupp Windeck's cruelties and protect their fellow Jews, who were the majority of prisoners in Monowitz now. They received aid from the communist political prisoners, with whom they formed an alliance. When Windeck's SS ally Rapportführer Remmele was transferred to another satellite camp in May 1943, this helped their cause by isolating Windeck from his protectors.[15]

But the balance of power reverted to the tyrant when a transport of six hundred prisoners from Mauthausen-Gusen arrived in Monowitz. The Mauthausen concentration camp complex in Austria was reputed to be one of the regime's harshest, with a large prisoner population who were put to extreme hard labor in a granite quarry. The consignment of six hundred sent to Monowitz in 1943 consisted entirely of green-triangle men, and there were some real savages among them. Windeck immediately began gathering them around him, strengthening his position and steering them into powerful roles as kapos and block seniors.

The Jews and communists resisted determinedly, but Windeck and his cronies were too powerful. Any prisoner who showed resistance was beaten— sometimes to death. The misery in Monowitz redoubled. But one by one Windeck's green men began to fall of their own accord; barbaric by nature, they couldn't restrain their behavior. One would go on a drunken bender, another would steal from the camp, yet another would pick a fight with an SS man or a civilian worker. Those who did so were removed and sent to the purgatory of Auschwitz's coal mining subcamps.[16] As the months went by, Jupp Windeck's new power base eroded away until eventually they were all gone.

It was Windeck's own corruption that brought on the final crisis. Gustl Herzog, in his position as clerk in the prisoner record office, discovered evidence that Windeck had acquired a precious necklace and was intending to mail it to his wife. This intelligence found its way to the camp Gestapo at Auschwitz I. Windeck was seized and sentenced to two weeks in the block 11 bunker, after which he was sent to a punishment company in Birkenau. Always a cunning operator and well-liked by the SS, within a few weeks he'd wrangled himself a position as camp senior in the Birkenau men's camp. But he never troubled Monowitz again.[17]

The Jewish Aryans regained their influence; the atmosphere among the prisoners became comradely again, they received their proper allowance of food, had showers once a week and fresh laundry once a month. There was order, and all that remained to worry about were the routine hazards of the SS, sickness, the ceaseless dangers of work, as well as the periodic selections of the ill and weak for the gas chambers. By contrast with what they had been through, it could almost be called civilization, albeit a civilization carved out with bleeding fingers inside the fences of hell.

14 | Resistance and Collaboration: The Death of Fritz Kleinmann

בֵּן

THE GREAT MACHINE IN which the concentration camps were the main components was a formidable but shockingly ramshackle work of engineering. Constructing it had been a process of extemporization—a component added here, a redesign there, parts bolted on. It ran at a juddering pace, misfiring, stuttering, consuming its human grist, pouring out bones and ashes, and ejecting an exhaust of nauseating smoke. The crusher was vast and growing all the time. The individual human, in drab blue and gray stripes, wasn't only physically impressed into the machine but morally and psychologically too. Beyond the Blockführers and kapos, the 380-volt barbed wire and watchtowers, the SS commandants and guard dogs, beyond the roads and rail tracks, the commandeered village and construction sites, the camps, the camp system, the hierarchy of the SS, beyond all this was a nation, a government, and a society teeming with human beings whose base, animal emotions—fear, spite, lust for gain or some imagined former greatness—empowered the system that kept the stripe-uniformed beings shut, helpless, inside the wire.

Their incarceration was intended to be the simple solution to the society's complex problems. The removal of its human toxins—criminals, left-wing activists, Jews, homosexuals—was supposed to bring back the nation's great days. But the cure was not a cure but a poison, slowly but surely bringing their nation to the ground. The inefficient labor of starved slaves, the cost of the system that enslaved them, the weakening of science and industry by the removal of geniuses because they were tainted by race, hamstrung the nation's economy. Becoming a pariah among nations had cost trade. Trying to solve these further problems by wars of conquest, more enslavement, more murder of the people falsely believed to be the root cause of the nation's woes, the crusher rattled on, day and night, grinding and destroying and slowly wearing itself out.

Fritz Kleinmann found the helplessness and hopelessness of being trapped in the machine intolerable. His father was safe for now, which lifted a great weight from his heart. But the injustices and insane cruelty of the system could make a sane man crazy, and a pious one curse God. They lived out their enslavement, and in most cases died their ignominious deaths, within fences and walls their fellow prisoners had built. Fritz himself, with meticulous skill, had raised the walls, helped create this prison out of open fields. Across the road, in the Buna Werke, other men like him made walls and roads and structures of steel, within which other slaves, male and female, would labor for the benefit of the Reich and IG Farben's bottom line. The very bricks and stones that Fritz laid had been molded and cut by yet other prisoners in stripes in the brick works and stone quarries run by the SS.[1]

From his earliest days in Buchenwald Fritz had learned that the key to survival was solidarity and cooperation. Deprivation and hunger bred hostility between prisoners, fracturing them along the lines of race, religion, and background, to the point where they would fight over an unfair portion of turnip soup, where a person might commit murder for a piece of bread. Even fathers and sons had been known to kill one another in the extremity of starvation. Only solidarity and friendship and acts of kindness were strong enough to keep humans alive for any length of time. Lone wolves and mavericks, or those who were isolated by their inability to understand German or Yiddish, never lasted long against the relentless terror of the SS and the green-triangle kapos.[2]

Bonding together made survival more likely, but nothing could safeguard it. Everywhere Fritz looked he saw the marks of abuse and deprivation and the signs of impending death in his fellow prisoners, even in himself.[3]

Even if there were no bruises or cuts or broken bones, there were sores and scabs, pallor and chapped skin, limping steps and gapped teeth. The inmates of Monowitz were able to shower once a week, but it was an ordeal. If a block senior was of the brutish kind and wished to get the business over quickly, his block inmates would have to strip in the bunk room then run naked to the shower block, wearing only shoes. After showering, only the first men out got dry towels; they were passed along, so if you lagged behind you got nothing but a soaking wet rag and had to walk back to the barrack dripping, even in the coldest winter weather. Pneumonia was endemic, and often fatal. There was a prisoner hospital but although it was large, taking up several barrack blocks, and well equipped by its prisoner staff,[4] treatment under the SS doctors was rudimentary, and it was a fearful place, often full of typhus patients. Nobody went there unless they had to; admissions were subject to selections, and if the patient was deemed unlikely to recover quickly, he went to the gas chambers or received a lethal injection.

Every day the prisoners lived with hunger. Food was distributed in the barrack, but there were only a few bowls provided, so the first to get their helping of soup had to wolf it down so as not to keep the others waiting. Any man who took his time would be shoved impatiently. Each morning their acorn coffee was served in the same bowls. If you managed to acquire your own spoon, it was as precious to you as jewels; you would guard it with your life, and as knives were unobtainable, you would extend its usefulness by sharpening the handle on a stone. There was no toilet paper in the latrines, so scrap paper was another valuable commodity; torn-up cement bags from the construction sites could be obtained from friends who worked there. Sometimes a newspaper might be acquired from a civilian—perhaps left lying around at the factory and smuggled back to camp—and pieces could be used or traded for food.

The people suffering this humiliation might be regarded by Germans as human garbage, but their nation's war economy was increasingly dependent on their labor. This was the new age of greatness that Hitler's Germany had brought into existence: a world in which a little square of waste paper became a currency with a tangible value, either to spend or to keep one's ass wiped.

Each man's body was subjected constantly to a hundred shocks and irritations. Having a decent pair of shoes was absolutely fundamental. The wooden clogs with which many prisoners in Buchenwald had been issued ruined a laboring man's feet in no time. But even regular shoes could be a prisoner's undoing. If they were too large, they chafed and caused blisters that were prone to infection. If they were too small, the problem was even worse. Socks were rare, and many improvised with strips of fabric torn from the tails of their camp-issue shirts. This in itself was a risk, because damaging SS property was sabotage and could earn you a period of starvation or twenty-five lashes on the Bock. With no scissors or clippers, toenails grew and grew until they broke or became ingrown.

Heads were shaved every two weeks by the camp barber. Partly this was to prevent lice, but it also served, like the striped uniforms, to make prisoners conspicuous. The barber used no soap or antiseptic, so every man's head and face had razor burn, pimples, and pustules, as well as ingrown hairs. Infections were common, and could lead to time in the hospital. Fritz was at least spared half the shaving ordeal—although twenty years old now, his beard had still not developed.

There was a camp dental station, but prisoners didn't go there if they could help it—only if a toothache became so bad that it had to be pulled. Loose fillings led to caries and gum diseases, exacerbated by scurvy brought on by lack of fruit or vegetables. Fortunately, neither Fritz nor Gustav had any problems with their teeth.[5] Gold teeth could be lifesavers or a deadly danger. Prisoners were murdered for them by certain kapos. But if the owner of a gold tooth possessed the strength of will to pull it out himself, it could be traded for luxuries. There was a fixed exchange rate among the civilian black marketeers at the Buna Werke: one gold tooth equalled one bottle of Wyborowa, a quality brand of Polish vodka. Within the camp, the tooth could buy five big loaves of *Kommisbrot** and a stick of margarine. Any of these could be traded onward for other things. In a world where each week, each day, or even each hour might be one's last, there was little point in storing up riches for some better or higher purpose. Anything that brought solace or comfort or a full stomach in the living moment was worth the price.

For the managers and board of IG Farben, on the rare occasions when they took any notice of how their slave workers were treated, the sacrifice was deemed worth it for the sake of their profits. Some of the staff felt guilt, but it was little and ineffective. Meanwhile, the company's accountants and direc-

---

* Military ration bread made from sourdough with a long shelf life

tors were conveniently blind to the huge quantities of their delousing chemical Zyklon B purchased by the SS, especially at Auschwitz.[6]

Fritz Kleinmann was in no doubt where the evil came from: "Let no one conclude that the prisoner hierarchy bears the blame for bringing about this state of affairs. Some of the functionary prisoners adapted themselves to SS practices for their own profit, but the sole responsibility belongs to the SS killing machinery, which achieved its perfection in Auschwitz."[7] Each prisoner who passed in through the gate could expect to survive, on average, for three to four months.[8] Fritz and his father had so far survived more than eight, along with less than a quarter of the comrades who had come with them from Buchenwald.

In the business of murder Auschwitz had achieved a kind of industrial perfection, but as a machine the system was flawed, inefficient, and subject to failure. Its very brutality created in some a will to resist, and its corruption produced the cracks and flaws that allowed resistance to thrive.

During his first summer in Auschwitz-Monowitz, when Jupp Windeck's dominance was at its height, the resilience and moral indignation that were defining parts of Fritz's character led him to become involved in the camp's underground resistance. In doing so he was putting his life in severe jeopardy. But he did that every day just by existing; every little scrape or misplaced glance or bout of freezing weather or contact with disease could start a chain reaction leading to incapacity and death. By resisting, it was at least possible to risk everything *for* something.

בן

It began with a conversation in a quiet corner of the barrack and ended in a new job.

Construction work in the camp itself was more or less complete by the summer of 1943, and the need for construction workers at the Buna Werke was declining. Fritz was at risk of outliving his usefulness. Certain friends of his decided that he could both be preserved and be of service to them.

They took Fritz aside and spoke to him in utmost secrecy, all of them Buchenwalders he'd known for years—men who had helped him to grow to manhood. There was Stefan Heymann, Jewish intellectual, war veteran, and communist, who'd been in the camps since 1933. In Buchenwald he'd been like a second father to Fritz and the other young boys, teaching them to survive, reading to them in the evenings inspiring passages from *Road to Life*. Also present was his other old friend Gustl Herzog, along with Erich Eisler, the Austrian antifascist. They had a task for him—a vital and potentially dangerous one.

Despite having known them for so long in Buchenwald, Fritz had only been partially aware of the covert side of their activities. Along with others, they had been involved in a Jewish-communist resistance against the SS, acquiring positions of influence in order to gain information and help their fellow prisoners to survive. It was partly through the efforts of this network that Fritz and Gustav had been moved to less dangerous work details, that Robert Siewert's builders' school had been set up, and it was through prisoners in the administration offices that Fritz had learned of the content of his mother's last letter and had advance warning that his father was listed for Auschwitz.

Since arriving here, these same Buchenwalders had worked their way into positions where they could resume their activities. The spur in their sides was the news of the uprising in the Warsaw ghetto in January 1943, when the Jews heroically but vainly fought back against the SS. The men in Monowitz discussed whether they ought to do something similar. Intelligence-gathering and sabotage were all very well—Fritz himself participated in such acts on the construction sites; a bag of cement might be dropped heavily so that it burst, or a hose surreptitiously hooked over the side of a truck loaded with cement bags and the spigot turned on full—but the organized resistance wanted to do more. They settled on a continuation of the work they had previously done in Buchenwald: saving as many lives as possible. While Gustl Herzog worked in the prisoner records office, Felix "Jupp" Rausch, who'd been a businessman in Vienna and had become a good friend of Fritz's father in Buchenwald, had a clerical job in the prisoner hospital; between them they were able to obtain all manner of intelligence about the other Auschwitz satellite camps, prisoner movements, selections, and special actions, as well as ensuring decent rations, acquiring medicines for the hospital, and educating the younger prisoners.[9] Other members of their group held similar positions or were kapos or block seniors. Most of the resisters were communists, who had long experience of acting covertly.

Now they wanted Fritz to join them. The role they had in mind was simple; they would arrange to have him transferred to one of the labor details in the Buna Werke, where he would come into contact with civilian workers. He'd shown himself good at making friends with civilians, and in the factories there were thousands of them. A place was found for him in Schlosserkommando 90—the locksmith section of the construction command. One morning after roll call, for the first time since arriving in Monowitz, he marched with the other prisoners and their SS guards out of the camp, across the main road, and along the lane leading to the Buna Werke.

It was only upon entering the site that one realized just how vast it was. The whole complex—a grid of streets and rail spurs—was divided into sections: the synthetic oil plant with all its supporting workshops, the Buna rubber factory, the power plant, and smaller subsections to manufacture and process chemicals. A person could stand on one of the main east-west streets and scarcely be able to make out its far end in the haze nearly three kilometers away. The cross streets, running north-south, were more than a kilometer long. The rectangular lots were packed with factory buildings, chimneys, workshops, depots, oil and chemical storage tanks, and weird structures of pipework looking like truncated sections of fairground rides. Most of it was still dormant—the structures built but the internal workings far from complete. Only the methanol plant was fully operational, while the rubber factory was reckoned to be at least a year away from production.

The place wasn't as busy as it would later become, but there were already several thousand men and women working in the factories. About a third of them were prisoners, the rest civilians. The locksmith section—which in fact undertook a variety of metalworking jobs in its workshop and around the factories—turned out to be a friendly, easygoing environment to work in. The prisoners were treated kindly by most of their kapos and encouraged to "work with the eyes," taking it slow and easy while keeping a sharp eye out for the slavedriver kapos.[10] Fritz's kapo was a sympathetic political prisoner, a former Dachau man, who had helped arrange his work placement.

Rather than being placed in a workshop, Fritz was put in a subsection on one of the main factory floors as a general assistant.[11] The German civilians here were mostly engineers, technical workers, and foremen, and the majority of their laborers were Polish and Russian prisoners, who found it hard to follow instructions in German and were treated abominably by their kapos. If the civilian foremen weren't satisfied with the workers' performance, IG Farben had them sent to Auschwitz I for "reeducation." By contrast, the German-speaking prisoners had it much easier; Fritz became known to the civilian foremen and was trusted by them.

He developed a friendly relationship with one German in particular. Again it started with discreet gifts of bread and cigarettes, or occasionally a newspaper. From time to time the man stopped by and chatted briefly. This was what Fritz was here for, and he listened eagerly to the man's news about the progress of the war, which flatly contradicted the propaganda dished out by the SS. It was going badly for Germany on all fronts; having lost Stalingrad, they were being battered ferociously by the Soviets. And in the Mediterranean German forces had been kicked out of North Africa by the British and Americans, who would soon be in Italy and driving north toward Germany.

It was clear to Fritz that this German was no Nazi; he hoped fervently that the war would end soon and that Germany would lose. Fritz cultivated the relationship, carrying back his news each day to his friends in the camp (along with the valuable gifts of bread and newspaper). Pleased with himself, he had little notion of the scale of the operation he'd become a part of, and although he knew it was hazardous, he couldn't have guessed just how quickly it would turn and bite him.

There was resistance in all the concentration camps, but the sheer malevolence and huge scale of the Auschwitz complex caused resistance to rise to a new level. At its most passive it gathered intelligence that could help prisoners survive; at its most militant it involved sabotage, escapes, and even violent revolt against the SS. But it was all uncoordinated, haphazard. What was needed was an organized network. On May 1, 1943—which besides being the international workers' day was a Nazi holiday when the SS operated a skeleton staff—a secret meeting had been convened in Auschwitz I, at which two groups of like-minded men of different nationalities agreed to cooperate and coordinate their resistance activities. They were dominated by a Polish group, including a number of former army officers, under the leadership of Jósef Cyrankiewicz, an educated and charismatic socialist from Galicia. Overcoming the anti-German and anti-Semitic objections from some of the Poles present at the meeting, Cyrankiewicz persuaded them to open up to cooperation with the Jews and with German and Austrian politicals. This would allow them to exploit all their various advantages—the Germans' language and understanding of Germany and the Nazis, which was vital in intelligence, combined with the fact that Polish prisoners were allowed to receive mail, which enabled them to bring in supplies and communicate with Polish partisans.

The newly formed international group chose to call themselves Kampf-gruppe Auschwitz—Battle Group Auschwitz—a measure of their militancy.[12]

Battle Group Auschwitz soon established contact with Stefan Heymann and the other Monowitz resisters. Their connection was aided by the constant shuffling of prisoners and labor details around the camps. The Monowitz group's main value was its ability to cultivate relationships with civilians. But the resistance also carried out more active tasks. Sabotage in the Buna Werke had been extensive and constant. Prisoners in the electricians' detail had managed to short-circuit a turbine in the power plant. Another group, taking advantage of the reduced guard on May 1, had caused an explosion in the half-complete synthetic fuel plant, while others destroyed fifty vehicles.[13] Such acts of sabotage—together with constant smaller acts and a general go-slow principle of work—had contributed greatly to delaying the start of production in the various factories.

While Fritz Kleinmann went back and forth between factory and camp each day, carrying his little snippets of intelligence, he was only dimly aware of his connection with this network. Battle Group Auschwitz and its allies were wary of all contacts—the camp Gestapo was constantly endeavoring to penetrate it and discover who its leaders and members were, and the work of spotting and weeding out informers was unending. This was especially vital when it came to the most sensitive resistance operation: the planning and execution of escapes.

בן

It was Saturday in June 1943, and the working day was over. At evening roll call, the prisoners in Monowitz stood to attention in the knowledge that tomorrow, although not a day of rest exactly, was at least a day of less toil and less danger.

Fritz stood in his place, uniform buttoned neatly, cap on straight and pulled to one side in the approved beret style, ready to whip it off mechanically at the "Caps off!" order. Everything was normal, the same slow, monotonous, grinding, day-in, day-out repetition he had known twice daily since October 1939, almost without variation.

The trained clock in his mind was anticipating the dismissal from the Rapportführer when he noticed a small knot of figures entering the square—two SS sergeants force-marching a man who limped and stumbled. They shoved and hit him like a prisoner, but he wasn't dressed as one. As they came closer, with a sickening jolt Fritz recognized his friend, the civilian from the factory. He'd been violently worked over, his face bloodied and swollen. Fritz also recognized the SS men; one was SS-Staff Sergeant Johann Taute, head of the Monowitz subdivision of the political department: the camp Gestapo. The other was Taute's subordinate SS-Sergeant Josef Hofer.

To Fritz's horror, they ordered the civilian to identify which prisoners he'd had contact with at the factory. He surveyed the thousands of faces before him, but Fritz, buried deep in the mass, was well out of sight. With the two SS men pushing him, the civilian walked along between the ranks, back and forth, studying the faces. He came along Fritz's row. Fritz stared straight ahead, heart thumping. The bruised, bloodshot eyes looked at him reluctantly, and a hand rose and pointed.

Fritz's father and friends watched in helpless dismay as he was seized and marched out of the ranks. Together with the civilian, he was shoved along, past his comrades, and out of the square.

Stefan Heymann and the other resisters were doubly anxious; how long did they have before Fritz was broken and the Gestapo came back for the rest of them? The roll call was dismissed and they went back to their blocks to wait and talk and try to plan for what was coming. As for why the Gestapo had singled out that particular civilian, they could only speculate.

Fritz was put under guard in a truck and driven out of the camp. It traveled the few kilometers to Auschwitz I, but instead of entering the camp compound Fritz was taken to the political department, which stood outside the fence opposite the SS hospital and adjacent to a small underground gas chamber. Inside the Gestapo building, Fritz was force-marched along a corridor by Sergeants Taute and Hofer and shoved into a large room.

Inside was a table with straps attached to it, and there were hooks embedded in the ceiling. Fritz contemplated these things in terror. He'd been long enough in the camps to guess what they were used for.

After a while an SS officer entered the room. He looked Fritz up and down with lively, smiling eyes in a gentle, patrician face. Prematurely bald and graying, on looks alone he might be a university professor or a genial clergyman.

Rarely can a man's appearance have been more at odds with his character; this affable-looking gentleman was SS-Lieutenant Maximilian Grabner, head of the Auschwitz Gestapo, and his reputation for cold, pitiless murder was unsurpassed in this or any other camp. When Grabner spoke, Fritz recognized his accent as that of the rural region near Vienna, but although his voice was eerily soft, his manner of speech was rough and uneducated. Those prisoners who had much contact with Grabner imagined him having been a cowherd in some Alpine farm. In fact he'd been an officer in the anti-communist arm of Chancellor Schuschnigg's security police, and after the Anschluss he had transitioned smoothly into the Gestapo.[14] The prisoners in Auschwitz were terrified of Maximilian Grabner, as were the SS who served under him. He regularly purged the hospital and the block 11 bunker—"dusting off" he called it—sending the inmates to the gas chambers or the Black Wall. He'd instituted a program of exterminating pregnant Polish women, and by the time Fritz encountered him he was reckoned personally responsible for over two thousand murders. One member of the Auschwitz resistance said of him at the time: "No one, not even the commandant, is as feared as Grabner."[15]

He studied Fritz a moment, then spoke. He said, quite matter-of-factly, that he knew prisoner 68629 to be involved in planning a large-scale escape from the Auschwitz-Monowitz camp, and that he had been doing so with the collaboration of the German civilian who had identified him. The Gestapo had been watching this civilian; his irregular behavior having caught their attention. What did the prisoner have to say about that?

Any expectations Fritz had had about the line his interrogation would take were confounded. He didn't know what to say. He couldn't deny knowing the civilian, but the stuff about an escape was a total mystery. Were the Gestapo just fishing, or did they have real information? If so, how, and what? "You will give me the names of the prisoners who are involved in this plot," Grabner said.

Taking Fritz's stunned silence for a refusal, Grabner nodded to Taute and Hofer.

The first blow of Hofer's cudgel didn't jolt a confession out of Fritz, and neither did the second or third. Realizing that Fritz would be harder to break than the civilian had been, they pushed him facedown on the table and fastened the straps, pinning him down. The cane rose and flashed down, whistling, lashing him across the buttocks. And again, and again, until his backside was lacerated and on fire with agony. Even in this extremity of fear and pain he kept count of the lashes, and he'd suffered twenty by the time they unstrapped him. Grabner ordered him again to admit his wrongdoing and give up the identities of the prisoners he was planning to help escape. Again Fritz gave no reply. What could he say? Again he was forced down on the table, again the straps were fastened, again the cane whistled in the air.

He lost track of how many times he was strapped to the table, but he doggedly kept count of the lashes: sixty agonizing cuts of the cane, sixty weals on his flesh.

When they unstrapped him and hauled him to his feet, Grabner demanded again: *confess, tell me the names.*

At some point, sooner rather than later, it must occur to any person trapped in this nightmare of pain and terror to just say anything to make it stop. Fritz could name several of his friends who were involved in some form of resistance, and would not be human if he didn't experience the overwhelming temptation to save himself. He could simply give Grabner their names—Stefan and Gustl and Jupp Rausch and the other resisters, his friends and mentors, condemning them to torture and death. Even though Fritz was smart enough to know that it wouldn't save his life, it would at least bring the torture to an end.

He said nothing. Grabner nodded at Taute and Hofer and indicated the hooks in the ceiling.

Fritz's hands were tied behind his back, so tightly that the circulation was cut off. The long end of the rope was thrown up over a hook, and the two sergeants hauled on it. Fritz's arms were wrenched upward and backward, and with an indescribable, blinding agony he was dragged off his feet. He hung with his toes a foot above the floor, his bodyweight twisting his shoulders in their sockets, filling his brain with blinding white light. So many times he had seen the poor souls suspended like this from the Goethe Oak. The experience of it was worse than could ever be imagined.

"Give me the names," Grabner repeated, again and again. Fritz hung there for nearly an hour, but all that came out of his mouth was inchoate squeaks and drool. "You won't live through this," said Grabner's voice in his ear. "Give up the names."

At a nod from Grabner, the rope was let go, and Fritz crashed to the floor. *Give up the names,* he was told, and it would be over. Still he said nothing. They dragged him up, hauled again on the rope, and raised him screaming into the air.

Three times they raised him off his feet by that infernal hook. By the third hoist, Grabner was losing patience. It was Saturday night, and he was keen to get home. This interrogation was wasting his precious leisure time. Fritz had hung for an hour and a half all told when they let go and he crashed to the floor for the third time. In his pain he was dimly aware of Grabner leaving the room. As he left he ordered the two sergeants to take the prisoner back to the camp. The interrogation would resume later.[16]

בן

Gustl Herzog was still up and about when he heard that Fritz was back. He rushed to meet him and found him being carried along by two Viennese friends, Fredl Lustig, who had worked with his father on the Buchenwald haulage column, and Max Matzner, another close friend of Gustav's, who had narrowly avoided death in the infamous Buchenwald typhus experiments.

Fritz couldn't stand; aside from the visible bruises and blood, he was in excruciating pain, his joints wrenched and twisted. Gustl told Lustig and Matzner to take him to the hospital, then went in search of the other resisters.

The prisoner hospital in Monowitz was extensive. Occupying a group of blocks in the northeast corner of the camp, it had several departments: medical, surgical, infectious diseases, and convalescence. Although an SS doctor was in overall charge, it was staffed mainly by prisoners, and each department had a block senior in charge.[17] By concentration camp standards, Monowitz's hospital was a good one, but like all others it suffered from a starvation of medical resources and was subject to regular selections for the gas chambers.

Fritz was taken to a room in the general medical block. He was half-paralyzed, his arms useless and senseless, his backside welted and bleeding, and his whole body shot through with pain. A Czech doctor gave him some strong painkillers and massaged his arms.

After a while, Gustl Herzog came in with Erich Eisler and Stefan Heymann. All three regarded Fritz with both pity and fear. When the doctor had gone, they questioned him anxiously about what the Gestapo had wanted with him. He told them about Grabner's accusations and the alleged escape plan. Had he given up any information? Of course not; he didn't know anything. But had he given Grabner any names—any at all? No, he hadn't. Despite his pain, his friends interrogated him over and over: *had he named any names at all?* No, he insisted; he'd told Grabner nothing.

Eventually they were satisfied. They were safe—for now. But Stefan and Erich were positive that Grabner wouldn't let the matter end there. If it hadn't been a Saturday, he'd have kept up Fritz's torture until he either confessed or died. It was a marvel that he'd let him come back to camp; presumably the cells in Auschwitz I's block 11 were jammed to bursting (as they usually were). Tomorrow, or maybe Monday, Grabner would send for Fritz again. The torture would resume, and sooner or later he would crack and start spilling out names. Something must be done to prevent that.

For the time being, they had Fritz moved to the infectious diseases block, where typhus and dysentery patients were kept; it was in the far corner of the camp, beside the shower block and adjoining the morgue. The SS doctor and his medical orderlies rarely went in there for fear of infection. Fritz was put in an isolation room. So long as he didn't pick up an infection, he'd be safe for the time being. But he couldn't hide in here forever, and his name would have to be entered in the hospital records. Otherwise, he'd be recorded as missing at morning roll call and a manhunt would be initiated. Whichever way they looked at the problem, there was only one solution: Fritz Kleinmann had to die.

With cooperation from Sepp Luger, the camp senior responsible for the hospital, the death of prisoner 68629 was recorded in the register. No details were required; the register provided only a single line for each entry, with admission number, prisoner number, name, dates of admission and departure, and reason for departure. In this column there were only three options: *Entlassen* (discharged); *nach Birkenau* for those selected for the gas chambers; or a stamped black cross denoting the dead. Once Fritz's death had been entered, Gustl Herzog recorded it in the general prisoner records office where he worked.[18]

Between them the conspirators broke the news to Fritz's many friends. Even his father could not be let into the secret—the risk was too great—and so Gustav was given the devastating news that his beloved son had died. After all they had been through together to survive this far, it was utterly heartbreaking. Gustav couldn't bring himself to record it in his diary, which had lain untouched for weeks.

While Gustav grieved and Fritz's friends absorbed this latest in a never-ending train of deaths, there remained the pressing matter of what to do with the living, breathing Fritz. While he began to recover from his injuries, he was kept in isolation in the hospital. Each time an inspection was carried out by the SS doctor or his male nurse, Fritz was helped out of his bed by his old Buchenwald friend Jule Meixner and hidden in the storeroom of the hospital laundry where he worked. All the while Fritz wondered what would become of him now. Watching the dysentery patients drag themselves to the latrine buckets in the outer room and the typhus patients writhing in their sweat-soaked beds in a febrile delirium, he knew he couldn't stay in this place much longer, injuries or no injuries. Word had come through from the Monowitz Gestapo that Grabner had dropped the investigation because of Fritz's death. It was time to move on.

Fritz was given the identity of a typhus patient who had just died. He was in no state of mind to recall the poor man's name—only that he was a Jew from Berlin, a relatively recent arrival whose prisoner number was up in the 112,000s. It was impossible to erase Fritz's tattoo or give him a new one with the dead man's number, so they just bandaged his forearm and hoped that no SS demanded to see it. Stefan Heymann spent a lot of time with him, and they grew closer than ever; he advised Fritz on how they would need to proceed and the precautions they would need to take when assigning him to a labor detail.

It was all one to Fritz; since his interrogation a lassitude had entered his soul and he no longer cared much whether he was discovered or not. The long grinding of grief, starvation, and hopelessness had worn down his resistance at last, and he had entered the mind state that led to becoming a Muselmann. He confessed to Stefan and his other friends that he was considering ending it all as soon as possible—it was so simple to rush the sentry line while on an outside work detail, or to throw himself on the electrified fence in the camp. One gunshot—a single fleeting instant—and the pain and wretchedness would all be over.[19]

Stefan had no patience with these thoughts. Couldn't Fritz imagine what committing suicide would do to his father? Gustav believed right now that his son was dead, but in time—perhaps soon—he would learn the truth and be overjoyed. But if he were to discover that Fritz had been alive all along and had then committed suicide—just imagine the utter devastation he would feel. After all they had survived together, the risks they had taken for each other, their shared endurance—for Fritz to not only cave in to the SS but to allow them to finish him off, it was too much. "They cannot grind us down like this," Gustav had said; endurance was all, misery was only for a time, hope and spirit were undying.

Fritz and Stefan talked it over at length. Stefan promised to do everything he could to keep Fritz safe in the hospital, to prevent his being selected for Birkenau. When he was well enough to go to work, a place would be found in some outside detail where he could remain obscure and unnoticed. Fritz trusted Stefan with his life, but he had grave doubts. People knew his face—including some of the SS. And sooner or later his father must find out. At least seven men in the resistance knew Fritz's secret; could they all keep it hidden forever from Gustav, who was their friend? Gustav was prominent in the camp now, well-known to the SS and the functionary prisoners, some of whom were hostile. His status made possession of so explosive a secret extremely dangerous for him. Moreover, he would find it hard to stay apart from his son and not acknowledge him. The incident with the Blockführer who had battered Fritz for claiming to be Gustav's son was a painful reminder of that fact. Gustav was conspicuous.

After three weeks, Fritz was recovered enough to leave the hospital. His friends smuggled him to block 48, where the senior was Chaim Goslawski, a member of the resistance. Like Fritz's father, Goslawski had been born in this part of the world, in the town of Sosnowiec, and his block was mainly popu-lated by German and Polish prisoners who didn't know Fritz.

The next day, Fritz went to work. A position had been found for him in a different section of the locksmith detail where he could pass unnoticed as a warehouseman; one of the kapos, a man named Paul Schmidt, was in on the secret and kept an eye on him. Marching out through the gates each morning and back in the evening, Fritz went through suffocating terror, expecting to be recognized by an SS guard or hostile kapo. He kept in the middle of the group, marching with his eyes fixed forward and his face expressionless while his heart pounded. Nobody noticed him, and as the weeks passed, he began to feel more settled at work. For the time being, his secret was safe.

אבא

One evening Gustav was sitting in the day room of block 7 when he was told that Gustl Herzog was outside, asking to see him.

Gustav stepped outside and found his old friend in a state of visibly sup-pressed eagerness. *Follow me*, he indicated, and led Gustav down the side of the building, away from the road. Behind the row of barrack blocks, in the space between it and the next row, stood a row of smaller buildings—two latrines, the Gestapo bunker, and a small bath house. Herzog led Gustav to the bath house, where the prisoner in charge was keeping watch at the door. They indicated that Gustav should go inside.

Wondering, he entered the building, inhaling the familiar smell of musty, soapless damp. In the gloom, he saw the shape of a man standing back in the shadows of the boiler room. The figure came forward, his features resolving in the half light, unbelievably, miraculously, into the face of Fritz. For Gustav, who never abandoned hope, to hold his son in his arms again, to inhale the smell of him, to hear his voice was beyond all hope, beyond everything.[20]

After that first reunion, they met whenever they could, always at night in the bath house. The bath supervisor was yet another veteran of the "Buchenwald school" who'd been with Fritz in the youth block. Now that his grief was gone, Gustav's mind was invaded by all the cares of fatherhood, redoubled now that Fritz was in so much more danger than he'd ever been in before. Gustl Herzog and the others assured him that they were doing all they could for Fritz, but would it be enough?

אב ובן

In the late fall of 1943, the gravest risk to Fritz's security was unexpectedly lifted when SS-Lieutenant Grabner was suddenly removed from his post.

For a long time, there had been questions in Berlin about Grabner's conduct of the Auschwitz Gestapo. Even by SS standards the number of deaths he ordered raised an eyebrow—not so much at the scale of the murder but the disorderly way in which it was done. In the minds of Himmler and his senior officers, the Final Solution—and killing generally—was an industrial business, to be conducted cleanly, efficiently, and systematically. It wasn't a game or a personal fetish. However, it was not Grabner's sadism or taste for murder that brought about his fall; it was his corruption. Like many senior concentration camp officers he had used his position to misappropriate property and enrich himself. He had done so on a colossal scale, stealing the valuables of Jews murdered in Birkenau and sending home whole suitcases crammed with loot. Unfortunately for him, the scale of his corruption drew the attention of an SS investigation. He was suspended from his post, and on December 1 was placed under arrest, along with fellow mass-murderer Gerhard Palitzsch. Grabner was permanently replaced, along with some of his accomplices.[21] SS-Lieutenant Colonel Rudolf Höss, commandant of Auschwitz, was one of them.

Höss's replacement, Arthur Liebehenschel, took up his post as commandant on November 11, 1943, and initiated a shake-up of the whole Auschwitz complex; staff were replaced, and order and discipline were imposed more firmly on the SS.[22]

Amid all this turmoil, there was little chance of one prisoner in Monowitz being taken much notice of by the camp Gestapo. Not only that, on the night of December 7, an accomplice of the dismissed SS officers started a fire in the main Gestapo building, destroying the records of their misdeeds.[23] Not long afterward, Fritz Kleinmann quietly came back to life. His entry in the camp register was reinstated, and the Berlin Jew who had died of typhus was forgotten.

But although the need for absolute secrecy had passed, Fritz still had to be careful; if he were noticed by any SS guards who had been aware of his death—especially the Gestapo sergeants Taute and Hofer—there would be trouble. But among the thousands in Monowitz, the hundreds of thousands who entered and were transferred back and forth between the Auschwitz camps, and the tens of thousands of dead, who would take notice of one prisoner's discreet resurrection?

As winter came on, Gustav used his position to achieve the unthinkable—he had Fritz transferred to join him in block 7. Now they could be together in the evenings without worrying about being seen by suspicious SS men. It was a socially tricky situation; because of his low status, Fritz wasn't permitted to sit in the block day room when his papa went there to talk with his friends; instead he had to sit on his bunk alone.

Still, at least it was warm and safe. It was certainly better than the place he'd been in before his death, where his block senior, a man named Paul Schäfer, hadn't been able to stomach the stench of men's bodies in the bunk room—an unavoidable ingredient of concentration camp barrack life—and had kept all the windows open to ventilate it, even in the cold weather. Simply for sadism's sake, he'd also turned off the heating, so the men's damp clothes wouldn't dry. If anyone was caught trying to keep warm by sleeping in his clothes, Schäfer would beat him up and confiscate his bread and margarine ration. Confinement in the bunk room of block 7 was luxury by comparison.

"And so the year of 1943 goes by," Gustav wrote. Winter was upon them again; snow began to fall, and the ground hardened. This would be his and Fritz's fifth winter since being taken from their home. That it would not be their last was both a blessing and a curse.

15 | The Kindness of Strangers

אחים

"CATCH!"

Fritz leapt in the air, stretching to reach the ball as it sailed over his head; it bounced off the bracket of one of the empty market stalls and skittered into the road. Fritz ran after it, whipped it up, and glanced up to see a policeman coming around the corner into Leopoldsgasse. The policeman stared hard at him, and he stood up straight, hiding the ball behind his back. Soccer wasn't allowed on the streets. When he'd gone, Fritz turned and ran back into the market, dropping the ball—just a tightly wrapped bundle of rags—onto the cobblestones and kicking it back toward his friends.

It was the end of the day and the last of the farmers were clearing away their unsold wares. As each one finished, he mounted his cart and chucked the reins, clopping off along the street. Fritz and his friends ran among the empty stalls, tossing the ball back and forth. Only Frau Capek the fruit seller was still at her post; she never packed up until it got dark. In the summer she would give the kids corn cobs. A lot of them were poor and would take all the free leftovers they could get—ends of sausage from the butcher, bread crusts from Herr König at the Anker bakery, whipped cream from Herr Reichert's cake shop in the Grosse Sperlgasse, just around the corner from the Sperlschule where they all went to school.

Fritz caught the ball as it came his way and was about to toss it back when they all heard the distant, familiar hooting of horns: *ta-raa ta-raa*. The fire truck was on its way to a fire. In a welter of excitement they ran back through the market and along Leopoldsgasse, following the sound, dodging among the passersby—the late housewives with their shopping, the Orthodox Jews in their black coats and beards hurrying home for the start of Shabbat before the light began to fade. "Wait!" Fritz turned and saw the little figure, legs pumping, running after him. Kurt! He'd forgotten all about him. He waited for his little brother, but by the time he caught up, Fritz's friends were out of sight and the fire truck was inaudible.

Kurt was only seven—a whole generation apart from Fritz, who was nearly fourteen, but they were close already, and Fritz let the kid tag along when he played with his friends, learning their games and the ways of the streets around the Karmelitermarkt and beyond. Kurt had his own gang of little pals, and Fritz's gang acted as their guardians.

Fritz noticed old Herr Löwy, who'd been blinded in the Great War, trying to cross the street, which was busy with trucks and heavy wagons from the coal sellers and breweries, clattering along pulled by massive Pinzgauer horses. Fritz took Herr Löwy's hand, waited for a gap, and helped him across. Then, beckoning Kurt to follow, he took off after his friends.

They caught up with them coming back along Taborstrasse, their faces streaked with cream and icing sugar. They hadn't found the fire, but they'd passed by Gross's confectioners in the Novaragasse and bagged about a ton of leftover cream cakes. One of them—his schoolfriend Leo Meth—had saved a cream slice and gave it to Fritz, who divided it with Kurt.

Cheeks bulging with pastry and cream, they walked back toward the Karmelitermarkt, Fritz holding Kurt by his sticky, sugary hand. Fritz enjoyed the comfort of comradeship; the fact that some of his friends were different, that while his parents neglected to go to synagogue, their parents stayed away from church, or that Christmas meant something slightly more to them than it did to him—these things seemed of no significance, and the thought that he and Leo and the other Jewish kids might ever be divided from their friends by these trivial things never crossed their minds.

It was a warm evening; summer was well on its way. Tomorrow was Saturday—perhaps they'd go swimming in the Danube Canal. Or they might join with the girls to play theater in the basement of number 17. Frau Dworschak the building supervisor—whose son Hans was one of Fritz's playmates—often let them light the place up with candles, and Herta and the other girls would put on a fashion show, dressing up in scavenged clothes and parading up and down like great ladies, or they'd all do a version of William Tell in front of an audience who paid two pennies each for admission. Fritz loved these burlesques.

Fritz and Kurt walked home in the warm summer dusk. Today had had been a good day in an unbroken string of good days. The kids of Vienna picked their joy from the streets like apples from a tree; all you had to do was reach up and it was there for the taking. Life was outside of time, invincible.

בן

Fritz was torn from a pleasant dream by the shrill screech of the camp senior's whistle. His eyes opened, staring into darkness, and his nostrils woke to the stench of three hundred unwashed bodies and three hundred sets of sweat-soured clothes. His brain, startled out of its bliss, registered the shock of his situation—as it did every dark pre-dawn morning.

The man in the bunk below climbed down and pulled on his jacket, as did about a dozen others who were on coffee duty. Fritz wrapped his blanket tightly about him and closed his eyes, settling into the straw mattress, squeezing the last embrace out of sleep and chasing the tatters of his dream.

An hour and a quarter later he was woken again by the bunk room lights flicking on. "All up!" barked the room orderly. "Up, up, up!" In an instant the three-tiered bunks sprouted legs, arms, bleary faces, clambering, treading on one another, pulling on striped uniforms. Fritz took down his mattress, shook it out, then folded his blanket and laid it all straight. After the men had splashed and scrubbed their faces in cold water in the washhouse—jam-packed with the inhabitants of the six surrounding blocks—and polished their shoes from the barrel of greasy boot-polish scavenged from the Buna Werke, they lined up in the bunk room for their acorn coffee, brought in in huge thirty-liter thermos canisters. They drank it standing up (sitting on the bunks was forbidden). Those who'd managed to save a bit of bread from the evening before ate it now, washing it down with the sweet, lukewarm coffee. The orderly inspected them to see that their bunks were in order, their uniforms presentable, and their shoes clean and polished.

The atmosphere was less anxious, more convivial than in any block Fritz had been in before. The *Prominenten* of block 7 looked after themselves in greater comfort. His previous block had been so overcrowded by an influx of new prisoners during the summer that they'd slept two to a bed.[1] The foremen, the kapos, the block senior, and the orderlies had treated the rest of them as second-class, especially the Jews. In block 7 there was more mutual respect, although Fritz, here only on sufferance and the influence of his father, was excluded.

At 5:45, still in darkness, they all trooped outside and formed rows in front of the building. All along the street prisoners were spilling out of their blocks and lining up to be counted by their block seniors. Every man had to be there, without exception. Not even the sick or the dead were excused—usually each block would produce at least one or two corpses of men who'd died in the night. They were carried out and laid down to be counted with the rest. The assembled prisoners marched along the street and wheeled into the roll-call square, lit by floodlights. Columns of hundreds came from each block, forming up on the open parade ground in orderly ranks of ten, each man with his assigned place within his block, each block in its assigned place among the others. The sick and the dead were carried along and put at the back.

The SS Blockführers prowled up and down the columns, looking for men out of place, lines not straight, counting up the prisoners of their block, taking a tally of the dead. Any infraction of perfect drill—especially if it led to a counting error—resulted in a beating; whole rows were made to lie down, stand up, lie down, until they got their lines perfectly straight. When the Blockführers were satisfied, they took their reports to the Rapportführer, who watched over the whole proceeding from a podium at the front. Then, while the prisoners continued to stand motionless—however cold or wet the weather—he went meticulously through the whole count.

By the time SS-Lieutenant Vinzenz Schöttl, the dough-faced director, arrived on the square to take roll call, they had been standing at attention for about an hour. Fritz watched warily as Schöttl took the podium; with the whole Auschwitz complex still going through the process of transitioning from the Höss-Grabner regime he was still afraid of being recognized and singled out; it was a fear that would never entirely leave, and recent events had put him more on edge than ever.

During the final days of the Grabner regime in September, an informer had been discovered among the prisoners.[2] The Gestapo were constantly putting out feelers to try and detect subversive activities, and the resisters had to be constantly vigilant. The ones to watch out for in particular were certain kinds of kapos and civilian workers. Fritz Beck, who was an orderly in block 7 and particularly alert to traitors, had made the discovery. Beck had learned from a fellow prisoner who was a clerk in the Monowitz Gestapo that Polish kapo Bolesław "Bolek" Smoliński—one of the heavy-handed kapos, a bigot and anti-Semite with a particular loathing for communists—was a stool pigeon working for SS-Sergeant Taute.

This vital intelligence was passed among the resisters. They realized at once the acute danger Smoliński presented; Curt Posener (known as Cupo), one of the old Buchenwalders, knew that Smoliński was friendly with the camp senior responsible for the prisoner hospital, which was a main nexus for the resistance. This was a terrible vulnerability. Cupo talked it over with Erich Eisler and Stefan Heymann. Eisler suggested that they try talking to Smoliński, to make him see the error of his ways. Stefan and Cupo argued strongly against this; it was far too dangerous. Nonetheless, for reasons which nobody would ever discover, Eisler disregarded the warnings and went ahead and talked to Smoliński. The reaction was instantaneous—Smoliński went straight to the Gestapo and gave them the names of several conspirators, including Erich Eisler and Curt Posener, as well as six others, including Walter Petzold and Walter Windmüller, both of whom were well-liked, highly respected functionary prisoners and members of the resistance. All were seized and taken to Auschwitz I, where they were put in the block 11 bunker and subjected to days of interrogation and torture. Despite being the Gestapo's informer, Smoliński was held with them.

Eventually Walter Petzold and Curt Posener were brought back to Monowitz, battered and physically broken. Like Fritz, they had resisted the torture and given up no information. Smoliński was also released and resumed his position. Walter Windmüller and Erich Eisler did not come back. Windmüller had succumbed to his injuries and died in the bunker. Poor Erich Eisler, who had outed himself as a resister by talking to Smoliński in the first place, was taken to the Black Wall and shot on October 21, 1943.[3] The rest were also shot. Eisler's death was heartbreakingly tragic. He had dedicated himself utterly to people's welfare; even before becoming a prisoner himself, he'd worked for the Rote Hilfe (Red Aid), a socialist organization that provided welfare to prisoners' families.[4] He'd been arrested in 1938 and sent to Dachau, then Buchenwald, where he'd become part of the circle of friends and resisters who now mourned him. In the end, it had been his humane temperament that was his downfall, thinking he could talk a man like Smoliński into behaving decently.

"Attention! Caps off!" yelled a sergeant's voice through the loudspeakers, and five thousand hands whipped the caps off five thousand heads and folded them neatly under their arms. They stood at attention while Schöttl checked through the assembled lists of prisoners, noting new arrivals, deaths, selections, and assignments.

Finally: "Caps on! Work details, move!"

The parade dissolved into chaos as each man ran to his allotted detail, coalescing into units and forming up in columns, counted off by their kapos. They marched along the street to the main gate, which swung open. Many were lethargic, Fritz noted—as always, there was a percentage who had reached the last of their strength; before long they would be selected for Birkenau or be among the corpses brought out to be counted at roll call.

As the columns passed, the prisoner orchestra, in their little building beside the gate, played stirring tunes. They were an international ensemble, led by a Dutch political, with a German Roma on violin, and the rest Jews from various countries. Yet it struck Fritz that they never seemed to play German tunes—only Austrian marches from the days of the empire. When his papa had been Fritz's age, he had marched to exactly these tunes on the parade grounds of Vienna, Cracow, and Kenty. He'd gone to war accompanied by the same martial airs. The camp orchestra were good musicians, and sometimes on a Sunday Schöttl permitted them to put on a concert for the more privileged prisoners on the roll-call square. It was a surreal sight—the motley musicians playing classical music to an audience of prisoners standing in uniforms, with SS officers in chairs to one side.

The sky was starting to grow light now as they marched along the road toward the checkpoint at the gates of the Buna Werke, each column guarded by an SS sergeant and sentries. Depending on where in the factory complex they worked, some of them had up to four kilometers to march, and then a twelve-hour shift and a four-kilometer march back to another several hours of roll call in the floodlit cold and rain. Each day the same as the last, each day another pit of gloom in an unbroken landscape of gray hopelessness.

Fritz went to his work in the warehouse: another day of moving stock about. As it turned out, this day was not entirely like all the others, although Fritz had no way of knowing it just yet.

He was chatting to another Jewish prisoner when one of the civilian welders who happened to be nearby broke in on their conversation. He was German and had noticed they were speaking his language. He hadn't come across many fellow Germans since coming to work here—most of the prisoners seemed to be Poles or other foreigners. Glancing at their prison uniforms he asked, rather impolitely and presumptuously, what crimes they had committed.

Fritz looked at the civilian in surprise. He was a youngish man who moved with a lame, halting manner suggesting some kind of disability. That would explain why he wasn't in the army. "Crime?" Fritz said. "We're Jews."

The man was mystified. "But the Führer would never lock up anyone who hasn't done anything wrong," he said.

"This is Auschwitz concentration camp," said Fritz. "Do you know what Auschwitz stands for?"

The man shrugged. "I've been in the army, on the Eastern Front. I've got no idea what's been going on at home." So that explained his lameness: wounded, presumably.

Fritz pointed out his and his friend's Jewish stars, explaining what they denoted, but the man refused to believe that that was the sole reason for their imprisonment. For Fritz, this blindness was stupefying—the man might have missed the escalation since 1941 while he was at the front, but where had he been since 1933 when the persecutions began, or 1938 when Kristallnacht happened and they started sending the Jews en masse to the concentration camps? Presumably he'd bought into the propaganda that Jews had merely been deported or emigrated of their own free will, and that those in the camps were criminals and terrorists.

Eventually Fritz accepted that it was hopeless and gave up trying to convince him of the truth. When the former soldier tried to restart the conversation again later, with the stunningly glib and pompous observation that everyone must pull together to defend home and Fatherland, and that even prisoners had their part to play, Fritz bit his tongue. Here was a man whose company he could grow extremely tired of very quickly indeed. The man went on and on, and at last Fritz couldn't stand it any longer. "Can't you see what's happening here?" he cried angrily, gesturing around him to take in the factories, Auschwitz, the whole system. Then he walked away.

But the civilian wouldn't leave the matter—or Fritz—alone. The whole business perplexed him, and throughout that day he came up to Fritz again and again, raising the matter of duty and Fatherland and that surely prisoners must be prisoners for a good reason. But despite his persistence, each time he raised the matter he sounded less sure of himself.

Eventually he fell silent, and for the next few days he went about his welding work in the factory without speaking. Then one morning he approached Fritz, quietly passed him a piece of bread and a large stick of sausage, then walked off. Surprised and puzzled, Fritz hid the gifts away, and as he did so he noticed that the bread was half a long loaf of *Wecken*, an Austrian bread made from very fine flour. He tore off a piece and put it in his mouth. It was blissful; nothing like the military Kommisbrot they were given in the camp. This was a taste of home and heaven—a reminder of the morsels he and his friends used to get at the close of day from the Anker bakery. There was a lot here, and the sausage was large; he would smuggle them back to camp and share with his father and friends.

Later the same morning, the civilian came back. "There aren't many Germans here," he said. "It's nice to have someone to talk to." He hesitated, and there was a look in his face Fritz hadn't seen before. On his way in to work that morning, he said, he'd seen a sight which had distressed him. Even as a veteran of the Eastern Front who was no stranger to atrocity, he'd been shaken by it. A prisoner's corpse was hanging on the barbed wire of the Monowitz camp. He'd been told it was a suicide, and not uncommon—prisoners would throw themselves on the fence and die either by electrocution or shooting. Fritz nodded; it was a common enough sight. The SS always left the bodies up for a few days to intimidate other prisoners. "This is not what I fought for," said the civilian. His voice shook with emotion, and Fritz saw tears in his eyes. "Not that. I want nothing to do with that."

Fritz was astounded—a German soldier standing before him, in tears over a dead concentration camp inmate. In Fritz's experience, Aryan Germans—soldiers, police, SS, green-triangle prisoners—were all of a kind: with few exceptions they were callous, bigoted, and brutal.

The man told Fritz his story. His name was Alfred Wocher. He was Bavarian-born but married to a Viennese woman, and his home was in Vienna—hence the Wecken loaf. Fritz had learned discretion and didn't mention that he was from Vienna too; instead he just listened while Wocher told him about serving in the Wehrmacht on the Eastern Front, how he'd been awarded the Iron Cross 1st and 2nd Class and reached the rank of sergeant. After being severely wounded he'd been sent home on indefinite leave; he would never be fit again for active service. He hadn't actually been discharged from the army but as a skilled welder he'd been sent to IG Farben to do civilian work.[5]

Back in camp that evening, Fritz went to the hospital to talk it over with Stefan Heymann; he described Alfred Wocher and repeated everything he'd said. Stefan was unsettled by the whole thing. He advised Fritz to be careful—you couldn't trust Germans, especially not a veteran soldier from Hitler's army. After Smoliński and the deaths of Erich Eisler and Walter Windmüller, the resistance was more wary than ever about potential informers. And surely Fritz had learned his lesson the hard way—the last time he'd become friendly with a civilian it had nearly cost him his life, besides putting his friends and his father through a world of grief and risk.

Fritz understood the danger all too well and had every reason not to trust this man Wocher. Therefore, given those facts, he would never understand why he did what he did the next day. He went back to work and, in defiance of Stefan's advice and his own good sense, continued conversing with the old soldier.

It wasn't as if he could easily keep away from him—Wocher came to him, usually because he wanted to get something off his chest, some query or other about Auschwitz. To Fritz it seemed suspiciously like probing. Wocher would bring copies of the *Völkischer Beobachter*, the official Nazi Party newspaper, to show Fritz what was going on in Germany. (Fritz didn't mind—newspaper torn into squares had a value in the camp, and it had to be said that wiping the asses of Jews was as good a use for the *Beobachter* as one could imagine.) Wocher brought Fritz gifts of bread and sausage, and one day he even offered to convey letters for him. If Fritz had anyone in the outside world he wanted to communicate with, he would get messages to them.

So there it was—entrapment. Or so it seemed. Fritz's instinct told him to test this man in some way. But to what purpose? If Wocher was a Nazi informer, what good would it do to prove it? Fritz discussed the matter again with Stefan Heymann. Knowing that Fritz would always go his own way, Stefan told him that it was up to him alone; he couldn't help him with this.

Not long afterward, Wocher happened to mention that he was about to go on leave and would be traveling through Brno and Prague—cities in what had formerly been Czechoslovakia, now German-occupied. Here was Fritz's opportunity; he came to work next day with a couple of letters directed to fictional addresses in both cities, claiming he had family there. He guessed that if Wocher was false, he naturally wouldn't bother trying to deliver the letters and wouldn't discover that the addresses weren't real.

When Wocher reappeared at work a few days later, he was livid. He'd tried to deliver both letters, and been unable to find either address. He'd guessed right away that Fritz had duped him—presumably for no better reason than to make a fool of him—and was hurt as well as angry. Fritz was apologetic, concealing his delight and relief; he was now almost sure that Wocher wasn't an agent provocateur.

Although he still didn't wholly trust the man, Fritz began to reveal more to him about what Auschwitz really was; gradually, over several days, he told Wocher about how Jews came in transports from Germany, Poland, France, the Netherlands, and countries in the east; about the selections in Birkenau; the children, the old, the unfit, and most of the women sent to the gas chambers, while the others were put to slave labor. Wocher had seen glimpses of it for himself; now he understood the long trains of closed cattle cars he'd seen coming in along the southeastern railroad past Monowitz, heading toward Oświęcim. Also, on one of the big factory floors he'd heard civilians talking about these things. He was beginning to realize that he'd missed a lot being in the army at the front.[6]

It was becoming harder to miss what was going on. Like a metastasizing cancer, Auschwitz was spreading and growing. With a new commandant in overall charge, sweeping organizational changes had been made, and Auschwitz III-Monowitz (its official name as of November 1943) became a principal camp along with Auschwitz I and Auschwitz II-Birkenau. Monowitz was now the administrative hub for a growing number of subcamps pustulating throughout the countryside around the Buna Werke. Accordingly it had a commandant installed above camp director Schöttl, a pallid, blank-eyed man called SS-Captain Heinrich Schwarz who liked to take a personal hand in the beating and murder of prisoners, working himself into a foaming rage in the process. Former commandant Rudolf Höss called Captain Schwarz "the choleric type, easily aroused and irascible" and praised his enthusiastic, meticulous devotion to enacting the Final Solution, often raging against Berlin if ever there was a lull in the number of transports of Jews.[7]

New transports for the IG Farben camps sometimes came directly to Monowitz now, and for the first time Fritz witnessed with his own eyes what he had previously only heard about—the bewildered people herded from the freight cars onto the ground near the camp, loaded down with luggage: men, women, and children, thinking they had come to be resettled.[8] Many were frightened, others happy and relieved to find friends again among the mass after days in the dark, suffocating cars. The healthy men were separated and marched to the camp. Meanwhile, the women, children, and elderly were put back on the train, which rolled on to Birkenau. In Monowitz the men were made to strip naked in the roll-call square, leaving all their clothes and belongings in a heap. Many tried to keep hold of precious possessions, but they were nearly always found out. Everything was taken to the special storage block for sorting and searching. This place, like its larger counterpart in Birkenau, was known as "Canada" (which was believed to be a land of riches). The prisoner detail responsible for handling the plunder were very thorough.[9] Working under close SS oversight, they searched through it like prospectors panning dirt, prying open seams to look for concealed valuables. Any that were found were often pocketed by the SS supervisors. Everything else was held in storage.

Among the new arrivals, Fritz took a particular interest in the Jews from the ghetto at Theresienstadt, many of whom had been deported there from Vienna. Fritz sought them out, looking for news of home. They had little to tell; they'd been away from Vienna a long time. More up-to-date news came when deportations directly from Vienna began arriving. Virtually all the registered Jews had gone from the city now, and the Nazi authorities had begun deporting those who fell in the no-man's-land between Jewish and Aryan—the *Mischlinge*, those who were born from the intermarriage of Jews and Aryans and were therefore both and neither. The Nuremberg Laws defined two categories of Mischling: those with two Jewish grandparents ("half Jewish") were of the first degree, and those with only one ("quarter Jewish") were of the second degree. The Nazis had never reached a consensus on how they felt about Mischlinge, especially whether those of the first degree should be treated as Jews if their parents practiced Christianity. Jews married to Aryans lived in a world of fearful uncertainty; those who had converted to Christianity could never be sure that the state would recognize their conversion or the special status they gained from their Aryan spouses.

With the extermination of the Jews approaching a climax, more and more Mischlinge were being deported to the camps. Fritz talked to those who came from Vienna but could get no more than general information about life there—nobody could tell him anything about his remaining relatives and friends, if any were still alive.

When Alfred Wocher mentioned that he would be going to Vienna on a short leave, Fritz saw his chance. He felt he could trust him now, and hoped the trust was reciprocated. Fritz gave him the address of his aunt Helene, who lived in Vienna-Döbling, a suburb on the northern outskirts, across the Danube Canal from Leopoldstadt. Helene had married an Aryan and been baptized a Christian, so had remained secure from the Nazis. Her son was Viktor, the cousin from whom Kurt had acquired his hunting knife, and her husband was a German officer. Fritz wanted her to know that he and his papa were still alive and well, and to pass the news on to any other surviving relatives. Wocher took the address and set off.

He returned a few days later. The mission hadn't been much more fruitful than the previous one. The address had been genuine enough, but the lady who'd answered the door to him had been decidedly unfriendly—she'd denied all knowledge of any Fritz Kleinmann and slammed the door in Wocher's face.

Much later, Fritz pieced together what had happened. What he hadn't realized was that when he was away from the factory, Alfred Wocher reverted to army uniform. His appearance on Aunt Helene's doorstep had scared the poor woman out of her wits. Her husband had died in the war, and she felt terrifyingly exposed without the protection his Aryan status had given her. What if the Nazis decided she was a Jew after all? When this total stranger in a Nazi sergeant's uniform came knocking on her door and mentioned Fritz being in Auschwitz, she'd thought her time had come, and she panicked.

One thing at least had come out of the affair: Fritz now trusted Alfred Wocher completely. With Christmas approaching, he was off to Vienna again. This time Fritz gave him some more addresses—a cousin and some friends of his papa's from the local neighborhood. He also gave him the address of Im Werd 11/16, his home, and a letter for his mother; despite everything he knew now about what was going on in the world, and despite having heard nothing from his mother or Herta for a year and a half, Fritz couldn't give up hope completely. He needed to believe that they were all right.

חברים

Leopoldstadt had lost its heart. It was still a populous area, but the excision of its Jewish people had taken the life quite literally out of it. Shops were still untenanted, businesses still boarded up. When Alfred Wocher ascended the stairs of the apartment building at Im Werd 11, the apartments where Jews had lived—around half of the twenty-three in the building—were unoccupied.[10] So much for the Nazi claim that Jews were taking up scarce living space that was needed for true Germans. There was no answer when he knocked on the door of number 16.[11] It had probably never been opened since Tini Kleinmann turned the key in the lock in June 1942. Wickerl Helmhacker, who'd overseen her eviction, was still living in the building. But so was Karl Novacek, an old friend of Gustav's. Karl worked as a cinema projectionist and was one of the handful of Aryan friends who had remained loyal to the Kleinmanns throughout the Nazi persecutions.[12] He was overjoyed to learn that Gustav and Fritz were still alive in body and spirit.

He wasn't alone. There were other true friends in the same street—Olga Steyskal, a shopkeeper who had an apartment in the building next door, and Franz Kral, a locksmith who lived in the next building along. The reaction was the same from all of them. As soon as they heard the news, Olga, Franz, and Karl hurried across the street to the Karmelitermarkt and came back with baskets of food for Wocher to take back to Auschwitz for Gustav and Fritz. Word also reached Fritz's cousin, Karoline Semlak—Lintschi, as she was better known—who lived a few streets away from the Karmelitermarkt. Lintschi was Aryan by marriage, but unlike poor Helene in Döbling she had no qualms about exposing her Jewish origins. She put together a package of food and wrote a letter in which she enclosed photographs of her children. The food assembled by the three friends, together with Lintschi's package and letter, filled two suitcases. Olga also wrote a letter for Gustav. She was deeply fond of him, as he was of her; there might have been sparks between them if he hadn't already been married.

It was an incongruous, improbable occasion: a group of Aryan friends and a converted Jew packing off a Bavarian soldier in Wehrmacht uniform with suitcases full of loving gifts for two Jews in Auschwitz. It was strangely beautiful, but it left Wocher with a problem: conveying all this bounty to Fritz in safety was going to be quite a challenge.

Somehow he overcame the problem, smuggling the gifts into the factory and passing them over to Fritz.[13] The food was very welcome, but even more so was the news of Lintschi and their friends. Fritz asked eagerly after his mother and sister, but Wocher shook his head gravely. Everyone he'd spoken to had said the same—Tini Kleinmann and her daughter had gone with the deportations to the Ostland and never been heard of since. Fritz's disappointment was bitter; his last hope had been taken away from him. But he still clung to the faint possibility that they weren't dead. Fritz's aunts, Jenni Rottenstein and Bertha Teperberg, had been deported too; after a few months' anxious suspense, in September 1942 they had both been summoned and put aboard one of the last Ostland transports to leave Vienna. Jenni had no family of her own other than her talking cat, but Bertha left behind her daughter and grandson. The two sisters went to their end together among the pines at Maly Trostinets.[14]

Fritz shared the food among his comrades in his work detail and took the news and the letters back to his papa. Despite the crushing news about Tini and Herta, Gustav was heartened to hear from his dear friends. His nature rebelled against giving up hope, and it gave him joy to think that he would be able to write to people he loved.

There was a much bleaker reaction from Gustl Herzog and Stefan Heymann when Fritz told them what he'd done; despite his own confidence in Alfred Wocher's trustworthiness, Stefan in particular was deeply suspicious. It was too soon after Erich and Walter and the others. He warned Fritz against any further involvement with the German. Fritz's respect for Stefan was great, but his longing for the old world and his family was greater.

16 | Far from Home

אבא

"DEAREST OLLY," Gustav wrote, "Your kind letter to me is received with many thanks, and you must forgive me for leaving you for so long with no word from me and Fritzl, but I have to take great care not to cause any trouble for you. For your kind package I thank you many times over, and also Franzl. It makes me so glad that I have such kind and good friends when I am so far from home."[1]

It felt good to be able to write without constraint. Today was the third day of the new year of 1944, and there was a faint whiff of hope in the air. His pencil darted rapidly across the ruled squares of the sketch paper.

"Believe me, dear Olly, through all the years I have always recalled the beautiful hours that I spent with you and all your dear ones, and have never forgotten you. As for me and Fritzl, the years have been hard, but I owe it to my will-power and energy that it was always my choice to keep going.

"If it should be granted to me to be in contact again with you and your dear ones, it will make up for what I have been missing—that for two and a half years I have had no news about my family . . . But I'm not letting my hair turn gray over it, because someday I will be reunited with them. As far as I am concerned, dear Olly, I am still the old Gustl, and intend to stay that way. And I get the same impression about you from your dear lines. . . . Anyhow, be assured, my dear, that wherever I am I am always thinking of you and all my dear friends—now I close with the fondest wishes and kisses. Your Gustl and Fritz.

"PS—Please give my regards to Franzl, Franzi, Karl, Gretl, as well as the Rittmann and Buritsch families."[2]

Gustav folded the sheets and put them in an envelope addressed to Olga Steyskal, Im Werd 9, Vienna. Fritz would smuggle it into the factory the next morning and pass it to his German friend. Once again his boy had surpassed himself for courage and initiative. There was no restraining him; all Gustav could do was hope he didn't bring trouble on himself again, or on his friends.

As the weeks went by, Fritz took letters to Fredl Wocher from other Viennese prisoners—mostly Jews with Aryan wives at home. Unlike Gustav's first letter to Olga, they took care to compose them so that they wouldn't incriminate either the sender or receiver if they were intercepted by the Gestapo.

This wasn't the only way in which Fritz and Gustav worked to benefit their comrades. Since the reorganization of the camps under the new commandant, on orders from Himmler Auschwitz had introduced bonus coupons for prisoners; worth 2 to 5 marks each, the coupons were given out for exemplary work and could be exchanged for luxury items like tobacco or toilet paper at the prisoner canteen. This was the only legitimate way for a prisoner to acquire money; in theory, the system was meant to increase the productivity of the most valuable workers, but in practice the bonuses were quickly adapted to the existing culture of favoritism and corruption among kapos. Although in the rest of Auschwitz they were paid to all categories of prisoner, in Monowitz they were given only to Aryans and confined to those with high-status occupations. Some kapos used them as a means of rewarding special favors rather than good work.[3]

Such bonuses provided a strong temptation to some prisoners to deviate from the general culture of resistance, in which one did as little work as one could get away with. For many, the temptation was increased by the fact that bonus coupons could be exchanged for visits to the camp brothel.

This facility—another of Himmler's initiatives to encourage productivity—had been created from a barrack block near the kitchens; known euphemistically as the *Frauenblock*,* it was enclosed within its own barbed wire fence and divided internally into single rooms.[4] The women were prisoners from Birkenau: German, Polish, Czech, none of them Jews. They had volunteered for this ordeal on the promise that they would be given their freedom in due course. The brothel was open for business in the evenings and all day Sunday; there was a waiting list for customers, and only Aryan prisoners with bonus

---

* Women's block

coupons could apply—block seniors, functionaries, kapos, and foremen would stand in line to enter their names in the Rapportführer's book, sitting at his table by the brothel door. On admission, the customer was given a prophylactic injection against venereal disease and an SS man assigned him a woman and a room. During the day, when the brothel was closed, the women could sometimes be seen taking walks outside the camp, each escorted by a Blockführer.

As a rule, the communist and socialist political prisoners declined to use the brothel, partly on principle but mainly because it would make them vulnerable to blackmail by the SS. As an official Aryan, Gustav received bonus coupons, but in the almost monk-like existence to which he had accustomed himself, he had little use for them. SS camp director Schöttl, who had perverse tastes, got vicarious thrills from listening to prisoners' detailed descriptions of their activities with the women; but although he tried several times to persuade Gustav to go to the brothel, he always declined, ruefully pointing out his advanced age. (He was only fifty-two, but by camp reckoning that made him a veritable graybeard; almost nobody lived that long.)

Since he didn't smoke either, Gustav had no pressing need for his bonus coupons. Instead he passed them to Fritz (who as a Jew received none of his own). Fritz had made friends with the kapos in charge of the kitchen and the store room where the clothes looted from prisoners were kept; both men were deeply corrupt, and both were addicted to the brothel. In return for Gustav's coupons they gave Fritz bread and margarine from the larder and good clothes from the Canada store—pullovers, gloves, scarves, anything to supplement the camp uniform and keep one warm. He took his bounty back to the block and shared it among his father and friends.

Around the middle of 1944 the women in the brothel were replaced by a new batch of younger Polish girls. The original group, who had endured months of degradation in the Frauenblock on the promise of freedom, were sent back to Birkenau. They were never set free.[5]

In mid-May 1944, the general character of Auschwitz began to alter noticeably. Gustav noted in his diary that Monowitz was receiving a constant stream of new prisoners and that they were, without exception, young Hungarian Jews. They brought with them a hollow-eyed melancholy, as well as news from the east which, by Gustav's reckoning, indicated that the war was going very badly for the Germans. His reckoning was correct.

✡

In March 1944, Germany had invaded its former ally, Hungary. The Hungarian government had grown alarmed by the steady crumbling of Germany's forces on the Eastern Front and in Italy and the imminent likelihood of an Anglo-American invasion of northwest Europe. Concerned about their image as collaborators in Nazi atrocities, the government had begun to withdraw its support from Germany and made secret overtures of peace to the Allies. In German eyes, it was a devastating betrayal, in part because Hungarian army divisions made up a large and valuable portion of Germany's fighting forces. Hitler responded with swift fury, invading the country, taking control of the administration, and retaining the use of the Hungarian divisions.

Hungary had a population of around 765,000 Jews.[6] Their lives had been blighted by exclusion and anti-Semitism—including forced conscription and expulsion from professions—but had so far remained safe from harm. Now, in an instant, they were cast into the pit.

Systematic Nazi persecution began on April 16—the first day of Passover, the traditional celebration of divine liberation from bondage.[7] Einsatzgruppe units, reinforced by the Hungarian gendarmerie (who threw themselves into the task with relish), began rounding up hundreds of thousands of Jews in zones across Hungary, herding them into makeshift camps and ghettos. It was rapidly, efficiently, and savagely done; the RSHA, the supreme security department of the SS, sent its two most experienced officers to exercise the Final Solution in Hungary: Adolf Eichmann, who had developed his expertise in deporting Jews from Vienna and honed it in the Netherlands and other conquered countries; and Rudolf Höss, the former commandant of Auschwitz.

The first RSHA transports left Budapest and Topolya* on April 29 and 30, arriving at Auschwitz on May 2. Between them they contained three thousand eight hundred Jewish men and women preselected as potential workers. After reselection in Birkenau, 486 men and 616 women were judged fit and registered; the rest went to the gas chambers.[8] They were the first trickle in a human flood. Work was being completed in Birkenau to heighten the camp's efficiency; the "old Jew-ramp" at Oświęcim would no longer suffice, and a rail

---

* Now Bačka Topola, Serbia; formerly part of Yugoslavia, ruled by Hungary 1941–4

spur had been hastily laid right into the Birkenau camp, with an unloading ramp nearly half a kilometer long. An additional spur went right to the gas chambers and crematoria, which were housed in extended enclosures at the rear of the main perimeter.

Rudolf Höss returned from Hungary on May 8 and took over as temporary senior commandant, especially to oversee the impending escalation.[9]

On Tuesday, May 16, 1944, the entire camp of Birkenau was put on lockdown. Prisoners were shut in their blocks under guard. The only exceptions were those in the Sonderkommando and, incongruously, the camp orchestra. Shortly afterward, a long train came steaming and squealing along the rail tracks, through the archway in the brick gatehouse, and rolled to a halt at the Birkenau ramp. It consisted of forty to fifty freight cars. The doors slid open, and from each car about a hundred people spilled out. Old and young, women, men, children, infants. Scarcely any of them had the faintest idea what manner of place they had come to; they'd been led to believe that their destination was a camp where they could live and work, and many disembarked with light hearts, tired and disorientated but hopeful. Some Hungarian Jews had been forced to labor in the killing fields of the Ostland during the alliance with Germany and knew well what atrocities had been done there, but even these few believed that the Nazis would treat Hungarians differently from Soviets.[10] As the striped uniforms of the Sonderkommando moved among them, no fear of death troubled them. The sound of music from the camp orchestra added to the atmosphere of harmlessness.

Then came the selection. Men and women over fifty years of age, anyone who was lame or sick, children, mothers and fathers with young children and infants, pregnant women, all these were sent to one side. Healthy men and women between sixteen and fifty years old—about a quarter of the total— were sent to the other.

As the day wore on, the process was repeated; two more trains completed their journey from Hungary at the Birkenau ramp. Two more selections, thousands of souls sent to left or right. Those designated fit for labor were labeled "Transit Jews" and put in a transit section of the vast camp. The elderly, the unwell, pregnant women, mothers with small children—were herded on to the low buildings among the trees where foul-smelling smoke streamed from the chimneys night and day.[11]

Around fifteen thousand Hungarian Jews entered Birkenau on those three trains; the exact number murdered would never be known, because not one of them—the dead or the enslaved—was ever registered as a prisoner of Auschwitz or received a number.[12] Even those assigned to the labor camps were not intended to survive long.

It was the beginning of a monstrous schedule that would mark the zenith— or rather the nadir—of Auschwitz as a place of extermination. Between May and July 1944, Eichmann's organization in Hungary sent 147 trains to Auschwitz, containing a total of 437,403 people, more than half the country's Jewish population.[13] The trains arrived in Birkenau at the rate of up to five a day, overwhelming the system. Additional gas chambers that had lain dormant for some time were put back into use. Four in all operated around the clock. Nine hundred overworked, traumatized Sonderkommando herded the panicked women, men, and children naked into the gas chambers and hauled out the corpses. The expanded Canada detail filled block after block with looted clothes, valuables, and suitcases of belongings. The crematoria couldn't cope with the sheer number of dead, and pits were dug in which to burn the bodies. The SS went into a frenzy of killing; so great was the rush to murder each newly arrived batch that gas chambers were often opened up hastily, while some victims were still breathing; those who moved were shot or clubbed to death; others were flung into the fire pits still alive.[14]

Many of the Hungarian Jews who survived the selections were sent to Monowitz. Gustav watched them arrive with bleak sympathy. "Many of them no longer have parents, because the parents are left behind in Birkenau," he wrote in his diary. Only a minority were like himself and Fritz—a father and son together, or a mother and daughter. Would they have the strength and luck to survive as he and Fritz had done? Looking at their broken state, it seemed unlikely. "Such a sad chapter," he wrote.

אבא

By the middle of 1944, Gustav and Fritz had been properly reunited. Gustav's upholstery detail had moved to premises in the Buna Werke, and he'd had Fritz transferred to work under him.[15] This was the level of influence he now enjoyed.

They'd had a hard time in the early months of the year. Winter was savage in this part of the world, with thick snow on the ground and outbreaks of fever and dysentery. Both of them had fallen sick and spent time in the hospital, where despite the presence of good friends among the functionaries they were in constant danger of being selected for liquidation. Gustav had been the first to fall ill and had been admitted to the hospital along with dozens of others on February 14. He was in for eight days, and only five days after his discharge a selection took place and several of the men who'd been admitted at the same time were sent to the gas chambers. Another outbreak of sickness in late March had put Fritz in the hospital for over two weeks; like his father he was lucky. Discharged in early April, he went back to work.[16]

Now that he was based in the factory, Gustav began getting to know Fredl Wocher personally. The man who had helped put him in touch with his old friends in Vienna now had his and Fritz's complete trust; he kept the lines of communication open and became a good friend to both of them.

For Fritz, being in his father's workshop meant a resumption of his apprenticeship in upholstery, which had been interrupted by the Anschluss of 1938. They worked under a German civilian master from Ludwigshafen. "He's all right," Gustav wrote, "and he supports us wherever he can. The man is anything but a Nazi."

The loyalties of Germans were coming under increasing pressure as the war unfolded. On June 6, the long-anticipated invasion of France by British, Canadian, and American forces began. Meanwhile, the Red Army pushed relentlessly from the east, while even more Allied armies advanced north through Italy. In early July the Red Army swept into the Ostland, encircling Minsk and capturing the region where the destroyed remains of Maly Trostinets lay (the small camp had been decommissioned and razed in October 1943, having served its purpose). On July 22, units advancing into the German General Government region of eastern Poland captured the huge concentration camp of Majdanek, which lay on the outskirts of the city of Lublin.

Majdanek was the first large-scale camp to be captured by the Allies. The Russian advance had been so rapid that the retreating SS had been forced to leave it virtually intact, complete with gas chambers and crematoria and the corpses of its victims. Eyewitness descriptions of Majdanek by Soviet and American reporters flew around the world, appearing in newspapers ranging

from *Pravda* to the *New York Times*. In the words of one Russian war correspondent, describing the functioning of the gas chambers and the vast quantities of plundered belongings, the horror of it was "too enormous and too
gruesome to be fully conceived."[17] By the end of that year the Soviet Union
had established a small memorial museum at Majdanek—the first to com-
memorate the Holocaust, founded while other concentration camps were still
in full operation.[18]

News also reached the outside world about the mass deportations of Jews
from Hungary, and pressure was growing on the Allied governments—who
already had quite detailed intelligence about the camps, including Auschwitz—
to do something directly to help. There were calls for bombing raids against
camp facilities and railroad networks. But the Allied air commanders considered and dismissed the calls; it was not a viable use of their resources, they
said—resources that were fully committed to mass bombing of strategic targets
and providing air support to the advancing armies. And that was that.[19] However, the SS didn't know this, and what was more, some of the camps were
located adjacent to strategic industrial facilities at high risk of bombing. With
the Third Reich shrinking, Auschwitz and the IG Farben Buna complex at
Monowitz were coming within striking distance of Allied long-range bombers.
The Auschwitz SS, who'd been discussing the matter since November 1943,
finally decided to implement some air raid precautions.[20] Air raid shelters were
set up at the Buna Werke and a blackout policy was implemented across the
Auschwitz complex.

At Monowitz, the task of equipping the factories against air raids fell in
part upon Gustav Kleinmann, who was taken off upholstery work and put
in charge of manufacturing blackout curtains. He was made a kapo and given
a workshop attached to the department where fiberglass pipe insulation was
made. He was provided with sewing machines and a team of twenty-four prisoners, mostly young Jewish women—"all well-behaved and reliable folk." He
used his position to have Fritz transferred along with him. While his father's
team made the curtains, Fritz helped the civilian fitters who installed them in
the factory buildings.

Gustav worked under the director of the insulation department, a good
civilian manager called Ganz "who gives me a completely free hand." Ganz
was a socialist, and after he discovered that Gustav had been a social democrat,
he would stop by the workshop to chat and share his lunch. Ganz was quite

different from his fellow manager, a man called Edlinger who lived in awe and terror of the Nazis; he wouldn't listen to the prisoners' stories, and insisted that the Führer knew what he was doing.

Edlinger wasn't alone. All unofficial contacts between prisoners and civilians had to be made cautiously because of the presence of stool pigeons. One of the civilian foremen, a man named Ackerl, was a thoroughgoing Nazi who reported any fraternization to the senior engineer, another loyal Nazi called Loch.

For every hostile force among the civilians, there was usually a sympathetic one. Some of the Polish women from the insulation workshop would smuggle bread and potatoes to the Jewish prisoners in the blackout workshop. Two young women in particular—Stepa Stanislawa and Danuta Jurewska—befriended the Jews and were unfailingly courageous in offering them help. Where they got the food from was a mystery, because their own rations were hardly plentiful. There were also two German women—Erika and Waltraud—who provided morsels of bread and sausage. They confessed that with the war going so badly for Germany, they feared that they might never see their homes again.

The women in Gustav's workshop, having been inside Birkenau, told Gustav all about what went on there—the transports from Hungary, the selections, the starvation and plundering. Four Hungarian tailors who were allotted to his curtain detail described the round-ups of Jews in Budapest. It had been like an unforeseen tornado, quicker and more ferocious than in Vienna. Despite the restrictions in Hungary, Jews had grown used to being able to keep the Shabbat and attend synagogue and had convinced themselves that the persecution stories coming out of Germany were exaggerated. Then the Nazis had come, and they had seen for themselves what it was like.

For nearly two years Gustav had absorbed the stories out of Birkenau, but this was a new and monstrous level of barbarism. "The stench of the burning corpses reaches as far as the town," Gustav wrote in his diary. "The four crematoria cannot cope; they are having to burn the rest in pyres." Every day he saw the transports pass by on the railroad from the southeast, which ran close to Monowitz, the long chains of freight and cattle cars closed tight. "But we know everything that's going on. They are all Hungarian Jews—and all this in the twentieth century."

בן

With Fritz helping, his civilian colleague Schubert fixed the last curtain to the office window. He explained to the manager how to use the curtains, but it was heavy going; Schubert was a *Volksdeutsche*—an ethnic German—from Poland and spoke German very badly.

He and Fritz packed their tools away. As they did so, one of the civilians passed some ends of bread to Schubert, with a nod at Fritz. Schubert took them discreetly, slipping them into Fritz's toolbox. Fritz heaved the stack of curtains onto his shoulder, picked up his toolbox, and together they walked out into the sunlight. On to the next building. There were hundreds upon hundreds of windows in the Buna Werke, spread across a vast area, and although there were other teams of fitters, it was still a mammoth undertaking. Some of the factories weren't even operational, and the work to complete them went on around the clock. After nearly two years, rubber production still hadn't begun. The inefficiency of slave labor and the constant erosion by small acts of sabotage were holding it back.

Fritz got on well with Schubert despite the difficulties of communication. His papa, who could speak Polish, got on with Schubert even better. He came from the town of Bielitz-Biala, where Gustav had worked as a baker's boy in the early years of the century, and where he had spent time in the military hospital in 1915 prior to his spell at Oświęcim.

Entering the next building, Schubert showed his pass to the supervisor, along with the paper that allowed Fritz to accompany him. The document bore the number of the work detail—114—and the number of prisoners Schubert was allowed to have with him. Fritz rather enjoyed being out and about like this—it was almost like a taste of freedom. A year had passed since his interrogation and torture by Grabner and his simulated death and resurrection, and there was no longer any fear of it coming back to haunt him. Each day he and Schubert returned to the workshop with their toolboxes full of scraps of bread to add to the pool of gifts to be shared among the prisoners. There were other curtain fitters who were just as kind as Schubert, including two Czechs—Frantisek and Pepitschko—who acted as message couriers for some of Fritz's Czech Jewish friends, just as Fredl Wocher did for him and his father. Whenever the two went on leave to Brno, they took letters to the prisoners' friends and brought back gifts of bacon and lard. All but the most strictly religious Jews received bacon with gratitude, having long abandoned the stricter elements of their faith.[21] Some, like Fritz, had abandoned faith itself, finding it impossible to sustain a belief in a God who loved the Jews.

The next building on the list was close to the main factory gates. There was a checkpoint just outside, manned by an SS corporal. Fritz didn't know his name; the prisoners called him "*Rotfuchs*"—Red Fox—because of his flaming red hair. He possessed a temper to match. As Fritz was passing by, Rotfuchs was staring in irritation at a group of Greek Jews standing idle inside the gates. Rotfuchs's anger got the better of him; he came in through the gates, marched up to the Greeks and started yelling at them to get back to work, battering them savagely with the butt of his rifle. None of them spoke German, and they had no idea what he was saying.

Fritz couldn't stop himself. He dropped everything and ran across, throwing himself between Rotfuchs and his victims. "You have to get back to the checkpoint," he said, and pointed toward the wide-open gate. "Prisoners might escape."

Any other SS man might have at least been given pause by this reminder of his duty, even by a Jewish prisoner. But not Rotfuchs. He turned apoplectic with rage. "I'll do as I please!" he screamed. There was the oily *schlick-clack* of his rifle being cocked, and the muzzle aimed at Fritz. So this was it; after all these years, it would end here.

Fritz Kleinmann would have become another in the endless string of Jews shot by the SS if it hadn't been for Herr Erdmann, one of the senior engineers, rushing forward at the very instant Rotfuchs took aim. As Erdmann snatched the rifle away, Fritz, without hesitation, turned on his heel and walked determinedly into a nearby materials store. He knew better than to hang around at the scene.

It could have gone either way; Fritz might have been shot anyway as a punishment, or at the very least suffered twenty-five lashes on the Bock. But it never came to that; Herr Erdmann lodged a formal complaint against Rotfuchs with IG Farben, with the result that the corporal was transferred to a different posting. The prisoners of Monowitz never saw him again.

Erdmann's action typified many Germans' feelings. Outside of the SS itself, there was little sympathy left for the Nazi regime; for many Germans, whatever national pride they had possessed, whatever Nazi ideology they had swallowed, the effect was being countered by the ever-worsening situation Hitler had brought upon Germany. Many were afraid of what would become of them, and for those who worked in and around Auschwitz, the more they learned about what the SS had really done—and was daily continuing to do—to the Jews, the less they could stomach it. Their acts of resistance were small—a little food, a blind eye turned—but they saved lives.

Even a few of those in the military were disposed to be kind. With his ability to move around the Buna Werke on curtain-fitting duties, Fritz was able to continue meeting up with Fredl Wocher, who had been moved to a different factory. On one occasion, Wocher introduced Fritz to two of his military friends, both NCOs in the Luftwaffe antiaircraft batteries stationed around the perimeter. They had more rations than they needed and gave Fritz several cans of meat and fish preserves, jam, and synthetic honey. More bounty for the pool to be shared among the prisoner laborers or smuggled into the camp.

These gifts were becoming more important than ever, because with Germany afflicted by shortages, all resources were being channeled to the military on the front lines; citizens in Germany were on rations, and prisoners in the concentration camps got almost nothing. The number of hopeless Muselmänner increased, and deaths from sickness and starvation escalated, as did the selections for the gas chambers. There was a limit to how far the surplus food collected by Fritz and his comrades could go, but at least it helped a few. At the suggestion of Gustl Herzog and Stefan Heymann, Fritz and his better-fed comrades donated all their camp-issued rations to other prisoners who were starving.

How to share out the rations and the extra food among such a large number was a matter of constant worry to Fritz, and the harsh choices it forced him to make would never cease to haunt him. "If we were to share it among so many, for each it would be no more than a drop of water on a hot stone." And to give food to a Muselmann, so starved that one look told you he would be dead within days, seemed like a waste. "Even today the thought torments me," said Fritz many years later, when he recalled his actions. Hardening his heart against the terminally weak and dying, he gave his spare food to the young. There were three boys in particular in his block, all of whom had lost their parents to the gas chambers. They were Walter Ansbacher, a sixteen-year-old from Augsburg, and fourteen-year-old Artus Fischmann from the Łodz ghetto; the third was Fritz's old schoolfriend, Leo Meth. Leo had initially escaped from the Nazis in Vienna by being sent to France, only to fall into the net after the German annexation of the Vichy zone. Fritz gave these boys his share of ration bread and soup, as well as a portion of the sausage and other morsels donated by the factory employees and the antiaircraft men. In his mind it was payback for the kindness he'd received from elders like Leo Moses when he was a vulnerable sixteen-year-old in Buchenwald.

Gustav also did what he could for young and needy prisoners. One day when a batch of new arrivals were being entered on the register, he heard the name Georg Koplowitz called. It sparked a memory from the distant past. After the death of Gustav's father and his own departure for Vienna, around 1908 Gustav's mother had moved to the town of Beuthen,* across the border in what was then the German Empire. There she worked for a Jewish family with the name Koplowitz; she'd been fond of them and remained with them until her death in 1928. Intrigued, Gustav tracked down this young man and discovered that he was in fact the son of the very same family, the sole survivor of the selection at Birkenau. Gustav took Georg under his wing, giving him surplus food each day and arranging for him to be provided with a safe position as a helper in the hospital under Felix Rausch.[22]

The circle of kindness was completed by British prisoners of war who worked in the factories. They were inmates of camp E715, a labor subcamp of Stalag VIII-B. Despite being within the SS-controlled Auschwitz zone and the inmates being employed as slave laborers in the Buna Werke, they were prisoners of the Wehrmacht, and it was Wehrmacht guards who escorted them to work and watched over them there. The POWs received regular welfare packages via the International Red Cross, and they shared some of the contents with the Auschwitz prisoners they worked with, along with news about the war, which they picked up from BBC broadcasts on secret radio sets in their camp. Fritz particularly remembered the chocolate, the English tea, and the Player's Navy Cut cigarettes. Given how priceless these last two commodities were to the average British soldier, it was an act of great generosity to share them. The British were appalled by the abuses they saw perpetrated by the SS and complained to their own guards about it. "The behavior of the English prisoners of war towards us quickly became the talk of the camp," Fritz recalled, "and the assistance they gave was of great value to many of our comrades."

---

* Now Bytom, Poland

Although the gifts from civilians, German soldiers, and POWs alike came quite readily, it was dangerous to be found in possession of them. There was one SS man in particular to beware of. SS-Sergeant Bernhard Rakers, Monowitz work detail leader, was both brutal and corrupt. He'd been transferred from Sachsenhausen as a punishment for embezzlement, and had continued in his habits. He ran the prisoner work details in the Buna Werke like his own little kingdom, intruding his presence even where it wasn't officially required, lining his pockets, and sexually harassing the women workers. He dished out savage punishments to prisoners and forced laborers alike.[23] Curt Posener said of him, "His grift in the workplace greatly exasperated even the senior Nazis among the IG Farben managers and engineers, because Rakers would not adhere to any rules."[24] Fritz, going about with contraband food concealed in his toolbox, was constantly aware of the risk of bumping into him. Rakers would often search prisoners, and the discovery any kind of contraband earned the culprit twenty-five lashes on the spot. There would be no official report—the contraband went straight into Rakers's pocket.

If a prisoner was caught with contraband by any other SS guard, the outcome was just as terrible—a whipping on the Bock at the very least, or a period of days without food or water in the standing cells in the bunker: tiny, claustrophobic rooms in which it was impossible to sit down.

But the known result of *not* collecting contraband food—slow starvation, sickness, and death over the course of a few months—was infinitely worse than the risk of punishment. And so Fritz and the others looked for new and better ways to acquire food. It was two Hungarian Jews who suggested the idea of the coats.

Jenö and Laczi Berkovits were brothers from Budapest, both young and both skilled tailors who'd been assigned to Gustav Kleinmann's blackout detail.[25] One day they approached Fritz and outlined their idea. The black fabric they were using to make curtains was thick and sturdy, coated on one side with waterproofing. One could make excellent raincoats from it. Such garments would be valuable trade goods, which could be exchanged for food on the black market. They could even be sold for cash to civilians in the factories.

Fritz had doubts. The curtain material was carefully stock controlled, the length of raw fabric tallied against the number of curtains produced. Even rejects had to be handed over to Herr Ganz. But Jenö and Laczi were enthusiastic and persuasive; they were positive they could siphon off a proportion of fabric. A skilled tailor could organize the usage of material so that the garments came more or less within the normal percentage of wastage. And with the number of curtains being produced, that would make a lot of coats.

Fritz consulted his father, who agreed to give the plan a trial. Between them the Berkovits brothers managed to turn out between four and six overcoats every day, without significantly increasing the overall consumption of material. Meanwhile the other workers in Gustav's shop had to work extra hard to keep curtain production up to speed. When it came to completing the coats, however, the brothers ran into a major problem: they had no buttons, nor anything that could be used as a substitute. The problem was solved when Pepitschko, one of the Czech curtain fitters, offered to bring back a supply on his next trip to Brno.

Fritz's Polish women friends from the insulation workshop, Danuta and Stepa, smuggled the finished coats out to their labor camp, where they sold them to fellow workers. The price per coat was either one kilo of bacon or half a liter of schnapps. Others were sold to civilians in the factories.

The danger of the scheme being discovered by the SS gradually increased as more and more civilians appeared wearing the distinctive black coats. But this risk was mitigated somewhat when the coats started becoming popular with German engineers and managers, who acquired a vested interest in turning a blind eye to the operation. And so the number of prisoners Fritz and his friends were able to help increased a little, and more lives were saved.

17 | Resistance and Betrayal

אח

FRITZ KLEINMANN DID EVERYTHING he could to help save lives but he craved a more direct form of resistance, and he was not alone. By the middle of 1944, he was already deeply involved.

Putting up an armed resistance against the SS was impossible without weapons and support. As things stood, the only way to achieve that would be to make contact with the Polish partisans operating from their hideouts in the Beskids mountains, about forty kilometers to the south. Getting basic messages to them was one thing, but developing a proper relationship would require a meeting in person. Somebody would have to escape.

Word was passed to the partisans, and at the beginning of May a five-man team of escapees was chosen by the resistance leadership. First up was Karl Peller, one of the old Buchenwalder Jews, a thirty-four-year-old butcher. Then there was Chaim Goslawski, the senior in block 48 who had looked after Fritz after his staged death. Goslawski was a Polish-born Jew who had arrived in Auschwitz from Sachsenhausen at the same time as the Buchenwalders.[1] He was a native of this region; if anyone could find a way to the partisans, it would be him. There was also a Jew from Berlin whose name Fritz never knew, plus two Poles known only to Fritz as "Szenek" and "Pawel," who worked in the camp kitchen.[2]

Fritz was brought into the circle by Goslawski. He wouldn't be among the escapees, but his help would be needed. He and Goslawski obtained civilian clothes from the Canada store, which the escapees would wear concealed under their camp uniforms. Meanwhile, other preparations were made, about which Fritz knew nothing.

On May 4, before morning roll call, Goslawski handed Fritz a small package, about the size of a loaf of bread, and instructed him to pass it to fellow conspirator Karl Peller, who worked on one of the Buna construction sites. As a block senior and functionary, Goslawski didn't go out with the labor details.[3] Fritz secreted it inside his uniform and they hurried off to roll call.

Later that morning, on his curtain-fitting rounds, Fritz managed to get to the site where Peller was at work and slipped the package to him. At noon, Szenek and Pawel arrived in the Buna Werke with the lunchtime soup for the prisoners. Fritz noticed that Chaim Goslawski had found some pretext to accompany them.

At roll call that evening, all five men—Peller, Goslawski, Szenek, Pawel, and the Berliner—were missing. They had walked out of the Buna Werke wearing their civilian disguises and disappeared. While the SS launched a search, an order was given that all prisoners were to remain standing on the roll-call square under guard.

There they remained as the hours ticked by, weary, aching. Midnight came and went, and the early hours of the morning wore away. Dawn found them still standing to attention, surrounded by a chain of armed sentries. Breakfast time approached, but there would be no bread or acorn coffee this morning. A whisper passed through the ranks; the SS were not only seeking the five missing men but also an unidentified prisoner who had been seen talking to Karl Peller on the construction site the previous morning. Fritz's heart shrank in his breast; if he were identified, it would be the bunker for him this time, and the Black Wall. But despite his fear, he inwardly rejoiced. The escape had been a success. Eventually the prisoners were ordered to march off to work, and away they went with empty bellies, exhausted, but uplifted by hope.

Days went by and it seemed that Fritz was safe. Nobody identified him to the SS. Three weeks passed with no word, and then the blow fell. The two Poles, Szenek and Pawel, along with the Berliner, were brought back to the camp. They had been arrested by a police patrol in Cracow on May 26, twenty-two days after their escape.[4] It was a shock and a mystery to the resistance, as Cracow was nowhere near the Beskids—almost in the opposite direction in fact. And where were Goslawski and Peller?

At roll call that evening, the three recaptured men were put on the Bock and lashed. And that, astonishingly, was the end of their punishment. Some time later, when a transport of several hundred Poles was sent from Auschwitz to Buchenwald, Szenek and Pawel were put on it.[5] The Berlin Jew remained in Monowitz.

There the matter seemed to end, with a question mark over the fates of Goslawski and Peller and whether they were now with the partisans. Eventually, having been too scared to speak while the two Poles were still in the camp, the Berliner revealed what had happened after the escape. The package Fritz had conveyed from Goslawski to Karl Peller had been at the root of it. It had been stuffed with cash and jewelry stolen from the Canada store, which was intended as a payment to the partisans to secure their assistance. A rendezvous had been prearranged, but Goslawski and Peller never got there; on the first night after their escape, both men were murdered by Szenek and Pawel. The motive was the fortune they were carrying. The Berliner had been too terrified to intervene. The next day, instead of cutting loose with their booty, the three decided to head for the rendezvous after all. When they got there, the partisans were waiting for them. They weren't happy; they'd been told to expect five men—where were the other two? Szenek and Pawel feigned ignorance, but the partisans weren't satisfied with their excuses and evasions. They sheltered the three men for a week, but when Goslawski and Peller still didn't show up, they called off the deal. Szenek, Pawel, and the Berliner were driven to Cracow and set loose. Lost and helpless, they simply wandered the streets until they were picked up by the police.

The Berliner's confession was passed to Paul Kozwara, the camp senior. "P. K.," as he was popularly known, was a tyrant, but a relatively benign one compared to the infamous Jupp Windeck (Kozwara liked to taunt the Muselmänner, for instance, but would whip any block senior he caught not distributing food fairly).[6] Kozwara passed the confession on to the SS administration.

Nothing happened for a few weeks. Then one day Szenek and Pawel reappeared in Monowitz, brought back from Buchenwald on SS orders. A gallows appeared on the roll-call square and the prisoners were ordered out on parade. Fritz and his comrades marched into the square as if it were roll call, but this was different. Lined up in front of the gallows was a cordon of SS troopers with machine-pistols leveled at the ranks of prisoners. Commandant Heinrich Schwarz and SS-Lieutenant Schöttl stood on the podium as the two Poles were marched in. "Caps off!" came the order over the loudspeakers. Fritz and eight thousand others whipped off their caps and tucked them under their arms. Schöttl read the sentences into the microphone: both prisoners were sentenced to death for escape and for two counts of murder.

First Szenek was led up to the gallows, then Pawel. In typical SS fashion there was no drop; they were strung up, legs kicking and bodies jerking, twitching with diminishing force as the minutes passed and they slowly strangled. Eventually they were still. Fritz and the others had to stand motionless throughout the spectacle, a stark warning to anyone who dared resist or escape.[7]

The whole affair not only weakened the resistance through the loss of Goslawski and Peller but also revived all the old tensions and mistrust between the Poles and the German Jews.

And it sowed suspicion in the SS. Not long after the hanging, they claimed to have uncovered an escape plot among the roofing detail in the construction command. The prisoners were taken to the Gestapo bunker and subjected to horrific torture. On Commandant Schwarz's orders, three of the suspects were hanged in a repeat of the same dreadful ritual. One of the victims was the brother of Freddi Diamant, the youngster who had been an unwilling sidekick of Jupp Windeck and was a friend of Fritz.[8]

More hangings followed—including three Russians accused of looting during the chaos following an air raid. In reality they had been searching for food in one of the bombed-out factory buildings. IG Farben's own security guards had caught them and turned them in to the SS. Attacks from the air were a new thing in summer 1944 and gave new heart to the resistance, a sign that the Allies were getting closer.

אחים

In the late afternoon of Sunday, August 20, 1944, the first bombs fell out of clear blue sky. They exploded in the central and eastern end of the Buna Werke, close enough to shake the ground under the feet of people in the Monowitz camp. One hundred and twenty-seven American B-17 Flying Fortress bombers, flying from a base in Italy, drawing a comb of vapor trails across the blue five miles above Auschwitz, rained 1,336 bombs, each one a quarter-tonne of steel and high explosive.[9]

The terrified SS hid in their bunkers, but the prisoners were not provided for. In the camps they watched the pillars of black smoke, heard the titanic roar of the explosions, and felt the concussion through their bodies. The Luftwaffe flak batteries around the perimeter plumed smoke in answer, flinging up shells toward the distant bombers. Prisoners working in the factories threw themselves to the floor and rejoiced.

"The bombing was really a happy day for us," one of them recalled years later. "We thought, they know all about us, they are making preparations to free us." Another prisoner recalled, "We really enjoyed the bombing . . . We wanted once to see a killed German. Then we could sleep better, after the humiliation never to be able to answer back."[10]

When the last echo died away and the bombers had gone, the ground in and around the Buna Werke was pocked with smoking craters. The buildings were dispersed over a vast area, and most of the bombs had failed to hit anything, but some found a mark. Buildings in the synthetic oil and aluminum production plants had been torn apart, as had various sheds, workshops, and offices. Some outlying bombs had landed in the various labor camps around the factory complex, including Monowitz. Altogether, around seventy-five prisoners were killed in the raid, and over one hundred and fifty injured.[11]

Seeing the SS terrified, seeing their invulnerability challenged by the American bombs, heartened many Jewish prisoners; on others it had the opposite effect. The young Italian Primo Levi, who had arrived in Monowitz in February, believed that the bombing hardened the will of the SS and brought about a solidarity between them and the German civilians in the Buna Werke; he even perceived it among the German green- and red-triangle prisoners: the criminals and politicals, some of whom recalled the Nazi propaganda about the influence of Jews on American and international policy. Levi despaired at the destruction in the factories, which he and his fellow slaves had to repair, and the interruption of the water and food supplies in the camp.[12]

The resistance did not despair, but they were disappointed. The appearance of bombers had prompted speculation that the Allies would start parachuting in soldiers and weapons. But they never came. In the days following the air raid, American airplanes were seen high overhead on a few occasions, but neither bombs nor parachutes fell; they were reconnaissance flights, carefully photographing the IG Farben works and the Auschwitz complex.

What particularly concerned the resistance was the relentless advance of the Red Army from the east and the prospect of the SS carrying out a last-minute mass liquidation of the whole camp, murdering all the prisoners before they could be liberated. Prisoners evacuated to Auschwitz from Majdanek before its liberation reported that all Jews in that camp had been murdered before the Red Army got there. Stefan Heymann and Gustl Herzog, who had planned in terms of a bloodless rescue, were shaken by this information.

The resistance drafted a letter addressed jointly to camp director Schöttl and Walther Dürrfeld, director of the IG Farben Buna Werke. It purported to be from a group of Polish partisans and informed the two men that their names were on a list of German war criminals that had been smuggled to the Allies. Their treatment after the war would depend on how they behaved toward the prisoners from now on, and they were explicitly warned against any liquidation attempt. The letter was smuggled out by a Czech civilian, Jiri Hubert, and mailed from the local post office.[13] It prompted a search for the letter's author by the Gestapo, who guessed that it originated in the camp. The search yielded nothing. Whether the letter had any effect or not remained to be seen.

Despite the executions, escape attempts didn't stop. In October four Monowitz prisoners on an outside work detail overpowered their SS guard, seizing his rifle, and destroying it before making their escape.[14] Other escapes were more elaborate. Fritz Sonnenschein was a relative newcomer to Monowitz, one of the Viennese Mischlinge; he was highly intelligent, and Gustl Herzog managed to maneuver him into a position doing clerical work in Schöttl's office. There he picked up information about upcoming selections, which enabled the resistance to conceal vulnerable prisoners. Sonnenschein was a man of extraordinary resource and courage. One day he walked out of the camp disguised in a stolen SS sergeant's uniform. He managed to get all the way to Vienna before the Nazis caught up with him, and he died in a shootout with Gestapo officers, defiant to the last.

Individual actions were inspiring, but the Jewish resistance needed more. Now that relations with the Polish prisoners had been soured, any further attempts to hook up with the partisans would be impossible. Instead, it was suggested that they try to make contact with the Soviet Red Army, which by winter 1944 had temporarily halted its advance, consolidating on a line running through Warsaw, west of Lublin, and about seventy to eighty kilometers east of Cracow. To stand any chance of contacting them, the resistance would need to establish a relationship with the Russian POWs held in Monowitz. There were several obstacles. The Russians were in a fenced-off section of the camp, in which they were subjected to "re-education" by the Nazis. But they worked in the Buna Werke, so they could be approached there via some of the Russian Jews who were known to the resistance. Another problem was that there were no loyal communists or Jews among them—they had all been shot immediately on capture—so there was little common ground. Nonetheless, Fritz Kleinmann and the others made the effort. Rudi Kahn, a German Jew who had been one of those Aryanized at the same time as Gustav, was a block senior in the Russian enclosure, and he helped. Eventually Rudi and some of his Russian friends succeeded in escaping. Everyone waited anxiously for news, and when none came they guessed he had evaded recapture.

This gave the resistance a glimmer of hope, but only a faint one. Listening to their discussions at meetings, gathering and weighing snippets of intelligence, Fritz felt a growing impatience. "It seemed to me too little to procure food, write letters, or to talk about resistance. If we were to be slain, we should at least take a few SS men with us." He turned this thought over and over in his mind, but with no idea how to accomplish it, he kept it to himself and said nothing to his friends.

אבא

There was a second air raid by the Americans on September 13. They came for the oil plant in the Buna Werke, which was proving to be one of Germany's most productive producers of synthetic fuel and therefore an important strategic target. Some of the bombers went off course and dropped their bombs mistakenly on Auschwitz I, where by good luck they hit the SS barracks, killing or badly injuring forty-three SS men; tragically a bomb fell on a sewing workshop, instantly killing forty prisoners, of whom twenty-three were Jews. Other stray bombs injured dozens more prisoners; a few fell on Birkenau, slightly damaging the rail tracks near the crematoria and killing about thirty civilian workers.[15] Only slight damage was done to the oil plant, but bombs injured around three hundred prisoner workers, who as always were barred from entering the shelters. They had to find their own hiding places or take their chances in the open.

Many of them were glad to do so. Weekly in Monowitz prisoners were selected for the gas chambers—around two thousand of them on October 17 alone.[16] In some prisoners' minds, the American bombs symbolized resistance, in some imminent liberation. How long could it be now?

"We are coming to winter again—already our sixth," Gustav wrote as the frost began to bite. "But we are still here, still our old selves." News from the outside kept reporting the same thing—the Russians were at a standstill near Cracow. "I keep thinking that our stay here will soon come to an end," wrote Gustav. How long could it drag on?

בן

"I want you to get me a gun."

Fredl Wocher was taken aback. He and Fritz often met up in the factory; normally Wocher would pass his friend some food or, on rare occasions when he'd been to Vienna, a letter or a package. This request was right out of left field.

"Can you do that for me?" Fritz asked urgently.

Wocher hesitated—he would have to think about it, he said relucantly. It was an extremely dangerous request.

"Think of all you've done for me," Fritz insisted. "This is no more dangerous than any of that."

Wocher wasn't convinced. A decorated German soldier smuggling guns for a Jewish prisoner? That wasn't merely dangerous, it was insane. Fritz was insistent; if there was a liquidation in Monowitz—as seemed increasingly probable—he wanted to be able to defend himself and his father.

A few days went by, and then they met again. To Fritz's disappointment, Wocher didn't have a gun for him. Instead he had an even more stunning suggestion. "We should escape together, you and I," Wocher said. He had it all planned out. Once free of the camp, they would head west and south, making for the mountain country of the Austrian Tyrol. It would be easy to hide out there. As a Bavarian, Wocher knew the region; he would be able to arrange a safe sanctuary among the peasant mountain farmers. Besides being a secure place to hide, it was right at the nexus between the two Allied fronts: American and British forces were pushing hard into northern Italy, while Patton's Third Army was driving through Alsace-Lorraine toward the Rhine and the German border. In no time, one or both of these advances would reach the Tyrol, and Fritz and Fredl would be liberated. It was better than waiting here and hoping to survive the Soviet onslaught. Wocher had fought against them and knew the pitiless violence of the Eastern Front: the mass murder, the callousness of the Red Army, which matched anything the SS was capable of.

Fritz thought it over. Wocher undeniably had a point. But it was out of the question for one simple reason: Fritz's papa couldn't make a grueling journey like that. Anyway, he probably wouldn't agree to go; there were people in the camp and in the Buna Werke who depended on him, and he wouldn't forsake them. And if Fritz went without him, as Fritz's kapo, Gustav would probably be held responsible for his escape, and subjected to interrogation by the Gestapo.

No, escape was impossible. But Fritz still wanted a gun. Could Wocher get him one?

The German reluctantly gave in. "All right," he said, "but I'll need money. And Reichsmarks won't do—make sure it's American dollars or Swiss francs."

בן

The first person Fritz tried was Gustl Täuber, who worked in the clothing store where they kept the garments taken from new prisoners. It was a haunting place, stuffy, filled with racks of coats and jackets, stacks of folded pants, sweaters, shirts, bundles and heaps of unsorted stuff, shoes, suitcases, each with a name and address painted—a Gustav or a Franz, a Shlomo or a Paul, Frieda, Emmanuel, Otto, Chaim, Helen, Mimi, Karl, Kurt, and the last names: Rauchmann, Klein, Rebstock, Askiew, Rosenberg, Abraham, Herzog, Engel, Zuckermann, Adler, Eisenstein, Deutsch, Burgiel; and over and over again: Israel and Sara. Each one with a truncated address in Vienna, Berlin, Hamburg, or just a number or birthdate. Every aisle between the racks and shelves redolent with their scents, their sweat and perfumes, mothballs and leather, serge, mildew, and decay.

Overseeing the store was Gustl Täuber, an old Buchenwalder. He was close to Fritz's father's age, a Jew from Jagielnice in Silesia,* born in the old

---

* Now Jagielnica, Poland

days of the German Empire.[17] Fritz had never liked him much; despite his long association with them all, Täuber was one of the very few who felt no bond of solidarity with his fellow prisoners and wouldn't put himself out for anyone. But he was Fritz's best hope of getting cash. They'd had a trading relationship for some time, Fritz giving Täuber his father's bonus coupons in exchange for warm clothes that Fritz distributed to prisoners in need. Täuber used the coupons to buy vodka and (as an Aryanized Jew) visits to the brothel.

Without giving any details, Fritz asked him for cash, knowing that there was often money found in the clothing. Täuber immediately shook his head. Fritz pleaded in desperation, but Täuber was immovable; he wasn't willing to put his privileges in jeopardy over some shady deal. This was a barefaced lie; he was happy enough to get involved in shady dealings when there was a brothel visit or a bottle of vodka in it for him.

From the clothing store Fritz went to the main bathhouse at the far end of the camp, next to the hospital. This was where new prisoners came for showers, disinfecting, and shaving. Cash and valuables that they had successfully concealed from the Canada searchers were often taken from them here. The bathhouse attendant was another old Buchenwalder, David Plaut, a Jewish salesman from Berlin.[18] Plaut was a decent friend, and Fritz's only remaining hope. Any pickings from the bathhouse were taken by the camp kapo, Emil Worgul, who was in overall charge, but Fritz reckoned Plaut, who did the actual work, must be able to sidetrack a little money for himself.

Again Fritz didn't explain the real reason he needed the money; instead he spun a yarn about wanting to buy vodka with which to bribe Worgul to give some of his comrades transfers to easier labor details. It was a compelling argument, and it worked. Plaut went to his hiding place and came back with a little roll of bills, all US dollars.

Next day at work, Fritz met with Fredl Wocher and passed him the money. There followed several days of anxious waiting. Then one day Wocher showed up at their meeting wearing an expression of mingled triumph and fear and handed Fritz a pistol. It was a military-issue Luger. Although Wocher said nothing about how he'd obtained it, Fritz guessed it came from one of his friends in the Luftwaffe flak batteries. He showed Fritz how it worked—how to extract the magazine and load it with bullets, how to cock it and operate the safety catch. There were a couple boxes of ammunition with it.[19]

Now came the problem of getting it back to camp. Contraband food was one thing; firearms were in a different league. Retreating to a hiding place, Fritz dropped his pants and tied the Luger to his thigh. The pants were so baggy there was no chance of the outline of the gun being noticed. The ammunition went in his pockets. That evening he marched back to camp feeling both excited and terrified.

Fritz went straight to the hospital and found Stefan Heymann. Beckoning him to follow, he led his friend behind a mountain of dirty laundry and showed him the Luger. Stefan was horrified. "Are you crazy? Get rid of that thing! If you get caught with that it won't just be you they kill—you're putting our whole operation at risk."

Hurt and indignant, Fritz replied: "You brought me up to be like this. You always taught me that I had to fight for my life."

Stefan had no answer to that. Over the next few days they talked again and again; Fritz explained his thinking and gradually wore Stefan down. He described how he'd got the pistol from Fredl Wocher and said he was sure he could get more guns if he had more money. Stefan agreed to help, but he insisted that the whole thing be properly organized within the resistance.

Eventually Stefan managed to scrape together $200. Fritz took it to Fredl Wocher, and another period of waiting followed. Then one day Wocher led Fritz to a discreet spot in the factory and showed him where he had hidden another Luger and two MP 40 machine pistols—the distinctive submachine guns with pistol grips and long magazines, used by the SS and German soldiers everywhere. Again there were several boxes of ammunition for all three weapons.

This would be a much bigger challenge to smuggle into the camp. Fritz planned it carefully; it would take several trips. He obtained one of the huge pails used to bring soup to the prisoners in the factory and built a false bottom into it, under which he hid the ammunition. The Luger was hidden easily enough, like the last time, but the machine pistols were a different matter. Having been tutored in their use and maintenance by Wocher, he dismantled the first weapon and tied as many of the parts as he could to his bare torso.

That evening he marched back to the camp, sweating under the eyes of the SS and kapos. With winter deepening and the nights drawing in, it was dark at the end of his shift, so there was little chance that they'd notice his unusually bulky shape. Then he had to stand through roll call with the heavy, lethal items strapped to him. It dragged on painfully slowly for hours, with ritual punishments and sick and injured to be accounted for. The moment it ended Fritz hurried along to the hospital laundry. Inside, his friend Jule Meixner was waiting for him. Fritz hurriedly stripped off his uniform, untied the gun components, and passed them to Jule, who hid them. For security, Fritz wasn't told exactly where—on the principle that nobody can give up a secret under torture if they don't know it in the first place—but he suspected it was somewhere inside the building.[20] Over the next several days, he repeated the dangerous operation until all the guns and ammunition were inside the camp.

Fritz felt pleased with himself; by bringing the Luger into the camp, he had forced Stefan's hand and presented the whole resistance group with a fait accompli. They would never have done it without him. Now at least if the worst rumors about Majdanek were manifest here, they would be able to fight back.

אבא

As the days of December went by, Gustav went on with his work, turning out blackout curtains and coats in parallel. With no direct involvement in the resistance, he had no idea of the dangerous venture his beloved, difficult son had embarked on. Gustav was looking forward to Christmas, because Wocher would be going to Vienna again on leave. There had been a long interlude, and Olly, Lintschi, and the others had probably fallen prey again to the belief he and Fritz must be dead.

On Monday, December 18, Gustav's workshop was busy with its output of curtains and coats when suddenly, over the soft, snickering clatter of sewing machines, they heard the rising moan of the air raid sirens, a pulsing, guttural howl echoing across the Buna Werke.[21] Within seconds, doors were slamming, feet running, voices raised. The SS and the civilians were making for the shelters. Gustav and his staff looked at one another—some terrified, some resigned. There was no shelter for them to go to. Some people had prepared themselves makeshift hiding places, but these would be of little use if a bomb fell close.

After a few minutes, with the last panicked footsteps dying away, the distant drone of the bombers and the thumping of the flak guns began. The noise rose to a crescendo, and with it came the first earthshaking concussions of bombs—the crash when they exploded in buildings, the pounding as they blasted craters in the open ground. Gustav lay flat; this wasn't a new terror for him; he'd spent whole weeks and months under near-constant bombardment in the trenches, and like every other veteran had learned to sit tight and wait for it to either pass or for one of the falling shells to find him and send him to oblivion. He knew well how useless and dangerous it was to panic. His great fear was always for Fritz, who was out on fitting work. Fritz had a hiding place among the buildings where he would at least be sheltered from flying debris.

Again the bombers were aiming for the synthetic oil plant but a lot of the explosions seemed farther away, as if they weren't hitting their target. Suddenly, the floor beneath Gustav was rocked by a titanic explosion. Windows shattered, and there was a cacophony of tearing metal and masonry.

Eventually the shuddering from the last, distant explosions died away. Dust floated in the air, and beyond the bubble of silence immediately around him Gustav could hear distant screams and yelling, the pounding of the flak guns stuttering to a halt, and the drone of the bombers receding. The all-clear began to sound.

Climbing to his feet, Gustav found the workshop in disarray: sewing machines shaken loose and toppled from their benches, chairs knocked over, dust everywhere, shards of glass from the broken windows. The men and women stood up, coughing and blinking.

As soon as he was satisfied that nobody was hurt, Gustav's first thought was for Fritz. He went outside, into the chaos of smoke and flame. Some buildings had been destroyed; there were dead prisoners scattered about in the open and among the rubble, injured men and women being helped out by their comrades.[22] There was no sign of Fritz. Gustav hurried through the smoke, heading for Fritz's hiding place, consumed by a rising sense of foreboding. Turning the corner, he reached the place. It wasn't there anymore—there was just a hill of broken brickwork and twisted metal. Gustav stared in shock and disbelief at the wreckage; nobody could have survived in there. His Fritzl—his pride and joy, his dear, sweet, loyal Fritzl—was gone.

Gustav turned away and wandered back to the workshop in a daze of grief.

SS men and civilians were emerging from their shelters. The sentries had panicked at the start of the raid and made for the bunkers; hardly any had stayed at their posts. The fences were down in a few places, and several prisoners had escaped. Gustav stood and watched a moment as the SS tried to restore order. He was about to turn away when he saw two figures in stripes walking toward him through the smoke, one carrying a large toolbox and moving with a familiar gait. Gustav could hardly believe his eyes. He ran and threw his arms around Fritz. "My boy, my Fritzl, you're alive!" he sobbed, kissing Fritz's face and hugging him, repeating over and over, "You're alive! My boy! It's a miracle!"

He took the astonished Fritz by the arm and led him to the smoking remains of his hiding place. "It's a miracle," he kept repeating. Gustav's faith in their good luck and fortitude, which had kept them alive and together for so long, was vindicated.

אם ובת

Another air raid fell on the Buna Werke the day after Christmas. The Americans had fixed on it as a prime target and wouldn't let up until they'd reduced it to a desert of rubble. But each time they only succeeded in knocking down a few buildings, wounding a handful of SS men or IG Farben managers, killing dozens of prisoners and slave laborers, and reducing productivity for a few days or weeks. Each time, droves of slaves were forced to clear the rubble, repair, and rebuild. They sabotaged what they could and worked as slowly as they dared, and between themselves and the bombs they ensured that the Buna Werke would never produce any buna rubber, and its other plants would never approach full capacity.

On January 2, 1945, Fredl Wocher returned from Vienna with letters and packages from Olga and Karl. "We get the greatest joy from knowing that we still have good friends at home," Gustav wrote in his diary. He and Fritz had the best of friends right here, in Fredl Wocher, who had proved himself true countless times, and in so many ways.

Fritz was growing worried about Wocher. With the Red Army not far away and likely to begin a new offensive any time now, Fritz tried to persuade his friend to disappear before they reached Auschwitz and discovered what had been happening here.

Wocher didn't see the need. "My conscience is clear," he said. "More than clear. Nothing will happen to me."

Fritz wasn't so sure. He reminded Wocher of the hatred the Russians felt for all Germans—which Wocher knew all too well from his service at the front. And Fritz pointed out that however the Soviet soldiers behaved, there were thousands of Russian prisoners in Auschwitz who would be thirsty for

vengeance. Not many German civilians or soldiers had been as good or con-
scientious as Sergeant Alfred Wocher, and he couldn't depend on there being
any discrimination once the wave of revenge began sweeping through the
camps. But Wocher was stubborn; he'd never run away before, and he wasn't
about to start now.

It was clear to Fritz that the end might come any day. His preparations
had been in train for two months. Thanks to him, the resistance had a cache
of weapons to defend themselves. Meanwhile, Fritz had taken the extra pre-
caution of equipping himself and his father for escape. Having dismissed the
idea of fleeing to the Tyrol, he had to accept that fighting might not be an
option either. Since November, on Fritz's initiative, he and his father had
been dodging the weekly head shaving and letting their hair grow. Roll call
was the only time prisoners routinely took their caps off in front of the SS,
and in the winter months the ritual always happened during darkness. Fritz
also acquired a cache of civilian clothes from David Plaut at the bathhouse,
which he hid in a toolshed in the camp. There were enough jackets and pants
for himself, his papa, and a few of their closest comrades.

For several months the Red Army had been content to hold the line
along the Vistula, consolidating, preparing, reinforcing. On January 12 they
launched their offensive—a colossal, well-planned assault along the whole
length of the front line in Poland, involving three armies made up of two and
a quarter million men. It was the final push, designed to drive the Germans
back into their Fatherland. It worked; the Wehrmacht and the Waffen-SS,
outnumbered more than four to one, fell back under the onslaught, holding out in a handful of fortified Polish cities. Frustratingly, the sector of
the front near Cracow moved slower than most. Each day the prisoners in
Auschwitz heard the distant thump of Russian guns, like a clock ticking away
the moments to deliverance.

On January 14, Alfred Wocher said a last good-bye to Gustav and Fritz.
He had been drafted into the Volkssturm. This hastily organized army, made
up of old men, underage boys, and disabled veterans, was tasked with conduct-
ing the last-ditch defense of the Reich. Any man capable of holding a rifle or
wielding an antitank grenade was called up for service. So Wocher would not
be found by the Russians at Auschwitz after all, and he was pleased to do this
final duty for his Fatherland. Whatever its crimes, it was Germany after all,

his home, a land full of women and children, and the Russians would tear it apart without mercy if they were permitted.

With winter deepening, the weather was deteriorating. There was thick snow on the ground, and on Monday, January 15, the day after Fredl Wocher's departure, Auschwitz awoke to thick fog. The prisoners in Monowitz were kept standing at roll call for several hours until the fog thinned enough for the SS to feel safe marching them to work.[23]

In the factories, work went on at full pace. The previous night, an American plane had flown over Monowitz and the Buna Werke at low altitude, illuminating the whole area with parachute flares and taking photographs. Photos taken the day before had shown nearly a thousand bomb craters in the factory complex and forty-four wrecked buildings, but the nighttime images revealed that repairs were well in hand and that the synthetic fuel plant—the most important of all—was virtually untouched.[24]

On January 17 the prisoners in Monowitz were held back at roll call again. They remained on standby throughout the morning, and in the afternoon they were marched to the factories. After only two and a half hours' work they were marched back again.

The SS were becoming extremely jittery. Each morning, the rumble of artillery was a little less distant. Cracow was still holding out, but on this day the chief of the General Government*—most of which had now fallen to the Red Army—was strafed and bombed by Russian planes while departing the city, turning his withdrawal into a rout. By evening, the Soviet guns were nearer still, and the Auschwitz commandant, SS-Major Richard Baer, gave orders to begin evacuating the camps.

Invalids were to be left behind, and any prisoner who resisted, delayed, or escaped was to be shot immediately.[25] "My dear ones!" wrote Jósef Cyrankiewicz, leader of the Auschwitz I resistance, to his partisan contacts in Cracow, "We are experiencing the evacuation. Chaos. Panic among the drunken SS."[26] He begged the partisans to arrange a visit to Auschwitz by the Red Cross, to prevent a massacre of the sick. In fact there wouldn't be time; the evacuation was well under way.

That same evening, all the patients in the prisoner hospital in Monowitz were examined by the doctors; those who were well enough to march were

---

* German-occupied southeast region of Poland

struck off the patient list. The rest—numbering over eight hundred—were left to the care of nineteen volunteer medical staff.[27]

The following day, Thursday, January 18, all eight thousand prisoners in Monowitz were kept standing on the square all day—hour after hour in the bone-aching cold. Fritz and Gustav, aware that the end was imminent, had put on their civilian clothes under their uniforms, ready to make a break for it the moment they got the opportunity. At least with their extra layers they were slightly less painfully cold than their comrades. Dusk began to gather.

Finally, at 4:30 PM, the SS guards came among them, ordering them into columns. With their limbs numb and joints seizing up, the prisoners were assembled like an army division into company-size units of about one hundred, further grouped into battalion-size units of around a thousand, which in turn formed three larger units, each containing up to three thousand. SS officers, Blockführers, and guards took command of each unit.[28] Anticipating trouble, every SS man had his rifle, pistol, or machine pistol ready in his hands. Fritz thought regretfully about his guns, concealed somewhere in the hospital laundry. It was impossible to get anywhere near them now. If he and his comrades were massacred, they'd have no chance of fighting back.

Disturbingly, SS-Sergeant Otto Moll was on hand. Moll wasn't part of the Monowitz guard battalion; notoriously he'd been director of the Birkenau gas chambers and crematoria. He walked among the waiting columns as they were issued with their meager marching rations, dishing out abuse while they got their bread, margarine, and jam. Moll, personally responsible for tens of thousands of murders, was a deeply unsettling presence in these circumstances. He stopped beside Gustav, drawn by something about his appearance, looked him up and down, then gave him two hard slaps across the face, left and right. Gustav staggered and recovered. Moll moved on.[29]

At last the order was given and the columns began to move. Tired already from standing in the bitter cold all day, they marched off the roll-call square, five abreast, wheeling left onto the camp street. Passing the barrack blocks, the kitchens, the little empty building where the camp orchestra had lived, the prisoners walked out through the open gateway. They were leaving a place which for some of them had been home for over two years. A few of the old survivors like Gustav and Fritz—especially Fritz—had helped build it from bare grassy fields; their comrades' blood had gone into its construction, and pain, blood, and terror had been the unrelenting life of the place ever since. But it was home nonetheless, by simple virtue of the animal urge to belong and attach oneself to the place where one ate and slept and shat; however much one hated it, it was where friends were, and where every stone and timber was familiar.

Where they were going, they had no idea. West, that was all they knew. All the Monowitz subcamps were on the move—over thirty-five thousand men and women taking to the snow-lined roads leading west from the town called Oświęcim.[30]

Part IV

Survival

18 | Death Train

אב ובן

FRITZ SAT CLOSE BESIDE HIS PAPA, huddling together for warmth. Around them sat their friends. It was early morning, and the cold was beyond imagining. They had no shelter, no food, no fires: just one another. They were bone weary; there were men among them who would never get to their feet again when this rest stop was over.

For the first few kilometers after leaving Monowitz, Fritz and Gustav and the other fitter, better-fed prisoners had helped their weaker comrades along. From the very start, the thousands of starved and sick had struggled to keep up with the march, slow as it was. If anyone lagged behind, he would be beaten by the SS with a rifle butt and driven onward. If he fell down in the middle of the pack, the semi-conscious marchers following behind would trample over him. Fritz and the others did what they could, but comradeship could only stretch so far. They were scarcely beyond Oświęcim when they ran out of strength and had to leave the weakest to fare as best they could. They just kept walking, father and son sticking close together, heads down, one foot in front of the other on the compacted snow and ice, hour after hour through darkness swirling with flecks of snow. They hugged their jackets tight around them and closed their ears to the sporadic gunshots from the rear of the column as stragglers were murdered.

To Fritz and Gustav it was like a repeat of the forced march, so many years ago, along the Blood Road to Buchenwald. But this was worse—infinitely, inconceivably worse. There had been an end in sight then; this march seemed doomed to go on forever. Close by Fritz a Blockführer marched, pistol in hand; Fritz could sense the man's terror of the pursuing Russians and the murderous feelings it provoked in his heart.

267

Dawn had broken, and by Gustav's reckoning they had trudged forty-two kilometers when they reached the outskirts of the town of Nikolai.* The column was directed off the road into an industrial area—an abandoned brickworks. The SS guards needed a rest almost as much as the wretched prisoners. Finding what shelter they could among the stacks of bricks and relics of the yard, the prisoners sat close for warmth.

Fritz and his papa stayed awake despite the weariness consuming them; they guessed that anyone who slept in this cold would never wake again. Talking with some comrades who had been in different parts of the column, they discovered that several Polish prisoners—including three of Fritz's friends—had slipped away and escaped. There were SS all along the column, but they couldn't be everywhere all the time, and in the darkness a person desperate or courageous enough could dodge away without being noticed.

"We should do that," Gustav said to Fritz. "We should make a run for it." Together they could make a go of it—Gustav spoke decent Polish, so they'd have no trouble finding their way and getting help. They could hook up with partisans or just head south toward Austria. But for all his preparations, all his determination to resist, Fritz's heart quailed as his papa talked. There was one very big problem: Fritz himself spoke no Polish. If they were separated, he'd be sunk. In Fritz's opinion, they should wait until they reached German soil, where they both spoke the language. There they could make a run for it, discard their camp uniforms, and become civilians. Gustav was dubious. Germany was still hundreds of kilometers away, and who could tell if they would ever reach it? They might succumb to exhaustion and a bullet by then—even assuming the SS intended them to survive that far.

Their discussion was cut short by the order to move. They'd only had a couple of hours, and no rest at all worth the name, when they hauled themselves to their feet. Some people who had slept remained where they were. Hypothermia had taken them, and their bodies were already beginning to freeze solid. There were others who were still alive but too weak to stand; the SS went among the crowds, kicking and chivvying, shooting dead any who couldn't be roused.[1]

There was confusion when another march of several thousand prisoners from the subcamp at Günthergrube crossed paths with the Monowitz march.

---

* Now Mikołów, Poland

While the Monowitz SS herded their charges on westward, their Günthergrube colleagues drove their columns of walking specters toward the Gleiwitz III subcamp.[2] Gustav, Fritz, and their comrades trudged on.

Behind them stretched a nightmare of trampled snow and scattered corpses, leading all the way back to Auschwitz. At this moment, the last evacuations were leaving Birkenau; over the next few days, the remaining SS would force Jews who had been too weak to evacuate to clear up and burn the stacks of corpses outside the gas chambers. Other teams prepared to dynamite the crematoria buildings, while elsewhere SS clerks were burning records. Some SS personnel, conscious of their crimes and their likely fate, were already wearing civilian clothes under their uniforms, pilfered from Birkenau's Canada section, where the incriminating mountains of loot were also being put to the torch. In the end the sheer weight of the crimes committed here would defy all efforts to erase the evidence.

The second leg of the march, from the brickyard at Nikolai, was a little shorter than the first. That same evening, twenty-four hours after leaving Monowitz behind, the column reached the town of Gleiwitz,* where there were several subcamps belonging to the Auschwitz system. The Monowitzers were herded into Gleiwitz II, a small enclosure that had housed around a thousand male and female inmates. The camp had served the Deutsche Gasrusswerke factory, which made carbon black, a highly toxic chemical compound used in rubber manufacture. The camp was deserted, the prisoners having been evacuated the previous day by their exceptionally panicky SS guards.[3] The Monowitz prisoners crammed themselves into the barrack blocks; they were overcrowded, given nothing to eat, but thankful at least for shelter, where they could sleep.

Two days and nights they remained in Gleiwitz while the SS organized their onward journey. Unlike the poor souls whose death marches would continue on foot all the way to Germany, the men of Monowitz would be going by train.

On January 21, a Sunday, they were rousted from their huts and marched to the city freight yard, where their transports were waiting on the track. Instead of the usual closed boxcars that had brought most of them to Auschwitz, the four long trains were made up of open-top freight cars, the type used for car-

---

* Now Gliwice, Poland

rying coal and gravel. They were of various sizes, some with sides only waist high, others higher than a man. After rations had been doled out—half a loaf of bread each, with one hundred grams of sausage—Fritz and Gustav climbed into one of the larger ones, along with more than 130 other men. They clambered up the sheer sides and dropped down with a clang on the steel floor, which echoed less with each pair of feet until the last few had to squeeze into gaps between the rest.

Every other car had a braking house, a little windowed hut raised above the level of the cars in which the brakemen took shelter. In each one an SS guard took post, armed with a rifle or machine pistol. "Anyone who puts his head above the sides will be shot," warned the Blockführer in charge of loading.

The train began to vibrate, and steam and smoke from the locomotive made a thick fog in the icy air. At last, with the clang and bang of couplings and shriek of wheels, the train began to move, dragging its load of four thousand souls.[4] As it built up speed, the men in the open cars were exposed to an abominable cold—a wind roared across the tops, dropping the temperature to twenty degrees below zero.*

אבא

The motion of the train rocked Gustav's body from side to side. He sat with his knees drawn up to his chest, with Fritz close beside him, hugged up against the terrible cold.

Beneath them, the wheels hissed on the rails, clanks and clangs from couplings, the sporadic jolts: the hissing-squealing-clanking-banging of steel-wheeled boxes on rails was a never-ending, nightmare music. The Holocaust was a crime made of journeys, crisscrossing Europe to the accompaniment of a tuneless score of protesting machinery.

After leaving Gleiwitz, the train had diverged from the other three, heading south toward Rybnik. The next morning they had stopped at Loslau† to take on hundreds more evacuated prisoners from the Charlottengrube subcamp.[5] After that, they had crossed into Czechoslovakia. Despite the warning from the Blockführer, Gustav had peeped over the side from time to time, gauging

---

* -4°F
† Now Wodzisław Śląski, Poland

the progress of their journey, noting when they passed through Oderberg,* and that they bypassed Brno altogether. The train never stopped but went painfully slowly, and so far it had taken two freezing nights and a day to cross Czechoslovakia. By Gustav's reckoning, the information they'd been given— that they were being taken to Mauthausen concentration camp—appeared to be correct. The thought was simultaneously thrilling and terrifying; Mauthausen's reputation was dire, and Gustav had witnessed the violent temperament of its criminal prisoners in the batch sent to Monowitz. But it was in Austria, in the beautiful hill country near Linz. *Austria!* Soon Gustav and his Fritzl would be on the soil of their homeland for the first time in over five years. And there they would almost certainly die. In Mauthausen they'd have none of the support system built up in Auschwitz, and would be subjected to an even harsher, even more murderous regime of kapos and SS.

That was if they made it that far. Even as Gustav turned the thoughts over in his mind, there was a stir among his fellow prisoners. Another had passed away. Weakness, sickness, and hypothermia were killing them off steadily. A friend of the dead man stripped the jacket and pants off the body and put them on over his own. The body was passed across the car and stacked in the corner with the other corpses, all stripped to their underwear and frozen solid. That corner also served as the latrine, and even in the cold the stench was abominable.

The deaths at least had the virtue of making more room to sit. Gustav looked around at the gaunt faces, the deep shadows beneath the eyes, the cheekbones whittled to ridges by starvation. Some had managed to eke out their ration, and as the fourth day of the journey passed, they nibbled their last crusts. Gustav and Fritz had none left. By the time they reached Mauthausen there would be nothing left of them but a carload of corpses. Gustav could already feel his strength slipping away, a slow ebb tide eroding his will. Only one thought was on his mind now: escape.

He spoke quietly to Fritz. The time would soon come when it would be too late; it had to be now. They had their disguises under their uniforms; if they could slip over the side during the night, they might not be noticed by the guards in the brake houses. Soon they would be in Austria, and language would be no problem at all. They could make their way to Vienna and find

---

* Now Bohumín, Czech Republic

a hiding place. Olly or Lintschi or one of their other good friends would take care of them. Fritz agreed eagerly.

That night they tested the watchfulness of the guards. With help from a couple of friends, they lifted a corpse from the stack, heaving the dead weight up to the rim of the sidewall, and pushed it over. As it went flailing away into the darkness, they waited for a yell from the brake house and a burst of gunfire . . . but nothing came. This would be easy. All they had to do was wait until they crossed into Austria.

The next morning—January 25, the fourth day since leaving Gleiwitz—the train reached Lundenburg,* just a few kilometers from the Austrian border. There, frustratingly, it halted. Hour followed hour followed hour, and nothing happened. A peek over the side showed that the whole train was surrounded by SS.

It was dusk when they finally started moving again. At some unknown, guessed-at time during the night, the Czech countryside gave way to Austria. Now was their time. Fritz nudged his papa and suggested that they make their break now, while it was dark. Gustav drifted awake from a doze, and tried to rise. He couldn't get up; his freezing, aching muscles were too weak. His strength was ebbing fast now. He looked at Fritz's eager face. His dear Fritzl, his pride and delight. "I can't do it," he said. Nothing Fritz said could raise him. "You have to go alone. Leave me and go."

Fritz was appalled at the mere idea. *If you want to keep living, you have to forget your father.* That was what Robert Siewert had said to him that day in Buchenwald. It had been impossible then, and it was impossible now. He had followed his papa to Auschwitz, and they had both survived because of it.

Gustav was insistent; he simply couldn't make it—he was old, the strength was gone from him at last. But Fritz refused to leave him behind.

When dawn came, they were in familiar snow-laden countryside. They were close to Vienna now and would quite likely pass through it. If they escaped then, would it matter that Gustav was so weak? They'd be home and dry within hours. But they never got the chance. After passing through Korneuburg the train steamed along the north bank of the Danube, and in broad daylight rolled into the northern suburbs and across the river into Leopoldstadt. They scarcely dared peek as, without halting, it passed the Nordbahnhof. Home was

---

* Now Břeclav, Czech Republic

achingly, heartbreakingly close. They hardly needed to peek to see the rim of the Riesenrad ferris wheel as they rolled by the west end of the Prater . . . and then it was past and gone, the train was rumbling over the Danube Canal, through the government district and the western suburbs, and back out into open countryside.

In the later morning they passed through the town of St. Pölten, and in the afternoon reached Amstetten, where the train halted. They were now little more than forty kilometers from Mauthausen.

When darkness fell, the journey resumed.

Gustav again urged Fritz to go. With each passing kilometer the situation in the car was getting worse, descending into savagery. Some of their comrades had reached the point where they would kill a friend for a piece of bread; several passed that point, strangling their fellow man for a single mouthful. They got water by fishing for snow with a tin cup dangled over the side on a string. Through cold, hunger, and murder, the corpses were piling up in the corner at the rate of eight to ten every day. Fritz had to go now, before it was too late, before they reached Mauthausen and the real murder began. This would be his last chance. By morning they would reach the end. Gustav pleaded, and at last Fritz gave way.

The pain of it would never leave him: "After five years of shared destiny, that I should now sever myself from my father," he recalled in anguish.

Within a few kilometers of leaving Amstetten behind, the train reached its maximum speed. Fritz peeled off the hateful striped uniform with its *Judenstern* and camp number and flung off the cap. He embraced his papa and kissed him, then with help from a friend he climbed the sidewall.

The full force of the subzero wind buffeted him and pierced his body like knives. The train shook and thundered. He peered anxiously toward the brake house. The moon was brighter now than it had been when they'd tested the guards' alertness: two days from the full, an eerie glow illuminating the white landscape and the trees flying past.[6] Gustav felt a last squeeze of his hand, then Fritz launched himself into the air. In an instant he was gone.

Sitting alone on the floor of the car, by the light of the moon Gustav wrote in his diary: "The lord God protect my boy. I cannot go, I am too weak. He wasn't shot at. I hope my boy will win through and find shelter with our dear ones."

The train sped on, hammering and clanking, as if the locomotive itself was desperate for this dreadful journey to be over. It was still dark when it passed through Linz, crossed the Danube again, and doubled back east toward the small town of Mauthausen.

בן

Fritz tumbled through the air, all sense of space and direction lost for a fleeting moment, then the ground hit him violently, jarring his bones and knocking the wind out of him. He rolled over and over and came to rest with the train wheels clattering past his face, not daring to move a muscle.

The last car rushed by and faded into the distance, leaving him alone in the snow-silence under the vault of stars. He looked around. He was lying in a thick bank of snow, which had cushioned his fall. Despite the pains in his limbs, he hadn't broken anything, and he got to his feet without difficulty. Shaking himself down, he started walking back along the railroad toward Amstetten.[7]

Nearing the town, his nerve failed him. There was nothing obviously wrong with his disguise, but he wasn't ready yet to face going into a busy town, even late in the evening. Leaving the railroad, he slithered down the embankment and struck out across an open field. It was hard going, with snow up to his hips, but eventually he came to a narrow back street on the edge of town. It was deserted. Warily, he stepped out, and followed it to the left, heading north. This was the only direction he could go; the only other way to bypass the town was to swim across the river Ybbs, which bounded it to the south.

Moving cautiously, Fritz managed to skirt around the north of the little town without meeting anyone and was soon on a country road winding eastward, parallel with the railroad. He walked through several small villages and hamlets, gradually working his way back in the direction of St. Pölten. It was slow going on the snow and ice, and strength wasn't on his side. He'd been walking for hours and had covered about fifteen kilometers when he reached the little town of Blindenmarkt, where the road converged with the railroad. He'd passed through this place the previous day. There was a small station where the trains from Linz to Vienna would stop. He was tired, and in his pocket were some Reichsmarks—his little stock of emergency cash scavenged in Monowitz.

On an impulse Fritz turned off the main road and walked to the station. It was still dark, so he found an empty cattle car standing on the tracks and crawled inside. It was too cold to sleep, but at least he could lie down out of the wind. Toward dawn, lights came on in the station windows. Fritz waited a few minutes, then pulled together his courage and dropped down from the car.

The station building was quiet, with just a solitary clerk behind the ticket window. Fritz wasn't familiar with the requirements for buying a train ticket under the Nazis. Would he be asked for papers? He approached the window and, as casually as he could, asked for a ticket to Vienna. The clerk, who wasn't accustomed to seeing strangers traveling this early, regarded him with some surprise (and suspicion, it seemed to Fritz). But he took Fritz's money without a word and gave him the ticket.

Fritz went into the deserted waiting room and sat down. After a few minutes, the clerk came in and lit the stove. Fritz moved closer to it gratefully. It was the first warmth he'd had since leaving Monowitz, and he was cold to the marrow. The life and heat flowing into his body was both heavenly and tortuous, filling the deadened nerves with pins and needles and awakening the aches of his journey.

He lost track of time and had no idea how long he'd been there when the Vienna train finally huffed its way to a stop outside the window. Fritz went out to the platform—still the only person there—and got into one of the third-class passenger cars.

It was full of German soldiers. There were no civilians at all—just a crowd of field-gray Wehrmacht uniforms. They were too busy talking, smoking, playing cards, and dozing to take any notice of him, and it was too late to get off again—which might just attract attention anyway—so he found a seat and sat down.

As the train moved off, Fritz felt like he was in an alien world. He was, in effect, a foreigner in his own homeland, with no idea of laws or protocol and little notion of how to behave like an ordinary civilian. If he'd known more about the ways of this new world, he would have realized right away that there was something very badly wrong here.

The soldiers continued to take no notice of him. After a couple of hours and a few more stops (at which nobody else got on), the train reached the station at St. Pölten, where it halted. Two German soldiers stepped aboard, both in the distinctive steel chains and gorgets of the Feldgendarmerie—the Wehrmacht military police. They came along the aisle. "Passes," they said. The soldiers took their identity cards and passes from their breast pockets. Fritz took out his ticket—it was all he had. The group of soldiers sitting near him bundled their documents and handed them all at once to the policeman. Desperately seizing his opportunity, Fritz slipped his ticket in among the sheaf of cards.

Shuffling through them, the policeman glanced in turn at each of the soldiers and handed back their documents. Then he came to the solitary rail ticket and frowned. He looked at Fritz and gestured peremptorily. "Papers," he said.

Heart pounding, Fritz made a show of rifling through his pockets. He shrugged helplessly. "I've lost them."

The policeman's frown deepened to grave suspicion. "Come with us."

Fritz's heart sank, but he knew better than to argue. He got up and followed the Feldgendarmes off the train. They led him out of the station to a Wehrmacht outpost, telling him they needed to establish his identity before they could let him continue on his journey.

They put him in a room where he was questioned sternly, although not aggressively, by an NCO who explained that his presence on the train had aroused curiosity. It dawned on Fritz that boarding that particular train had been a terrible error. If he'd known the ways of the world outside the concentration camps, he would have recognized, as soon as it pulled in at Blindenmarkt, that the train was a front-line special, taking troops home on leave, and he'd have known better than to board it. If he'd waited, a regular train would have come along, on which his civilian attire would have blended in instead of standing out like a beacon.

"What is your name?"

"Fritz Kleinmann." He saw no point in lying about that, at least. It was a perfectly acceptable German name and hardly unique.

"Where are your papers?"

"I must have lost them."

"Home address?"

On the spur of the moment, Fritz gave a fictional street address in a town near Weimar. The NCO wrote it down and stood up.

"Stay there," he said, and left the room.

He was gone a long time, and when he reappeared he was accompanied by a superior. They had checked—the address Fritz had given did not exist. He was asked to give his real address. Claiming a faulty memory, Fritz gave them a different address. They checked it, and again found it was false. By now, Fritz was just desperately playing for time. The Feldgendarmes went through the charade again, disposing of a third fake address before finally losing their patience.

Two guards were summoned and ordered to take Herr Kleinmann to the security section at the local Wehrmacht barracks.

They drove him through the streets to a small barrack complex, where he was taken to a building resembling a Gestapo bunker, with an office and cells. Fortunately, it wasn't the Gestapo—just a regular Wehrmacht garrison. An officer looked over the note from the Feldgendarmerie and asked Fritz to identify himself. "If you lie to me, I will lock you up." What else could Fritz do? He gave a fourth imaginary address. It was checked, and he was placed under formal arrest. The officer was calm and quiet. He didn't yell or rage or threaten torture; he simply directed his men to lock Herr Kleinmann in a cell. "Perhaps the truth will come to you in there," he said.

The cell was large, with three soldiers already in residence waiting to be court-martialed for minor offenses. Fritz fell into desultory conversation with them, explaining that he was a civilian who'd lost his papers and was waiting for verification.

It was pleasantly warm in the cell, with a bed for each man, a table and chairs, and a basin and toilet in the corner. Fritz hadn't been in such a comfortable environment in years. When an orderly brought their evening meals—the first hot food Fritz had had in nearly a week, and his first full meal for as long as he could remember—he had to fight down his ravening hunger, forcing himself to eat in normal mouthfuls rather than gobbling it down like a dog.

After dinner, when Fritz turned back the blanket on his bed, he could hardly believe his eyes—there were sheets underneath. *Sheets!* What kind of a cell was this? Easing his exhausted body into bed was little short of heaven, and he slept soundly and blissfully through the night.

The next morning was, if possible, even better. The orderly brought breakfast, and simple as it was by the standards of the regular world, it was enough to make Fritz's head spin. There was *real* hot coffee, bread, margarine, sausage, and plenty of it. While his cellmates chatted idly, Fritz kept his head down and concentrated on the food.

Shortly afterward, he was brought before the officer again, who demanded to know who Fritz really was. As the questioning went on, Fritz began to realize that the officer was working on the theory that he was an army deserter. His age, appearance, and accent were all consistent with it, as were the circumstances of his apprehension. Believing that he'd caught his prisoner in a minor deception, it didn't occur to the officer to look for an enormous one—that this young man with the full head of dark hair, chiseled features, civilian dress, and Viennese accent might actually be a Jew on the run from a concentration camp. Perhaps there was some hope in that.

Fritz refused to answer any further questions and was put back in his cell. Perhaps his years in the camps had institutionalized him, or perhaps it was just the food and warmth and the comfortable bed, but he felt contented in there. Lunch consisted of a simple but very good stew and a piece of bread.

Despite these luxuries, the part of Fritz's mind that had kept him alive in the camps was fully aware of the danger he was in, and as the day wore on, he groped around for a way out. After dinner that evening, while his cellmates were busy talking, he surreptitiously pilfered a stick of shaving soap from one of them, and ate it. By the next morning, he was violently unwell: hot, sweating, and with terrible diarrhea.[8] His cellmates called the guard, and Fritz was carried out.

They took him to a military hospital. During the examination—which discovered nothing more serious than stomach cramps and a raised temperature—he managed to conceal the tattooed number on his left forearm. He was put in a side ward by himself and kept under observation.

It was even better in the hospital than in the cell: crisp white bedlinen, female nurses bringing him tea and medication. After a while he was able to eat, although the diarrhea persisted. Illness was a small price to pay for this degree of comfort and the postponement of his interrogation. A doctor who visited him on the third day, evidently sharing the assumption that Fritz was a deserter, mentioned that there was a sentry outside the door with a machine-pistol, so he'd better not be thinking of making a run for it.

After several days in the hospital, Fritz's fever had passed and the diarrhea was gone. Fritz was immediately returned to the barracks security section. He was met by the officer, whose patience was wearing thin. "It's time for this case to be closed," he said. "If you don't confess, I shall hand you over to the Gestapo." Fritz said nothing. The officer, seething with frustration, ordered him back to his cell. "Two more days," he promised, "and then I'm done with you."

When the two days had expired, Fritz was brought back to the interrogation room.

"I have guessed who you are now," said the officer, to Fritz's alarm. "You are an Austrian émigré; you are on a mission on behalf of the English and have been dropped by parachute to engage in covert operations." Having delivered this astonishing revelation, the officer stated flatly: "You will be treated as a spy."

Fritz was horrified; this was worse than if he'd been identified as a concentration camp escapee. He denied the accusation strenuously, but the officer refused to listen. In his mind, only a trained secret agent would be sneaking about in the way Fritz had been, associating with German troops, and able to resist interrogation for so long. No deserter or civilian could do that. Despite his strident denials, Fritz was force-marched back to his cell. Suddenly it didn't feel quite so congenial. Should he confess? No, that would be asking for a death sentence; he'd be returned to the SS and shot or hanged. But the outcome would be the same if they believed him to be a spy. On the other hand, even if he confessed, would they believe him now? The officer's notion of him as a German Austrian was so fixed, even if he saw his tattoo he might not believe it.

The next day, Fritz was taken before the officer once more. He noticed that two armed soldiers were waiting there. "I'm through with your denials," the officer announced, "and I'm done with you. You are going to Mauthausen."

19 | Mauthausen

בן

FRITZ FELT THE PINCH of cold steel round his wrists as the handcuffs snapped shut. "If you make any attempt to escape," said the officer, "you will be shot immediately."

His three-man escort—an NCO and two privates—marched him to the station. There they all boarded a train bound for Linz. For the third time, Fritz traveled the familiar route: St. Pölten to Blindenmarkt to Amstetten . . . At some point the train must have passed by the spot where he had made his leap. It was unidentifiable now in the light of day with the snow starting to thaw. How vivid it all was in his memory. But no more vivid than his pleasant interlude in St. Pölten; like a blissful vacation, he would always remember it as lasting little more than a week, when in fact it had been closer to three.[1] Three weeks of eating well, resting in safety, and having his health restored.

At Linz they changed to a local train for the short journey to Mauthausen, crossing the Danube and doubling back along the north bank. Mauthausen itself was a pleasant little town, nestled in a bow of the Danube beneath rolling green hills checkered with fields and woods. Fritz was marched through it, two paces ahead of the NCO and the soldiers, who kept their rifles trained on his back. The locals, accustomed to living in the shadow of the place that lay out of sight in the hills above the town, paid them no heed.

A winding road led up the valley to the camp. When it came in sight, it was like no concentration camp Fritz had ever seen. He'd heard about it from prisoners transferred to Monowitz, but its appearance was still remarkable—Mauthausen was more like a fortress than a camp, with high, thick stone walls topped by walkways and studded with gun emplacements. There was an angle in the wall, in which there stood a massive, beetling stone gatehouse flanked at one corner by a squat round tower and at the other by an enormous square turret four stories high. Off to one side, emerging through the melting snow, was a fruit garden, and tucked under the wall was an enclosure containing SS barrack buildings. Somewhere within those walls were Fritz's father and friends. Or so he hoped. One could only imagine how harsh the selections would be in such a camp. But Fritz had faith in his father's strength, and in the destiny that bound them together; deep down he was certain they would be reunited here—much sooner than they had expected. Fritz would certainly have a story to tell.

Instead of taking him through this imposing gate, his Wehrmacht guards turned left and marched him along the road parallel to the outer wall, past the fruit garden. Mauthausen was built on a steep hill, and on the slope just below, Fritz saw a second camp, smaller and more conventional in appearance, with barbed wire fences and basic watch towers. At the corner of the stone wall, the road swung sharply right, and the ground on one side fell steeply away, ending in a sheer drop into a vast, deep pit lined with jagged cliff faces.

Fritz was looking down into the place that gave Mauthausen its evil name: the granite quarry. Wider and many times deeper than the limestone quarry at Buchenwald, its bottom was a hive of long work sheds teeming with slaves and echoing to the tinkling clangor of picks and chisels on stone; the far rim fell away with the slope of the hill, and on that side was a broad, steep staircase cut into the rock, curving upward in one enormous flight of 186 steps from the bottom of the pit to the rim. Up it hundreds of prisoners were climbing, each carrying a square block of granite on his back. They called it the Stair of Death, and it was the symbol of all that was hideous about Mauthausen.

Unlike the little Buchenwald quarry, whose main purpose had been to provide materials for the camp itself, this was a full-scale industrial operation run by the German construction materials company DESt* in conjunction with the SS; the granite extracted here was destined for the monumental building projects conceived by Adolf Hitler. The Führer's grandiose vision required stone in enormous quantities, and thousands of prisoners had died extracting and carrying it. The Stair of Death was the epitome of SS thinking—why install a more efficient mechanical conveyor when criminal and Jewish labor was so cheap and the process so satisfyingly punishing? Injuries and fatalities were constant—the slightest misstep on the staircase would send a man and

---

* Deutsche Erd- und Steinwerke (German Earth- and Stoneworks)

his granite block tumbling among the others, setting them off like dominoes, breaking limbs and crushing bodies.

The road around the main camp ran a little way along the edge of the quarry, then turned right into the administrative section, a compound of low barrack huts. Here Fritz's Wehrmacht guards handed him over to the SS and departed.

Fritz had been expecting an interrogation and a beating but received neither. An SS sergeant marched him to the main gatehouse. This was another titanic construction of stone, a bit like the Buchenwald gatehouse, but built from granite and much more intimidating, with two towers crowned by glazed watch offices decked with floodlights and machine guns. This was the main entrance to the prisoners' part of the camp (the gatehouse he'd seen at the front led into a courtyard containing the SS garages).

Passing through the gate, Fritz found himself looking at a surprisingly small and ordinary interior; it was smaller than Monowitz and filled with rows of similarly basic single-story wooden barrack blocks on either side of a narrow roll-call ground. The sergeant disappeared through a door into the gatehouse, ordering Fritz to wait by the wall.

A few prisoners were hanging around there. One came over and asked Fritz who he was and what he'd been brought here for. Fritz told him his name and that he was from Vienna. The man walked away and came back a few moments later with another prisoner, who had an air of authority and knowingness, clearly some kind of functionary. He was Viennese and had been in Mauthausen for several years. He studied Fritz, chatted a little. Mauthausen was pretty bad, he said, but the one thing you really didn't want to be was a Jew. Jews lasted no time at all here. With that, he walked off.

After a few more minutes, the SS sergeant emerged from the gatehouse and, out of the blue, demanded to know whether Fritz had an Auschwitz tattoo. Taken aback, Fritz said no, and to prove it, rolled up his right sleeve. The sergeant—who evidently didn't know much about Auschwitz practices—seemed satisfied and put Fritz in the custody of a functionary prisoner who took him to the bathhouse.

There he met the Viennese prisoner again. This time he introduced himself properly; his name was Josef Kohl, though everyone called him Pepi for short. Fritz would later learn that Pepi Kohl was the leader of Mauthausen's resistance. Feeling instantly at ease with him, Fritz admitted the truth for the first time since his escape. Some of the truth, anyway: the fact that he'd been in Buchenwald and Auschwitz, and the story of his escape from the transport, right up to his arrest. He kept quiet about being Jewish; any hope he had of surviving here would depend on that fact remaining hidden. Thank goodness his papa was marked as Aryan.

For the third time Fritz went through the ritual of being a new prisoner: the shower, the confiscation of his clothes and belongings, the shaving of his head, and finally registration at the prisoner records office. Mauthausen added its own nuances to the system, but the only really significant novelty was that he went through it alone. The camp took in only eight other prisoners that day, and they came in later.

As his details were being taken, Fritz was told that the sole reason he was brought here was his refusal to give a home address. It was too late for that now. Perhaps acting on advice from Pepi Kohl, Fritz admitted the truth and was entered on the records as a transferee from Auschwitz who had been in the camp system since October 2, 1939. Better that than be subjected to torture by the camp Gestapo—a certain fate if he'd continued to keep silent. The interlude between his escape and his arrival was of no interest to the SS here. Neither was his tattoo; it was noted as a distinguishing feature, but the number wasn't taken down. He told them he was a German Aryan "protective custody" prisoner, and the clerk didn't bat an eye. Fritz was entered on the record accordingly and assigned the prisoner number 130039.[2]

No detailed records had come from Auschwitz, and no inquiries could be made. Auschwitz no longer existed; it had fallen to the Red Army on January 27, less than ten days after the evacuation (the same day Fritz boarded the soldiers' train at Blindenmarkt). The only souls remaining in Monowitz had been the few hundred half-dead specters in the hospital and their carers, and many of those hadn't survived long after liberation. Auschwitz and all its secrets were now part of history.[3]

Fritz gave the name of his cousin Lintschi as his next of kin, and his real Vienna address. Lintschi was officially Aryan, and there was nobody left at Im Werd 11/16 who could be endangered by association with him. When it came to his trade, he calculated his chances. He'd acquired a lot of varied skills in the camps, but which ones should he admit to? It didn't look as if there was much call for construction workers here, and he guessed that any surplus labor would wind up in the quarry. He told them he was a heating engineer.[4] It was half true—he'd helped build and fit out the heating plants at both Buchenwald and Monowitz, and he'd learned from his papa how easy it could be to bluff one's way into a trade.

Although Fritz's escape bid had failed in the end, it had done one thing for him: given him respite, during which he'd eaten well and rested, building up his health and strength. He knew well what an advantage this would give him in surviving what was to come.

Fritz was assigned to block 12, at the end of the main walled enclosure. It was unsettlingly close to the camp bunker, which had a gas chamber and crematorium attached. In the next section of the camp, separated by a wall, was the quarantine area and block 20—Mauthausen's own Death Block, where hundreds of Soviet prisoners of war were kept in appalling conditions, starved and put to murderous hard labor. Fritz learned that there had been a major escape from the Death Block two weeks earlier; the whole camp had been awakened by machine gun fire after the Russians used wet blankets to short the electric fence enclosing that side of the camp. Many had been killed, but four hundred had managed to escape. They were desperate and weak, and for days afterward the local people heard gunshots from the woods as the Russians were hunted down and murdered by the SS.[5]

The camp was horribly overcrowded, with some blocks intended for three hundred prisoners holding many times that number. Mauthausen, Buchenwald, and the other concentration camps on Reich soil had been receiving countless transports of prisoners evacuated from Auschwitz and its subcamps.

Fritz, finding his feet in this new place, was looking forward to his reunion with his papa and friends, who must be somewhere among the multitude. But as he asked around he couldn't find anyone who knew where they were or who recognized their names. Wherever he inquired, he could find no trace of them. As far as he could gather, although there had been transports from Auschwitz nobody knew of any that had arrived on or around January 26.

His father simply wasn't here. Neither were any of their old friends from Monowitz. It was as if they had never been here. But if that was the case, where on Earth were they? Fritz had heard dreadful stories about SS atrocities in Poland and the Ostland—about whole transports of Jews murdered in the forests. Was that what had happened to the Auschwitz transport? Was that the fate Fritz had escaped?

אבא

Fritz was gone, launched over the side into the freezing night. Pray God he would find his way to home and safety. Gustav sat with his back against the car wall. He was so weak and tired. He'd had no food for days and only a mouthful of snow for moisture. "One man will kill another for a little scrap of bread," he wrote in his diary. "We are veritable artists of hunger . . . we fish for snow with a mug tied to a string dangled out of the car."

Later that night the train with its freight of dying men and frozen corpses crossed the Danube and pulled in at the Mauthausen ramp. The train was surrounded by an SS cordon and stood waiting. Hours ticked by; dawn came, and then the morning wore away. Inside the cars, the men who still had strength and wits wondered what was happening. There appeared to be some kind of dispute going on.

A team of prisoners from the camp came along the train, and to the ravenous delight of the men aboard they handed out bread and canned food. There was little of it—half a loaf and one can between five men—and it was devoured in no time.

Eventually, with night drawing in again, the train began to groan and move, heading back the way it had come. Mauthausen's commandant, with his camp full to bursting, had refused to receive the transport.[6] It crossed the Danube and as it passed through Linz, it turned west. Where they were being taken, they had no idea, other than that they were heading in the general direction of the German border. In a matter of hours they would be in Bavaria, and if the train carried on in a straight line it would bring them to Munich. That could mean only one thing: Dachau.

Gustav became aware of voices raised in urgent debate. A dozen of his comrades—including several of the old Buchenwalders—had been inspired by Fritz's example and were talking of escape. They appealed to Gustav and to Paul Schmidt, who had been Fritz's kapo in the Buna Werke and had helped conceal him after his faked death. But Gustav could no more face it than when Fritz had tried to persuade him, and Schmidt also declined to go. As the train left Linz behind, twelve of them climbed the sidewall and leapt over. Despite the scale of the exodus there were no shots. The SS seemed oblivious; if more prisoners had had the strength, the train might have reached its destination empty except for the corpses.

Whatever the destination was, it wasn't Dachau. Passing into Bavaria, the train veered due north. Day followed night—and another, and another. By the fifth day since leaving Mauthausen behind, they were in the German province of Thuringia and appeared to be heading directly for Weimar. Was Gustav going back to Buchenwald? That would be a strange return. But no—the train kept steaming northward, bypassing Weimar, and on Sunday, February 4— two weeks to the day since leaving Gleiwitz—it pulled into the freight yard at Nordhausen, an industrial town on the southern fringe of the Harz mountains.[7]

It was met by SS and a Sonderkommando from the nearby Mittelbau-Dora concentration camp. Gustav and the other exhausted, wasted prisoners climbed over the sidewalls with difficulty. Once the living had disembarked, the dead were lifted out. By the end of the process, 766 corpses lay stacked on the ground. Gustav had seen some terrible things, but this was among the worst. "Starved and murdered," he wrote in his diary later, "some frozen to death, and the whole thing not to be described." Many of the survivors were hardly in better condition than the dead—around six hundred of them died in the two days following their arrival, out of a little over three thousand who had survived the transport.[8]

Tucked in a fold in a wooded ridge north of Nordhausen, the concentration camp had originally been founded in 1943 as a satellite of Buchenwald, code-named Dora. In October 1944 it had become a main camp and given the name Mittelbau.[9] It was about the size of the main camp at Buchenwald, but the buildings were laid out haphazardly and the place was dreadfully over-crowded, with over 19,300 prisoners crammed into its barrack blocks.

The new arrivals went through the registration procedure, Gustav receiving prisoner number 106498.[10] Assigned to blocks, they gave all their attention to the food—"the first warm meal since the start of our fourteen-day odyssey," Gustav noted. Each man got half a loaf, a portion of margarine, and a chunk of sausage, "on which we pounce like hungry wolves."

Gustav remained in the Mittelbau-Dora camp for only two days. Then he was selected for transfer to one of the smaller satellite camps. There were no transports, so they had to march the whole way, skirting the hill on which Mittelbau-Dora was built and following the valley northwest to a concentration camp beside the railroad on the edge of the village of Ellrich—a walk of fourteen kilometers.

Ellrich concentration camp was by some margin the worst Gustav had yet experienced. It wasn't large, but it contained around eight thousand prisoners in wretchedly insanitary conditions. Despite intakes from elsewhere, the population was constantly falling due to the horrific death toll from starvation and disease. From around a hundred deaths per month the previous fall the fatality rate had escalated to nearly five hundred in January. There were no washing or laundry facilities, with the result that lice were endemic; an attempted delousing program in the fall had simply resulted in destroying hundreds of prisoners' uniforms, which had never been replaced. When Gustav and the others arrived on February 6, they were confronted by the sight of filthy inmates, many of them in rags, some of them naked but for their underwear. The "unclothed" were excused from work and restricted to half rations; as a result they were rapidly starving to death.[11]

Gustav's group was given two days' rest then put to work. Perhaps it was because he was weakened by increasing age, the general wear and tear of five and a half years in the camps, or the torment of the journey from Auschwitz; more likely it was the sheer unmitigated hell of this place that shattered Gustav like nothing had shattered him before. Every day, reveille came at 3 AM. In the depth of winter it felt like the middle of the night.[12] The reason for starting at this unholy hour quickly became apparent. After a typically long drawn-out roll call, the work details marched to the railroad that ran by the camp, where they boarded a train and traveled back in the direction of the main Mittelbau-Dora camp. Halfway was a village called Woffleben; this was where the main work site was located, in a series of tunnels bored into the roots of the hills on which the main camp stood.[13]

It resembled a quarry, with stepped cliff faces cut into the hillside; at the base, great openings like the entrances to aircraft hangars had been excavated. The whole outer area of the tunnels was covered with scaffolding elaborately draped in camouflage. The work that went on inside, in the deeps of the earth, was top secret and, for the forced laborers, absolute hell.

The Mittelbau complex had been established in response to the Allied bombing campaign against Germany's armaments industry. It was one of a number of locations where arms production had been moved underground, out of reach of the bombs. In the Woffleben tunnels under the Mittelbau hills—carved out at appalling human cost by prisoner labor—they were manufacturing V-2 ballistic missiles, the most advanced and most terrifying of Hitler's secret weapons.

The labor detail into which Gustav was drafted was busily delving new tunnels just to the west of the main complex. He was put with a group consisting mostly of Russian prisoners of war, doing the backbreaking work of laying railroad tracks underground. The kapos and engineers under whom they worked were true slavedrivers, harassing and lashing out with canes at anyone and everyone who caught their eye. Gustav had known nothing like it since the quarry at Buchenwald. This was worse; day after day it went on, without friends, on rations that wouldn't sustain a bed-bound invalid: two bowls of thin soup each day, with a piece of bread. For two weeks in a row they had to make do without the bread, just the watery soup alone, on which to endure a shift lasting from dawn until 7:30 in the evening. He lived in filth, and within weeks he was as wasted and riddled with lice as the rest.

Ellrich's camp director was SS-Sergeant Otto Brinkmann, a little weasel of a man who was both a sadist and unfit for his responsibility. He'd been posted here by the former commandant of Mittelbau-Dora, SS-Major Förschner, who had treated Ellrich like a trash can into which he shed his unwanted SS personnel and those prisoners who were least likely to survive. Förschner had since been replaced by Richard Baer, the former commandant of Auschwitz, who escalated the system of repression still further.[14] At evening roll call in Ellrich, when the men were exhausted to the point of collapse, Brinkmann forced the prisoners to do exercises, lying down on the sharp stones of the unmade parade ground.

By Gustav's reckoning, fifty to sixty people a day were dying of starvation and abuse—"the perfect bone mill." But there was a grit in him that even now would not submit. "One can scarcely drag oneself along," he wrote, "but I have made a pact with myself that I will survive to the end. I take Gandhi, the Indian freedom fighter, as my model. He is so thin and yet lives. And every day I say a prayer to myself: *Gustl, do not despair. Grit your teeth—the SS murderers must not beat you.*"

He thought of the line he'd put in his poem "Quarry Kaleidoscope" five years earlier:

> Smack!—down on all fours he lies,
> But still the dog just will not die.

Recalling that image of resistance now, he wrote: "I think to myself, the dogs will make it to the end." His faith in that outcome was a rock, as firm as his belief that his boy was safe, that Fritzl must have reached Vienna by now.

בן

Fritz looked despondently at his food: a hunk of bread not much bigger than his hand and a small bowl of thin turnip stew. That, along with a mug of acorn coffee, was his ration, meant to sustain him through the whole day's labor. Sometimes he got extra stew, but it wouldn't hold his soul to his body for long. Looking at his wrists, they were already visibly thinner. He could feel the sharpening of the bones in his face. Little more than a month had passed since his arrival at Mauthausen, but he had never felt so abandoned, so devoid of friendship and support. Those bonds that had sustained him through Buchenwald and Auschwitz were no longer there; he had cut them away when he jumped from the train.

Pepi Kohl was a force for good in Mauthausen, but Fritz was no longer in the main camp. He'd been transferred to a subcamp at the village of Gusen, four kilometers away. The path that had brought him here was, in its own way, even stranger than the one that had brought him to Mauthausen in the first place. In early March, with Germany fighting for its very existence and desperately short of men, the camp commandant, SS-Colonel Franz Ziereis, had announced that German and Austrian prisoners who were of Aryan blood could earn their freedom by volunteering for the SS. They would form special units, be provided with uniforms and weapons, and would fight alongside the regular SS for the survival of the Fatherland.[15]

At a meeting of the Mauthausen resistance, Pepi Kohl and the other leaders agreed that around 120 suitable prisoners should volunteer. They guessed that the SS leadership would attempt to use these units as cannon fodder or turn them against their fellow prisoners.[16] By infiltrating resisters into their ranks, they could turn the SS's own scheme against them; at the crucial moment, the volunteers would turn their weapons on the regular SS.

Among the "volunteers" Pepi chose was Fritz Kleinmann. He was officially Aryan and had the air of a fighter. Fritz was deeply reluctant; after years of being abused and tortured by the SS, the very thought of putting on their uniform and joining their ranks sickened him, even if it was done with the best of motives. But Pepi was insistent and wasn't the sort of man to be easily denied. So Fritz Kleinmann, Viennese Jew, went along with the others to the commandant's office and signed up for the SS Death's Head special unit.[17]

Fritz and his comrades were taken from the camp and posted to a nearby training school, where they began a hasty program of indoctrination and instruction. Other volunteers may have been able to focus on the ends and live with what they were doing, but Fritz couldn't. The whole thing felt so profoundly wrong that he began to misbehave, with the intention of getting kicked out. It was a dangerous thing to do—knowing the SS and given the extremely tense circumstances, it was potentially a path to a bullet in the back of the head or a gallows. In fact it earned him punishment and—just as he desired—dismissal from the unit. He became a prisoner again and was sent back to the camp. His SS career was over before it had properly begun.

He'd been back in Mauthausen no more than a few days when on March 15 he was transferred to the subcamp at Gusen. Fritz was one of a batch of 284 skilled workers moved that day, all of them perfect strangers to whom he felt little attachment. They were a cosmopolitan selection—Jews, politicals, and protective custody prisoners from all the lands of the Reich: Polish, French, German, Austrian, Belgian, Greek, Russian, Dutch. Besides Fritz (in the guise of heating engineer), there were electricians, fitters, plumbers, painters, metalworkers, and a large group of general mechanics, plus one solitary Ukrainian aircraft mechanic.[18]

The subcamp of Gusen II accommodated around ten thousand prisoners, many of them technical workers. It was one of three subcamps supplying labor to the secret underground aircraft factories that had been constructed in tunnels bored under the hills. As at Mittelbau-Dora, this was another attempt to shield armaments production from Allied bombing. The factories under Gusen and the neighboring village of St. Georgen were operated by the firms of Steyr-Daimler-Puch and Messerschmitt.[19] Fritz and the others were assigned to labor battalion Ba III, a code name for a subunit working in the B8 "Bergkristall" aircraft plant in the tunnels by St. Georgen, where Messerschmitt built fuselages for its ultra-advanced Me 262 jet fighter.[20]

The relationship with Pepi Kohl and his resistance group that Fritz had begun in Mauthausen had been severed before having a chance to develop any further, and in Gusen he felt utterly isolated: "Here I was on my own, without any contact with any other group." A despondency like that which had pushed him toward thoughts of suicide in Monowitz took hold of him again, and he scarcely noticed the passage of days through March and April 1945; they did not stick in his memory other than as a hellish blur. The prisoners labored in the tunnels and wasted away through lack of nourishment, while the SS and the green-triangle kapos murdered them at will. Besides those killed on the spot, during March alone nearly three thousand were declared unfit for work and despatched to Mauthausen, where most of them died. When a truckload of food was delivered to the camp by the International Committee of the Red Cross, the SS plundered it, taking the best for themselves, then pierced the remaining cans of food and condensed milk; laughing, they threw the leaking cans among the prisoners. Yet despite the death rate, the population grew rapidly as more and more death marches from evacuated camps across Austria were brought in.[21] They died in thousands, and their unburied corpses piled up in the camps.

Physically as well as mentally Fritz had altered from the undersized boy of 1940; during his time in Robert Siewert's construction detail in Buchenwald, then the Buna Werke and the Monowitz resistance, he'd had a passable diet, and was now 170 centimeters tall.* But the conditions in Mauthausen-Gusen eroded him in two months from the lean, healthy state he'd been in when he left the Wehrmacht barracks in St. Pölten, starvation whittling the flesh from his bones until by late April 1945 he resembled the spectral, skeletal Muselmänner of Auschwitz.

And yet he did not give up as they had. In Gusen at least there was an end in sight, if Fritz could just cling on by his bony fingers long enough to see it. As the end of April approached, so did the sounds of war—the familiar thumping of artillery and crackle of gunfire in the far distance. The Americans were coming.

The Mauthausen SS leadership and their seniors in Berlin had planned for this. They had no intention of letting their top secret jet fighter production facility and their tens of thousands of skilled workers fall into enemy hands. On April 14, Heinrich Himmler sent a telegram to all concentration camp commandants insisting that "No prisoner may fall alive into the hands of the enemy."[22] In Himmler's mind, that meant evacuation (except in certain special cases where he planned to bargain with the Allies), and his telegram said so. But in the minds of Ernst Kaltenbrunner, head of the RSHA, and Mauthausen commandant Franz Ziereis, it was understood to mean a total liquidation. This

---

* Five feet, seven inches

had long been the intention, and as far as they were concerned it remained so. Ziereis laid his plans accordingly.

At 10:45 in the morning on April 28, the air raid sirens sounded in Gusen I and II, which were right next-door to each other. It was a Saturday, but the prisoners had not yet been sent to work. As soon as the alarm went off, the SS and kapos began urgently herding the tens of thousands of prisoners from both camps toward the Kellerbau tunnels. The only ones left behind were seven hundred invalids in the hospital, who were too sick to be moved.[23]

There were two sets of underground works at Gusen—the Bergkristall tunnels near the village of St. Georgen, where Fritz and the other Gusen II prisoners worked, and the Kellerbau tunnels, immediately to the north of the camps. It was toward these that the prisoners were shepherded. They filed in through one of the tunnel entrances—a huge maw as wide and high as a railroad tunnel.

Inside, the granite and concrete walls were danker and colder than the Bergkristall tunnels, which were cut into sandstone (and therefore less stable and more prone to collapse). Due to the expense of excavating in this rock, and the presence of underground springs that flooded them, the Kellerbau tunnel system had never been fully completed, and Messerschmitt had moved most of its aircraft production to Bergkristall.[24] But Kellerbau remained more convenient as an air raid shelter for the camps. Fritz and thousands of fellow prisoners stood in the damp chill and waited, listening for the sounds of bombers and the thump of explosions. The minutes passed, and nothing happened.

Those among them who were most observant, and most familiar with Kellerbau, might have noticed as they filed in that two of the three entrances to the tunnels had been bricked up, leaving only this one open. Even the sharpest-eyed were unaware that, after they had entered, SS machine-gunners set up positions outside. The prisoners were also ignorant of the fact that over the previous few days, this last entrance had been mined with explosives. The task had been organized by the DESt plant manager in charge of tunnel construction, a civilian named Paul Wolfram, on orders from Commandant Ziereis. The operation was codenamed *Feuerzeug*—lighter. Wolfram and his colleagues were told that their own and their families' lives would be in jeopardy if they botched the job or revealed the secret.[25] Wolfram had laced the entrance with all the explosives he had in stock. According to his calculations, it wouldn't be sufficient, so the charge was supplemented by a couple of dozen aerial bombs and two truckloads of marine mines. During the night before the air raid alert, the explosives had been wired up. Once all the prisoners were inside and the machine-gunners were ready to prevent any escaping, the tunnel entrance was to be blown. The prisoners would be trapped inside and suffocate to death.

20 | The End of Days

אבא

BY THE CLOSE OF MARCH, when he'd been at Ellrich about a month and a half, things had improved a little for Gustav; not much, but just enough to nourish his iron will and keep his body bound to his soul. He'd been taken off track-laying and was working in the tunnels as a carpenter. His kapo was a decent man named Erich who had secret sources of food for himself and gave Gustav his soup ration.[1] Nonetheless, like everyone, Gustav was starving and grew more filthy and infested with lice with every passing day. He lived his days underground, and the society in which he lived likewise descended into the fourth circle of the pit of Hell: most of the slaves were on the brink of death from starvation, the stronger preying on the weak, robbing them of their meager rations. The only plentiful thing was corpses, and there had been occurrences of cannibalism. Over a thousand prisoners had died in March, and a further sixteen hundred walking skeletons had been sent by the SS to an army barracks in Nordhausen that served as a dump for the spent and useless.[2]

In April, with American forces only days away, the SS began pulling the plug. On April 3, all work was halted and final preparations began for the evacuation of Mittelbau-Dora and its subcamps. That same night, the British Royal Air Force firebombed Nordhausen, hitting the barracks and killing hundreds of the sick prisoners. The raid spurred on the SS evacuation, which began the next day. That night the RAF bombers visited again, razing the town and adding more prisoners to the death toll.[3]

The evacuation of Ellrich began on April 4 and took until the next day to complete. All the prisoners who were fit to move were loaded into cattle cars.

As the final train prepared to leave on April 5, the last SS man to depart the camp personally shot the dozen or so remaining sick prisoners. The SS left the camp empty, and when the US 104th Infantry Division reached Ellrich a week later they found not a living soul.[4]

אבא

Gustav thought back on the journey from Auschwitz. The weather was far milder now, and they were in closed cars. Gustav had room to sit, and they even got a little food. Not nearly as much as they should have received, however—supply cars stocked with bread and canned food had been coupled to the rear of the train when it left Ellrich, but at some point they had been disconnected; peering through gaps in the car side, the prisoners could see that the food cars were no longer there. A little relief came around the fourth day when the train stopped off at a town in which there was a bread factory, where they were intended to pick up rations. Gustav met an English prisoner of war who gave him two kilos of bread and pumpernickel—enough to keep him and his comrades going for three days.[5]

The train had come far into the north of Germany, past Hanover and on in the direction of Bremen. On April 9 it reached its final destination: the small town of Bergen, the unloading place for Bergen-Belsen concentration camp.

With the ring of enemies closing in more and more tightly, the SS, under Himmler's instructions, was determined to hold on to its prisoners, who were intended to serve one final purpose—as hostages.

Bergen-Belsen was one of the last handful of concentration camps remaining on German-held soil. By the time Gustav Kleinmann arrived, the camp, designed for only a few thousand, had swollen beyond all sense or reason, and despite thousands of deaths every month from starvation and disease—seven thousand in February, eighteen thousand in March, nine thousand in the first days of April—the living population had climbed to over sixty thousand souls, existing among piles of unburied corpses in an atmosphere rife with typhus. In Himmler's peculiar mind, he was saving them, trying to win favor with the Allies by showing himself merciful to the Jews rather than the architect of their mass murder.[6]

Into this boiling mass of humanity, Gustav and the other survivors of Mittelbau-Ellrich were to be driven. Many had not survived the journey, and there was the usual cargo of corpses to be unloaded from the train. As they marched from the station toward the camp, an astonishing thing happened that was both terrible and wonderful. The column of ghosts met another marching in the same direction; they were all Hungarian Jews—men, women, children, all starving and wretched. Many of the Ellrich survivors were Hungarian also, and to Gustav's wonder, first one person then another and another from one column recognized relatives in the other. They broke ranks and ran to them, calling their names. Beloved friends, mothers, sisters, fathers, children, long separated and thinking their dear ones dead, found them again on the road to Belsen. It was both joyous and heartrending, and Gustav could not find the words to describe what he saw—"one can only imagine such a reunion." What he would not give to be so reunited with Tini and Herta and Fritz. But not here, not in this place.

There were no anchors left, no touchstones, no certainties; even the regime of the camp system had broken down. Bergen-Belsen was full to bursting, and the fifteen thousand who arrived from the Mittelbau camps were turned away by the commandant, Josef Kramer. Their SS escorts found accommodation for them at a Wehrmacht panzer training school a kilometer away, between Belsen and Hohne. Its barracks were pressed into service as an overflow concentration camp, designated Belsen Camp 2, under the command of SS-Captain Franz Hössler, who had accompanied the transports from Mittelbau.[7] This man was notorious; a thuggish-looking individual with a jutting chin and sunken mouth, before Mittelbau Hössler had been in command of one of the women's sections in Auschwitz-Birkenau, participating in selections and gassings and countless acts of individual murder and brutality. It had been Hössler who had selected the women "volunteers" sent to the Monowitz brothel.[8]

Physically the barracks in the panzer training school were a pleasant change for the prisoners; clean, airy white buildings set around asphalt squares dispersed among pleasant woodland. The Wehrmacht staff—now consisting of a Hungarian regiment—supplemented the SS guards and helped manage the prisoners. The rations they were given were better quality, but the quantities were pathetically inadequate for so many people. Gustav and his comrades were reduced to foraging potato and turnip peelings from the garbage bins outside the barrack kitchens—"anything to relieve the hunger," he noted in his diary. In all his time in the camps, he had never been surrounded by so much tight-pressed humanity—or seen helpless starvation on such a scale. The faith that had kept him going was beginning to ebb away. What made him special? Why should he make it to the end when all these thousands had not or would not?

In their own way, the Hungarian troops were as brutal as the SS. Most of the officers were well-groomed, with pomaded hair, and had instilled in their mostly illiterate men an anti-Semitic fascist ideology that was on a par with anything the SS could provide. They were callous and apt to shoot inmates for entertainment. Their main duty, aside from keeping the prisoners under general guard, was to protect the kitchens, and they would stand in the square between the barracks taking shots at the prisoners foraging for food, killing dozens of them; in the main camp it was the same, with hundreds shot each day.[9] Some of the Hungarian troops retained a mystic devotion to the Nazi cause. One Jewish woman encountered a Hungarian near the perimeter of the camp; seeing her Star of David, he regretted that the work of exterminating the Jews had not yet been completed, telling her that Hitler would return, "and again we shall fight side by side."[10]

On the first night in Belsen Camp 2, Gustav stood vigil in the upper story of his building. Looking out the window toward the south, he saw the dark sky glowing orange. It looked to him as if a town—possibly Celle, twenty or so kilometers away—was in flames. Even as Gustav watched, it flashed and erupted with explosions. That wasn't aerial bombing—that was a battle front.[11] His sinking heart began to rise. "I think to myself, now the liberators must be here soon—and I have faith again. I think to myself still, the lord God does not forsake us."

On April 12, with the tacit consent of Commandant Kramer, local Wehrmacht commanders made contact with the British forces advancing toward them and negotiated for the peaceful surrender of Bergen-Belsen. In order to contain the epidemic of typhus, a zone of several kilometers around the camp would become neutral territory.

In the barracks, Gustav noticed that most of the Hungarian soldiers had begun wearing white armbands as a token of neutrality. Even some of the SS were doing the same—including the camp leader, SS-Corporal Sommer, whom Gustav had known in Auschwitz as "one of the bloodhounds." At last Gustav felt sure that the prisoners would be handed over to the British without bloodshed. "It is high time," he wrote, because the SS "wanted to make of us a St. Bartholomew's Night massacre under English illumination, but the Hungarian colonel didn't want any part of it, and so they have left us alone."

Two days later, on April 14, Gustav saw the first British tanks in the distance. In the barracks there was unconstrained joy, and the celebrations went on all night. Soon they would be set free.

חברים

Captain Derrick Sington struggled to make himself heard over the convoy of tanks clanking and roaring along the road leading through the town of Winsen an der Aller. Following a race to catch up with the tanks and scout cars of the 23rd Hussars leading the advance, Sington had found the regiment's intelligence officer and was trying to inform him of his special mission over the din of military traffic.

Derrick Sington was commander of the No. 14 Amplifying Unit of the British Army Intelligence Corps. Equipped with light trucks mounted with loudspeakers, the unit's role was to disseminate information and propaganda. His commanding officer had ordered him to proceed with the advance column of the 63rd Anti-Tank Regiment, Royal Artillery, to the concentration camp at Bergen-Belsen. That regiment would be establishing and taking control of a neutral zone surrounding the camp. The prisoners—or "internees" as the British were officially calling them—must not be allowed to leave the zone. Information from the Wehrmacht indicated a typhus epidemic in the camp, and it could not be allowed to spread into the areas behind the British front line. Once the camp had been secured, Captain Sington was to take his loudspeaker truck inside and make the requisite announcement to the inmates. As a German-speaker, he would also act as an interpreter for Lieutenant Colonel Taylor, commander of the 63rd AT, who would be in overall command of the zone.[12]

Yelling at the top of his voice over the clattering squeal of tracks and roaring engines, Sington explained all this to the Hussars intelligence officer, who leaned out of the turret of his tank with his hand cupped over his ear. He nodded and told Sington to fall into line. Sington jumped back into his seat, gestured to his driver, and they pulled into the road, joining the flow of armored vehicles.

Beyond Winsen, the column passed through open countryside that gave way to thick woodlands of firs, whose powerful scent mingled with the exhaust fumes and the stench of burning. The infantry advancing ahead of the armor were torching the undergrowth on either side with flamethrowers. There had been a tough fight for Winsen, with tanks lost to unseen German 88-mm guns, so they weren't taking any chances today. If there were snipers concealed in the thickets, they'd soon be flushed out.

Not far up the road, Sington saw the first warning notices—DANGER TYPHUS—marking the perimeter of the neutral zone. Sington pulled over and was met by two German NCOs, who handed him a note written in bad English inviting him to meet the Wehrmacht commandant at Bergen-Belsen. Meanwhile, the column of Sherman and Comet tanks carried on rolling.

Sington followed them, and as the road swung eastward he spotted the camp—an enclosure of high barbed-wire fences and watch towers cut out of the forest, flanking the left-hand side of the road for about one and a half kilometers. Sington's truck pulled off the road at the main gate, where he was met by a small group of very smartly dressed enemy officers: one in the field-gray of the Wehrmacht, a highly decorated Hungarian captain in khaki, and a bulky, fleshy-faced SS officer with a simian jaw and a scar on his cheek. This man proved to be SS-Captain Josef Kramer, commandant of Bergen-Belsen.

The Englishman introduced himself. While they waited for the arrival of Colonel Taylor, Sington fell into polite conversation with Kramer. He asked him how many prisoners were in the camp; Kramer answered forty thousand here, and an additional fifteen thousand in Camp 2 up the road. And what kind of prisoners were they? "Habitual criminals and homosexuals," said Kramer, looking furtively at the Englishman. Sington said nothing in answer to this but later noted that he had "reason to believe it was an incomplete statement."[13]

Their conversation was mercifully cut short by the arrival of Colonel Taylor's jeep. He ordered Sington to go into the camp and make his announcement, then roared on up the road toward Bergen.

After a show of reluctance, Kramer allowed the barrier to be lifted, then at Sington's invitation he climbed up on the running board of the loudspeaker truck, and they drove in through the gates. With Kramer giving directions, the truck passed through the first compound, containing the SS facilities, then on through the inner gate into the main camp.

To Sington, who had tried many times to imagine what the inside of a concentration camp would be like, it was unlike anything he had pictured. There was a straight street through the center, with separately enclosed compounds on either side, each filled with wooden barrack blocks. The place was suffused with "a smell of ordure" that reminded Sington of "the smell of a monkey-house" in a zoo; "sad blue smoke floated like a ground mist between the low buildings." The excited inmates "crowded to the barbed wire fences . . . with their shaven heads and their obscenely striped penitentiary suits, which were so dehumanising." Sington had been with the advance from Normandy through France, Belgium, and Holland, and had witnessed gratitude from many different liberated peoples; but the cheers from these skeletal, wasted ghosts, "these clowns in their terrible motley, who had once been Polish officers, land-workers in the Ukraine, Budapest doctors, and students in France, impelled a stronger emotion, and I had to fight back my tears."[14]

He drove through, stopping his truck at intervals, the loudspeakers blaring out the announcement that the camp zone was in quarantine under British administration. The SS had surrendered control and would now withdraw; the Hungarian regiment would remain, but under direct command of the British Army. Prisoners must not leave the area due to risk of spreading typhus. Food and medical supplies were being rushed to the camp with all haste.

It was greeted with explosions of joy. The inmates spilled out of the compounds, surrounding the truck. Kramer was alarmed, and he wasn't the only one. A Hungarian soldier began firing his rifle directly over the heads of the prisoners. Sington jumped out of his truck. "Stop shooting!" he ordered, pulling his revolver, and the soldier lowered his rifle. But no sooner had the shooting stopped than, to Sington's amazement, a band of men in prisoner uniforms armed with cudgels ran into the crowd, lashing and beating the prisoners with appalling brutality. Sington, who had no idea of the existence of kapos and block seniors, was stunned by this spectacle. One poor skeletal wretch was on the ground, but still the kapo kept up the rain of blows.

When they arrived back at the main gate, Sington said to Kramer, "You've made a fine hell here."[15]

Sington hadn't seen the half of it. His brief tour had shown him only the throng of survivors, and it would be a day or two before he finally discovered the burial pits, the crematorium, and the grounds strewn and stacked with thousands of naked, emaciated corpses.

Pulling out of the gate, he turned his truck toward Camp 2, to repeat his round of announcements.

אבא

There had been celebrations the day before when Gustav saw the tanks in the distance. Today, the British column had come rolling up the main Bergen road, passing by the camp, and little seemed to happen. Then the loudspeaker truck arrived. Captain Sington's announcement was drowned out by cheering.

The prisoners in Camp 2, although in a dreadful state, weren't nearly as wretched as those in the main camp. As soon as the loudspeaker truck departed, the lynchings began. Hundreds of men, exalted in their fury and encouraged by their strength in numbers, singled out the individuals who had tortured them. Gustav watched dispassionately as certain SS guards and green-triangle block seniors were strung up or beaten to death. Gustav saw at least two murderers from Auschwitz-Monowitz die and felt no pity or remorse for it. The Hungarian troops made no move to intercede. That afternoon, when the killing was done, the remaining SS were made to remove the bodies and buried them the next day with their own hands.

On April 17, the British began taking records of all the surviving prisoners in Camp 2, ordering them by nationality; Bergen-Belsen had been transformed into a displaced persons camp, and the inmates were being prepared for repatriation. Gustav remained with the Hungarian Jews; he'd made many good friends among them, and with his long experience of the camps they had chosen him to be a room senior.

It was a liberation and yet not a liberation. Gustav and his comrades were no longer under the heel of the SS; the British brought in food and medical supplies, and they ate well and began to recover their health. It was very different from the main camp, where the inmates were in such a terrible state that thousands died in the weeks following liberation. Yet they were all still prisoners. Because of the quarantine, the Hungarian soldiers were under orders from the British to prevent anyone from leaving. As far as Camp 2 was concerned, this was preposterous—the was no typhus here, and no need to keep the prisoners incarcerated. Gustav began to chafe, longing to experience freedom again after all these years.

His first priority, though, was to let his family know that he was alive and well. He wasn't the only one. The liberation of Belsen was a huge international story; there were newsreels and radio reports, and the papers were full of it. Across Europe and in Britain and America, the relatives of people taken by the Nazis heard the reports and sent desperate inquiries. Periodically, Captain Sington's loudspeaker truck would tour the camp, broadcasting the names of people whose families had inquired.[16]

Gustav thought of Edith and Kurt. He hadn't seen Edith since her departure for England in early 1939 and had heard no news of her since the beginning of the war. Kurt too had been cut off since December 1941. Gustav wrote a message detailing his whereabouts and block number. Providing Edith's last known address in Leeds, he entrusted it—along with the thousands of messages from other inmates—to the British administration.[17]

Meanwhile, the British got on with the enormous task of looking after the liberated people. The main camp was the first priority. Food and water were brought in, and medical staff began their work of trying to save as many lives as possible. Handling the dead blasted the minds of those who witnessed it. The corpses lay in heaps in the thousands, and the half-dead, half-living moved around them as if they weren't there, stepping over them, sitting down to their scraps leaning against stacks of the dead.[18] Great pits were excavated, dozens of meters long and several meters deep. At first the SS were forced to carry the dead into the pits by hand, jeered at and cursed by survivors; a few SS men made a run for the forest, but they were shot down and their comrades had to drag their bodies back. Into the pits they went, along with their victims.[19] The task proved overwhelming in the end; there were just too many bodies to bury by hand, and the bulldozers that had dug the pits had to push the stacks of decomposing corpses into them. It took nearly two weeks before the last were buried.[20]

The main camp was gradually evacuated, and the survivors moved to the clean, solid buildings of the panzer training school; the former Camp 2 was converted into a huge hospital, named Bergen-Hohne. The transfer would take about a month, due to the weakness of most of the survivors. As the infected, insanitary, broken-down wooden barracks in the main camp were emptied, they were burned down with flamethrowers.

Experts in typhus and famine relief were brought in, along with general medical staff. It was traumatic for all of them. One English nurse who arrived on April 19 felt shame and remorse that, having heard of the existence of such camps as early as 1934, she had never realized—and hadn't wanted to realize—that they could be like this. She and her colleagues were "stirred with a cold anger against those primarily responsible, the Germans, an anger which grew daily at Belsen."[21] Others were shocked by how abuse and extreme degradation had reduced many survivors to an animalistic state, fighting for food, eating voraciously from bowls that they had just used as bedpans, with only a wipe with a rag between uses, living among rotting corpses without noticing the choking stench.[22]

It was measure of the state of these survivors that the Mittelbau transferees, wasted and starved as they were, were considered relatively fit and healthy. The influx from the main camp raised a problem for them: it brought typhus into their vicinity. The infected were put in a set of buildings that were cordoned off, but their presence still increased the risk that it would spread throughout the barracks.

Gustav was not alone in desperately wanting to leave this terrible, haunted place. He wasn't sick, but like everyone else he was under quarantine. Also, there was still fighting going on outside the neutral zone, and it was still dangerous out there. Nonetheless, Gustav was itching to go.

On April 25, the first repatriation transports were allowed to leave. Those who departed were a selection of French, Belgian, and Dutch survivors. The way to their homelands lay to the west, in liberated countries. Those who came from Germany, Austria, Poland, Russia, and Hungary would have to wait, regardless of their state of health. Their countries were either war zones or still in German hands. Some were now Soviet-occupied territory, and repatriation would present a whole new world of difficulties. Moreover, within German-held territory there were still concentration camps not yet liberated—Mauthausen-Gusen, for one, where at that very moment the SS leadership were plotting to murder all the prisoners by trapping them in the tunnels.

Gustav watched the transports go with longing. It gave him hope, but as the days passed and no further transports left, he started growing impatient. It was now over two weeks since the British had liberated the camp. It didn't matter that it was irrational, that Austria wasn't yet free, Gustav was sure he could find his way home. He believed that Fritz would be in Vienna now, waiting for him. Gustav needed to get back there somehow.

He waited until the weekend was over, and on the morning of Monday, April 30, Gustav set out. Taking his few belongings and a little food, he walked out of his barrack block and along the asphalt path, heading for the road. A Hungarian soldier stepped in front of him, rifle raised. Where did he think he was going? Gustav told him he was leaving, going home. There was a look in the soldier's eyes no different from the expression Gustav had seen in hundreds of SS guards—the look of an anti-Semitic fascist regarding a Jewish prisoner. Until two weeks ago this soldier had been fighting alongside the Nazis. Gustav went to walk past him. The soldier swung his rifle-butt and smacked Gustav in the chest. "Try that again and I'll shoot you," he said.

Gustav staggered, then turned and went back to his barrack. He was trapped in this place, liberated but not free.

בן

Fritz stood waiting amid the dense crowd of prisoners in the chilly, dripping, cavernous tunnel, wondering what was going on. Minutes ticked by, but there were no sounds of airplanes, no thump of explosions: just the echoing susurrus of tens of thousands of prisoners breathing and murmuring to one another. Hours passed. The prisoners, who were accustomed to standing at roll calls that dragged on just like this, thought little of it. A false alarm, presumably. At least they weren't having to work.

Most of them would never learn the true reason why they'd been lured into the tunnels, would never be aware of the complications that kept them standing there for so many hours. The explosive charges, bombs, and mines embedded around the entrance were failing to detonate. Paul Wolfram, the DESt manager in charge of blowing up the tunnel entrance, would later claim that it was reluctance on his part to commit mass murder, adding that the bombs and mines had no detonators. Commandant Ziereis—who spent much of this period drunk—claimed that he had reservations about the whole business. But a story among some of the survivors claimed that a Polish prisoner named Władysława Palonka, an electrician, had discovered the detonation wires and cut them.[23]

At 4:00 PM the all-clear sounded, and the prisoners who had walked in unknowingly to their deaths walked out again and filed back to their blocks in the camps. For the time being they were safe, rescued at the last minute either by an uncharacteristic failure of the SS's murderous instincts or an ingenious act of daring by a resourceful prisoner. Had it succeeded, it would have killed over twenty thousand and would have been one of the largest single acts of mass murder in the history of Europe.[24]

Routine resumed for a couple days, but on Tuesday, May 1, the prisoners were not sent to work. For Fritz there was a sense of déjà vu; the mood among the SS was like at Monowitz in the middle of January, but now the panic was deeper.

On May 3, all the SS guards disappeared from the camp. The fanatical Nazis among them had gone off intending to fight a last-ditch defense in the mountains, while the rest shed their uniforms and went into hiding among the civilian populations in the cities. Command of Mauthausen-Gusen was officially handed over to the Vienna civil police force, and camp administration fell to the Luftwaffe. They were aided by a detachment of the Vienna fire service who had come here as political prisoners in 1944.[25] There would be no evacuation from Mauthausen. There was nowhere left to go.

The Allies were closing in on Austria from three directions. In the south, the 15th Army Group—an international force of Americans, British, Canadians, Poles, Indians, New Zealanders, and one Jewish Brigade—was pushing into the South Tyrol, the mountainous borderland between Italy and Austria. It was here that the Nazis had been hoping to make a last stand in an imaginary "Alpine Fortress" that they had never gotten around to creating.

In the east, the Red Army had crossed the Hungarian-Austrian border at the end of March and immediately began moving to encircle Vienna. By April 6, the city was surrounded by two Soviet armies and under siege. The German forces remaining in Vienna—around forty thousand troops with only twenty-six functioning tanks—were hopelessly insufficient to defend it against the vastly superior Soviet force, and the siege was short lived. By April 7, Soviet troops were in the southern part of the inner city, and on April 10 the Germans evacuated the districts east of the Danube Canal, including Leopoldstadt. The Danube bridges were captured, and on April 13, the last SS armored unit abandoned the city.[26] Vienna was liberated from the Nazis seven years almost to the day since Hitler had held his bogus plebiscite to consolidate his political grip on Austria. Now he was trapped in his Berlin bunker and his grand Reich was reduced to a tiny, bleeding stump.

The third spearhead into Austria came from the northwest, where the American 65th Infantry Division, part of General Patton's Third Army, crossed the Bavarian stretch of the Danube on April 27 against stiff German resistance. Forced to hold back his desired drive into Austria at several points due to an agreement with the Soviet Union, Patton juggled his divisions and sent his

XII Corps into Austria north of the Danube, less than a hundred kilometers northwest of Linz and Mauthausen. They faced heavy fighting from fanatical German forces who had taken to hanging deserters from roadside trees.[27] Leading the American advance was the 11th Armored Division, and on May 5, as the advance pushed down the Danube, the very tip of the spearpoint consisted of a patrol from the 41st Cavalry Reconnaissance Squadron and a platoon from the 55th Armored Infantry Battalion. Probing the Danube valley east of Linz they came to the villages of St. Georgen and Gusen, and first laid eyes on the camps.

For sheer horror, Mauthausen and Gusen rivaled Bergen-Belsen, which had been liberated three weeks earlier. Like Belsen, Mauthausen had been a sink into which the SS concentration camps had drained. Tens of thousands of prisoners had been transferred here, and the death rate had spiraled to over nine thousand a month. The walking cadavers in striped uniforms who greeted the American liberators were found to be living among tens of thousands of their unburied, half-buried, or half-burned dead. The stench of it was what stuck in the minds of the GIs. "The smell and the stink of the dead and the dying, the smell and the stink of the starving," recalled one officer. "Yes, it is the smell, the odor of the death camp that makes it burn in the nostrils and memory. I will always smell Mauthausen."[28]

Olive-green tanks bearing the white American star, scarred and weathered, rolled into the camp compounds. In Gusen I, Sergeant Albert J. Kosiek from Chicago stood on top of his Sherman and yelled in English to the crowd of emaciated prisoners, "Brothers, you are free!"[29] His announcement was translated into all the prisoners' languages by a representative of the International Red Cross; bursts of various national anthems came from the crowd, and the Volkssturm officer in command of the German guards presented his sword to Sergeant Kosiek.

In Gusen II, Fritz Kleinmann greeted his liberation without any overwhelming joy. He was too weak and demoralized to celebrate with any fervor. The typical life expectancy for a prisoner in Mauthausen-Gusen was four months, even if he began from a state of robust health. Fritz, having been only passably healthy when he arrived, had experienced three months. He was scarcely alive, little more than bones shrouded in skin, marked with bruises and sores.

The spirit of resistance and the system of support that had kept Fritz going in Buchenwald and Auschwitz had been absent in Mauthausen-Gusen. He had no real comrades, only fellow sufferers. "I was utterly demolished there," he wrote.[30] Now that he was free, he was too weak and sick to go home, if there was even a home to return to.

אבא

Nursing his bruised ribs, Gustav walked back to his block. Getting out of Bergen-Belsen was going to be trickier than he'd anticipated. He talked it over with a fellow Viennese, a man named Josef Berger, who was also desperate to go home.

That afternoon, the two men left the building and hung around, watching the sentries. At last came the moment they were waiting for: the changing of the guard. While the soldiers were distracted, Gustav and Josef made a dash for it—not toward the road this time but in the direction of the woodlands fringing the northern and western edges of the camp. They were between sentry posts when there was a shout in Hungarian and the crack of a rifle, the bullet snapping over their heads. Another shot zipped past, and they both threw themselves flat on the ground. Bullets thwacked into the turf around them, and they crawled on. As soon as there was a pause in the shooting, the two men jumped to their feet and made a break for the woods, dodging, hurling themselves among the trees and out the other side. They ran on through the Russian section of the camp and into the forest on the far side.

After a kilometer or so, Gustav and Josef stopped to catch their breath. There were no sounds of pursuit; just birdsong and the muffled silence of the forest. They sank down to rest. Gustav looked around him, gazed up at the sky, and inhaled the fir-scented air. The very smell of it gave him joy; it was the scent of freedom. "Finally free!" he wrote in his diary. "The air around us is indescribable." For the first time in years, the atmosphere was untainted by the odors of death and labor and unwashed human hordes.

They weren't safe yet; they had to keep going. The front lines lay east, so for the time being they turned their backs on their homeland and pressed on west by north through the forest. All afternoon and into the evening they walked, passing several tiny hamlets scattered among the woods—German places, where they didn't dare ask for help. Eventually, after around twenty kilometers, they emerged from the forest into the small village of Osterheide. On the outskirts there was a large prisoner of war camp—Stalag XI—that had been liberated by the British the day after Belsen.[31] It had been evacuated several days ago and was in the process of being converted into an internment camp for Nazi party members. However, there was still a population of Russian POWs, who gave the itinerant Viennese bed and board for the night.

Next morning, May 1, Gustav and Josef walked on into the nearby town of Bad Fallingbostel, which was in British hands. It was a small, pleasant spa town, choked with refugees and troops. Gustav and Josef presented themselves to the British authorities in charge but were told that nothing could be done for them right away—they ought to be in one of the displaced persons camps for refugees and former camp inmates. They tried applying to the German mayor's office, where they fared much better, assigned accommodation in a hotel and a food ration.

Gustav found himself a week's employment as a saddler with a local uphol-sterer named Brokman. For the first time in seven years, he worked for decent pay, earned his bread, and was treated as a citizen. He began to recover from the ordeal he'd been through. In his room at the hotel, he brought out the little green notebook that had accompanied him since the early days. On the first page was the entry: "Arrived in Buchenwald on the 2nd October 1939 after a two-day train journey. From Weimar train station we ran to the camp . . ." So began the record of his captivity. Now he started recording his liberty.

"At last one is a free man, and can do as one pleases," he wrote. "Only one thing nags at me, and that is the uncertainty about my family at home."

It would continue to prey on his mind, so long as the remnants of the Nazi regime remained, still fighting, across the territory between himself and his homeland.

21 | The Long Way Home

מִשְׁפָּחָה

PETER PALTENHOFFER, LOOKING OUT the front window of the apartment, could see all of London laid out before him. The grandly named Spring Mansions—a genteel three-story Victorian townhouse—stood at the corner of Gondar Gardens, where the road dropped down a steep hill. Just beyond, the line of the railroad could be seen, and beyond that the Kilburn High Road, which cut a straight line all the way to Westminster in the bomb-scarred heart of London.

The war was all but over, but the wounds would take a long time to heal. Peter had missed a lot of it. He had been evacuated for a while to a farm near Gloucester in the west of England. Little of it stuck in his memory—the walks to church on a Sunday (their hosts were not Jewish), the gander that would bite his backside when he ran to the outhouse, the country lanes. His memories before that were even more cloudy, and when he came home to his parents and his baby sister, Joan, it was no longer the same place—his parents had left Leeds and moved to this little apartment in London.

Peter had known nothing in his short life but England and the war. He was British by birth, language, and accent; his parents, conscious of the hostility to all things German in this country, never spoke anything but English in the house.

Bringing Peter back from Gloucestershire had turned out to be premature. Although the Blitz had finished, a rash of devastating V-2 rockets had hit the capital. There was never any warning, just a massive explosion. Nonetheless, his mother would grab him and Joan and rush them to the shelter, snatching the gas masks off the hall table in passing.

309

As Peter watched, a mailman wheeled his bicycle up the hill and posted a bundle of letters through the street door. A few minutes passed, then he heard footsteps racing up the stairs, and his mother's excited voice. She appeared holding an opened letter. The envelope was covered with scratched-out and rewritten addresses. Peter couldn't make out what the excitement was about; she just kept repeating that her father—Peter's grandfather—was alive. *Alive.*

מִשְׁפָּחָה

Edith wrote immediately to Kurt to tell him the news.

Kurt was fifteen now, prospering at school, growing into the community of New Bedford, and becoming more American all the time. He sold war bonds, went to camp, and rose to be an Eagle Scout. Vienna was draining out of him. He was forgetting his old self, forgetting his mother language. But his life was idyllic.

Elated by the news, he tried writing to his father via the International Red Cross, and when no reply came, Judge Barnet contacted his acquaintance Leverett Saltonstall, United States senator for Massachusetts, seeking help. Sam Barnet was amazed that Kurt's father was still alive: "Dear Lev," he wrote, "I know that you will agree with me . . . that only through the intervention of God himself could anyone have lived through six years of slavery in any concentration camp." He asked his friend to inquire about opening a channel of communication.[1]

The senator's response was not encouraging. Communication with displaced persons was simply not feasible. Kurt's message to his father via the Red Cross was the best hope.[2] Weeks went by, and no further messages came.

בֵּן

In the days following liberation, the US Army began bringing medical aid to the survivors of Mauthausen and Gusen. Thousands who were beyond saving died in those first days.

Fritz Kleinmann was among those whose grip on life still held, despite his desperate condition. When the medical assessments began, he was interviewed by an American officer. To Fritz's surprise, he revealed that he had been born in Vienna, in Leopoldstadt. Pleased by this connection between them, the officer found Fritz a place on an emergency evacuation transport. He was taken first to the town of Gallneukirchen, near Linz. After a night there, he was put on another transport to Regensburg in southern Bavaria, where there was an American military hospital. He arrived around the same time as the news that Germany had surrendered; Hitler and Himmler were dead, and the war in Europe was over.

Regensburg was a beautiful, ancient city that had come through the war with little harm. Allied bombing had raised an inferno in the surrounding region, but only a few bombs had fallen on Regensburg itself. The US Army's 107th Evacuation Hospital had arrived just over a week before Fritz's arrival and was housed in tents and buildings on the bank of the Regen where it flowed into the Danube. As well as serving the US forces advancing into Austria, it treated German civilians injured by mines, a fair number of GIs who'd wounded themselves fooling around with captured German weapons, and at least one survivor of Mauthausen-Gusen concentration camp.[3]

When Fritz was checked in, he was scarcely alive; his weight was recorded as only thirty-six kilograms.* The hideous, miraculous, haphazard chain of events that had allowed him to evade death for five and a half years had nearly finished him off at the end.

Resting on his cot in the hospital tent, Fritz knew it was all over; the ordeal that had begun on that day in March 1938 when the Luftwaffe dropped their snowstorm of propaganda leaflets all over Vienna, when the Nazi troops marched into the city, when the days of terror for the Jews began, was finished.

Except it wasn't. The journey that had begun that day would not be complete until he returned to Vienna and discovered whether it was still his home. And as for the nightmare—why, that would never end so long as life and memory lasted. The dead remained dead, the living were scarred, and their numbers and their histories would stand for all time as a memorial.

Leaving the future to take care of itself for the moment, Fritz focused on regaining his strength. The American doctors gave him a diet of cookies, milk pudding, and a strength-building concoction whose ingredients he never knew. By the end of two weeks he had gained ten kilos.† He was still severely underweight, but he felt strong enough to travel and could feel the pull of home. The hospital—which was a mobile unit—was already packing up to move to

---

* Seventy-nine pounds
† Twenty-two pounds

a new station, and his request to be discharged was granted. He went to the city hall in Regensburg, where he was issued with civilian clothes and listed for a transport back to Austria.

On May 26, Fritz Kleinmann passed through Linz and arrived at the demarcation line between the American and Soviet zones of occupation at the small town of Enns, which stood on the south bank of the Danube, opposite Gusen and Mauthausen. At St. Valentin he caught a train. Yet again he took the railroad journey through Amstetten, through Blindenmarkt, and through St. Pölten. This time he met no interference.

At last, on Monday, May 28, 1945, Fritz set foot in Vienna: five years, seven months, and twenty-eight days since leaving it on the transport bound for Buchenwald. His train came in at the Westbahnhof, the very same station from which he had departed on that terrible day. Fritz later discovered that of the 1,035 Jewish men who had been on that Buchenwald transport, only twenty-six were still alive.

Vienna hadn't suffered in the recent fighting the way Budapest, Berlin, or Stalingrad had. There had been no all-costs defense, no wholesale destruction, no savage fight from street to street. It had fallen in just a few days, and although there were pockets of battle damage and areas that had been bombed, much of the city was scarcely touched. However, it was Fritz's luck that the route he walked from the station to the city was one of the worst hit, giving him the disconcerting impression that Vienna had been mostly destroyed.

It was late in the evening, and the darkness of a summer night was settling over the buildings when he reached the Danube Canal. The buildings on the Leopoldstadt side were badly damaged by bombs, and the once handsome Salztor bridge was just a jagged stump protruding from the bank. Fritz crossed by another bridge and eventually found himself in the Karmelitermarkt, the hub and heart of his former life.

The stalls had been packed away, the cobblestones were bare, and it was as it had been on those evenings long ago when he and his friends had played here in their innocence, kicking a rag ball around, watching out for the police, being warned off by the lamplighters for climbing the gas lamp poles. He could recall the cream cakes, the pink *Mannerschnitte* wafers, the bread crusts and ends of sausages, the shopkeepers and stallholders, Jews and non-Jews driving their trade side by side, thriving without hate or hostility, their children playing in a single rushing, laughing society. Now half of that world, half of what had made this place alive, was gone. They were ashes from the Auschwitz ovens floating down the Vistula, bones in the soil under the pine needles of Maly Trostinets, or scattered to the world—Palestine, England, the Americas, the Far East. Aside from a tiny handful like Fritz, they would never come back to the Karmelitermarkt.[4]

When he reached the old apartment building at Im Werd 11, he found the outer door locked. There was a Soviet-imposed curfew that began at 8:00 PM, and all buildings were closed up. He hammered on the door, and it was opened by the familiar figure of Frau Ziegler, the building caretaker. She greeted him with amazement. Everyone had thought him and his father dead. She let him in but wouldn't allow him up to the old apartment; there were new people living there now who had been bombed out of their home. There were no Kleinmanns here anymore.

On his first night back in Vienna, Fritz slept on Frau Ziegler's floor. When he rose the next morning and went out, he found that the news of his return had preceded him. *The Kleinmann boy is back.* He didn't find Olly Steyskal or any of his other loyal friends that morning, but he did run into Josefa Hirschler, the caretaker of Olly's apartment building. She greeted him warmly and invited him to take his first Viennese breakfast with her and her children, Fritz's old friends Helli and Fritzi. He was begrimed from his journey across Austria, so she sent him out to the back courtyard to clean up. He found a bowl waiting for him filled with hot water.

As he splashed his face and scrubbed at his neck, he felt that a new life was beginning for him. But it was a new life alone, without any family. His little brother in America, his sister in England, his mother and Herta gone, almost certainly dead in the east, and as for his father—where in the world was he?

אבא

Gustav had found himself a good life in Bad Fallingbostel; he had work and was eating well. He'd made friends with a German woman from Aachen and she gave him extra food. He had additional work making rucksacks for some Serbian army officers who had been prisoners of war. They seemed well supplied and gave him lots of cigarettes.[5]

Despite his comfortable existence, he wasn't quite content. "I feel much stronger," he wrote, but "Dear Lord, if only I were in Vienna with my son."

Gustav still doggedly believed that Fritz must have made it home after jumping from the train.

Several other liberated Viennese had drifted into Fallingbostel and formed a tiny community. They all felt homesick. When the news came that the war had ended, there was nothing more to hold them here. So, less than two weeks after his arrival, on May 13 Gustav and his new Viennese friends left Fallingbostel and began the long trek. They were joined by two women from Aachen; the first leg of their way home lay on the same southward route.[6]

The first day they walked only as far as Essel, on the road to Hanover, where they found a barn to sleep in. They went slowly, finding food and shelter wherever they could, passing to the east of Hanover to the forested, mountainous country south of Hildesheim. Gustav appreciated the slowness of the journey, relishing the freedom and the beautiful scenery. They had been four days on the road when they reached the town of Alfeld, northwest of the Harz mountains, where they paused. Gustav was delighted to bump into an old friend, Fritz Scholz, who'd been a political prisoner in Buchenwald and was now chief of police in Alfeld, no less. Hearing about the long journey Gustav had before him, Scholz gave him a bicycle.

The next day Gustav and his friends traveled on, walking, cycling, hitching rides as chance offered. They altered their direction; if they continued south, they would soon reach Nordhausen and the environs of Mittelbau and Ellrich. Instead they struck out southeast, passing to the north of the Harz mountains and avoiding the scene of some of Gustav's most unpleasant memories.

In Stapelburg, Gustav spent his first night in a decent bed. The pace picked up, and at noon on May 20 the traveling party reached the city of Halle in Saxony, where they registered at the police station to receive an allocation of food. In Halle Gustav was unexpectedly reunited with many more old comrades from both Monowitz and Buchenwald.[7] Among the latter was his good friend and Fritz's mentor Robert Siewert, who had survived in Buchenwald right to the end and had come back to his old hometown to begin rebuilding its communist party.

Halle proved to be something of a gathering place for concentration camp survivors, and Gustav decided to stay for a while. They received good care and plenty to eat, and there was an established Austrian committee. Robert Siewert gave a public talk on conditions in Buchenwald—beginning his lifelong task of helping to keep the memory of the Holocaust alive and in the forefront of public awareness.

Pleased to be in the company of so many comrades, Gustav stayed in Halle for a month. On June 20, the journey resumed. He and his companions passed through the city of Leipzig, which was in ruins; bombed heavily by both the British and Americans, it had lost tens of thousands of historic buildings and thousands of human lives. Gustav and his friends hurried on to Zwickau, which was in American hands but about to be handed over to the Soviets.

Having swept in a wide easterly arc (thereby avoiding Weimar and Buchenwald), the route now veered a little west of south, passing by the Czech border and heading into Bavaria. Cycling through forest and mountains, Gustav exulted in the beauty of nature. "This area is glorious," he wrote in his diary during one of their frequent halts. "Nothing but mountains everywhere. I feel as if I have been born again."

On June 29, they reached Regensburg, where they had a friendly reception. Gustav had no idea that Fritz had been here just over a month earlier. After staying a couple days, they moved on to Passau, on the confluence of the Danube and the Inn, right by the Austrian border. On July 2 Gustav rode his bicycle over the Danube bridge and passed into Austria, welcomed home by the pealing of church bells striking noon.

The next day the Austrian exiles reached Linz in pouring rain, after dark. It was too late to find accommodation, so they spent the night in an air raid shelter. The next day they registered at the government office and received their ration cards. Provided with an apartment belonging to a Dr. Klemenz, who had fled, they spent several days in the city.

Although he was on home soil and Vienna was only a train ride away, Gustav's footsteps slowed again. After traveling so far, he suddenly felt no great urgency to reach home. He was enjoying himself, and although he never confessed as much to his diary, there must have been nagging at the back of his mind the thought that he might find distressing news there, including the full truth about what had happened to Tini and Herta. And what if his faith was mistaken, and Fritz wasn't there?

In truth, Gustav was enjoying his freedom. For the first time ever—not only since the camps but for the first time in his whole life—he was completely at liberty, without responsibility or cares or fear, free to go as he pleased and take his time drinking in the sights and smelling the flowers.

One day, taking advantage of the beautiful weather, he took a day trip up into the mountains with one of his companions.[8] Acting on an impulse, they went to the village of Mauthausen, where yet another old camp comrade, Walter Petzold from Auschwitz, was now chief of police. They walked up the hill and had a look at the concentration camp, its formidable stone enclosure now deserted. Gustav was curious to see the place from which the inmates of the death train had been turned away. Had he known that Fritz had spent three months here, and that it had nearly killed him, he might have regarded it in a different light.

They stayed in Mauthausen two days before moving on. Like Germany, Austria was divided into occupation zones, and on July 11, they crossed the "green border" for the first time, passing from the American into the Soviet zone. Gustav found the Russians "very courteous to us concentration camp survivors." He made friends with a Soviet officer who had fought at Stalingrad.

Weeks went by, and still he was in no mood to hurry home. Through the rest of July and August, he lingered in central Austria, and it was only when the summer began to wane that he finally steered his bicycle toward the final homeward leg.

On a day in September, Gustav Kleinmann entered Vienna. He saw the areas of devastation, the massive concrete flak towers looming over the pretty parks, and he saw all the familiar landmarks. The Karmelitermarkt was still there, and the apartment buildings of Im Werd overlooking it, and his old workshop on the first floor of number 11, under new occupancy now. He went into number 9, up to the second floor, and knocked on the door of Olly's apartment. And there she was, his dearest, truest friend, smiling at him in astonished joy, welcoming him home.

In the same building Gustav found the person he had most longed to see, living in an apartment he had been allowed to occupy until its owner returned—his boy, his Fritzl, his son, his companion, his pride and delight. Gustav enfolded his boy in his arms. Out of their shared hardship, out of their separation and suffering, out of the nightmare, of all the millions who had perished, blind fortune had played a large part in singling them out and preserving them, but it was solidarity, love, and faith that had got them through it and brought them safely home again.

Epilogue: Jewish Blood

Vienna, June 1954

An American GI stood by the west bank of the Danube Canal, looking across the water toward Leopoldstadt. He wore dress uniform, with the chevron of a private first class on his sleeve, below the division shoulder patch. He was a soldier of the 1st Infantry Division—the Big Red One, whose troops had been among the first to hit Omaha Beach on D-Day. This soldier was way too young to have been there on that day: he'd been just a schoolboy in 1944. Now he was grown tall and handsome, the very image of a United States soldier. He was stationed in Kitzingen, Bavaria, with the Allied occupying force, and had taken advantage of a one-week furlough to take a look at Vienna, the city where he'd been born.

It was familiar yet different. The city was bringing itself back to life, healing its wounds. Most of the bridges had been destroyed in the war, and even nine years on only a few had been rebuilt. The one before him, the Augartenbrücke, was one of them. It stood right by the boundary between the American zone—which covered the northwest city and suburbs—and the International sector in the city center. Across the canal, Leopoldstadt lay in the Soviet zone.

The GI approached the Soviet checkpoint and showed his identification. They waved him through, and Private First Class Kurt Kleinmann walked out across the broad bridge, under the shadow of the grand old Rossauer Kaserne, the Austrian military barracks where his parents had been married in 1917, toward the old Second District that had once been his home and his world.

Many of the familiar buildings were scarred, and some were covered in scaffolding, still under repair. But the place was all still recognizable, still as

317

fresh in his mind as the day he'd left. How his life had changed since then, and how it had changed him.

After high school, Kurt had gone to college in Providence, Rhode Island, to study pharmacy. He'd graduated in 1952, and after studying toward a degree in pharmacology at Ohio State in 1953, he'd been drafted into the army. He was a product of America as much as of Vienna now. His family was there—not only the Barnets, who had become family in all but name, but also his sister, who now lived in Connecticut. Edith and Richard had stayed in London for three years after the war, but in 1948, with sponsorship from Judge Barnet, they had finally made it to the United States, leaving England behind for good.

The Paltenhoffers adapted rapidly to American life. When they arrived, Peter and Joan—aged eight and six—had been English children with "Oxford accents" (according to the New Bedford paper), but that didn't last long. Determined to fit in, Richard and Edith had discarded the name Paltenhoffer and taken a new last name—Patten. For six years they lived in America as residents, but just last month, in May 1954, they had finally become United States citizens.[1]

Being drafted into the army had been the first step on the road leading Kurt back to the land of his birth for the first time since 1941. Although Germany had been partitioned and made nominally independent in 1949, Austria was still under occupation, and it showed. The country had suffered badly in the postwar years, with economic depression and bad harvests. The Soviet Union and the West played out their Cold War in the area, and lately there had been fears about all-out conflict breaking out as it had in Korea.

Kurt strolled along the Donaustrasse and up the Grosse Schiffgasse, surprised at how well he remembered it all. Then came the familiar turn right and left, and there it was. The Karmelitermarkt opened up before him, its stalls laid out in rows on the cobbles, the clock on its slender tower in the center, and the shops and apartment buildings of Leopoldsgasse and Im Werd on either side.

He was an alien here now. The sense of foreignness was almost palpable—he couldn't even speak the language anymore. His command of German had been gradually lost along the American journey to manhood. But paradoxically, he was an alien who had come home.

The old building at number 11 looked the same, but it wasn't home anymore. Instead Kurt entered the building next door, climbed the stairs to the second floor, and knocked on the door of Olga's apartment; the same one as all those years ago. And there was his father, older, more lined, with more gray in his hair, but still that same old smile on the lean face with its trim mustache. And there was Olga herself, loyal, wonderful Olly. She was Frau Kleinmann now, Kurt's stepmother.

Kurt visited many times during that summer. Sitting around the kitchen table, the four of them—Gustav and Olly, Kurt in his incongruous US Army uniform, together with Fritz—talked as best they could. As time passed, Kurt found that a little of his German came back: just enough to get by, but not enough for a proper conversation.

It was hard to recover the lost years. His father didn't want to talk about his time in the camps, and Kurt's relationship with Fritz wasn't what it had been. Raised an all-American boy in the postwar world, Kurt was dismayed by his brother's communist sympathies. Fritz had acquired his politics partly by inheritance from their father's prewar socialism, and partly in the camps from heroes like Robert Siewert and Stefan Heymann. Life as a worker in postwar Austria had confirmed him in his left-wing principles. There were also religious differences. None of the family aside from Kurt had ever been very devout in their Judaism, but Fritz had abandoned his religion entirely somewhere along the Auschwitz road.[2]

"No talk about politics or religion," decreed Gustav, and they stuck to safer subjects.

מִשְׁפָּחָה

On their return to Vienna in 1945, Gustav and Fritz had faced the problem of adjustment, not just to freedom but to the new world and their new circumstances within it.

Even finding somewhere to live was a challenge in the bomb-damaged, Soviet-controlled city, despite the reduction of its population by war, migration, and mass murder. Gustav stayed in Olly Steyskal's apartment, and remained there until he married her in 1948, the same year he managed to reestablish his upholstery business.

There was still anti-Semitism, but it had gone underground again, expressed in muttering and insinuation. Of the 183,000 Jews who had lived in Vienna in March 1938, more than two-thirds had managed to emigrate by November

1941: nearly 31,000 to Britain, 29,000 to the United States, 12,000 to South America, 21,000 to Asia and Australia, and just over 9,000 to Palestine. A further 21,647 had emigrated to European nations that had subsequently come under Nazi rule. Nearly all went to the camps, along with 43,421 Jews deported directly from Vienna to Auschwitz, Łodz, Theresienstadt, and Minsk between 1941 and 1944, and the uncounted thousands sent to Dachau and Buchenwald from 1938 to 1940.[3]

After the Shoah, Vienna still had a Jewish community, which gradually recovered its identity and held on to its heritage, but in scale it was a mere fragment of what it had been. The synagogues had been destroyed or stood in ruins, and only a few were ever restored. The Stadttempel in the ancient Jewish quarter, where Kurt Kleinmann had sung as a boy, and which had been gutted by stormtroopers on Kristallnacht, would eventually be restored in 1949, and the Israelitische Kultusgemeinde was revived in its traditional role at the center of Jewish cultural life.

By 1946 Fritz had managed to get an apartment in their old building, and he settled there briefly.[4] He was unable to work for the first few months due to poor health and lived on a disability pension. He and his father discussed at length what they should do about Kurt. Should they bring him home? Edith had her own family now, but Kurt was still only fifteen, and they missed him. But what was there for him here? His mother was dead, and his father aging and poor. They concluded that Kurt was better off where he was; the Barnets were good people, and rich, and he was happy in America. So Gustav and Fritz carried on together, supporting each other as they had for so many years.

One of the delights of those postwar years was their reunion with Alfred Wocher. The tough, courageous old German sergeant had survived the inferno of the last defense of the Reich and tracked down his old Auschwitz friends in Vienna. He visited them many times. "For us concentration camp inmates, Wocher had fulfilled more than his duty," Fritz recalled. "Through his conduct he gave us courage and faith, and thus contributed decisively to our surviving Auschwitz. Nobody rewarded him for it. We the survivors are indebted to him."

While his father tried to forget what he had seen and suffered in the camps (his diary had been more an aid to helping him survive it than an attempt to record it for posterity), and would only talk about it with reluctance, Fritz was of an entirely different disposition. He remembered it vividly and deliberately.

And he carried a burning detestation of the former Nazis who still lived in Vienna. He heard the mutterings around Im Werd—*See, the Kleinmann Jew is back again*—and while his father tried to live peacefully alongside the collaborators, Fritz wouldn't acknowledge their existence or speak to anyone who had sided with Nazis. They were mystified by this, and one of the neighbors who had betrayed them to the SS actually complained to Gustav, "Your son won't say hello to us!" Willful ignorance about the Shoah was such that this man couldn't grasp the evil of what he had done.

There were occasional reprisals against collaborators by younger Jewish men, and Fritz became involved. There was an Aryan neighbor, Sepp Leitner, who'd been a member of the 89th SS-Standarte "Holzweber," which had been based in Vienna and had taken part in the destruction of the synagogues on Kristallnacht. Fritz confronted Leitner and beat him up. He was arrested for it by the police, but the Soviet authorities, who approved of summary justice for fascists, ordered his release.

Fritz struggled to come to terms with what Austria had become; in Buchenwald he had listened to the Austrian *Prominenten* debate the future once the Nazis were defeated. They had conceived of Austria as a democratic socialist utopia, and Fritz had longed for that. But most of those men were dead now, and Austria was far from utopian. Things improved in 1955, when the occupying powers departed and Austria regained the independence it had lost in 1938, becoming a democracy again and resuming the constitutional system it had lost with the Austrofascist takeover in 1934.

After working for five years as a lathe operator for a company run by the USIA—the Soviet authority that controlled the Austrian and former German factories in their zone—Fritz took evening classes, and around 1956 joined his company's trade union. Fritz's family life was unsettled for a while; he had two marriages, from which came a son, Peter, and a stepson, Ernst. Gustav, meanwhile, was content to be back in his old trade and married to Olly. Immediately after returning to Vienna, he had considered leaving behind the painful memories altogether and had registered with the American Jewish Joint Distribution Committee, with a view to emigrating to the United States.[5] But it had come to nothing, and in 1947 the window of opportunity had closed. He would remain Viennese to the end of his days.

In 1964 Gustav retired, having carried on working to the ripe age of seventy-three. One of his last jobs was providing upholstery for the Austrian pavilion at that year's New York World's Fair. In 1966, he and Olly visited the United States. They stayed with Edith and Richard in Hartford, Connecticut, and spent time with Kurt and his wife, Diane. Although Gustav scarcely understood a word of English, he now had five all-American grandchildren and three great-grandchildren. He posed for photographs with the little ones on his knees, beaming contentedly, surrounded once more by love and family.

Gustav Kleinmann died on May 1, 1976, the day before his eighty-fifth birthday. He had been severely ill for some time, yet his prodigious inner strength had kept him going in his final days.

Two years later, Fritz, who was only in his mid-fifties, had to take early retirement; he had moved on from technical work and become first a time-and-motion officer and then a works estimator. But he couldn't sustain a working life. The torture he had endured in the Gestapo dungeon at Auschwitz had left him with permanent back injuries that, despite spinal operations, eventually caused partial paralysis. Nonetheless, Fritz Kleinmann had his father's toughness, and he lived a long life, passing away on January 20, 2009, aged eighty-five.

After the war ended, the victorious Allies convened a succession of trials against the perpetrators of the Shoah, including those at Nuremberg in 1945–6 and at Dachau in 1945–7. Many criminals were executed or imprisoned, and the concepts of *genocide* and *crimes against humanity* entered the statutes of international law.

But once those trials were over, shadows began to fall over the atrocities perpetrated by Nazi Germany—particularly within Germany itself. Those who had lived through it and had colluded with it either actively or passively tried to draw a veil over the past and forget it. By the end of the 1950s a young generation of Germans had been raised on a cushion of lies—that the Jews had mostly just emigrated, that there had been atrocities on all sides during the war, and that those committed by Germany had been no worse than those by the Allies. These young people knew almost nothing of the Holocaust, and the names of Auschwitz and Sobibor, Buchenwald and Belsen, were obscure or unknown to them. Most of the Nazi murderers remained free, many still living in Germany.

That changed in 1963, when the landmark Auschwitz trials began in Frankfurt. The man responsible was Fritz Bauer, a Jewish state attorney, who had himself been a political prisoner in a concentration camp. Bauer had helped trace Adolf Eichmann in Argentina, leading to his capture by Mossad. In Frankfurt, Bauer instituted proceedings against twenty-two former SS men accused of carrying out atrocities at Auschwitz. The witnesses who gave depositions for the Frankfurt trials included over two hundred surviving inmates, of whom ninety were Jews.[6] Among them were Gustav and Fritz Kleinmann, who were interviewed by the prosecutors in April and May 1963, giving written statements.[7] Their fellow witnesses included their old friends and comrades Stefan Heymann, Felix Rausch, and Gustl Herzog. Among those on trial were members of the camp Gestapo, Blockführers, and camp administration. Some were acquitted; others received sentences ranging from three years to life. More important than the individual sentences, the Frankfurt trials forced Germany's eyes open and ensured that the nation—and the world—would not forget the Holocaust, as did the trial of Eichmann in Jerusalem in 1961.

Fritz Kleinmann continued doing his part. In 1987 he was invited by a friend, the political scientist Reinhold Gärtner, to give a public talk about his experiences. The audience was a group about to set out on a study trip to Auschwitz-Birkenau—young and old, from various classes and political alignments. Fritz would be one of four survivors speaking over the course of two days. "For days before it, I could not sleep; the images from my concentration camp imprisonment welled up more intensely than ever before." The event—which included extracts from his father's diary read by a Viennese actor—moved Fritz profoundly, and overwhelmed the audience. He came back and gave his talk again and again to new parties for over a decade.

A few years after that first event, Fritz was persuaded by Reinhold to explore his memories further, by writing a memoir that was later published in a book.[8] Even after all the decades, Fritz still burned with indignation and anger about the atrocities visited on him and his people, but it was countered by the love he still felt for those who had helped him survive: Robert Siewert, Stefan Heymann, Leo Moses, and all the rest. He pored over the handful of old documents he had preserved. He still had the photograph of himself taken in 1939 for his J-Karte—the identity card stamp with a large red J, although he had destroyed the rest of the detested document immediately after returning home in 1945. And he still possessed the photograph taken of him in Buchenwald in 1940. There he was, glaring into the lens, wearing the loaned, ill-fitting suit and incongruous shaved scalp. His mother had kept the photo and passed it on to a relative before being deported to Maly Trostinets, perhaps guessing that she would not be coming back.

And there was the diary. His father had revealed its existence to him shortly after their reunion in Vienna in 1945. Turning back its dog-eared cover, there was the first page, yellowed, covered with his father's angular pencil strokes, fading now after all these years. "Arrived in Buchenwald on the 2nd October 1939 after a two-day train journey. From Weimar station we ran to the camp . . ." The vividness of the images seared Fritz's mind. The quarry, hauling the stone-laden wagon up the tracks—"*Left*–two–three! *Left*–two–three!"—the corpses in the mud, a man running between the sentries and dropping with a bullet in his back, bloody streaks across a man strapped to the Bock, hanging from the beam in the Gestapo bunker with his arms twisting out of their sockets, the weight of the Luger in his palm, the agonizing cold of the open car between Gleiwitz and Amstetten . . . and the poem, "Quarry Kaleidoscope," with its unforgettable central image:

> It rattles, the crusher, day out and day in,
> It rattles and rattles and breaks up the stone,
> Chews it to gravel and hour by hour
> Eats shovel by shovel in its guzzling maw.
> And those who feed it with toil and with care,
> They know it just eats, but will never be through.
> It first eats the stone and then eats them too.

But it hadn't crushed them all. A few, like the tall prisoner in the poem, had managed to outlast the machine, to keep going until the stone crusher clattered itself to a halt, malfunctioning, choked by its own appetite.

In the end the Kleinmann family not only survived but prospered; through courage, love, solidarity, and blind luck, they outlasted the people who had tried to destroy them. They and their descendants spread and multiplied, perpetuating through the generations the love and unity that had helped them through the darkest of times. They took their past with them, understanding that the living must gather the memories of the dead and carry them into the safety of the future.

Bibliography
and Sources

Interviews

Conducted by the author
Kurt Kleinmann: March–April 2016, July 2017
Peter Patten: April 2016, July 2017

Archived
Fritz Kleinmann: February 1997: interview 28129, Visual History Archive: University of Southern California Shoah Foundation Institute

Archive and Unpublished Sources

AFB   Findbüch for Victims of National Socialism, Austria: www.findbuch.at/en (retrieved February 21, 2017)

ABM   Archives of Auschwitz-Birkenau Museum, Oświęcim, Poland

AJJ   American Jewish Joint Distribution Committee Archives, New York

AWK   Testimonies from Kristallnacht: Wiener Library, London: available online at www.wienerlibrarycollections.co.uk/novemberpogrom/testimonies-and-reports/overview (retrieved February 19, 2017)

BWM   Belohnungakten des Weltkrieges 1914–1918: Mannschaftsbelohnungsanträge No 45348, Box 21: Austrian State Archives, Vienna

DFK   Letters, photographs, and documents from the archive of Fritz Kleinmann

DKK   Letters and documents in possession of Kurt Kleinmann

DOW   Dokumentationsarchiv des Österreichischen Widerstandes, Vienna: some records available online at www.doew.at/personensuche (retrieved April 14, 2017)

DPP   Documents and photographs in possession of Peter Patten

DRG   Documents and photographs in possession of Reinhold Gärtner

FDR   FDR Presidential Library, Hyde Park, New York

FTD   Records of the Frankfurt Auschwitz trials: Fritz Bauer Institut, Frankfurt am Main, Germany

GRO   Records of births, marriages, and deaths for England and Wales: General Register Office, Southport, UK

HOI   Home Office: Aliens Department: Internees Index, 1939–1947: HO 396: National Archives, Kew, London

IKA   Archiv der Israelitischen Kultusgemeinde, Vienna

ITS   Documents on victims of Nazi persecution: ITS Digital Archive: International Tracing Service, Bad Arolsen, Germany

LJL   Leeds Jewish Refugee Committee: case files: WYL5044/12: West Yorkshire Archive Service, Leeds, UK

LJW   Leeds Jewish Refugee Committee: correspondence and papers: Collection 599: Wiener Library, London

MTW   Maly Trostinec witness correspondence, 1962–67: World Jewish Congress Collection: Box C213-05: American Jewish Archives, Cincinnati

PGB   Prisoner record archive: KZ-Gedenkstätte Buchenwald, Weimar

PGD   Prisoner record archive: KZ-Gedenkstätte Dachau, Dachau

PGM   Prisoner record archive: KZ-Gedenkstätte Mauthausen Research Center, Vienna

PNY   Passenger Lists of Vessels Arriving at New York: Microfilm Publication M237, 675: National Archives and Records Administration, Washington, DC

TAE   Trial of Adolf Eichmann: District Court Sessions: State of Israel Ministry of Justice: available online at www.nizkor.org (retrieved March 19, 2016)

WLO   *Adolph Lehmanns Adressbuch*: Wienbibliothek Digital: www.digital.wienbibliothek.at/wbrobv/periodical/titleinfo/5311 (retrieved May 20, 2017)

YVP   Papers and documents: Yad Vashem, Jerusalem: some available online at www.yadvashem.org

YVS   Central Database of Shoah Victims' Names: Yad Vashem, Jerusalem: available online at yvng.yadvashem.org (retrieved April 14, 2017)

Books and Articles

Aarons, Mark. *War Criminals Welcome: Australia, a Sanctuary for Fugitive War Criminals Since 1945*. Melbourne: Black Inc, 2001.

Arad, Yitzhak, Israel Gutman, and Abraham Margaliot. *Documents on the Holocaust*, 8th ed. Translated by Lea Ben Dor. London and Jerusalem: University of Nebraska Press and Yad Vashem, 1999.

Bardgett, Suzanne, and David Cesarani, eds. *Belsen 1945: New Historical Perspectives*. London: Vallentine Mitchell, 2006.

Barton, Waltraud, ed. *Ermordet in Maly Trostinec: Die österreichischen Opfer der Shoa in Weißrussland*. Vienna: New Academic Press, 2012.

Bentwich, Norman. "The Destruction of the Jewish Community in Austria 1938–1942." In *The Jews of Austria*, edited by Josef Fraenkel, 467–78. London: Valentine, Mitchell, 1970.

Berkley, George E. *Vienna and Its Jews: The Tragedy of Success, 1880s–1980s*. Cambridge, MA: Abt Books, 1988.

Browning, Christopher. *The Origins of the Final Solution*. London: Arrow, 2005.

Burkitt, Nicholas Mark. *British Society and the Jews*. University of Exeter: PhD dissertation, 2011.

Cesarani, David. *Eichmann: His Life and Crimes*. London: Vintage, 2005.

Cesarani, David. *Final Solution: The Fate of the Jews 1933–49*. London: Macmillan, 2016.

Czech, Danuta. *Auschwitz Chronicle: 1939–1945*. London: I. B. Taurus, 1990.

Czeike, Felix. *Historisches Lexikon Wien*, 6 vols. Vienna: Kremayr & Scheriau, 1992–7.

Długoborski, Wacław, and Franciszek Piper, eds. *Auschwitz 1940–1945: Studien der Geschichte des Konzentrations- und Vernichtungslagers Auschwitz*, 5 vols. Oświęcim: Verlag des Staatlichen Museums Auschwitz-Birkenau, 1999.

Dobosiewicz, Stanisław. *Mauthausen-Gusen: Obóz zagłady*. Warsaw: Wydawn, 1977.

Dror, Michael. "News from the Archives." *Yad Vashem Jerusalem* 81 (October 2016): 22.

Dutch, Oswald. *Thus Died Austria*. London: E. Arnold, 1938.

Fein, Erich, and Karl Flanner. *Rot-Weiss-Rot in Buchenwald*. Vienna: Europaverlag, 1987.

Foreign Office (UK). *Papers Concerning the Treatment of German Nationals in Germany, 1938–1939*. London: HMSO, 1939.

Friedländer, Saul. *Nazi Germany and the Jews: vol. 1: The Years of Persecution, 1933–1939*. London: Weidenfeld and Nicolson, 1997.

Friedman, Saul S. *No Haven for the Oppressed: United States Policy Toward Jewish Refugees, 1938–1945*. Detroit: Wayne State University Press, 1973.

Frieser, Karl-Heinz. *The Eastern Front, 1943–1944*. Translated by Barry Smerin and Barbara Wilson. Oxford: Clarendon Press, 2017.

Gärtner, Reinhold, and Fritz Kleinmann. *Doch der Hund will nicht krepieren: Tagebuchnotizen aus Auschwitz*. Innsbruck: Innsbruck University Press, 2012.

Gedye, G. E. R. *Fallen Bastions: the Central European Tragedy*. London: Gollancz, 1939.

Gemeinesames Zentralnachweisbureau. *Nachrichten über Verwundete und Kranke Nr 190 ausgegeben am 6.1.1915; Nr 203 ausgegeben am 11.1.1915*. Vienna: k. k. Hof und Staatsdockerei, 1915.

Gerhardt, Uta, and Thomas Karlauf, eds. *The Night of Broken Glass: Eyewitness Accounts of Kristallnacht.* Translated by Robert Simmons and Nick Somers, 36–55. Cambridge: Polity Press, 2012.

Gerlach, Christian. *Kalkulierte Morde: Die deutsche Wirtschafts- und Vernichtungspolitik in Weißrußland 1941 bis 1944.* Hamburg: Hamburger Edition, 1999.

Gilbert, Martin. *The Holocaust: The Jewish Tragedy.* London: Collins, 1986.

Gilbert, Martin. *Auschwitz and the Allies.* London: Joseph, 1981.

Gilbert, Martin. *The Routledge Atlas of the Holocaust,* 3rd ed. London: Routledge, 2002.

Gillman, Peter, and Leni Gillman. *"Collar the Lot!" How Britain Interned and Expelled Its Wartime Refugees.* London: Quartet, 1980.

Gold, Hugo. *Geschichte der Juden in Wien: ein Gedenkbuch.* Tel Aviv: Olamenu, 1966.

Goltman, Pierre. *Six mois en enfer.* Paris: Éditions le Manuscrit.

Gottwaldt, Alfred, and Diana Schulle. *Die «Judendeportationen» aus dem Deutschen Reich 1941–1945.* Wiesbaden: Marixverlag, 2005.

Grenville, Anthony. "Anglo-Jewry and the Jewish refugees from Nazism." *Association of Jewish Refugees Journal* (December 2012). Available online at www.ajr.org.uk/index.cfm/section.journal/issue.Dec12/article=11572 (retrieved July 18, 2017).

Gutman, Yisrael, and Michael Berenbaum, eds. *Anatomy of the Auschwitz Death Camp.* Bloomington: Indiana University Press, 1994.

Hackett, David A., ed. and trans. *The Buchenwald Report.* Boulder, CO: Westview Press, 1995.

Haunschmied, Rudolf A., Jan-Ruth Mills, and Siegi Witzany-Durda. *St. Georgen - Gusen - Mauthausen: Concentration Camp Mauthausen Reconsidered.* Norderstedt: Books on Demand, 2007.

Hayes, Peter. *Industry and Ideology: IG Farben in the Nazi Era.* Cambridge: Cambridge University Press, 2001.

Hecht, Dieter J. "'Der König rief, und alle, alle kamen:' Jewish military chaplains on duty in the Austro-Hungarian army during World War I." *Jewish Culture and History* 17/3 (2016): 203–16.

Heimann-Jelinek, Felicitas, Lothar Hölbling, and Ingo Zechner. *Ordnung muss sein: Das Archiv der Israelitischen Kultusgemeinde Wien.* Vienna: Jüdisches Museum Wien, 2007.

Heller, Peter. "Preface to a Diary on the Internment of Refugees in England in the Year of 1940." In *Exile and Displacement,* edited by Lauren Levine Enzie, 163–79. New York: Peter Lang, 2001.

Horsky, Monika. *Man muß darüber reden. Schüler fragen KZ-Häftlinge.* Wien: Ephelant Verlag, 1988.

Jones, Nigel. *Countdown to Valkyrie: The July Plot to Assassinate Hitler*. London: Frontline, 2008.

Keegan, John. *The First World War*. London: Hutchinson, 1998.

Kershaw, Roger. "Collar the lot! Britain's policy of internment during the Second World War." UK National Archives Blog, July 2, 2015. blog.nationalarchives.gov.uk/blog /collar-lot-britains-policy-internment-second-world-war (retrieved July 18, 2017).

K.u.k. Kriegsministerium. *Verlustliste Nr 209 ausgegeben am 13.7.1915*. Vienna: k. k. Hof und Staatsdockerei, 1915.

K.u.k. Kriegsministerium. *Verlustliste Nr 244 ausgegeben am 21.8.1915*. Vienna: k. k. Hof und Staatsdockerei, 1915.

Kurzweil, Edith. *Nazi Laws and Jewish Lives*. London: Transaction, 2004.

Langbein, Hermann. *Against All Hope: Resistance in the Nazi Concentration Camps, 1938–1945*. Translated by Harry Zohn. London: Constable, 1994.

Langbein, Hermann. *People in Auschwitz*. Translated by Harry Zohn. Chapel Hill: University of North Carolina Press, 2004.

Le Chêne, Evelyn. *Mauthausen: The History of a Death Camp*. Bath: Chivers, 1971.

Levi, Primo. *Survival in Auschwitz and The Reawakening: Two Memoirs*. New York: Summit, 1986; previously publ. 1960, 1965.

Loewenberg, Peter. "The *Kristallnacht* as a Public Degradation Ritual." In *The Origins of the Holocaust*, edited by Michael Marrus, 582–96. London: Meckler, 1989.

London, Louise. *Whitehall and the Jews, 1933–1948: British Immigration Policy, Jewish Refugees and the Holocaust*. Cambridge: Cambridge University Press, 2000.

Lowenthal, Marvin. *The Jews of Germany*. London: L. Drummond, 1939.

Lucas, James. *Fighting Troops of the Austro-Hungarian Army, 1868–1914*. Tunbridge Wells: Spellmount, 1987.

Maier, Ruth. *Ruth Maier's Diary: A Young Girl's Life under Nazism*. Translated by Jamie Bulloch. London: Harvill Secker, 2009.

Mazzenga, Maria, ed. *American Religious Responses to Kristallnacht*. New York: Palgrave Macmillan, 2009.

Megargee, Geoffrey P., ed. *The United States Holocaust Memorial Museum Encyclopedia of Camps and Ghettos, 1933–1945*: 4 vols. Bloomington: Indiana University Press, 2009.

Pendas, Devin O. *The Frankfurt Auschwitz Trial, 1963–1965*. Cambridge: Cambridge University Press, 2006.

Phillips, Raymond. *Trial of Josef Kramer and Forty-Four Others: The Belsen Trial*. London: W. Hodge, 1949.

Plänkers, Tomas. *Ernst Federn: Vertreibung und Rückkehr. Interviews zur Geschichte Ernst Federns und der Psychoanalyse.* Tübingen: Diskord, 1994.

Pukrop, Marco. "Die SS-Karrieren von Dr. Wilhelm Berndt und Dr. Walter Döhrn. Ein Beitrag zu den unbekannten KZ-Ärzten der Vorkriegszeit." In *Werkstatt-Geschichte* 62 (2012): 76–93.

Rabinovici, Doron. *Eichmann's Jews: The Jewish Administration of Holocaust Vienna, 1938–1945.* Translated by Nick Somers. Cambridge: Polity Press, 2011.

Rees, Laurence. *The Holocaust: A New History.* London: Viking, 2017.

Rosenkranz, Herbert. "The Anschluss and the Tragedy of Austrian Jewry 1938–1945." In *The Jews of Austria*, edited by Josef Fraenkel, 479–545. London: Valentine, Mitchell, 1970.

Sagel-Grande, Irene, H. H. Fuchs, and C. F. Rüter. *Justiz und NS-Verbrechen: Sammlung Deutscher Strafurteile wegen Nationalsozialistischer Tötungsverbrechen 1945–1966: Band XIX.* Amsterdam: University Press Amsterdam, 1978.

Schindler, John R. *Fall of the Double Eagle: The Battle for Galicia and the Demise of Austria-Hungary.* Lincoln: University of Nebraska Press, 2015.

Silverman, Jerry. *The Undying Flame: Ballads and Songs of the Holocaust.* Syracuse, NY: Syracuse University Press, 2002.

Sington, Derrick. *Belsen Uncovered.* London: Duckworth, 1946.

Stein, Harry, compiler. *Buchenwald Concentration Camp 1937–1945.* Edited by Gedenkstätte Buchenwald. Göttingen: Wallstein Verlag, 2004.

Taylor, Melissa Jane. *"Experts in Misery"? American Consuls in Austria, Jewish Refugees and Restrictionist Immigration Policy, 1938–1941.* University of South Carolina: PhD Dissertation, 2006.

Teichova, Alice. "Banking in Austria." In *Handbook on the History of European Banks*, edited by Manfred Pohl. Aldershot: Edward Elgar, 1994.

Trimble, Lee, with Jeremy Dronfield. *Beyond the Call.* New York: Berkley, 2015.

van Pelt, Robert Jan, and Debórah Dwork. *Auschwitz: 1270 to the Present.* New Haven, CT: Yale University Press, 1996.

van Pelt, Robert Jan. *The Case for Auschwitz: Evidence from the Irving Trial.* Bloomington: Indiana University Press, 2016.

Wachsmann, Nikolaus. *KL: A History of the Nazi Concentration Camps.* London: Little, Brown, 2015.

Wagner, Bernd C. *IG Auschwitz: Zwangsarbeit und Vernichtung von Häftlingen des Lagers Monowitz 1941–1945.* Munich: K. G. Saur, 2000.

Wallner, Peter. *By Order of the Gestapo: A Record of Life in Dachau and Buchenwald Concentration Camps.* London: John Murray, 1941.

Walter, John. *Luger: The Story of the World's Most Famous Handgun.* Stroud: History Press, 2016.

Wasserstein, Bernard. *Britain and the Jews of Europe, 1939–1945,* 2nd ed. London: Leicester University Press, 1999.

Watson, Alexander. *Ring of Steel: Germany and Austria-Hungary at War, 1914–1918.* London: Penguin, 2014.

Weinzierl, Erika. "Christen und Juden nach der NS-Machtergreifung in Österreich." In *Anschluß 1938,* 175–205. Vienna: Verlag für Geschichte und Politik, 1981.

Werber, Jack, and William B. Helmreich. *Saving Children.* London: Transaction, 1996.

Wünschmann, Kim. *Before Auschwitz: Jewish Prisoners in the Prewar Concentration Camps.* Cambridge, MA: Harvard University Press, 2015.

Wyman, David S. *America and the Holocaust,* 13 vols. London: Garland, 1990.

Zalewski, Andrew. *Galician Portraits: In Search of Jewish Roots.* Jenkintown, PA: Thelzo Press, 2012.

Zucker, Bat-Ami. *In Search of Refuge: Jews and US Consuls in Nazi Germany, 1933–1941.* London: Vallentine Mitchell, 2001.

Acknowledgments

THIS BOOK COULD NOT HAVE BEEN WRITTEN without its primary source material—Gustav Kleinmann's concentration camp diary and Fritz Kleinmann's memoir, which came to me through Professor Reinhold Gärtner of University of Innsbruck. Reinhold helped Fritz publish both documents in the book *Doch der Hund will nicht krepieren* (Innsbruck University Press, 2012), and has provided indispensable cooperation in my initial research for this book, for which I thank him.

I am profoundly grateful to Kurt Kleinmann, who lived through the Anschluss and the Nazi occupation of Vienna, for the many hours of interviews and months of correspondence. Without Kurt's generous and tireless help, this tale would have been far less rich in depth and detail. Peter Patten, Gustav's grandson, has also very kindly contributed interviews and correspondence. I am grateful also to Rachel Schine, who helped put me in touch with the American branch of the family. The Austrian side of the family has also provided support. The encouragement of Peter Kleinmann, Victor Zehetbauer and his father, Ernst, as well as Richard Wilczek, has been indispensable.

A draft English translation of *Doch der Hund* prepared by John Rie was my first contact with this story and provided a vital foundation for creating my own translation of Gustav's diary and Fritz's memoir. For the preparation of the Hebrew section titles, I am grateful for the expert advice given by Keren Joseph-Browning.

Many archives and their archivists have provided me with guidance, documents, and images, and have patiently dealt with my queries. I am grateful to all of them. They include the Austrian State Archive, Vienna, for documents on Gustav Kleinmann's WWI record; Ewa Bazan, head of the Bureau for Former Prisoners at Auschwitz-Birkenau Memorial Museum; Douglas Ballman and Georgiana Gomez, access supervisor, University of Southern California

Shoah Foundation Institute for Visual History and Education, for providing a transcript of Fritz Kleinmann's 1997 interview and helping with photographs; Johannes Beermann, archivist, Fritz Bauer Institut, Goethe-Universität, Frankfurt am Main, for Fritz's and Gustav's witness statements from the Frankfurt Auschwitz trials; Cambridge University Library; Judy Farrar, archives and special collections librarian, Claire T. Carney Library, University of Massachusetts, Dartmouth, for information on Samuel Barnet; Harriet Harmer, archive assistant, West Yorkshire Archive Service, Leeds, UK, for documents on Edith Kleinmann and Richard Paltenhoffer; Elisa Ho, archivist and special projects coordinator, The Jacob Rader Marcus Center of the American Jewish Archives, Cincinnati, for documents on Maly Trostinets; Heike Müller, International Tracing Service, Bad Arolsen, Germany, for documents relating to the Kleinmanns' incarceration in various concentration camps; Katharina Kniefacz, KZ-Gedenkstätte Mauthausen Research Center, Vienna, for prisoner records on Fritz Kleinmann; Albert Knoll, archivist, KZ-Gedenkstätte Dachau, for information on Richard Paltenhoffer; Kimberly Kwan, volunteer, Gedenkstätte Buchenwald, for information on the Kleinmanns and Richard Paltenhoffer; Susanne Uslu-Pauer, head of department, Archive of the Israelitische Kultusgemeinde, Vienna; and the Wiener Library, London.

Finally, I am grateful to my literary agent, Andrew Lownie, for first bringing the Kleinmann story to my attention, and to Yuval Taylor of Chicago Review Press, for believing in the book and bringing his enthusiasm to the project. As ever, my partner, Kate, has provided the constant, patient moral support that has sustained me through every book I have ever written.

—*Jeremy Dronfield, December 2017*

Notes

Prologue

1. Moon phase data from www.timeanddate.com/moon/austria/amstetten ?month=1&year=1945.

Chapter 1: "When Jewish Blood Drips from the Knife . . ."

1. One occasion was in 1926, when Gustav was forced to come to a legal agreement to repay his creditor in installments (*Wiener Zeitung*, September 12, 1926, p. 14; October 3, 1926, p. 1). The debt was held jointly with his brother-in-law and fellow upholsterer, Rudolf Popper, who was married to Tini's elder sister, Charlotte.

2. Due to shifting borders, Gustav's home village of Zabłocie has at various times been in Silesia, but in his childhood it was in Galicia.

3. *Im Werd* means "in the island" in Middle High German. The island is the land between the Danube Canal and the river Danube, Vienna's Second District, Leopoldstadt, historically a center of Jewish settlement.

4. Printed in *Die Stimme*, March 11, 1938, p. 1; see also Gedye, *Fallen Bastions*, pp. 287–9 for an eyewitness account of events in Vienna that day.

5. Austria already had a form of Fascism in place; Schuschnigg's Fatherland Front ruled repressively, suppressing not only the Nazi Party but also the Social Democrats and workers' movements. However, it was not especially anti-Semitic. Estimates of the number of Jews in Austria vary; Gilbert (*Routledge Atlas of the Holocaust*, p. 22) gives it as 183,000, while Bentwich ("Destruction," p. 467) places it at 191,000, based on the 1934 census.

6. *TIME* cover story, March 21, 1938.

7. *Die Stimme*, March 11, 1938, p. 1. The notion of being "German" was about language and culture and had existed long before the country called Germany, created in 1871 from a cluster of independent kingdoms and duchies that did not include the German regions that were part of the Austro-Hungarian Empire. The newly unified state became the German Empire, which in 1918 became a republic.

8. Some people of Jewish descent considered themselves entirely German; Peter Wallner, a Viennese, stated, "nor was I ever a Jew, though all four of my grandparents were Jewish." But when the Nazis came he was persecuted with the rest; "For according to the Nuremberg Laws I am a Jew" (Wallner, *By Order*, pp. 17–18). Under the Nuremberg Laws of 1935 a person was defined as Jewish, regardless of religion, if they had more than two Jewish grandparents.

9. Fritz Kleinmann recalls this in his 1997 interview, and remarks that his father kept his politics out of family life, especially after 1934.

10. *Die Stimme*, March 11, 1938, p. 1.

11. *Jüdische Presse*, March 11, 1938, p. 1. For both Jewish papers, that day's edition would be the last they would ever print.

12. The scenes in the streets on this day are described by George Gedye (*Fallen Bastions*, pp. 287–96), a British journalist for the *Daily Telegraph* and *New York Times* who lived in Vienna. The Austrian Youth (Österreichisches Jungvolk) was the youth arm of Schuschnigg's Fatherland Front party. In 1938 it had about 350,000 members.

13. For this reason, Schuschnigg had cynically set the minimum age for voting in the plebiscite at twenty-four; most Nazis were below that age.

14. *The Times*, March 11, 1938, p. 14; also *Neues Wiener Tagblatt (Tages-Ausgabe)*, March 11, 1938, p. 1.

15. Gedye (*Fallen Bastions*, pp. 290–3) describes the scenes as the evening progressed.

16. Gedye, *Fallen Bastions*, p. 290; *The Times*, March 12, 1938, p. 12.

17. Quoted in Gedye, *Fallen Bastions*, pp. 10, 293, and *The Times*, March 12, 1938, p. 12. According to *The Times*, newspapers in Berlin that evening claimed that Germany had quashed "treason" by the "Marxist rats" in the Austrian government who had been carrying out "harrowing cruelties" against the people, who were fleeing to the German border in large numbers. With these untruths the Nazis justified their move to take over Austria.

18. The synagogue that evening is described as *"überfüllt"*—overcrowded, jam-packed (Gold, *Geschichte*, p. 77). According to Gold the venue was the synagogue in Tempelgasse in the Second District, but Weinzierl ("Christen und Juden," pp. 197–8) states that it was the Stadttempel.

19. Gedye, *Fallen Bastions*, p. 295.

20. Ibid. The hostility to Catholics (and to some Protestant churches) stemmed from a long-standing antagonism over issues such as Nazi attempts to suppress the Old Testament and de-Judaize Christianity, as well as the churches' recognition of non-Aryan Christian converts and the Vatican's condemnation of racism, plus continued interaction between Aryans and Jews in Catholic regions of Germany (Cesarani, *Final Solution*, pp. 114–6, 136).

21. Quoted in Cesarani, *Final Solution*, p. 148.

22. Dutch, *Thus Died Austria*, pp. 231–2; see also *Neues Wiener Tagblatt (Tages Ausgabe)*, March 12, 1938, p. 3; *Banater Deutsche Zeitung*, March 13, 1938, p. 5; *The Times*, March 14, 1938, p. 14.

23. *Neues Wiener Tagblatt (Tages Ausgabe)*, March 12, 1938, p. 3.

24. Gedye, *Fallen Bastions*, p. 282.

25. *Arbeitersturm*, March 13, 1938, p. 5; *The Times*, April 17, 1938, p. 14.

26. It isn't certain which police station this was. The most likely is Leopoldsgasse, a station of the Schutzpolizei Gruppenkommando Ost, the uniformed Reich police (*Reichsamter und Reichsbehörden in der Ostmark*, p. 207, AFB).

27. Based on Fritz Kleinmann's memoir; also testimony of Kurt Kleinmann and Edith's son Peter Patten; additional details from various contemporary sources.

28. Evidence of Moritz Fleischmann, vol. 1, session 17, TAE; Berkley, *Vienna*, p. 259; Lowenthal, *Jews of Germany*, p. 430; see also *The Times*, March 31, 1938, p. 13; April 7, 1938, p.13.

29. Gedye, *Fallen Bastions*, p. 354.

30. *The Times*, April 8, 1938, p. 12; April 11, 1938, p. 11; also Gedye, *Fallen Bastions*, p. 9.

31. *The Times*, April 11, 1938, p. 12. Even the ballot paper itself was a work of propaganda, with a big circle in the center for yes and a little one off to the side for no.

32. *The Times*, April 12, 1938, p. 14.

33. *The Times*, April 9, 1938, p. 11.

34. *The Times*, March 23, 1938, p. 13; March 26, 1938, p. 11; April 30, 1938, p. 11.

35. Bentwich, "Destruction," p. 470.

36. Ibid.; Rosenkranz, "Anschluss," p. 484.

37. Concentration camps had been a part of the Nazi regime since 1933. Dachau, established in a disused factory, was the first dedicated concentration camp. By summer 1938 there were four major operational camps in Germany (plus some smaller ones): Dachau, Buchenwald, Sachsenhausen, and Flossenbürg, with several more opened shortly after, including Mauthausen in Austria, which opened in August 1938 (see Wachsmann, *KL*; Cesarani, *Final Solution*; Rees, *The Holocaust*). It was initially to Dachau and Buchenwald that the Jews of Vienna were sent.

38. Reich Ministry of the Interior regulations, August 17, 1938, in Arad et al. *Documents*, pp. 98–99.

39. Testimony B.306, AWK.

40. One Jewish witness said: "During August in general people still went to cafés and cinemas, and in September it appeared as if the Jewish question had been forgotten, even swastikas disappeared" (testimony B.95, AWK).

41. This was the story according to the Brussels correspondent for *The Times* (October 27, 1938, p. 13). Associated Press via the *Chicago Tribune* (October 27, 1938, p. 15) added the detail about the camera and increased the number of Nazis involved

to four, and added the anonymous claim that the Nazis had been knocked down and kicked.

42. *Neues Wiener Tagblatt*, October 26, 1938, p. 1.
43. *Völkischer Beobachter*, October 26, 1938, p. 1, quoted in Marrus, *Origins*, p. 585.
44. *Neues Wiener Tagblatt*, November 8, 1938, p. 1.
45. "Night of broken glass" is the usual translation, but "crystal" is more accurate.
46. Telegram from Reinhard Heydrich to all police headquarters, November 10, 1938, in Arad et al., *Documents*, pp. 102–4.
47. UK Consul-General in Vienna, letter, November 11, 1938, in Foreign Office, *Papers*, p. 16.

Chapter 2: Traitors to the People

1. The Polizeiamt Leopoldstadt, headquarters of the local uniformed police, was at Ausstellungsstrasse 171 (*Reichsamter und Reichsbehörden in der Ostmark*, p. 204, AFB).
2. Memoir of Fritz Kleinmann in Gärtner and Kleinmann, *Doch der Hund*, p. 188; additional details: witness testimonies B.24 (anon.), B.62 (Alfred Schechter), B.143 (Carl Löwenstein), AWK; also: testimonies of Siegfried Merecki (Manuscript 166 (156)), Margarete Neff (Manuscript 93 (205)) in Gerhardt and Karlauf, *Night of Broken Glass*; Wallner, *By Order of the Gestapo*.
3. UK Consul-General in Vienna, letter, November 11, 1938, in Foreign Office, *Papers*, p. 16.
4. The exact number of documented arrests is 6,547 (Taylor, *"Experts in Misery"?*, p. 48).
5. B.62 (Alfred Schechter), AWK. At this time, Mauthausen camp was for convicts; Jews were not imprisoned there prior to the war, but it was believed at the time that they were (e.g. *The Scotsman*, November 14, 1938; cf. Wünschmann, *Before Auschwitz*, p. 183).
6. B.143 (Carl Löwenstein), AWK.
7. *New York Times*, November 15, 26, 1938, p. 1.
8. Quoted in Swiss *National Zeitung*, November 16, 1938.
9. Quoted by Kyle Jantzen in Mazzenga, *American Religious Responses*, p. 44.
10. *Spectator*, November 18, 1938, p. 836.
11. *Westdeutscher Beobachter* (Cologne), November 11, 1938.
12. Ibid.
13. Unnamed German newspaper, quoted by UK Consul-General in Vienna, November 11, 1938, in Foreign Office, *Papers*, p. 15.
14. Cesarani, *Final Solution*, p. 199.
15. *Spectator*, November 18, 1938, p. 836.

16. Cesarani, *Eichmann*, p. 60ff. It was a position of enormous authority for a mere *Untersturmführer* (second lieutenant). Eichmann had only just been commissioned, having acquired his expertise with the SD while only a clerical NCO. In June he was promoted to *Obersturmführer* (first lieutenant).

17. Quoted in Cesarani, *Final Solution*, p. 207.

18. Rabinovici, *Eichmann's Jews*; Cesarani, *Final Solution*, p. 147ff.

19. Évian invitation, quoted in Friedländer, *Nazi Germany and the Jews*, p. 248.

20. *Spectator*, July 29, 1938, p. 189.

21. Ibid., p. 190.

22. *Spectator*, August 19, 1938, p. 294.

23. *Neues Wiener Tagblatt*, November 16, 1938, p. 2.

24. Adolf Hitler, speech to the Reichstag, January 30, 1939, quoted in *The Times*, January 31, 1939, p. 14; also in Arad et al., *Documents*, p. 132.

25. *Chicago Tribune*, November 21, 1938, p. 2.

26. *Chicago Tribune*, November 20, 1938, p. 3.

27. *Daily Telegraph*, November 22, 1938; also House of Commons *Hansard*, November 21, 1938, vol. 341, cc1428–83.

28. Testimony B.226, AWK.

29. *The Times*, December 3–12, 1938.

30. Fritz Kleinmann, 1997 interview.

31. *Manchester Guardian*, December 15, p. 11; March 18, p. 18.

32. Letter from Leeds JRC to Overseas Settlement Dept., JRC, London, June 7, 1940, LJL. From whom the affidavits came isn't known; the Kleinmanns had several relatives and friends in New York, New Jersey, and Massachusetts (see later chapters).

33. *The Times*, classified ads, 1938–9 *passim*.

34. London, *Whitehall*, p. 79.

35. *The Times*, November 8, 1938, p. 4.

36. It isn't clear what the connection was. In his 1997 interview, Fritz Kleinmann is vague about it: The contact was "*man von einem Burschen in unserem Haus.*"

37. The system could only cope with investigating a limited number of applicants; women applying to be servants were easier to vet than men, and so over half of the Jews entering Britain in 1938–9 were women (Cesarani, *Final Solution*, p. 158). Britain's Home Office expedited the process by having Jewish refugee agencies process the applications, which increased the rate to four hundred a week (ibid., p. 214).

38. Letter from British Consul-General, November 11, 1938, in Foreign Office, *Papers*, p. 15.

39. This building, at Wallnerstrasse 8, now houses the Vienna Stock Exchange.

40. Maier, *Ruth Maier's Diary*, p. 110.

41. M. Mitzmann, "A Visit To Germany, Austria and Poland in 1939," document 0.2/151, YVP.
42. Ibid.
43. This is the probable reason. He states (in *Doch der Hund*, p. 70, and in unpublished notes) that his *Kennkarte* was issued in August 1939; for unknown reasons, the place of issue was Schwechat, a town on the outskirts of Vienna.
44. Stein, *Buchenwald*, pp. 115-6; Gärtner and Kleinmann, *Doch der Hund*, pp. 80-1.
45. Fritz recalled (1997 interview) that the third man was called Schwarz, although no record has been found of a person of that name living in Im Werd 11. Fritz was unable to recall the name of the fourth member of the group (the building's Nazi leader).
46. The dialog here is from interviews given by Fritz and Kurt Kleinmann. They both recalled these scenes quite vividly.
47. Buchenwald personal record card 1.1.5.3/6283389, ITS.

Chapter 3: Blood and Stone: Konzentrationslager Buchenwald

1. This account is based primarily on Gustav Kleinmann's diary and Fritz's recollections, with additional circumstantial details from other sources (e.g., Werber, *Saving Children*, pp. 1-3, 32-6; Stein, *Buchenwald*, pp. 115-6; testimonies B.82, B.192, B.203, AWK).
2. Fritz Kleinmann (in *Doch der Hund*, p. 12) gives a figure of 1,048 Viennese Jews in this transport, but other sources (Stein, *Buchenwald*, p. 116) give 1,035.
3. Stein, *Buchenwald*, pp. 27-8.
4. The camp was intended to be called Konzentrationslager Ettersberg, but strident local objections to this appropriation of the cultural history of the place made Himmler relent and name it Buchenwald instead.
5. See e.g. testimony B.203, AWK.
6. KZ Buchenwald (its remains now preserved as a memorial) is 8.1 kilometers (5 miles) from Weimar train station. In October 1939 it was still in its initial expansion phase, having begun in July 1937.
7. Gärtner and Kleinmann, *Doch der Hund*, p. 15n.
8. Stein, *Buchenwald*, p. 35.
9. Buchenwald personal record cards 1.1.5.3/6283389, 1.1.5.3/6283376, ITS. There were no tattoos; this practice began at Auschwitz in November 1941 and was not employed at any other camps (Wachsmann, *KL*, p. 284).
10. Werber, *Saving Children*, p. 36.
11. Testimony B.192, AWK.
12. Protective custody, *Schutzhaft*, had been introduced in Germany in February 1933 (a month after Hitler came to power). *Schutzhäftlinge* were political prisoners.

The basic concentration camp badge was an inverted triangle, the color of which denoted a category: red for political prisoners, green for criminals, pink for homosexuals, black for "asocials" (the disabled, addicts, Roma, pacifists, etc.), and purple for Jehovah's Witnesses. For Jewish prisoners the category badge was combined with a second, yellow, triangle, making up a Star of David; if the Jewish prisoner didn't fit into any of the other categories, both triangles were yellow.

13. Emil Carlebach, in Hackett, *Buchenwald Report*, pp. 162–3.

14. This is not the same as the "little camp" set up in 1943 to the north of the barracks (Stein, *Buchenwald*, pp. 149–51). There is a detailed description of the original little camp in 1939–40 by inmate Felix Rausch in Hackett, *Buchenwald Report*, pp. 271–6.

15. Hackett, *Buchenwald Report*, pp. 113–4. Following *Kristallnacht*, new arrivals totaled 10,098. However, the camp population actually decreased thereafter, with over 9,000 departures due to release, transfer, or death (about 2,000 deaths in total in 1938–9, not including those who died between Weimar and the camp; ibid., p. 109). The prisoner population of Buchenwald declined steeply from 1938–9, exploding again with the autumn 1939 intake (8,707 during September–October).

16. Gustav never revealed how he kept his diary hidden. Fritz wrote many years later: "I know that my father risked his life with this diary. None of the other prisoners had encouraged him to do this, as he was putting not only himself but all of us at risk. And even today, questions remain unanswered: Where did my father hide the diary? How did he get it through the controls? . . . My father neither wished nor was able to burden me or the other prisoners with this knowledge" (*Doch der Hund*, pp. 12–13). However, Gustav did reveal that at one point, when he was a room orderly in his barrack block, he hid it inside the bunks, and when he was on outdoor work details he generally carried it on his person (Fritz Kleinmann, 1997 interview).

17. This account is based primarily on Gustav Kleinmann's diary and Fritz's recollections, with additional circumstantial details from other sources (e.g. Hackett, *Buchenwald Report*; Stein, *Buchenwald*; testimony B.192, AWK).

18. The *kapo* system was invented in the early days of Dachau. In Himmler's words, the *kapo*'s task "is to see that the work gets done . . . As soon as we are no longer satisfied with him, he is no longer a kapo and returns to the other inmates. He knows that they will beat him to death his first night back" (quoted in Rees, *Holocaust*, p. 79).

19. The word used by Gustav for their assignment is *Lorefahrer*. A *Lore* was a dump wagon used for hauling stone from the quarry (Stein, *Buchenwald*, p. 96). The weight of the wagon is estimated as follows: 4.9 short tons (US) = 4.4 long tons = 4.5 metric tonnes. Based on size of wagon and density of broken limestone = 1,554 kg/m^3. Different sources give the number of men assigned to pull each wagon as between sixteen and twenty-six.

20. Gustav refers to this place as the *Todes-Holzbaracke* (death barrack), probably a nickname for a building used for sick Jews after they were barred from the prisoners' infirmary (block 2, in the southwest corner of the camp facing onto the roll-call square) in September 1939 (see Emil Carlebach in Hackett, *Buchenwald Report*, p. 162).

21. Stein, *Buchenwald*, p. 96.

22. Stefan Heymann in Hackett, *Buchenwald Report*, p. 253.

23. The putsch (coup) began on November 8, 1923, when Hitler and his followers crashed a meeting of the Bavarian State Commissioner in the Bürgerbräukeller. The next day they marched through Munich; they were shot at by police, and sixteen were killed. Hitler was imprisoned for treason, with a very lenient sentence from a sympathetic judge. While in prison, he wrote *Mein Kampf*.

24. Jones, *Countdown*, pp. 103–5.

25. Hitler, who saw it as an opportunity for war propaganda, alleged that the plot had been concocted with the cooperation of British intelligence agents. Georg Elser was eventually murdered in Dachau in April 1945.

26. Wachsmann, *KL*, p. 220.

27. Hackett, *Buchenwald Report*, p. 51; Stein, *Buchenwald*, p. 119.

28. Hackett, *Buchenwald Report*, pp. 231, 252–3; Wachsmann, *KL*, p. 220.

29. Fritz Kleinmann, quoted in Horsky, *Man muß darüber reden*, pp. 48–9, reproduced in Gärtner and Kleinmann, *Doch der Hund*, p. 16n.

30. Stein, *Buchenwald*, pp. 52, 108–9; Testimony B.192, AWK.

31. Born in 1914, Paul Heller had qualified not long before his arrest. He later served as a doctor in Auschwitz. He survived the Holocaust and immigrated to the United States. "He was a very decent man. If he could help a person, he would," recalled one of his fellow prisoners (obituary, *Chicago Tribune*, September 29, 2001).

32. Burkett, *Buchenwald Report*, pp. 60–4.

33. Prisoner Walter Poller, quoted in Pukrop, "Die SS-Karrieren von Dr. Wilhelm Berndt," p. 79.

34. In his account of this episode (*Doch der Hund*, p. 48), Fritz seems to imply that his "weeping and desperate" (*weinender und verzweifelter*) voice was an act.

35. Gustav's diary is hard to interpret here: "*[Am] nächsten Tag kriege [ich] einen Posten als Reiniger im Klosett, habe 4 Öfen zu heizen . . .*" The *Klosett* might have been the latrine in the little camp, or perhaps in the main camp barrack blocks, which had earlier been out of order due to a water shortage (Stein, *Buchenwald*, p. 86). The *Öfen* (ovens or furnaces) are harder to pinpoint; most likely they were part of the kitchens or the shower block. They were not crematorium ovens, which Buchenwald did not acquire until summer 1942 (ibid., p. 141).

36. Gärtner and Kleinmann, *Doch der Hund*, pp. 47, 49. Fritz gives his height at this time as 145 cm (about 4 feet 9 inches). But in the 1938 family photograph, when he was fourteen, he is measurably only slightly shorter than the adult Edith (who

was 5 feet 2 inches according to her passport: DPP). He must have grown a little in the following eighteen months, so must have been over five feet tall (over 152 cm) by late 1939.

Chapter 4: The Stone Crusher

1. Note of employment, undated, LJL; England and Wales census, 1911; description and details in passenger list, SS *Carinthia*, October 2, 1936, PNY; General Register Office 1939 Register, National Archives, Kew, London. Morris and Rebecca Brostoff were born in Białystok (now in Poland) around 1878 and immigrated to Britain prior to 1911. In 1939 they lived at 373 Street Lane.
2. Record card 46/01063-4, HOI. No record card for Richard Paltenhoffer from this time has been found, but he was presumably also put in Category C at this time.
3. Wachsmann, *KL*, pp. 147–51; Cesarani, *Final Solution*, pp. 164-5; Wünschmann, *Before Auschwitz*, p. 186.
4. Arriving in Dachau on June 24, 1938, Richard Paltenhoffer was prisoner number 16865 (prisoner records, PGD). He was transferred to Buchenwald on September 23, 1938, where he was assigned prisoner number 9520 and placed first in block 16, then block 14 (prisoner record, PGB).
5. Wachsmann, *KL*, pp. 181–4.
6. Ibid., p. 186.
7. A. R. Samuel, letter to David Makovski, May 25, 1939, LJW; marriage certificate, GRO; Motague Burton, letter to D. Makovski, February 26, 1940, LJL; Burkitt, *British Society*, p. 108. The company was Rakusen Ltd, which still exists. Richard's first lodgings were at 9 Brunswick Terrace. There was no universal health care in the UK until 1948.
8. Biographical history, LJW; Grenville, "Anglo-Jewry."
9. B. Neuwirth, letter to Richard Paltenhoffer, February 16, 1940; Control Committee, letter to Registrar of Marriages, February 20, 1940, LJL.
10. Gustav recorded all these imprecations in his poem, "Quarry Kaleidoscope" (see later in this chapter).
11. Altogether, 1,235 prisoners died in Buchenwald in 1939, the majority of them in the last quarter of the year (Hackett, *Buchenwald Report*, p. 114).
12. The sequence of events at this period (including the precise assignments to barracks) differs somewhat between Gustav's diary and Fritz's recollections. The account given here reconciles the two.
13. The Goethe Oak was damaged by an Allied bomb in 1944 and was felled. However, its stump is still there.
14. Fritz Kleinmann, 1997 interview. Jewishness in itself was not sufficient cause to be sent to the camps until much later; at this time, the Nazi regime was focused

on forcing Jews to emigrate, including those being held in the camps, who were released if they obtained the necessary emigration papers.

15. From "Quarry Kaleidoscope" by Gustav Kleinmann. I have translated Gustav's German as faithfully as possible:

> Klick-klack Hammerschlag,
> klick-klack Jammertag.
> Sklavenseelen, Elendsknochen,
> dalli und den Stein gebrochen.

16. Gustav's original:

> Klick-klack Hammerschlag,
> klick-klack Jammertag.
> Sieh nur diesen Jammerlappen
> winselnd um die Steine tappen.

17. Gustav and Fritz both record Herzog's first name as "Hans" but according to Stein (Buchenwald, p. 299) it was Johann. For other eyewitness accounts of Herzog's character and behavior, see statements given in Hackett, Buchenwald Report, pp. 159, 174–5, 234. Although rumored to have later been murdered by a former prisoner, Herzog went on to have a long criminal career.

18. Gustav's original:

> Klatsch – er liegt auf allen Vieren,
> doch der Hund will nicht krepieren!

19. Gustav's original is much more perfectly structured than my translation:

> Es rattert der Brecher tagaus und tagein,
> er rattert und rattert und bricht das Gestein,
> zermalt es zu Schotter und Stunde auf Stund'
> frißt Schaufel um Schaufel sein gieriger Mund.
> Und die, die ihn füttern mit Müh und mit Fleiß,
> sie wissen er frißt nur – doch satt wird er nie.
> Erst frißt er die Steine und dann frißt er sie.

Chapter 5: The Road to Life

1. Kurzweil, Nazi Laws, p. 153.
2. Report in Arad, Documents, pp. 143–4.
3. Rabinovici, Eichmann's Jews, p. 87ff.
4. Fritz and Gustav never understood where Tini got the money from, as she wasn't allowed to work. In fact she did get occasional jobs (letters to Kurt, 1941, DKK), and otherwise presumably depended on charity and better-off relatives.

5. Passenger list, SS *Veendam*, January 24, 1940, PNY; United States census, 1940, NARA. Bettina's mother, Netti, who was Hungarian-born, appears to have been a sister of Tini's mother, Eva née Schwarz (Bettina Bienenwald, birth record, October 20, 1899, Geburtsbuch and Geburtsanziegen, IKA).

6. Transport list, Vienna/Nisko, October 10, 1939, DOW.

7. Alfred Bienenwald, US passport application, 1919, NARA. Bettina and Alfred were born illegitimately, their father being Emmanuel Bienenwald from Lemberg (a.k.a. Lwów, Lviv).

8. United States census, 1940, NARA.

9. US State Department memo, June 26, 1940, in Wyman, *America and the Holocaust*, vol. 4, p. 1; also ibid., p. v.

10. Bertha Rothenstein birth record, April 29, 1887, Geburtsbuch, IKA; *Lehmann's Adressbuch* for Vienna for 1938, WLO; casualty reports, *Illustrierte Kronen Zeitung*, June 4, 1915, p. 6; K.u.k. Kriegsministerium, *Verlustliste 209*, p. 54.

11. Gärtner and Kleinmann, *Doch der Hund*, p. 69; Buchenwald personal record card 1.1.5.3/6283376, ITS. For consistency, Jeanette's surname is spelled *Rottenstein* here. In fact it was always spelled Rothenstein, whereas Tini's was Rottenstein. Jeanette was born in 1890 (Jeanette Rothenstein birth record, July 13, 1890, Geburtsbuch, IKA).

12. Fritz transferred into the garden detail on April 5, 1940 (prisoner record card, 1.1.5.3/6283377, ITS).

13. Hackmann was appointed adjutant in 1939 and served until 1941 (Stein, *Buchenwald*, pp. 44–5, 307; Hackett, *Buchenwald Report*, p. 34). His first name is variously given as Hermann and Heinrich. He was later convicted by the SS for embezzlement.

14. Fritz (*Doch der Hund*, p. 50) refers to Oranienburg and Lichtenburg as if they were a single camp. In fact, the former was north of Berlin and the latter was between Berlin and Dresden. Oranienburg closed in 1934—presumably occasioning Moses's transfer to Lichtenburg, which became an all-women's camp in 1937 and closed altogether in 1939 (Wachsmann, *KL*, pp. 38–88).

15. Gustav Herzog was born in Vienna, January 12, 1908 (entry for Gustav Herzog, 68485, AMP).

16. Wünschmann, *Before Auschwitz*, p. 220.

17. Stefan Heymann was born in Mannheim, Germany, March 14, 1896 (entry for Stefan Heymann, 68488, AMP).

18. Anton Makarenko, *Road to Life: An Epic of Education (A Pedagogical Poem)*, vol. 2, ch. 1. Translation available online at www.marxistsfr.org/reference/archive/makarenko/works/road2/ch01.html (retrieved May 2, 2017).

19. Fritz Kleinmann, in Gärtner and Kleinmann, *Doch der Hund*, p. 54.

20. Hackett, *Buchenwald Report*, pp. 42, 336; Gärtner and Kleinmann, *Doch der Hund*, p. 55.
21. Stein, *Buchenwald* (German edition), p. 78.
22. Stein, *Buchenwald*, pp. 78–9.
23. Ibid., p. 90.
24. Gärtner and Kleinmann, *Doch der Hund*, p. 57. Schmidt's general temperament and habits are documented by many witnesses quoted in Hackett, *Buchenwald Report*.

Chapter 6: A Favorable Decision

1. Gillman, *Collar the Lot*, pp. 78–9. The term "fifth column" originated during the Spanish Civil War (1936–39), when a general told the press that he had four columns of troops plus a "fifth column" within the enemy camp.
2. Kershaw, "Collar the lot."
3. Gillman, *Collar the Lot*, p. 153; Kershaw, "Collar the lot."
4. Gillman, *Collar the Lot*, pp. 167ff, 173ff; Kershaw, "Collar the lot."
5. Winston Churchill, House of Commons, June 4, 1940, *Hansard* vol. 364 c. 794.
6. Wasserstein, *Britain and the Jews*, p. 108.
7. Quoted in Wasserstein, *Britain and the Jews*, p. 83.
8. The address was 15 Reginald Terrace (various letters, LJL). At the time of their marriage, Richard had had lodgings at number 4 (marriage certificate, GRO). The Victorian houses in Reginald Terrace were demolished in the 1980s.
9. Leeds JRC, letter to Home Office, March 18, 1940, LJL. Mrs. Green lived at 57 St. Martin's Garden.
10. Wasserstein, *Britain and the Jews*, p. 83.
11. JRC, letters, June 7 and 13, 1940, LJL.
12. Gillman, *Collar the Lot*, pp. 113, 133. Six months in, Edith would have been visibly pregnant, but she also happened to be armed with a certificate from her physician, Dr. Rummelsberg (April 24, 1940, LJL), presumably obtained for some purpose connected with her work or emigration application.
13. London, *Whitehall*, p. 171.
14. There is no record of where Richard Paltenhoffer was interned. His case file appears to have been among the majority that were later routinely destroyed by the Home Office (discovery.nationalarchives.gov.uk/details/r/C9246: retrieved September 30, 2017).
15. Joint Secretary, letter to Edith Paltenhoffer, August 30, 1940, LJL.
16. Joint Secretary, letter to Edith Paltenhoffer, September 4, 1940, LJL.
17. Home Office, letter to Leeds JRC, September 16, 1940, LJL.
18. Home Office, letter to Leeds JRC, September 23, 1940, LJL. Richard's release had been approved on September 16 (Record card 270/00271, HOI).
19. Victor Cazalet, House of Commons, August 22, 1940, *Hansard* vol. 364 c. 1534.

20. Rhys Davies, House of Commons, August 22, 1940, *Hansard* vol. 364 c. 1529.
21. Quoted in Silverman, *Undying Flame*, p. 15.
22. Quoted in Silverman, *Undying Flame*, p. 15.
23. Manfred Langer, in Hackett, *Buchenwald Report*, pp. 169–70.
24. Quoted in Silverman, *Undying Flame*, p. 15. Leopoldi survived the Holocaust, but Löhner-Beda was murdered in Auschwitz in 1942.
25. This grove was later the site of a special enclosure whose inmates were isolated and kept secret from the rest of the camp. They included many VIP prisoners who were enemies of the Nazi regime.
26. Hackett, *Buchenwald Report*, p. 42.
27. Fritz appears to have been transferred to the construction detail on August 20, 1940, after four months in the garden (prisoner record card, 1.1.5.3/6283377, ITS). He does not specify which garages he worked on. There were two: a smaller one with a gas station close to the admin block and the main camp, and a larger complex further southeast near the officers' housing and the main construction yard. It was probably the latter.
28. In Gärtner and Kleinmann, *Doch der Hund*, p. 72.
29. Fritz refers to this as the Heizwerk Nord; it was probably attached to the SS bath facility.
30. Many years later, Fritz learned the name of the friendly Styrian; he was Othmar Wanke (Gärtner and Kleinmann, *Doch der Hund*, p. 76).
31. The *Prominenten* of block 17 were of middling status. The Nazi regime kept its highest ranking political prisoners—former prime ministers, presidents, and monarchs of conquered countries—in isolation, often in special secret compounds within concentration camps. Buchenwald's was a walled compound in the spruce grove in front of the SS barracks.
32. Gedenkstätte Buchenwald, www.buchenwald.de/en/1218 (retrieved May 14, 2017); Ulrich Weinzierl, *Die Welt*, April 1, 2005. Transferred to Dachau in October 1940, Fritz Grünbaum died there on January 14, 1941, from cardiac paralysis, according to the death certificate (ibid.), although in fact his death was caused by abuse and starvation.
33. Plänkers, *Ernst Federn*, p. 158. Ernst Federn survived in Buchenwald until liberation in 1945; he continued his career in psychoanalysis and died in 2007.
34. In Gärtner and Kleinmann, *Doch der Hund*, p. 59.
35. His motivation is unclear. Fellow prisoner Emil Carlebach (in Hackett, *Buchenwald Report*, p. 164) states that Hans Kunke was killed "on the first day of work" in the quarry, whereas Fritz Kleimann (*Doch der Hund*, p. 64) states that Kunke was transferred to the quarry in mid-April, but is vague about his date of death. Stein (*Buchenwald*, p. 300) gives it as October 31, 1940. For further

information about Hans Kunke and his wife, Stefanie, see the online resource *Steine der Erinnerung in Liesing*, www.steine23.at (retrieved May 15, 2017).

36. Gärtner and Kleinmann, *Doch der Hund*, p. 64; Stein, *Buchenwald*, pp. 131, 293.
37. Wachsmann, *KL*, pp. 224–5.
38. Ibid., p. 225. Cremation is forbidden in Jewish law, and cremated remains are prohibited from cemeteries. However, exceptions are made for those cremated against their will, and ashes sent back from the concentration camps were permitted into Jewish cemeteries from the start.
39. Tini Kleinmann, letter to German Jewish Aid Committee, New York, March 1941, DKK.
40. Margaret E. Jones, letter to AFSC, November 1940, in Wyman, *America and the Holocaust*, vol. 4, p. 3.
41. The consuls themselves, who didn't have to face the applicants, were generally callous and even supported anti-Semitic immigration restrictions despite speaking publicly against Nazi anti-Semitism (Zucker, *In Search*, pp. 172–4). The Vienna consulate was more sympathetic than most and willing to bend the rules a little (ibid., p. 167).
42. Tini Kleinmann, letter to German Jewish Aid Committee, New York, March 1941, DKK.

Chapter 7: The New World

1. This episode is based in part on interviews with Kurt Kleinmann, accounts written by him, and letters from Tini Kleinmann, July 1941, DKK; notes by Fritz Kleinmann, DRG; also data from passenger and crew list, SS *Siboney*, March 27, 1941, PNY.
2. The passenger list records Irmgard Salomon as having blonde hair and blue eyes, which would be unusual but not at all unknown for a Jewish child; however, in this case it seems to be clerical laziness, as every passenger on the same page (mostly German and Hungarian Jews of all ages) is entered with the same dittoed physical description (fair, blonde, blue eyes) with only the heights varying.

   Kurt remembers Irmgard and Karl being respectively two years younger and two years older than him. In fact Irmgard was eleven (the same age) and Karl fourteen (three years older), although the latter's small size may have misled Kurt.
3. There is an account of such a departure from Vienna in Maier, *Ruth Maier's Diary*, pp. 112–3. If Kurt's train left in the evening, Tini and Herta would not have been allowed to accompany him to the station at all, due to the curfew; a non-Jewish friend or relative would have had to accompany him.

4. Passenger and crew list, SS *Siboney*, March 27, 1941, PNY. Kurt recalls that the ship docked at Ellis Island and remained there for about two hours, but the immigrants did not go ashore. It appears that medical examinations were carried out aboard ship, and notes were added by the examiner to the ship's passenger list.

5. Efforts have been made by the author, by Kurt himself, and by the One Thousand Children organization to trace Karl Kohn and Irmgard Salomon, but no information has yet been found about their subsequent lives.

6. Samuel Barnet was born in New York, November 27, 1890, and according to his 1942 draft card he was five feet four and a half inches tall, with gray hair and a "dark" complexion (records of the Selective Service System, Record Group Number 147: NARA).

7. United States census, 1940.

8. Records of the Selective Service System, Record Group Number M1509: NARA; genealogical note on Mollie Copeland Byer, www.wikitree.com/wiki/Byer-16 (retrieved May 22, 2017).

9. United States census, 1940, NARA; Samuel Barnet draft card, 1942, records of the Selective Service System, Record Group Number 147: NARA.

Chapter 8: Unworthy of Life

1. In all the accounts of this murder (Gustav Kleinmann's diary; Emil Carlebach, Herbert Mindus in Hackett, *Buchenwald Report*, pp. 164, 171–2; Fein and Flanner, *Rot-Weiss-Rot*, p. 74) no mention is made of what triggered Abraham's actions.

2. Herbert Mindus (in Hackett, *Buchenwald Report*, pp. 171–2) states that Hamber was in the construction detail and implies that the incident occurred on the SS garage site. However, Mindus's account was written four years later, whereas Gustav Kleinmann's diary account is contemporary and probably more accurate, albeit less detailed; Gustav states that Hamber was in the haulage column (see also Fein and Flanner, *Rot-Weiss-Rot*, p. 74) and that the incident took place in an excavated part of the *Wirtschaftsamt* (economic affairs department). Some accounts (Stein, *Buchenwald*, p. 288) date the incident to late 1940; in fact it was spring 1941.

3. Cesarani, *Final Solution*, p. 317; Stein, *Buchenwald*, pp. 81–3; Kleinmann in Gärtner and Kleinmann, *Doch der Hund*, pp. 77–9.

4. His registered name appears to have been Edmund (Stein, *Buchenwald*, p. 298), but everyone knew him as Eduard (e.g., Fritz Kleinmann in *Doch der Hund*, p. 81; Mindus in *Buchenwald Report*, p. 171).

5. Emil Carlebach in Hackett, *Buchenwald Report*, p. 164.

6. Ibid.

7. Stein, *Buchenwald*, p. 298.

8. Ibid., p. 59.

9. Otto Kipp in Hackett, *Buchenwald Report*, p. 212.

10. Gustav is enigmatic on this point; he clearly uses the word *Aktion*, meaning a campaign or special operation (the Nazis themselves typically used this word as a euphemism for mass killings), implying that he had in mind some kind of concerted resistance among the haulage column, led by Eduard Hamber, which withered and died with the murders of the witnesses. However, his writing is extremely elliptical—probably because, while keeping a diary would probably be fatal for him if found out, the consequences would be even worse if it contained evidence of anti-SS activities.

11. Personal record cards 1.1.5.3/6283389, 1.1.5.3/6283376, ITS. The record indicates four packages signed for during 1941—one each for Gustav and Fritz on May 3, one for Fritz on October 22, and one for Gustav on November 16. All contained items of clothing.

12. Gustav writes: *Wir sind die Unzertrennlichen*—"We are the inseparables." There is no exact equivalent of the noun *Unzertrennlichen* in English. In German it is used for the bird species known in English as lovebirds, and is also the German title of the David Cronenberg film *Dead Ringers*.

13. Tini, letter to Kurt, July 15, 1941, DKK.

14. Order of May 14, 1941, quoted in Gold, *Geschichte der Juden*, pp. 106–7.

15. Cesarani, *Final Solution*, p. 443.

16. *New Republic*, quoted in Zucker, *In Search*, p. 178.

17. Friedman, *No Haven*, pp. 30, 246n.

18. Ibid., pp. 113–4.

19. Rabinovici, *Eichmann's Jews*, p. 136.

20. Cesarani, *Final Solution*, p. 418.

21. Tini, letter to Kurt, August 5, 1941, DKK.

22. Tini, letter to Kurt, July 15, 1941, DKK.

23. Tini, letters to Kurt, July–August 1941, DKK.

24. William L. Shirer, quoted in Cesarani, *Final Solution*, p. 285.

25. Stein, *Buchenwald*, pp. 124–6; Wachsmann, *KL*, pp. 248–58; Cesarani, *Final Solution*, pp. 284–6.

26. SS-Doctor Waldemar Hoven, quoted in Stein, *Buchenwald*, p. 124.

27. Gustav gives the date as August 1941; he is normally totally reliable on dates, but it seems that he described the events of spring and summer 1941 retrospectively—probably at the end of the year—and his chronology and figures are sometimes unreliable for this period.

28. SS nurse Ferdinand Römhild, quoted in Stein, *Buchenwald*, p. 126.

29. Wachsmann, *KL*, p. 260.

30. Gustav Kleinmann's diary says that this occurred on June 15. This is impossible, as war between Germany and the USSR did not begin until June 22. Clearly this

is another instance of his misattributing the date of a 1941 event due to writing about it from memory (see note 27 above). Aside from the date, all the other details of his account are corroborated by multiple sources.

31. Stein, *Buchenwald*, pp. 121–4; Hackett, *Buchenwald Report*, p. 236ff; Wachsmann, *KL*, p. 258ff.

32. Stein, *Buchenwald*, p. 85; Wachsmann, *KL*, p. 277ff.

33. Stein, *Buchenwald*, pp. 121–3.

34. Gustav uses the word *Justifizierungen*, a euphemism sometimes used for judicial murder, for which there is no exact English equivalent—adjustment, judgment, or adjudication are near translations.

35. Fritz Kleinmann in *Doch der Hund*, p. 21n.

36. Wachsmann, *KL*, pp. 270–71. A similar effect had been observed among the Einsatzgruppen death squads on the Eastern Front; shooting large numbers of victims at close range over a long period traumatized even hardened, dedicated SS men (Cesarani, *Final Solution*, p. 390). This was one of the reasons for the move toward using gas chambers in concentration camps, and forcing teams of prisoners—the Sonderkommandos—to handle the victims.

37. Stein, *Buchenwald*, p. 58-9; witness statements in Hackett, *Buchenwald Report*, pp. 71, 210, 230; Wachsmann, *KL*, p. 435.

38. Stein, *Buchenwald*, p. 58.

39. Ibid., pp. 200–203; Wachsmann, *KL*, p. 435.

40. Stein, *Buchenwald*, p. 200–3; Hackett, *Buchenwald Report*, p. 71ff.

41. Fritz Kleinmann, in Gärtner and Kleinmann, *Doch der Hund*, pp. 79–80.

42. Tini sent Fritz one pair of socks in late October 1941, and Gustav a sweater in November (personal record cards 1.1.5.3/6283389, 1.1.5.3/6283376, ITS).

43. *Völkischer Beobachter* quoted in Cesarani, *Final Solution*, p. 421.

44. Rees, *Holocaust*, p. 231; Cesarani, *Final Solution*, p. 421ff; notes on accession no. 2005.506.3, United States Holocaust Memorial Museum, collections. www.ushmm.org/search/catalog/irn523540 (retrieved May 30, 2017).

45. Rabinovici, *Eichmann's Jews*, pp. 110-1.

46. Tini Kleinmann, letter to Sam Barnet, July 19, 1941, DKK.

47. Fritz Kleinmann in Gärtner and Kleinmann, *Doch der Hund*, p. 83.

48. Rees, *Holocaust*, p. 231; Cesarani, *Final Solution*, p. 422ff.

49. Order from Heinrich Müller, RSHA, October 23, 1941, in Arad et al., *Documents*, pp. 153-4.

Chapter 9: A Thousand Kisses

1. Dror, "News," p. 22. Arnold Frankfurter, born in 1881, died in 1942 in Buchenwald on either February 14 (Czeike, *Historisches Lexikon Wien*, vol. 2, p. 357) or

March 10 or 19 (Heimann-Jelinek et al., *Ordnung*, p. 152). He married Gustav Kleinmann and Tini Rottenstein in Vienna on May 8, 1917 (Hecht, "Der König rief," pp. 209–10).

2. Fritz Kleinmann in Gärtner and Kleinmann, *Doch der Hund*, p. 82.
3. Cesarani, *Final Solution*, pp. 445–9.
4. Stein, *Buchenwald*, p. 128.
5. Ibid., p. 146.
6. Hermann Einziger in Hackett, *Buchenwald Report*, p. 189.
7. Gustav is specific that Greuel was the SS sergeant involved. Confusingly, he seems to say that this incident occurred on a "gravel transport from the crusher." However, it occurs within the context of his writing about transporting tree trunks from the forest. Presumably his team was doing both jobs alternately. The fact that some of Gustav's men were not carrying anything on this occasion suggests that this occurred during log-carrying rather than gravel transport (which would have been by wagon).
8. Robert Siewert and Josef Schappe in Hackett, *Buchenwald Report*, pp. 153, 160.
9. Fritz says that Leopold Moses went to Natzweiler in 1941 (in Gärtner and Kleinmann, *Doch der Hund*, p. 50). However, the newly established Natzweiler had only a small number of prisoners (transferred from Sachsenhausen) at that time; it began to receive large transports in spring 1942 (Jean-Marc Dreyfus in Megargee, *USHMM Encyclopedia*, vol. 1B, p. 1007).
10. Fritz Kleinmann, in Gärtner and Kleinmann, *Doch der Hund*, p. 82. (Tini's original letter, which Fritz never saw, was not preserved.)
11. Former Soviet territory under German rule was divided into Reichskommissariat Ostland and Reichskommissariat Ukraine. East of these zones was a larger area that was the rear of the German front line, which was not designated for "resettlement."
12. This narrative is reconstructed from various sources. The instructions for deportees from the Altreich and Ostmark to the Ostland are outlined in Cesarani, *Final Solution*, p. 428; Browning, *Origins*, p. 381; memorandum in Arad, *Documents*, pp. 159–61. The instruction leaflet issued to transport supervisors through the IKG in Vienna is quoted in full in Gold, *Geschichte*, pp. 108–9. The viewpoint of a deportee is given in the testimony of Viennese survivor Wolf Seiler (deported May 6, 1942), document 854, DOW.
13. Transports of Jews to the Ostland began in November 1941; there were seven that month from various German cities, including one from Vienna (Alfred Gottwaldt, "Logik und Logistik von 1300 Eisenbahnkilometern" in Barton, *Ermordet*, p. 54). The program was interrupted due to the logistical demands of the Wehrmacht, which was fighting to stabilize the front line and needed all the rail capacity available. The transports resumed in May 1942; between then and October there were

nine from Vienna, leaving weekly in late May and June (ibid.; see also Gottwaldt and Schulle, *Die Judendeportation*; Sagel-Grande et al., *Justiz*, pp. 192–6).

14. Gärtner and Kleinmann, *Doch der Hund*, p. 69; Buchenwald personal record card 1.1.5.3/6283376, ITS.

15. Bertha Rothenstein birth record, April 29, 1887, Geburtsbuch, IKA; *Lehmann's Adressbuch* for Vienna for 1938, WLO; casualty reports, *Illustrierte Kronen Zeitung*, June 4, 1915, p. 6; K.u.k. Kriegsministerium, *Verlustliste 209*, p. 54.

16. How long Tini and Herta Kleinmann were held in the Sammellager (holding camp) in the Sperlschule isn't known; some waited a week or more between arrest or notification and deportation. As Tini's and Herta's deportation serial numbers were quite high (see note 18), they were presumably notified quite late and would not have been held for long.

17. Loading could take over five hours (e.g., police report on transport Da 230, October 1942, DOW).

18. The deportees are listed in the Gestapo departure list for Transport 26 (Da 206), June 9, 1942, 1.2.1.1/11203406, ITS; limited data also available in Erfassung der Österreichischen Holocaustopfer (Database of Austrian victims of the Holocaust), DOW and YVS.

19. Tini Rottenstein was born January 2, 1893, in the apartment building at Kleine Stadtgutgasse 6, near the Praterstern (Geburtsbuch 1893, IKA).

20. The Aspangbahnhof was demolished in 1976. A small square—Platz der Opfer der Deportation (Deportation Victims' Square)—now stands on the site, along with a memorial to the thousands of deportees who left Vienna from the station.

21. The route is given in Alfred Gottwaldt, "Logik und Logistik von 1300 Eisenbahnkilometern" in Barton, *Ermordet*, pp. 48–51. Timings are estimated from the Vienna police report on transport Da 230, October 1942, DOW.

22. When the war began, the SS-Totenkopfverbände (Death's Head units) division was placed under the overall command of the Waffen-SS. Veteran guard personnel were sent to fight on the Eastern Front. They were replaced in the camps by new volunteers and conscripts. The Death's Head insignia was worn on the caps of all SS men, but the SS-TV wore it on their collar tabs also.

23. Sipo-SD was the informal name of the combined units of the SS Sicherheitspolizei (Sipo, security police) and Sicherheitsdienst (SD, intelligence). The Sipo, which combined the Gestapo and the criminal police, was defunct by this time, having been absorbed into the Reich Main Security Office (RSHA), but the term was still used for the combined police-SD units operating in the eastern territories.

24. Testimony of survivor Wolf Seiler (deported May 6, 1942), document 854, DOW; testimony of Isaak Grünberg (deported October 5, 1942), quoted in Gottwaldt, "Logik und Logistik von 1300 Eisenbahnkilometern" in Barton, *Ermordet*, p. 49.

25. Alfred Gottwaldt, "Logik und Logistik von 1300 Eisenbahnkilometern" in Barton, *Ermordet*, p. 51.

26. The transport that left Vienna on Tuesday, June 9, is recorded as arriving at Minsk on either Saturday, June 13 or Monday, June 15; rail records indicate the former date, whereas a report by SS-Lieutenant Arlt (June 16, 1942: file 136 M.38, YVP) indicates the latter. Holocaust deniers have taken this as casting doubt on the evidence for the massacres at Maly Trostinets. In fact it was due to industrial relations; as of May 1942, railroad workers in Minsk were not required to work weekends, and trains arriving on a Saturday were parked at Kojdanów station outside the city until Monday morning (Alfred Gottwaldt, "Logik und Logistik von 1300 Eisenbahnkilometern" in Barton, *Ermordet*, p. 51).

27. Letter to Kurt, August 5, 1941, DKK.

28. Sources used here include secondary accounts (Sybille Steinbacher, "Deportiert von Wien nach Minsk" in Barton, *Ermordet*, pp. 31–8; Sagel-Grande et al., *Justiz*, pp. 192–6; Gerlach, *Kalkulierte Morde*, pp. 747–60; Petra Rentrop, "Maly Trostinez als Tatort der «Endlösung»" in Barton, *Ermordet*, pp. 57–71; Aarons, *War Criminals Welcome*, pp. 71–6), official reports (SS-Lieutenant Arlt, June 16, 1942: file 136 M.38, YVP), and personal testimonies of survivors (Wolf Seiler, document 854, DOW; Isaak Grünberg, quoted in various preceding citations).

29. Petra Rentrop, "Maly Trostinez als Tatort der «Endlösung»" in Barton, *Ermordet*, p. 64.

30. Cesarani, *Final Solution*, p. 356ff.

31. Sybille Steinbacher, "Deportiert von Wien nach Minsk" in Barton, *Ermordet*, pp. 31–8; Sagel-Grande et al., *Justiz*, pp. 192–6; Gerlach, *Kalkulierte Morde*, pp. 747–60; Petra Rentrop, "Maly Trostinez als Tatort der «Endlösung»" in Barton, *Ermordet*, pp. 57–71. Maly Trostinets concentration camp is rarely mentioned in general Holocaust histories; even the mammoth four-volume *United States Holocaust Memorial Museum Encyclopedia of Camps and Ghettos* (ed. Megargee) does not have an entry for it, just a few references in the entry for the Minsk ghetto (vol. 2B, pp. 1234, 1236). There are many variant spellings of the name in the literature—in modern Belarusian it is Małý Trościeniec; other variants include Trostenets; Trostinets; Trostinec; Trostenez; Trastsianiets; Trascianec. In German it is sometimes referred to as Klein Trostenez.

32. Sometimes the selection for the camp would be made here if it hadn't already been done at the station (testimony of Wolf Seiler, document 854, DOW).

33. Sagel-Grande et al., *Justiz*, p. 194.

34. Aarons, *War Criminals*, pp. 72–4.

35. Sagel-Grande et al., *Justiz*, p. 194.

36. Aarons, *War Criminals Welcome*, pp. 72–4.

37. Petra Rentrop, "Maly Trostinez als Tatort der «Endlösung»" in Barton, *Ermordet*, p. 65. There may in fact have been up to eight gas vans in Belarus, but only three or four appear to have been used at Maly Trostinets (Gerlach, *Kalkulierte Morde*, pp. 765–6).

38. Sagel-Grande et al., *Justiz*, pp. 194–5.

39. SS-Lieutenant Arlt, June 16, 1942: file 136 M.38, YVP.

40. Tini refers to this rowing outing and to her own childhood in her last letter to Kurt, July 15, 1941, DKK.

41. Altogether, according to the Dokumentationsarchiv des österreichischen Widerstandes (www.doew.at), about nine thousand Jews were deported from Vienna to Maly Trostinets. Only seventeen are known to have survived. The total numbers killed at Maly Trostinets are not known for certain, but it is estimated that over two hundred thousand German, Austrian, and Belarusian Jews and Soviet prisoners of war were murdered there between 1941 and 1943, when the camp was shut down (Gilbert, *Holocaust*, p. 886, n. 38).

Chapter 10: A Trip to Death

1. An account given after the war by prisoner Hermann Einziger (in Hackett, *Buchenwald Report*, p. 189) states that this occurred in April, and that the labor detail was carrying the logs to the camp by hand. However, Gustav's diary (which returns to its usual chronological reliability in 1942) suggests that it was later in the year (mid to late summer) and although sketchy it implies that the logs were being loaded (i.e., onto a wagon) rather than carried and stacked. Einziger says Friedmann was from Mannheim; Gustav says he was from Kassel. Neither offers any further details about him.

2. The ban on Jews being admitted to the infirmary had been lifted at some point; the precise date isn't known.

3. Stein, *Buchenwald*, pp. 138–9; Ludwig Scheinbrunn in Hackett, *Buchenwald Report*, pp. 215–6.

4. Stein, *Buchenwald*, pp. 36–7; Hackett, *Buchenwald Report*, p. 313.

5. Order of October 5, 1942, quoted in Stein, *Buchenwald*, p. 128.

6. Stein, *Buchenwald*, pp. 128–9.

7. This was a full week after the drafting of the list on October 8 (Stefan Heymann in Hackett, *Buchenwald Report*, p. 342).

8. Fritz (in *Doch der Hund*, p. 86) says there were eighty men to a car; however, Commandant Pister had ordered a train from the railway company consisting of ten cattle/freight cars and one passenger car for SS personnel (Stein, *Buchenwald Report*, pp. 128–9). Fritz also gives the date of departure as October 18 and of arrival at Auschwitz as October 20; his dates are off by one day.

9. Gustav uses the stock expression *Himmelfahrtskommando*, which translates literally as "trip to Heaven mission" and is the German equivalent of "suicide mission" or "kamikaze order."

Chapter 11: A Town Called Oświęcim

1. Men in Austria-Hungary were drafted into the army in the spring of the year in which they turned twenty-one; infantrymen did three years' full-time service, followed by ten years in the reserves (Lucas, *Fighting Troops*, p. 22). Gustav Kleinmann turned twenty-one on May 2, 1912. The kaiserlich und königlich (k.u.k.) Armee (Imperial and Royal Army) was made up of troops from all over the empire.
2. Lucas, *Fighting Troops*, pp. 25–6.
3. Schindler, *Fall*, p. 13. The suggested phrases are (German) "Alles Erdreich ist Österreich untertan" and (Latin) "Austria erit in orbe ultima."
4. Lucas, *Fighting Troop*, p. 210.
5. The 12th Infantry Division was part of First Army's support force and was attached to X Corps for the advance.
6. Schindler, *Fall*, p. 171. In 1914, the north and west of what is now Poland was part of the German Empire, and the south (comprising Galicia) belonged to Austria-Hungary. Central modern Poland (including Warsaw) was part of the Russian Empire. Thus Austria's border with Russia was to the north and east.
7. Ibid., p. 172ff.
8. Ibid., pp. 200–39.
9. Watson, *Ring of Steel*, pp. 193–5.
10. Watson, *Ring of Steel*, pp. 200–1; Zalewski, *Galician Portraits*, pp. 205–6.
11. Keegan, *First World War*, p. 192.
12. Gemeinesames Zentralnachweisbureau, *Nachrichten Nr 190*, p. 24; *Nr 203*, p. 25. The exact circumstances of Gustav's wound are not known, other than that he was shot. The two reports cited indicate respectively that he was shot in the left lower leg (*linken Unterschenkel*, January 6, Biala) and left forearm (*linken Unterarm*, January 11, Oświęcim); either one of these was a misprint or he was wounded in both at the same time. Simultaneous wounds in the left arm and left leg sometimes happened when a soldier was kneeling to fire his rifle. The fact that he suffered a bullet wound to the lower body suggests that it probably occurred during an attack or raid rather than while in trenches.
13. Van Pelt and Dwork, *Auschwitz*, p. 59.
14. Ibid.
15. The report describing Gustav's actions (Award application, 3 Feldkompanie, Infanterieregiment 56, February 27, 1915, BWM) indicates that this was entirely on

Gustav and Aleksiak's own initiative, which suggests that their sergeant and/or platoon officer was absent, most likely killed in the assault.

16. Austro-Hungarian Army report, February 26, 1915, *Amtliche Kriegs-Depeschen*, vol. 2 (Berlin: Nationaler Verlag, 1915): reproduced online at www.stahlgewitter .com/15_02_26.htm (retrieved October 1, 2017).

17. Award application, 3 Feldkompanie, Infanterieregiment 56, February 27, 1915, BWM.

18. *Wiener Zeitung*, April 7, 1915, pp. 5–6. Altogether, nineteen men of the 56th were awarded the Silver Medal for Bravery 1st Class (Silberne Tapferkeitsmedaille erster Klasse) while ninety-seven received the 2nd Class.

19. K.u.k. Kriegsministerium, *Verlustliste 244*, p. 21. The official list of wounded doesn't specify how Gustav received this wound or where it was located (nor indeed which hospital he was in); he is merely listed as "*verwundeten.*" Family oral history says it was in the lung.

20. Tini Rottenstein birth record, January 2, 1893, Geburtsbuch and Geburtsanzeigen, IKA.

21. This is the substance of speeches given by Rabbi Arnold Frankfurter at this time, including at weddings, as quoted by Hecht in "Der König rief," pp. 212–3, which specifically mentions Gustav and Tini's wedding.

22. Watson, *Ring of Steel*, pp. 503–6.

23. Prior to 1944, when a rail spur and loading ramp were constructed in the Birkenau camp, prisoners arriving at Auschwitz disembarked at a spur near Auschwitz I, and prior to that at the train station in the town, and marched to the camps.

24. Czech, *Auschwitz Chronicle*, p. 255.

25. There were 405 men on the transport list, but only 404 were admitted to Auschwitz (Czech, *Auschwitz Chronicle*, p. 255). Presumably one had died en route.

26. In 1944, Auschwitz I acquired a purpose-built admissions building outside the camp entrance (van Pelt and Dwork, *Auschwitz*, pp. 222–5; Czech, *Auschwitz Chronicle*, p. 601). Prior to that date there were only the regular facilities inside the camp.

27. The first gassings in Germany, using trucks and gas chambers, had occurred in 1939 as part of the T4 euthanasia program (Cesarani, *Final Solution*, pp. 283–5). The first experimental gassings with Zyklon B at Auschwitz were done in August 1941 in Auschwitz I; the use of crematoria for gassings soon followed, and the specialized gas chambers came into use in Auschwitz-Birkenau in early 1942 (Wachsmann, *KL*, pp. 267–8, 301–2; Franciszek Piper in Megargee,*USHMM Encyclopedia*, vol. 1A, pp. 206, 210). By late 1942, rumors about gassings in camps had spread through the concentration camp system and among local populations.

28. *Eine Laus dein Tod*—this message was painted on walls throughout the Auschwitz complex.

29. Delousing of uniforms was done by fumigation with Zyklon B. This was the original intended purpose of this poison gas infamously adapted by the SS for use in the killing gas chambers. For that purpose, the SS asked the manufacturer (a subsidiary of IG Farben) to remove the noxious warning smell that was normally added to it (Hayes, *Industry*, p. 363).

30. The first recipients of tattooed numbers were Soviet POWs, beginning in fall of 1941 (Wachsmann, *KL*, p. 284). No other concentration camp used tattooing.

31. Arrivals list, October 19, 1942, ABM.

32. The numbering Auschwitz I, II, and III was not introduced until November 1943 (Florian Schmaltz in Megargee, *USHMM Encyclopedia*, p. 216), but is used here for clarity and consistency.

33. Franciszek Piper in Megargee, *USHMM Encyclopedia*, p. 210. Auschwitz-Birkenau (Auschwitz II) began construction in October 1941 and was operational in early 1942. It continued expanding over the next few years.

34. Gustav uses the phrase *schwarze Mauer* rather than the more commonly used *schwarze Wand*. Both mean the same. It was named for the black-painted screen that protected the brick wall from bullet strikes.

35. Gustav does not comment on this return to Auschwitz in his diary (which is admittedly written extremely sketchily during the initial period at Auschwitz, recording only the barest facts). Neither does Fritz ever refer to it in his memoir or interview; possibly Gustav didn't mention to Fritz the fact that he had been in the hospital here during World War I. It is possible that Gustav didn't remember his previous time at Auschwitz, but this is unlikely; he was familiar with the general area from his upbringing and had been stationed in the district at the time when the Zasole barracks were being constructed. He would remember it well.

36. Czech, *Auschwitz Chronicle*, p. 259.

37. Höss, quoted in Langbein, *People*, pp. 391–2.

38. Quoted in Langbein, *People*, p. 392. From November 1942 SS-Sergeant Gerhard Palitzsch became increasingly unbalanced due to the death of his wife. They lived in a house near the camp, and Palitzsch, who was involved in corruption, obtained clothes stolen from the prisoners in Birkenau. In October 1942 she contracted typhus—probably from lice carried in these clothes—and died. Palitzsch took to drinking heavily and his behavior became erratic (ibid., pp. 408–10).

39. Czech, *Auschwitz Chronicle*, pp. 255–60.

40. Ibid., p. 261. The 186 women from Ravensbrück were declared fit and assigned work separately from the men (ibid., pp. 261–2).

41. In Gärtner and Kleinmann, *Doch der Hund*, p. 90. Fritz says that they stayed only a week in Auschwitz I, and in their testimony to the Frankfurt trials both he and

Gustav stated the time as eight days (Abt 461 Nr 37638/84/15904–6; Abt 461 Nr 37638/83/15661–3, FTD); in fact it was eleven days (Czech, *Auschwitz Chronicle,* pp. 255, 260–1).

42. The truth of this is uncertain. There was a heavy demand for workers for construction of the new Monowitz camp, and the records imply that the intention all along had been to send the transferred prisoners to work there (Czech, *Auschwitz Chronicle,* p. 255). However, the record is unclear, and Fritz and Gustav had the impression that they were all slated for execution. Certainly that was the purpose of their selection at Buchenwald—hence the retention of construction workers.

Chapter 12: Auschwitz-Monowitz

1. At this time the camp was officially referred to as the Buna labor camp (or as "Camp IV" by IG Farben management—see Wagner, *IG Auschwitz,* p. 96), later as Monowitz concentration camp or Auschwitz III. The later names are used here for clarity.

2. By early September 1942 the Monowitz camp had been completely laid out, but construction hadn't progressed beyond a small number of barracks (between two and eight, according to sources). The rest of the camp buildings had been delayed in order to expedite construction of the Buna Werke factory. The camp officially opened for reception of prisoners on October 28 (Wagner, *IG Auschwitz,* pp. 95–7).

3. The IG Farben Buna Werke was named for the brand of synthetic rubber intended to be produced there. Among other applications, rubber was vital in aircraft and vehicle manufacture, e.g., tires and various shock-absorbing components.

4. Florian Schmaltz in Megargee, *USHMM Encyclopedia* vol. 1A, pp. 216–7; Gärtner and Kleinmann, *Doch der Hund,* p. 92. Eventually camp inmates would make up about a third of the Buna Werke's total workforce, the rest made up of paid workers from Germany or occupied countries (Hayes, *Industry,* p. 358), many of whom would be drafted labor from enforced schemes such as France's Service du Travail Obligatoire.

5. Florian Schmaltz in Megargee, *USHMM Encyclopedia* vol. 1A, p. 216. Figures cited in various sources for this vary enormously, from two thousand down to just six hundred (Wagner, *IG Auschwitz,* p. 97).

6. Hayes, *Industry,* pp. 354–8; Florian Schmaltz in Megargee, *USHMM Encyclopedia* vol. 1A, p. 216; Wagner, *IG Auschwitz,* pp. 94–6.

Chapter 13: The End of Gustav Kleinmann, Jew

1. Wachsmann, *KL*, pp. 49–52; Joseph Robert White in Megargee, *USHMM Encyclopedia* vol. 1A, pp. 64–6. Esterwegen and the other Emsland camps were shut down in 1936.
2. Lehmann directory name listings, 1891, WLO; Teichova, "Banking in Austria," p. 4.
3. Wagner, *IG Auschwitz*, p. 107.
4. The origin of the term—which is mainly associated with Auschwitz but was used in other camps as well—is not known. (See Yisrael Gutman in Gutman and Berenbaum, *Anatomy*, p. 20; Wachsmann, *KL*, pp. 209–10, 685 n. 117; Wladyslaw Fejkiel quoted in Langbein, *People*, p. 91.) By the time the concentration camps were liberated in 1944–5, most long-term prisoners had been turned into Muselmänner, and they became emblematic of the Holocaust's victims. But they existed in the camps as early as 1939.
5. Hayes, *Industry*, p. 358.
6. Herzog was a clerk from mid-1943, and head of the office from January to October 1944 (Herzog, Frankfurt trials statement, Abt 461 Nr 37638/84/15891-2, FTD).
7. Detailed plan and layout of buildings by Irena Strzelecka and Piotr Setkiewicz, "Bau, Ausbau und Entwicklung des KL Auschwitz" in Długoborski and Piper, *Auschwitz 1940-1945*, vol. 1, pp. 128–30.
8. Wachsmann, *KL*, p. 210.
9. Primo Levi, who was a prisoner in Auschwitz III-Monowitz from February 1944, said of block 7 that "no ordinary Häftling [prisoner] has ever entered" (Levi, *Survival*, p. 32).
10. Wagner, *IG Auschwitz*, pp. 117, 121–2; Langbein, *People*, pp. 150–1.
11. Quoted in Wachsmann, *KL*, p. 515.
12. Wagner, *IG Auschwitz*, pp. 121–2.
13. Ibid., p. 117.
14. Freddi Diamant, quoted in Langbein, *People*, p. 151.
15. Irena Strzelecka and Piotr Setkiewicz, "Bau, Ausbau und Entwicklung des KL Auschwitz" in Długoborski and Piper, *Auschwitz 1940-1945*, vol. 1, p. 135.
16. By the end of 1943 Auschwitz had three satellite camps dedicated to coal mining: Fürstengrube, Janinagrube, and Jawischowitz. They ranged from around fifteen to one hundred kilometers distant from the main Auschwitz camp (entries in Megargee, USHMM Encyclopedia, vol. 1A, pp. 221, 239, 253, 255).
17. Wagner, *IG Auschwitz*, p. 118.

Chapter 14: Resistance and Collaboration: The Death of Fritz Kleinmann

1. Wachsmann, *KL*, pp. 206–7.
2. Fritz Kleinmann in Gärtner and Kleinmann, *Doch der Hund*, p. 108.

3. The following details are described at length by Fritz Kleinmann in Gärtner and Kleinmann, *Doch der Hund*, pp. 108–12.

4. Langbein, *People*, p. 142; Irena Strzelecka and Piotr Setkiewicz, "Bau, Ausbau und Entwicklung des KL Auschwitz" in Długoborski and Piper, *Auschwitz 1940–1945*, vol. 1, p. 128.

5. Gustav did attend the Monowitz dental station in August 1944, but apparently his teeth were in good shape (dental station records, August 2–15, 1944, ABM).

6. Hayes, *Industry*, pp. 361–2.

7. Fritz Kleinmann in Gärtner and Kleinmann, *Doch der Hund*, p. 112; author's translation.

8. Florian Schmaltz in Megargee, *USHMM Encyclopedia* vol. 1A, p. 217.

9. Henryk Świebocki, "Die Entstehung und die Entwicklung der Konspiration im Lager" in Długoborski and Piper, *Auschwitz 1940–1945*, vol. 4, pp. 150–3.

10. Goltman, *Six mois*, pp. 89–90.

11. Fritz states that he worked as *Transportarbeiter*, transport worker (*Doch der Hund*, p. 113), but doesn't elucidate; this was quite a broad label and probably denotes fetching and carrying for locksmith technicians within the factory.

12. Hermann Langbein in Gutman and Berenbaum, *Anatomy*, pp. 490–1; Henryk Świebocki, "Die Entstehung und die Entwicklung der Konspiration im Lager" in Długoborski and Piper, *Auschwitz 1940–1945*, vol. 4, pp. 153–4.

13. Florian Schmaltz in Megargee, *USHMM Encyclopedia* vol. 1A, p. 217.

14. Langbein, *People*, pp. 31, 185, 322, 329–335.

15. Ibid., p. 329.

16. In his memoir and interview, Fritz says only that he was taken to the political department, without specifying whether it was the main department at Auschwitz I or the sub-department in Monowitz. The involvement of Grabner and the seriousness of the charge suggests that it was probably the main department. On the other hand, at the end of the interrogation he says that Grabner "went back to Auschwitz with the civilian" (*Doch der Hund*, p. 114); but he also writes that Taute and Hofer took him "back to the camp" (ibid.), which again suggests Auschwitz I as the scene of the torture. Overall, the balance of evidence favors the latter. In his 1963 statement for the Frankfurt trials (Abt 461 Nr 37638/83/15663, FTD), Fritz stated that this incident occurred in June 1944; as Grabner left Auschwitz in late 1943, this is probably a transcription error for June 1943.

17. Wagner, *IG Auschwitz*, pp. 163–92; Irena Strzelecka and Piotr Setkiewicz, "Bau, Ausbau und Entwicklung des KL Auschwitz" in Długoborski and Piper, *Auschwitz 1940–1945*, vol. 1, p. 128.

18. The entry recording Fritz Kleinmann's death has not come to light; presumably it was among the majority of Auschwitz records destroyed before liberation of the

camp. Some hospital registers have survived (and have the format described), but this one is apparently lost or the entry was later removed.

19. In his published recollections Fritz makes no mention of his suicidal thoughts at this time, but in his 1997 interview he describes them at some length and with strong emotion.

20. Fritz is unclear about exactly how long it was before his father was told about his survival. In his written memoir, he implies that it was shortly after his transfer from the hospital to block 48, whereas in his 1997 interview he is vague, implying that through necessity the secret was kept for a long time.

21. Czech, *Auschwitz Chronicle*, pp. 537, 542.

22. Langbein, People, p. 40; Wachsmann, *KL*, pp. 388–9; Czech, *Auschwitz Chronicle*, pp. 537, 812.

23. Prisoner resistance report, December 9, 1943, quoted in Czech, *Auschwitz Chronicle*, p. 542. There followed a period of conflict between the camp Gestapo and the new commandant, who deeply disapproved of the anarchic operation the Gestapo had been running.

Chapter 15: The Kindness of Strangers

1. Wagner, *IG Auschwitz*, p. 333.

2. The version of this incident given by Fritz Kleinmann differs in some details from the version in Gustav's diary, and both differ from the Gestapo records (as quoted in Czech, *Auschwitz Chronicle*, pp. 481–2). The account given here is a synthesis of the three.

3. Gustav recorded in his diary that both Eisler and Windmüller were shot (see also Czech, *Auschwitz Chronicle*, p. 482); presumably this was the story that came back to Monowitz at the time.

4. Not to be confused with the Rote Hilfe eV, a socialist aid organization founded in 1975. The original Rote Hilfe was founded in 1921 as an affiliate of the International Red Aid. It was banned under the Nazis and later disbanded. Many of its activists ended up in concentration camps.

5. Fritz does not specify whether Wocher had been discharged from the army or not. However, a reference to his wearing uniform when away from the factory indicates that he had not.

6. It is not known exactly what Alfred Wocher's duties were on the Eastern Front, or what unit he was in, but it is difficult to believe that he was not aware of the mass murders of Jews carried out there. By no means were the Waffen-SS and Einsatzgruppen the only organizations involved; Wehrmacht units took part too, and even if Wocher was nowhere near any such events, he must have heard reports. It may be that he perceived those things differently, and that he was only affected

at last by witnessing the persecution and murder of people who were German-born and spoke German.

7. Langbein, *People*, pp. 321-2.

8. There was never a "ramp" at Monowitz, and the railroad did not enter the camp; from 1942 onward, standard procedure was that transports went to the "old Jew-ramp" at Oświęcim train station, or to a spur near Auschwitz I, and from 1944 to the ramp inside Birkenau. However, Fritz Kleinmann (*Doch der Hund*, pp. 129-30) suggests that some transports were unloaded at or near Monowitz, presumably in open ground near the camp, and that men selected for Monowitz arrived with their luggage.

9. In Birkenau, two whole sections of the camp, known in camp slang as Kanada I and II, comprising thirty-six barrack blocks, were used for storage of loot. Officially the sorting details were called Aufräumungskommando ("cleaning-up commando") but the unofficial name "Kanada Kommando" became so entrenched that the SS used it as well (Andrzej Strezelecki in Gutman and Berenbaum, *Anatomy*, pp. 250-2).

10. There were twenty-three apartments in Im Werd 11; by 1941 and 1942 only twelve were still occupied (Lehmann directory house listings, Im Werd, 1938, 1941-2, WLO).

11. Although he makes no mention of it in his written memoir, Fritz says in his 1997 interview that he hoped Wocher would be able to find his mother and gave him a letter for her.

12. He is listed as "Bildwurfmeister" in Lehmann directory listings, Im Werd, 1942, WLO. Karl Novacek is not the same man as the Friedrich Novacek who lived in the same building and was one of the friends who betrayed Gustav and Fritz in 1938 and 1939. It is not known whether Karl and Friedrich were related.

13. Fritz gives no details how this was accomplished; since there were two cases of foodstuffs, he must have done it in multiple small installments.

14. Transport list, Da 227, September 14, 1942, DOW. Transport Da 227 arrived at Minsk two days later, and as was usual the deportees were taken straight to Maly Trostinets (Alfred Gottwaldt, "Logik und Logistik von 1300 Eisenbahnkilometern" in Barton, *Ermordet*, p. 54).

Chapter 16: Far from Home

1. Gustav Kleinmann, letter to Olga Steyskal, January 3, 1944, DFK.

2. Gustav Kleinmann, letter to Olga Steyskal, January 3, 1944, DFK. These last named families are probably those of Rudolf Rittmann, a Reichsbahn employee, and Franz Burič, a master tailor, both of whom had apartments in the same building as Olga Steyskal (Lehmann directory name listings, 1942, WLO).

3. Langbein, *People*, p. 25; Fritz Kleinmann in Gärtner and Kleinmann, *Doch der Hund*, pp. 129–30.

4. Fritz Kleinmann in Gärtner and Kleinmann, *Doch der Hund*, pp. 129–30; Wagner, *IG Auschwitz*, pp. 101, 103; Levi, *Suvival*, p. 32.

5. Fritz Kleinmann in Gärtner and Kleinmann, *Doch der Hund*, p. 132; Wagner, *IG Auschwitz*, p. 101.

6. Cesarani, *Final Solution*, p. 702. About 320,000 of Hungary's Jews had formerly been citizens of neighboring countries before Germany had carved off parts of them and given them to its Hungarian ally.

7. Ibid., p. 707.

8. Danuta Czech, "Kalendarium der wichtigsten Ereignisse aus der Geschichte des KL Auschwitz" in Długoborski and Piper, *Auschwitz*, vol. 5, p. 201; *Auschwitz Chronicle*, p. 618.

9. Wachsmann, *KL*, p. 458; Danuta Czech, "Kalendarium der wichtigsten Ereignisse aus der Geschichte des KL Auschwitz" in Długoborski and Piper, *Auschwitz*, vol. 5, p. 202.

10. Rees, *Holocaust*, pp. 381–2.

11. Danuta Czech, "Kalendarium der wichtigsten Ereignisse aus der Geschichte des KL Auschwitz" in Długoborski and Piper, *Auschwitz*, vol. 5, p. 203; Wachsmann, *KL*, pp. 457–61; Cesarani, *Final Solution*, pp. 707–11; Rees, *Holocaust*, pp. 381–5; Czech, *Auschwitz Chronicle*, p. 627.

12. Danuta Czech, "Kalendarium der wichtigsten Ereignisse aus der Geschichte des KL Auschwitz" in Długoborski and Piper, *Auschwitz*, vol. 5, p. 203.

13. Cesarani, *Final Solution*, p. 710.

14. Wachsmann, *KL*, pp. 460–1.

15. This appears to have happened around May 1944, as Gustav refers to it immediately after his description of the Hungarian Jews. In Fritz's memoir, he implies that it occurred before Christmas 1943, but the diary seems to rule this out.

16. Auschwitz III-Monowitz hospital admissions list, February–March 1944, pp. 288, 346, ABM. Gustav's illness isn't named in the hospital record (which records only name, number, dates, and either discharge, death, or "*nach Birkenau*"), and he doesn't refer to this episode in his diary, which jumps directly from October 1943 to May 1944. Fritz doesn't mention either episode in either his memoir or interview.

17. Konstantin Simonov, quoted in Rees, *Holocaust*, p. 405. Other death camps in the region, such as Sobibór and Treblinka, had been decommissioned in October 1943, at the same time time as Maly Trostinets.

18. The museum at Majdanek still exists (www.majdanek.eu/en/mission).

19. The other practical arguments were that aerial bombing was not precise enough to be effective. To be sure of hitting the gas chambers at Auschwitz, for instance, would have required such a magnitude of ordnance dropped over such a wide area

that thousands of prisoners in Birkenau would probably have been killed, without any certainty that the gas chambers would be hit. Bombing the rail network leading to the camps was similarly problematic. Railroads were extremely difficult to hit from high altitude, and wherever they were destroyed as part of the strategic campaign the Germans simply diverted traffic and usually had the tracks repaired and in service again within twenty-four hours or less. For overviews of the arguments on both sides, see Gilbert, *Auschwitz and the Allies*; David S. Wyman, "Why Auschwitz Wasn't Bombed" in Gutman and Berenbaum, *Anatomy*, pp. 569–87; Wachsmann, *KL*, 494–6.

As for the question "Why didn't the Allies *do something* to halt the Holocaust?" this author's answer is that they did; they waged—and eventually won, at the cost of millions of Allied lives—a total war of destruction against the state that was perpetrating it.

20. Air raid precautions in Auschwitz had been discussed at a meeting of the camp command on November 9, 1943, including imposition of blackout, but nothing was apparently done until well into 1944 (van Pelt, *Case for Auschwitz*, p. 328).

21. Fritz specifically says bacon—*Speck*—in his memoir (*Doch der Hund*, p. 139). Some stricter Jews traded nonkosher foods for bread if they could, and there were Hasidic rabbis in Monowitz who refused all nonkosher food; they quickly starved to death (Wollheim Memorial oral histories: online at www.wollheim-memorial .de/en/juedische_religion_und_zionistische_aktivitaet_en; retrieved July 4, 2017).

22. Fritz mentions this encounter in *Doch der Hund* (p. 142) without identifying the young man more specifically. He appears to have been prisoner number 106468, who appears in the Auschwitz III-Monowitz hospital record (ABM) but not in any other surviving Auschwitz records. This serial number was one of a batch issued on March 6, 1943, to Jews deported from Germany (Czech, *Auschwitz Chronicle*, p. 347).

23. Wagner, *IG Auschwitz*, p. 108.

24. Quoted in Wagner, *IG Auschwitz*, p. 108. Eventually Rakers was relieved of his position on instructions from the IG Farben management.

25. Fritz identifies them only by the names Jenö and Laczi. Surviving Auschwitz records show that two Jewish brothers arrived together on a transport from Hungary at about this time: Jenö and Alexander Berkovits (prisoner numbers A-4005 and A-4004; Monowitz hospital records and work register, ABM).

Chapter 17: Resistance and Betrayal

1. Personal details: arrivals list, October 19, 1942, ABM; prisoner card, Chaim Goslawski, 69976, ABM.

2. Without explanation, Fritz indicates that "Pawel" was also known as "Tadek." These were apparently false names. The real names of the Poles were Zenon Milaczewski (number 10433) and Jan Tomczyk (number 126261); the "Berliner" was apparently Polish-born Riwen Zurkowski (number unknown), who had presumably lived in Berlin (Czech, *Auschwitz Chronicle*, p. 619).

3. Fritz doesn't explain why Goslawski couldn't give the package directly to Peller at roll call. Possibly the construction workers were subjected to greater scrutiny when entering the factory enclosure; or the two men, being in separate blocks, didn't have the chance to communicate before roll call; or the package was arranged in haste and there wasn't time before Peller left for work. The date is given as May 4 (Czech, *Auschwitz Chronicle*, p. 619) or May 3 (Jan Tomczyk's prisoner record, ABM).

4. Monowitz commandant's office notification in Czech, *Auschwitz Chronicle*, p. 634.

5. Date unknown. Thirteen Poles were transferred to Buchenwald on June 1, 1944 (Czech, *Auschwitz Chronicle*, p. 638), and several transports of Poles went between August and December 1944 (Stein, *Buchenwald*, pp. 156, 166; Danuta Czech, "Kalendarium der wichtigsten Ereignisse aus der Geschichte des KL Auschwitz" in Długoborski and Piper, *Auschwitz*, vol. 5, p. 231).

6. Langbein, *People*, pp. 151–2.

7. The date of the execution is unclear. It may have been as late as December. The date of death of Zenon Milaczewski (one of the Poles known to Fritz as "Szenek" and "Pawel") is given in the Monowitz hospital death book (ABM) as December 16, 1944.

8. Fritz states that two men were hanged but according to Gustav Herzog, there were three; aside from Diamant, their names were Weiss and Felltmann (Frankfurt trials statement, Abt 461 Nr 37638/84/15893, FTD).

9. Gilbert, *Auschwitz and the Allies*, p. 307. Gilbert states that the raid began at 10:32 PM, but this seems highly unlikely, as US bombing raids were normally performed in daylight. Czech (*Auschwitz Chronicle*, p. 692) gives the time as "late afternoon."

10. Arie Hassenberg, quoted in Gilbert, *Auschwitz and the Allies*, p. 308.

11. Gilbert, *Auschwitz and the Allies*, p. 308; testimony of Siegfried Pinkus, Nuremberg Military Tribunal: NI-10820: Nuremberg Documents, quoted in Wollheim Memorial, www.wollheim-memorial.de/en/luftangriffe_en (retrieved July 5, 2017).

12. Levi, *Survival*, pp. 137–8.

13. Henryk Świebocki, "Die Entstehung und die Entwicklung der Konspiration im Lager" in Długoborski and Piper, *Auschwitz 1940–1945*, vol. 4, pp. 151–2n.

14. Czech, *Auschwitz Chronicle*, p. 722.

15. Gilbert, *Auschwitz and the Allies*, p. 315ff.

16. Ibid., p. 326.

17. Prisoner number 68705, arrivals list, October 19, 1942, Monowitz hospital records, ABM.

18. Prisoner number 68615, listed in arrivals list, October 19, 1942, ABM.

19. Fritz doesn't identify the weapon as a Luger, but that's almost certainly what it was. In *Doch der Hund* (p. 158) he describes it as an "0.8 mm pistol," which is clearly an error, as there has never been any such weapon. He may have meant 0.8 cm (8 mm), but that is not a standard caliber either (9 mm and 7.65 mm were the standards at the time). The model number of the military-issue Luger was P.08 (for 1908, when it was first introduced), which might account for Fritz's error of memory. Fritz surmised that the weapon came from Wocher's friends in the Luftwaffe flak units, and such units were issued with the Luger P.08 well into World War II, when higher-status army and SS units had switched to the Walther P.38 (Walter, *Luger*, ch. 12).

20. In *Doch der Hund* (p. 159) Fritz says that he had no knowledge of where Meixner hid the guns, but in his 1997 interview he says that it must have been somewhere in the hospital laundry.

21. In his memoir, Fritz mistakenly gives the date of this raid as November 18. There was no air raid on that date. Altogether there were four during 1944: August 20, September 13, December 18, and December 26 (Gilbert, *Auschwitz and the Allies*, pp. 307–333).

22. Although many of the bombs fell in open ground, and a few on the surrounding camps, the December 18 raid succeeded in doing very heavy damage to several buildings in the Buna Werke (Gilbert, *Auschwitz and the Allies*, pp. 331–2).

23. Czech, *Auschwitz Chronicle*, p. 780.

24. Ibid., pp. 778–9.

25. Ibid, pp. 782–3.

26. Jósef Cyrankiewicz, January 17, 1945, quoted in Czech, *Auschwitz Chronicle*, p. 783.

27. Czech, *Auschwitz Chronicle*, pp. 785, 786–7.

28. Gustav Kleinmann's diary indicates units of one hundred, whereas other records specify one thousand as the unit size (Czech, *Auschwitz Chronicle*, p. 786), and Fritz Kleinmann's memoir mentions three groups of about three thousand; the inference is that the units were organized hierarchically, in military style.

29. Gustav specifically identifies Moll. He was based at Birkenau, and no record has been found of his presence at Monowitz at this time. Possibly it was a flying visit to check on the evacuation.

30. On January 15, 1945, the total number of prisoners in Auschwitz III-Monowitz and its subcamps was 33,037 men and 2,044 women (Czech, *Auschwitz Chronicle*, p. 779).

Chapter 18: Death Train

1. Altogether, fifty prisoners were shot dead during the march (Czech, *Auschwitz Chronicle*, p. 786n).
2. Stanislawa Iwaszko in Megargee, *USHMM Encyclopedia*, vol. 1A, p. 250; Czech, *Auschwitz Chronicle*, p. 788.
3. Irena Strzelecka in Megargee, *USHMM Encyclopedia*, vol. 1A, pp. 243–4.
4. Four trains left Gleiwitz that day, carrying prisoners from several Auschwitz sub-camps besides Monowitz. The Monowitz prisoners were split between different trains. Each had a different destination: the concentration camps of Sachsenhausen, Gross-Rosen, Mauthausen, and Buchenwald (Czech, *Auschwitz Chronicle*, p. 797).
5. Czech, *Auschwitz Chronicle*, p. 791.
6. Moon phase data from www.timeanddate.com/moon/austria/amstetten ?month=1&year=1945.
7. In his 1997 interview, Fritz says that he discarded his camp uniform after jumping, but in his written memoir he places it before. This seems more likely, since his uniform would be of value to the other prisoners to fend off the cold.
8. Eating regular soap would probably not have much effect (although the carbolic soap in use at the time might do so). Shaving soap, however, if of the hard type, contains potassium hydroxide, which is highly toxic and produces severe gastro-intestinal symptoms if ingested.

Chapter 19: Mauthausen

1. Mauthausen arrivals list, February 15, 1945, 1.1.26.1/1307365, ITS. Fritz jumped from the train on January 26, 1945 (per Gustav's diary), but was not entered on the records at Mauthausen until February 15, 1945 (Mauthausen transport list, AMM-Y-50-03-16, PGM)—eleven days later than would be indicated by his own reckoning of his time in custody in St. Pölten. Gustav's record of the escape date agrees (give or take one day) with the Mauthausen record, which indicates that Fritz's transfer from Auschwitz officially took place on January 25 (Mauthausen prisoner record card, AMM-Y-Karteikarten, PGM). There is thus a gap of twenty-one days between Fritz's *official* arrival at Mauthausen and his actual arrival.
2. Prisoner record card AMM-Y-Karteikarten, PGM; Mauthausen arrivals list, February 15, 1945, 1.1.26.1/1307365, ITS. Mauthausen received no documentation from Auschwitz about the transport of prisoners (for reasons explained later in the chapter); hence the fact that Fritz was able to pass himself off as Aryan.
3. The liberation of Auschwitz attracted little attention in the international press at the time, despite Soviet attempts to publicize it (they were keen to propagandize it as an example of the inevitable end-point of capitalism). In the eyes of the press it was a rerun of the previous summer's revelations about Majdanek, and the whole

affair was overshadowed by coverage of the climactic Yalta conference of February 4–11. On February 16 (the day after Fritz Kleinmann entered Mauthausen) the first Western Allied serviceman to see inside Auschwitz after its liberation, Captain Robert M. Trimble of USAAF Eastern Command, was given a guided tour of Birkenau by Soviet officers (Trimble and Dronfield, *Beyond the Call*, p. 63ff.).

4. Prisoner record card AMM-Y-Karteikarten, PGM; Mauthausen arrivals list, February 15, 1945, 1.1.26.1/1307365, ITS.

5. Testimony of local priest Josef Radgeb, quoted in museum guide at www .mauthausen-memorial.org/en/Visit/Virtual-Tour#map||23 (retrieved July 10, 2017).

6. Czech, *Auschwitz Chronicle*, p. 797.

7. According to an account cited in Czech, *Auschwitz Chronicles*, p. 797n, the transport reached Nordhausen on January 28. This seems highly unlikely, since it had arrived at Mauthausen on January 26 and was kept a whole day there. Gustav Kleinmann gives February 4 as the date, and in this part of his diary his dates are all accurate.

8. The figure of 766 comes from Gustav's diary; the other figures are from Czech, *Auschwitz Chronicle*, p. 797n.

9. Michael J. Neufeld in Megargee, *USHMM Encyclopedia*, vol. 1B, pp. 966–71.

10. Mittelbau-Dora prisoner list, p. 434, 1.1.27.1/2536866, ITS.

11. Michael J. Neufeld in Megargee, *USHMM Encyclopedia*, vol. 1B, pp. 979–81.

12. According to Neufeld (in Megargee, *USHMM Encyclopedia*, vol. 1B, p. 980), this extremely early start was practiced during the summer months, but Gustav Kleinmann's diary states that it was the case in February to March 1945.

13. A small camp had been established by this time at Woffleben (camp B-12) to save the journey time for workers from Ellrich (Michael J. Neufeld in Megargee, *USHMM Encyclopedia*, vol. 1B, p. 981); however, Gustav and most of the other prisoners were not among those transferred here, and they continued having to make the journey to and from the site each day.

14. Michael J. Neufeld in Megargee, *USHMM Encyclopedia*, vol. 1B, pp. 969, 980. In his diary, Gustav gives Brinkmann's first name as Hans; other sources give it as Otto.

15. Langbein, *Against All Hope*, pp. 374–5.

16. An alternative theory is that the SS intended to use the volunteers as decoys, to draw enemy fire while the real SS made their escape (Le Chêne, *Mauthausen*, p. 155).

17. Fritz makes no mention of this episode in either his written memoir or his 1997 interview and does not appear to have told his family about it after the war. However, he did talk about it in a 1976 interview with fellow Austrian Auschwitz survivor and resistance member Hermann Langbein (Langbein, *Against All Hope*, p. 374).

18. Prisoner record card AMM-Y-Karteikarten, PGM; Gusen II transfer list, March 15, 1945, 1.1.26.1/1310718; Mauthausen transfer list, March 15, 1945, 1.1.26.1/1280723; Gusen II prisoner register, p. 82, 1.1.26.1/1307473, ITS. Langbein's sources (*Against All Hope*, p. 384) indicate that the plan to infiltrate the SS units occurred in "mid-March" 1945, but the episode must have been in early March, before Fritz's transfer to Gusen on March 15.

19. Robert G. Waite in Megargee, *USHMM Encyclopedia*, vol. 1B, pp. 919–21.

20. Gusen II transfer list, March 15, 1945, 1.1.26.1/1310718, ITS; Haunschmied et al., *St Georgen-Gusen-Mauthausen*, pp. 144, 172. In his memoir (*Doch der Hund*, p. 170), which is very sketchy at this point, Fritz erroneously identifies the aircraft as Me 109.

21. Haunschmied et al., *St Georgen-Gusen-Mauthausen*, pp. 198, 210–1.

22. Quoted in Dobosiewicz, *Mauthausen-Gusen: obóz zagłady*, p. 384.

23. Dobosiewicz, *Mauthausen-Gusen: obóz zagłady*, p. 386.

24. Haunschmied et al., *St Georgen-Gusen-Mauthausen*, p. 134ff.

25. Ibid., p. 219ff.

Chapter 20: The End of Days

1. Gustav gives no further details about Erich or his sources of food; presumably, as with Fritz Kleinmann's system of contacts in the Buna Werke, it came from civilians employed in armament production in the tunnel complex.

2. Michael J. Neufeld in Megargee, *USHMM Encyclopedia*, vol. 1B, p. 980.

3. Ibid., p. 970.

4. Ibid., p. 980.

5. In his diary, Gustav writes that this stopover was at Schneverdingen, a town to the north of Munster. This seems unlikely, since it would have necessitated immediately doubling back south to the ultimate destination, which was Bergen-Belsen. However, given the chaotic nature of concentration camp evacuations at this time, that would not be out of the question.

6. David Cesarani, "A Brief History of Bergen-Belsen" in Bardgett and Cesarani, *Belsen 1945*, pp. 19–20.

7. Sington, *Belsen Uncovered*, pp. 14, 18, 28; Phillips, *Trial*, p. 195.

8. Langbein, *People*, p. 406.

9. Josef Rosenhaft, quoted in Sington, *Belsen Uncovered*, pp. 180–1; testimony of Harold le Druillenec in Phillips, *Trial*, p. 62.

10. Quoted in Sington, *Belsen Uncovered*, p. 182.

11. An American air raid on Celle on April 8 killed many concentration camp prisoners en route to Belsen; there followed a massacre of prisoners by local SS and townspeople of Celle. In all, three thousand were killed. This could not be what Gustav

witnessed, which was on the night of April 10/11. What he saw must have been fighting in the vicinity of Celle, which was liberated by British forces on April 12.

12. Testimony of Captain Derrick A. Sington in Phillips, *Trial*, pp. 47–53; Sington, *Belsen Uncovered*, pp. 11–3.

13. Testimony of Captain Derrick A. Sington in Phillips, *Trial*, pp. 47, 51; Sington, *Belsen Uncovered*, pp. 14–5.

14. Sington, *Belsen Uncovered*, p. 16.

15. Ibid., p. 18.

16. Ibid., p. 187.

17. The original message itself has not survived, but Edith did receive it. It told her little other than that her father was alive and in block 83 of Bergen-Belsen (Samuel Barnet, letter to Leverett Saltonstall, June 1, 1945, War Refugee Board 0558 Folder 7: Requests for Specific Aid, FDR).

18. Molly Silva Jones in "Eyewitness Accounts" in Bardgett and Cesarani, *Belsen 1945*, p. 57.

19. Major Dick Williams, "The First Day in the Camp" in Bardgett and Cesarani, *Belsen 1945*, p. 30.

20. Ben Shepard, "The Medical Relief Effort at Belsen" in Bardgett and Cesarani, *Belsen 1945*, p. 39.

21. Molly Silva Jones in "Eyewitness Accounts" in Bardgett and Cesarani, *Belsen 1945*, p. 55.

22. Gerald Raperport in "Eyewitness Accounts" in Bardgett and Cesarani, *Belsen 1945*, pp. 58–9.

23. Haunschmied ct al., *St Georgen-Gusen-Mauthausen*, p. 219ff; Dobosiewicz, *Mauthausen-Gusen: obóz zagłady*, p. 387.

24. It is unclear how many prisoners were herded into the Kellerbau tunnels, partly because of widely varying figures for the number of prisoners in the Mauthausen complex at the time. The total prisoner population of Mauthausen and Gusen has been given variously as 21,000 (Robert G. Waite in Megargee, *USHMM Encyclopedia*, vol. 1B, p. 902), 40,000 (Haunschmied et al., *St Georgen-Gusen-Mauthausen*, p. 203), and 63,798 (Le Chêne, *Mauthausen*, pp. 169–70). Furthermore, not all went to the tunnels—such as the seven hundred who were too sick to be moved.

25. Fritz Kleinmann in *Doch der Hund*, p. 171; Langbein, *Against All Hope*, p. 374; Le Chêne, *Mauthausen*, p. 165.

26. Krisztián Ungváry, "The Hungarian Theatre of War" in Frieser, *Eastern Front*, pp. 950–4.

27. Le Chêne, *Mauthausen*, pp. 163–4.

28. George Dyer, quoted in Le Chêne, *Mauthausen*, p. 165.

29. Haunschmied et al., *St Georgen-Gusen-Mauthausen*, p. 226.

30. Quoted in Langbein, *Against All Hope*, p. 82.

31. In his diary, Gustav erroneously identifies this place as Ostenholz, a village to the southwest of Bergen-Belsen, well away from the route he and Josef Berger took, which did not have a POW camp near it.

Chapter 21: The Long Way Home

1. Samuel Barnet, letter to Leverett Saltonstall, June 1, 1945, War Refugee Board 0558 Folder 7: Requests for Specific Aid, FDR.
2. O'Dwyer, letter to Samuel Barnet, June 9, 1945, War Refugee Board 0558 Folder 7: Requests for Specific Aid, FDR.
3. Fritz does not identify the hospital, but it must have been the 107th EH, which established a facility at Regensburg on April 30, 1945, and remained there until May 20 (www.med-dept.com/unit-histories/107th-evacuation-hospital; retrieved July 16, 2017). No other American military hospital units have been identified in Regensburg at that time.
4. In later years, Fritz recorded the names and fates of fifty-five Jewish and non-Jewish children who had been playmates in the Karmelitermarkt before 1938 (*Doch der Hund*, p. 179). Of the twenty-five Jews, five, including Fritz himself, survived the camps, and eight, including Kurt and Edith Kleinmann, either emigrated or hid. Twelve were murdered in the concentration camps. Of the thirty non-Jewish children, nineteen stayed in or around Vienna throughout the war, and eleven served in the Wehrmacht during the war; of these, only three survived.
5. Gustav had apparently taken up smoking since leaving Auschwitz; Fritz mentions that his father had no use for his bonus coupons because he neither smoked nor wished to use the brothel.
6. Gustav gives the women's names as Elly Offermann and Gerti Zimmermann, but no further information about them. He doesn't name any of his other traveling companions, except for one, identified only in one place as "G."
7. Gustav names one of them as Fritz Heymann; this may be a mistaken reference to Stefan Heymann. There was a Fritz Heymann in Monowitz, but neither Fritz nor Gustav Kleinmann ever refer to him in their writings.
8. Gustav identifies this man only as "G."

Epilogue: Jewish Blood

1. Naturalization records for Richard and Edith Patten, May 14, 1954: Connecticut District Court Naturalization Indexes, 1851-1992: NARA microfilm publication M2081.
2. On their testimony for the Frankfurt Auschwitz trials given in 1963, Gustav gave his religion as "Mosaic" (Jewish) and Fritz as "no religious affiliation" (Abt 461 Nr 37638/84/15904–6; Abt 461 Nr 37638/83/15661–3, FTD).

3. Statistics given in Gold, *Geschichte der Juden*, pp. 133–4.
4. Israelitische Kultusgemeinde list of surviving Jews in Vienna, 1946, 3.1.1.3/78805412, ITS. This document gives Gustav's address as Im Werd 9 (Olly's building) and Fritz's as Im Werd 11 (their old home) but doesn't give apartment numbers.
5. Displaced person registration card for Gustav Kleinmann, file 1655, AJJ.
6. Pendas, *Frankfurt Auschwitz Trial*, pp. 101–2.
7. Trials of Burger et al. and Mulka et al., Frankfurt, 1963; testimony of Gustav Kleinmann (Abt 461 Nr 37638/84/15904–6, FTD) and Fritz Kleinmann (Abt 461 Nr 37638/83/15661–3, FTD). Gustav was interviewed mainly about the death march and camp senior Jupp Windeck; Fritz's statement is mostly concerned with Windeck and SS-Sergeant Bernhard Rakers.
8. Along with his father's diary and commentaries by Reinhold Gärtner, Fritz's memoir was included in the book *Doch der Hund will nicht krepieren* (Innsbruck University Press, 1995, 2012).

Index